STU[illegible] ACCOMPANY

MICRO ECONOMICS

SCARCITY, WANTS, AND CHOICES

SEVENTH CANADIAN EDITION

McCONNELL ■ BRUE ■ BARBIERO

WILLIAM B. WALSTAD
University of Nebraska, Lincoln

ROBERT C. BINGHAM

TORBEN ANDERSEN
Red Deer College

McGraw-Hill Ryerson Limited

Toronto Montreal New York Auckland Bogotá Caracas
Lisbon London Madrid Mexico Milan New Delhi
San Juan Singapore Sydney Tokyo

Study Guide to accompany
MICROECONOMICS: Scarcity, Wants, and Choices
Seventh Canadian Edition

ISBN: 0-07-552615-8

2 3 4 5 6 7 8 9 10 W 5 4 3 2 1 0 9 8 7

Printed and bound in Canada

Senior Editor: Jennifer Mix

Developmental Editor: Daphne Scriabin

Contents

Preface

Welcome to the study of economics. This ***Study Guide*** is intended to accompany and complement the textbook, ***Microeconomics***, 7th Canadian edition, by McConnell, Brue and Barbiero. The design of the ***Study Guide*** is based on the conviction that active study is superior to passive study. To benefit from an aerobics class, you must not only watch the instructor's demonstrations--you must do the exercises yourself. To learn carpentry you cannot merely read a book--you must practice using the tools. Learning economics is a lot like aerobics or carpentry: you must do exercises, and you must handle the tools.

The ***Study Guide*** lets you practice using the tools of economics, and gives you feedback along the way. It provides a range of questions that require verbal, numerical, and graphical answers. These are the three main modes of analysis in economics, and skill in all three areas will likely be expected of you on your economics exams.

I hope that you will work extensively with this ***Study Guide***, and that as a result, you have more success, and more fun, in your economics course.

What the Study Guide Is

For each chapter in the text there is a chapter in the ***Study Guide.*** Each ***Study Guide*** chapter has eleven sections. The first five sections identify and explain the basic content of each chapter.

1. An introduction relates the chapter to other chapters, and identifies what topics are of special importance.
2. A checklist states your learning objectives.
3. A chapter outline summarizes all of the essential points in the chapter.
4. A list of terms and concepts indicate what you need a working knowledge of in the chapter. (There is also a Glossary at the end of the ***Study Guide***).
5. Selected hints and tips alert you to common pitfalls, points you cannot afford to overlook, etc.

The final sections provide questions and answers:

6. Fill-in questions.
7. Problems and projects.
8. True-false questions.
9. Multiple-choice questions.
10. Discussion questions.
11. Answers to all fill-in questions, true-false questions, multiple-choice questions, and most of the problems.

A Bit of Advice

Try to work several times each week with both the text and the ***Study Guide***. Economics is absorbed most effectively in small, frequent doses.

You might find it useful to preview the ***Study Guide*** introduction, chapter outline and checklist before tackling a new chapter in the textbook. However, most of your time with the ***Study Guide*** should come after reading the chapter in the textbook, and probably after your instructor has dealt with the material in class.

Make a serious attempt to answer a question before looking at its solution. Evaluate your results to assess your areas of strength and weakness. If you don't have time to do all of the questions, choose ones that seem more important given your instructor's emphasis.

When reviewing for exams, you will not have time to re-read all of the textbook chapters. Use the compact summaries in the ***Study Guide*** for quick review and to zero in on key areas that you might need to review in more detail in the textbook.

Acknowledgements

I thank Cyril Grant, William Walstad, and the late Robert Bingham, whose work on other editions of the ***Study Guide*** made my work much easier. Thanks to Tom Barbiero for preparing a fine text for Canadian students, and for encouraging me along the way. The McGraw-Hill Ryerson team was most helpful: especially Jennifer Mix early on, and later, Daphne Scriabin.

At home, Sheila, Niels, Katie, and Alison were infinitely patient. Finally, thanks to my students at Red Deer College who have taught me a great deal about what is important in introductory economics.

Torben Andersen

PART 1

An Introduction to Economics

CHAPTER 1

The Nature and Method of Economics

Chapter 1 introduces you to economics--the study of how people decide how to use scarce productive resources to satisfy material wants. Knowledge of economics is important because it is essential for well-informed citizenship and has many practical applications to personal decisions. This chapter explains the nature of the subject and describes the different methods that economists use to study economic questions.

Descriptive or *empirical economics* refers to economic knowledge obtained by gathering relevant facts or data. *Economic theory* involves the derivation of principles by methods of *induction* or *deduction*. *Economic policy* entails the formulation of policies or recommended solutions to economic problems.

The heart of the chapter is the discussion of economic principles in the economic theory section. These principles are generalizations meant to closely approximate our complex world. Because the economist cannot employ laboratory experiments to test the generalizations, these principles are imprecise and subject to exceptions. Economics is a science, but not an exact science. Economic principles are not, in themselves, answers to economic problems but are tools to analyse these problems and find solutions for them. Though economic principles are inexact, we rely on them in order to predict and understand economic phenomena.

Our society has five widely accepted goals: economic growth, full employment, price level stability, equitable income distribution, and a balance in foreign trade. The economic policy controversies that our society must grapple with often centre on how these goals should be interpreted, and on the relative importance of different goals, given that there are often trade-offs between goals. Such questions move us from economic theory and positive economics, which investigates *what is*, to normative economics, which incorporates subjective or value-laden views of *what ought to be*. Many of the apparent disagreements among economists are over normative policy issues and involve deciding which economic goals for our economy are most important in making the case for a policy solution.

Economics is divided into two broad categories: microeconomics and macroeconomics. Microeconomics studies the behaviour of individual economic units such as business firms or households, and concentrates on the determination of output and prices in markets for particular goods. Macroeconomics studies the determinants of economy-wide aggregates, such as Canada's national output, or unemployment rates. Common to both microeconomics and macroeconomics is the economic perspective that in the face of scarcity people act according to rational self-interest, and make choices as if they are based on benefit-cost comparisons.

Clear thinking about economic questions requires that the beginning student avoid many pitfalls. Errors of commission and omission can occur from bias, loaded terminology, imprecise definitions, fallacies of composition, and confusing correlation with causation. Awareness of these pitfalls will help you think more objectively about economic issues.

Checklist

When you have studied this chapter, you should be able to:

- ☐ Write the formal definition of economics.
- ☐ Give two reasons for studying economics.
- ☐ Define descriptive economics, economic theory, and economic policy.
- ☐ Distinguish between induction and deduction in

economic reasoning.

- ☐ Explain what an economic principle is and how economic principles are obtained.
- ☐ Discuss how economic principles are generalizations and abstractions.
- ☐ Explain what the "other things equal" (*ceteris paribus*) assumption is and why this assumption is employed in economics.
- ☐ Distinguish between macroeconomics and microeconomics.
- ☐ Distinguish between positive economics and normative economics and provide examples of both.
- ☐ Identify the five economic goals.
- ☐ Recognize the "pitfalls to straight thinking" when confronted with examples.
- ☐ Outline the three basic steps in economic policy formulation.
- ☐ Describe the economic perspective.

Chapter Outline

1. Economics is concerned with the efficient use of limited productive resources to achieve maximum satisfaction of human material wants.

2. In order to comprehend some of the present-day problems of their society citizens must have an understanding of economic principles. Economics also has personal applications for business executives, consumers and workers.

3. Economists gather relevant facts to develop *economic principles* which will increase our understanding of the economy and help to formulate policies which will solve economic problems.

(a) *Descriptive economics* is the gathering of relevant facts about the production, exchange, and consumption of goods and services.

(b) *Economic theory* is the analysis of the facts and the derivation of economic principles.

(1) These principles may be derived by either *inductive* or *deductive* methods.

(2) Economic principles are also called laws, theories, and models.

(3) Each of these principles is a generalization.

(4) Economics employs the *ceteris paribus* (or "other things equal") assumption to obtain these generalizations.

(5) These principles are also abstractions from reality; appropriate abstraction is necessary for theories to be practical.

(6) Economists test their hypotheses by comparing theoretical predictions with relevant facts.

(7) Economists can derive principles of economic behaviour at the macroeconomic or the microeconomic level.

(c) *Economic policy* involves the application of economic principles to reach specific goals.

(1) The three steps in policy design are stating the goals, analyzing the effects of alternative policies for achieving the chosen goals, and evaluating the effects of the selected policies after their implementation.

(2) At least five major economic goals are widely accepted in Canada: economic growth, full employment, price level stability, an equitable distribution of income, and a balance of trade.

(3) Economic goals may be complementary or conflicting; when goals are in conflict, value judgments must be made about what is most important.

(4) Positive economics concerns *what is*, or the scientific analysis of economic behaviour; normative economics suggests *what ought to be* in offering answers to policy questions.

4. Pitfalls encountered by beginning students in studying and applying economic principles include:

(a) bias or preconceived beliefs not warranted by facts;

(b) loaded terminology or the use of terms in a way that appeals to emotions and leads to a nonobjective analysis of the issues;

(c) the definition of terms by economists different from the way these terms are ordinarily used;

(d) the fallacy of composition or the assumption that what is true of the part is necessarily true of the whole;

(e) the *post hoc* fallacy, or the mistaken belief that when one event precedes another, the first event is the cause of the second.

5. The economic perspective is a cost benefit perspective. It is described in three inter-related ideas:

(a) Scarcity of resources forces people, either as individuals or in groups, to make choices.

(b) People behave as rational decision-makers who make choices based on their self-interest.

(c) People make such choices by comparing marginal costs and marginal benefits.

Terms and Concepts

ceteris paribus **or "other things being equal" assumption**
choices
correlation and causation
descriptive economics
economics
economic goals
economic perspective
economic policy
economic theory
fallacy of composition
hypothesis
induction and deduction
macroeconomics and microeconomics
policy economics
positive and normative economics
post hoc, ergo propter hoc **or "after this, therefore because of this" fallacy**
principles or generalizations
scarcity
trade-offs
wants

Hints and Tips

1. Some students have difficulty with the claim that economics is a science, especially because its theories are inexact. Economics is a science by virtue of its methodology. That economic generalizations are inexact does not disqualify economics from being a science, nor does it negate the value of these generalizations. Think of generalizations from cancer research, or from meteorology. Scientists have demonstrated an important link between smoking and lung cancer, even though the knowledge is not exact enough to identify which smokers will get cancer. Meteorologists are not always correct in their weather forecasts, but most of us pay attention to these forecasts because they are generally better than the forecasts we could generate ourselves without the benefit of the inexact science of meteorology.

2. One way for you to remember each type of pitfall to objective thinking in economics is to associate each one with a specific example. Choose examples that are funny, or that have personal application.

Fill-In Questions

1. Economics is concerned with the __________ use of __________ resources to attain the __________ of human material wants.

2. Economics, like other sciences, begins with the facts found in the world around us.

(a) The gathering of relevant facts is the part of economics called __________ economics.

(b) Economic __________ involves deriving general principles about the economic behaviour of people and institutions. When economists develop economic principles from studying facts, they are using the __________ method; whereas the __________ method uses facts to test hypotheses or predictions derived from economic theories.

(c) The formulation of recommended solutions to economic problems is referred to as __________ .

3. The economic principles (often called __________, or __________) derived from facts are all __________ about human economic behaviour and, as such, necessarily involve __________ from reality.

4. Economists hypothesize that the number of units of a particular good a consumer purchases depends upon the price of that good, and several other factors such as income and tastes. To isolate the relationship between the price of the good and the quantity purchased economists often assume that these other factors are constant and do not change and this is termed the __________ assumption.

5. Macroeconomics deals with the economy __________. Micro-economics deals with the behaviour of __________ economic units.

6. The three steps involved in the formulation of economic policy are:

(a) ______________________________________

(b) ______________________________________

(c) ______________________________________

7. Five economic goals that are widely accepted in Canada include:

(a) ______________________________________

(b) ______________________________________

(c) ______________________________________

(d) ______________________________________

(e) ______________________________________

8. Increases in economic growth that promote full employment would be an example of a set of (conflicting, complementary) __________ economic goals. Efforts to achieve an equitable distribution of income that reduce economic growth would be an example of a set of __________ economic goals.

9. Two different types of statements can be made about economic topics. A (positive, normative) __________ statement explains *what is* by offering a scientific proposition about economic behaviour that is based on economic theory and facts. A __________ statement includes a value judgment about an economic policy or the economy that suggests *what ought to be*. Many of the reported disagreements among economists usually involve __________ statements.

10. There are many obstacles to logical consistency in economic reasoning. For example, the conclusion that "what is true for an individual must necessarily be true of the group" is known as the fallacy of __________. The conclusion that because one event precedes another the first is necessarily the cause of the second is known as the __________ fallacy.

11. The economic perspective is a __________ perspective that has three interrelated features: (1) It recognizes that scarcity requires __________; (2) that people make decisions in a __________ manner based on their __________; and (3) that weighing the costs and benefits of a decision is based on __________ analysis.

Problems and Projects

1. Below are five statements. Each of them is an example of one of the pitfalls frequently encountered in the study of economics. Indicate, in the space following each statement, the type of pitfall involved.

(a) The Second World War resulted in forty five years of economic expansion in Canada. ____________________

b) "An unemployed worker can find a job if he or she looks diligently and conscientiously for employment; therefore, all unemployed workers can find employment if they are diligent and conscientious in looking for a job." ____________________

(c) "Just tell me when rain will be needed and I will schedule my vacation for that week." ____________________

(d) "The players, not the team owners, deserve to benefit from the recent explosion in revenues experienced by the National Basketball League; after all, it is the players that fans pay to see." ____________________

(e) " The North American Free Trade Agreement will make Canadian workers pawns of the powerful corporations who can move their sweat shops to Mexico." ____________________

2. Below is a list of economic statements. Indicate in the space beside each whether they are positive (P) or normative (N). Then in lines (g) through (j), write two of your own examples of positive statements and two examples of normative economic statements.

(a) Tuition fee increases are causing university enrolments to decrease. _____

(b) The supply management system in agriculture protects our small family farms from unfair competition by large corporate agricultural enterprises. ____

(c) Higher income tax rates reduce the number of people willing to be employed. ____

(d) The Unemployment Insurance program is too generous because it gives people the incentive to quit their jobs. ____

(e) Free trade can improve the standard of living of a country. ____

(f) The federal government should do more to eliminate regional disparity in Canada. ____

(g) P ______________________________

(h) P ______________________________

(i) N ______________________________

(j) N ______________________________

3. Below is an exercise in making graphs. On the graph, plot the economic relationships contained in the table that follows. Be sure to label each axis of the graph and to indicate the units of measurement and scale used on each axis. Graph national income on the horizontal axis and consumption expenditures on the vertical axis; connect the seven points and label the curve "Consumption Schedule."

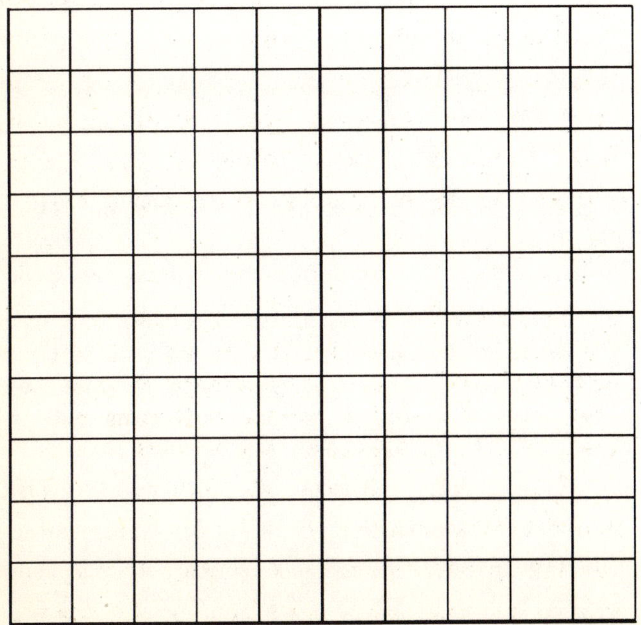

National Income (billions)	Consumption expenditures (billions)
$600	$660
650	700
700	740
750	780
800	820
850	860
900	900

There is a(n) (direct, inverse) __________ relationship between national income and consumption expenditures, and the Consumption Schedule is a(n) (up-, down-) __________ sloping curve.

True-False

Circle T if the statement is true, F if it is false.

1. Economics deals with the activities by which people earn their living and try to improve their standard of living. **T F**

2. The study of economics provides the student with specific skills which are highly valued by businesses. **T F**

3. Gathering the relevant economic facts from which economic principles are derived is the part of economics called economic analysis. **T F**

4. In economics, the terms "law," "principle," and "theory," mean essentially the same thing. **T F**

5. The "other things equal" or *ceteris paribus* assumption is made in order to simplify the reasoning process. **T F**

6. The first step in the formulation of an economic policy, the statement of the goal or desired result, may be an occasion for disagreement because different people may have different and conflicting goals. **T F**

7. Making value judgments as to preferred goals of an economy is known as positive economic analysis. **T F**

8. Normative statements are expressions about desired states of the economy as seen by the speaker. **T F**

9. The statement: "Increased patent protection for the Canadian pharmaceutical industry will result in increased investment by that industry in Canada" is a positive statement. **T F**

10. Rational self-interest is the same thing as being selfish. **T F**

11. The economic perspective views individuals or institutions as making rational choices based on the analysis of the costs and benefits of the decision. **T F**

12. Complete equity in regional income per person and sustained national economic growth may be conflicting goals for any economy. **T F**

13. Microeconomic analysis is concerned with the behaviour of individual households and business firms. **T F**

14. Scarcity is caused by the fact that people make choices. **T F**

15. In economics the word "marginal" means additional, or extra. **T F**

Multiple-Choice

Circle the letter that corresponds to the best answer.

1. Which statement is the best one to complete a short definition of economics? "Economics is the study of:
(a) how businesses maximize profits."
(b) the triumph of the capitalistic system over communism."
(c) monetary transactions."
(d) the efficient use of scarce resources."

2. Economics is a practical field of study in several ways. Which one of the following is *not* an element of its practicality?
(a) every person affects and is affected by the operation of the economy
(b) every person has to earn a living in some manner, and economics develops skills and trains the student in the art of making a living
(c) every person in a democracy is confronted with its political problems and many of them are economic in nature
(d) every person who understands the overall operation of the economy is in a better position to solve personal economic problems

3. One economic principle states that, *ceteris paribus*, the lower the price of a commodity the greater will be the quantity of the commodity consumers will wish to purchase. On the basis of this principle alone, it can be concluded that
(a) if the price of mink coats is falls, one can conclude that more mink coats will be purchased by consumers
(b) if the price of mink coats falls, there must have been a decrease in the demand for clothes made of fur
(c) if the price of mink coats falls and there are no important changes in the other factors affecting their demand, consumers will probably purchase more mink coats than they did at the higher price
(d) if more mink coats are purchased this month than last month, it is because the price of mink coats has fallen

4. An economic model is *not*:
(a) an ideal type of economy or economic policy that we should strive to achieve
(b) a tool economists employ to enable them to predict
(c) one or a collection of economic principles
(d) an explanation of how the economy or a part of the economy functions in its essential details

5. Which of the following is *not* among the dangers encountered in the construction or application of an economic model?
(a) it may contain irrelevant facts and be more complex than necessary
(b) it may come to be accepted as "what ought to be" rather than as "what is"
(c) it may be overly simplified and so be a very poor approximation of the reality it explains
(d) it may result in a conclusion that is unacceptable to people

6. A theory in economics is:
(a) useless if simplifying assumptions are used
(b) of little use because it is too abstract
(c) useful if the predictions of the theory correspond to actual economic occurrences
(d) would never contradict another economic theory if both were derived using the rules of logic

7. The method of reasoning in which economic principles are derived from an analysis of historical data is called:
(a) descriptive economics
(b) hypothesis testing
(c) induction
(d) deduction

8. An economic theory may contain all but which of the following?
(a) predictions that are deduced from that theory
(b) definitions that clearly set out the variables included in the model
(c) statements of the relationships among the variables in the model
(d) normative statements as to the most preferred outcomes

9. During World War II, Canada employed price controls to prevent inflation; this was referred to as "a fascist and arbitrary restriction of economic freedom" by some and as "a necessary and democratic means of preventing ruinous inflation" by others. Both labels are examples of
(a) economic bias
(b) the fallacy of composition
(c) the misuse of common-sense definitions
(d) loaded terminology

10. If one individual decides to consume less beef, there will be little or no effect on beef prices. To argue, therefore, that if all individuals do likewise there should be little or no effect on beef prices is an example of:
(a) the *post hoc, ergo propter hoc* fallacy
(b) the fallacy of composition
(c) an oversimplified generalization
(d) using loaded terminology

11. The Great Depression that began in 1929 was preceded by a stock market crash. To argue that the depression was then caused by the decline in the stock market is an example of:
(a) the *post hoc, ergo propter hoc* fallacy
(b) the fallacy of composition
(c) the *ceteris paribus* assumption
(d) using loaded terminology

12. Which of the following would be studied in microeconomics?
(a) the output of the entire economy
(b) the national unemployment rate
(c) the effect of money supply changes on the Consumer Price Index
(d) the price and output of apples

13. If economic growth tends to produce a more equitable distribution of income among people in a nation, then the relationship between these two economic goals appears to be:
(a) deductive
(b) conflicting
(c) complementary
(d) mutually exclusive

14. To say that two economic goals are conflicting means that:
(a) there is a tradeoff in the achievement of the goals
(b) these goals are not accepted as goals
(c) the achievement of one goal results in achievement of the other goal
(d) it is impossible to quantify both goals

15. Which of the following is a macroeconomic topic?
(a) the effect of cigarette tax reductions on cigarette consumption
(b) the effect of government set stumpage fees on the amount of lumber being exported to the United States
(c) the effect of the cod fishery closure on the economy of the Maritimes
(d) the effect of the Free Trade Agreement on the price of computers in Canada

16. When studying the relationship between two variables economists frequently assume that "other things are equal." This is the use of:
(a) the *post hoc, ergo propter hoc* fallacy
(b) the fallacy of composition
(c) *ceteris paribus* assumption
(d) using loaded terminology

Discussion Questions

1. Define economics in both a less and a more sophisticated way. In your second definition, explain the meaning of "resources" and "wants."

2. What is a "laboratory experiment under controlled conditions?" Why are such experiments not normally possible in economics? What does economics have instead of a laboratory?

3. What is the relationship between facts and theory?

4. Define and explain the relationships between descriptive economics, economic theory, and applied economics.

5. Why are economic principles and models necessarily generalizations and abstractions?

6. Sketch a map showing me how to get from your home to the nearest grocery store. In what ways is your map realistic, and in what ways is it unrealistic (abstract)? Would your map necessarily be more helpful to me in finding the store if it was more realistic? Would it be worth making it more realistic? How do these issues concerning your map relate to issues concerning economic theories?

7. What does it mean to say that economic principles can be used for prediction and control?

8. Explain each of the following:
(a) fallacy of composition;
(b) loaded terminology;
(c) the *post hoc, ergo propter hoc* fallacy.

9. Explain briefly the difference between:
(a) macroeconomics and microeconomics;
(b) deduction and induction;
(c) correlation and causation.

10. In the discussion in Box 1-2, exactly what economic perspective was used to understand the behaviour of fast-food customers?

Answers

Fill-in questions

1. efficient, scarce resources, maximum satisfaction

2. (a) descriptive; (b) theory, inductive, deductive; (c) economic policy

3. theories, laws (or models), generalizations, abstractions

4. "other things equal" (*ceteris paribus*)

5. in aggregate (as a whole), individual

6. (a) stating goals; (b) analysing policy options; (c) evaluating policy effectiveness

7. (a) full employment; (b) economic growth; (c) reasonable price stability; (d) viable balance of payments; (e) equitable distribution of rising incomes

8. complementary, conflicting or mutually exclusive

9. positive; normative; normative

10. fallacy of composition; *post hoc, ergo propter hoc*

11. cost-benefit; choices, rational, self-interest, marginal

Problems and projects

1. (a) *post hoc ergo propter hoc* fallacy; (b) the fallacy of composition; (c) confusing correlation and causation; (d) bias; (e) loaded terminology

2. (a) P; (b) N; (c) P; (d) N; (e)P; (f) N

3. direct, up

True-False

1. T	**2.** F	**3.** F	**4.** T	**5.** T	**6.** T
7. F	**8.** T	**9.** T	**10.** F	**11.** T	**12.** T
13. T	**14.** F	**15.** T			

Multiple-choice

1. (d)	**2.** (b)	**3.** (c)	**4.** (a)	**5.** (d)	**6.** (c)
7. (c)	**8.** (d)	**9.** (d)	**10.** (b)	**11.** (a)	**12.** (d)
13. (c)	**14.** (a)	**15.** (c)	**16.** (c)		

APPENDIX TO CHAPTER 1

Graphs and Their Meaning

This appendix introduces you to graphing in economics. Graphs help illustrate and simplify the economic theories and models that are presented throughout this book. The old saying that "a picture is worth a thousand words" applies to economics; graphs are the way that economists "picture" relationships between economic variables.

You will need to master the basics of graphing if these "pictures" are to be of any help to you. The appendix explains how to achieve that mastery. It begins by showing you how to construct a graph from a table of data on two variables, such as income and consumption. Economists usually, but not always, place the independent variable (income) on the horizontal axis and the dependent variable (consumption) on the vertical axis of the graph. Once the data points are plotted and a line drawn to connect the plotted points, you can determine whether there is a direct or inverse relationship between the variables. Identifying whether the relationship between variables is direct or inverse is an essential skill that is used repeatedly in this book.

A typical economic graph shows the relationship between two variables: a dependent variable and an independent variable. The curve is drawn based on the *ceteris paribus* condition. If any other variable that influences the dependent variable happens to change, then it is necessary to plot a whole new curve through a different set of points. This is termed a shift in the curve.

The data in a graph or a table can be written in an equation. In the case of a straight line relationship, the equation can be found by determining the values of the slope and the vertical intercept from the line in a graph or data in a table. From such a linear equation, you can find the value of the dependent variable for any given level of the independent variable.

The slope of a line often has economic meaning, because slopes inherently measure effects of marginal changes. Marginal analysis is central to economics. Some graphs used in the book are nonlinear. With nonlinear curves, the slope of the line is no longer constant throughout but varies as one moves along the curve. This slope can be estimated at a point by determining the slope of a straight line that is drawn tangent to the curve at that point. Similar calculations can be made for other points to see how the slope changes along the curve.

Checklist

When you have studied this appendix, you should be able to:

- ☐ Understand why economists use graphs.
- ☐ Construct a graph of two variables using the numerical data from a table.
- ☐ Construct a table with two variables from an algebraic function or from data on a graph.
- ☐ Distinguish between a direct and an inverse relationship when given data on two variables.
- ☐ Identify dependent and independent variables in economic examples and graphs.
- ☐ Calculate the slope of a straight line between two points and determine the vertical intercept for the line.
- ☐ Write a linear equation using the slope of a line and the vertical intercept, and when given values for the independent variable, determine values for the independent variable.
- ☐ Estimate the slope of a nonlinear curve at a point using a line that is tangent to the curve at that point.

Appendix Outline

1. A graph is a visual representation of the relationship between variables and serves as an aid in describing economic theories and models.

2. To construct a simple graph, plot numerical data about two variables from a table. The tabular data can be

obtained from the mathematical expression of the relationship between the variables.
(a) Each graph has a horizontal and a vertical axis that can be labelled for each variable and then scaled for the range of the data points that will be measured on the axis. Arithmetic graphs are used extensively in the text and possess the characteristic that along a given axis equal distances represent equal numerical values.
(b) Data points are plotted on the graph by drawing perpendiculars from the scaled points on the two axes to the place on the graph where the perpendiculars intersect.
(c) A line or curve can then be drawn to connect the points plotted on the graph.

3. A graph provides information about relationships between variables.
(a) A line that is upward sloping to the right on a graph indicates a positive or direct relationship between two variables: an increase in one is associated with an increase in the other; a decrease in one is associated with an increase in the other.
(b) A line that is downward sloping to the right means that there is a negative or inverse relationship between the two variables because the variables are changing in opposite directions: an increase in one is associated with a decrease in the other; a decrease in one is associated with an increase in the other.

4. Economists are often concerned with determining cause and effect in economic events.
(a) A dependent variable changes (increases or decreases) because of a change in another variable.
(b) An independent variable produces or "causes" the change in the dependent variable.
(c) In a graph, mathematicians place an independent variable on the horizontal axis and a dependent variable on the vertical axis; economists are more arbitrary about which variable is placed on an axis.

5. Economic graphs are simplifications of economic relationships. When graphs are plotted, there is usually an implicit assumption made that all other factors are being held constant. This "other things equal" or *ceteris paribus* assumption is used to simplify the analysis so the study can focus on the two variables of interest.

6. A slope and intercept can be calculated for a straight line and written in the form of a linear equation.
(a) The slope of a straight line is the ratio of the vertical change to the horizontal change between two points. Roughly, the slope measures the change in the dependent variable as a result of a one unit change in the independent variable. A positive slope indicates that the relationship between two variables is direct; a negative slope means there is an inverse relationship between the variables.
(b) Where the line intersects the vertical axis of the graph is the vertical intercept.
(c) A linear equation is written as $y = a + bx$. Once the values for the intercept a and the slope b are calculated, then given any value of the independent variable x, the value of the dependent variable y can be determined.

7. The slope of a straight line is constant, but the slope of a nonlinear curve changes throughout. To estimate the slope of a nonlinear curve at a point, the slope of a line tangent to the curve at that point is calculated.

Appendix Terms and Concepts

dependent and independent variables
direct and inverse relationships
slope of a straight line
tangent
vertical and horizontal axes
vertical intercept

Hints and Tips

1. The text includes a number of graphs of real world data showing relationships between two variables. Global Perspective 2-1 in Chapter 2 is an example. These graphs often take the form of a "scatter diagram" with a "best-fitting line." That is, the data points may be somewhat scattered, rather than lying exactly on a curve. Though a precise relationship is not evident in the data, the data may show a discernible tendency or pattern, indicating that the variables are related. The best-fitting line is located to show this pattern. If you take a statistics course you will learn the precise techniques and criteria for determining such best-fitting lines, and for judging when you can be reasonably sure that the points in a scatter diagram do indicate some relationship. For the time being you need only have an intuitive or informal understanding of a "best-fitting line."

Fill-In Questions

1. The relationship between two economic variables can be visualized with the aid of a two-dimensional graph.

(a) Customarily, the (dependent, independent) __________ variable is placed on the horizontal axis and the __________ variable is placed on the vertical axis. The __________ variable is said to change because of a change in the __________ variable. In (economics, mathematics) __________ the axis designations are sometimes arbitrary.

(b) The vertical and horizontal (scales, ranges) __________ on the graph are calibrated to reflect the __________ of values in a table of data points on which the graph is based.

(c) Other variables, beyond the two in the graph, that might affect the economic relationship are assumed to be (changing, held constant) __________. *Ceteris paribus* also means that other variables are __________.

2. The graph of a straight line that slopes downward to the right indicates that there is (a direct, an inverse) __________ relationship between the two variables. A graph of a straight line that slopes upward to the right tells us that the relationship is (direct, inverse) __________. When the value of one variable increases and the value of the other variable increases, then the relationship is __________; when the value of one increases, while the other decreases, the relationship is __________.

3. The slope of a straight line between two points is defined as the ratio of the (vertical, horizontal) __________ change to the __________ change. When two variables move in the same direction, the slope will be (negative, positive) __________; when the variables move in opposite directions, the slope will be __________. The point at which the line meets the vertical axis is called the __________.

4. We can express the graph of a straight line with a linear equation that can be written as $y = a + bx$.

(a) a is the (slope, intercept) __________ and b is the __________.

(b) y is the (dependent, independent) __________ variable and x is the __________ variable.

(c) If a was 2, b was 4, and x was 5, then y would be __________. If the value of x changed to 7, then y would be __________. If the value of x changed to 3, then y would be __________.

5. The slope of a (straight line, nonlinear) __________ curve is constant throughout; the slope of a __________ curve varies from point to point. An estimate of the slope of a nonlinear curve at a point can be made by calculating the slope of a straight line that is __________ to the point on the curve.

Problems and Projects

1. The data below represent the relationship between the mortgage interest rate and the number of new houses built.

Mortgage Rate (% per year)	Housing Starts (thousands per year)
12	70,000
10	90.000
8	110,000
6	130,000
4	150,000

(a) Which variable is dependent? __________ Which is independent? __________

(b) On the axes of the graph below, set up the scales to best suit these data. Label each axis of the graph (including the units of measurement).

(c) Plot the five data points given in the table.

(d) The relationship between the mortgage interest rate and housing starts is (direct, inverse) __________, and the curve is (up-, down-) __________ sloping.

2. (a) Based on the relationship found in question 1, what is the effect on housing starts if the mortgage rate increases by 1%, *ceteris paribus*?

(b) If household incomes rise, new homes would become (more, less) __________ affordable, so there would be (more, fewer) __________ new housing starts at the same interest rate as before. On the graph, this causes a (leftward, rightward) __________ (movement along, shift of) __________ the curve in question 1.

(c) If lumber prices increase, new homes would become (more, less) __________ affordable, so there would be (more, fewer) __________ new housing starts at the same interest rate as before. On the graph, this causes a (leftward, rightward) __________ (movement along, shift of) __________ the curve in question 1.

3. The Hammerheads, a very mediocre club band, have just released a CD of their music. They will immediately sell 10 copies to their parents and friends. Thereafter, they can sell 4 copies for each performance they give in a club.

(a) Based on this information, complete the table below.

Performances	CD Sales
0	
5	____
10	____
15	____
20	____

(b) Which variable is dependent? __________ Which is independent? __________

(c) Plot the data on the graph below.

CD Sales

Performances

(d) The vertical intercept value is __________.

(e) The slope value is __________.

(f) Write the equation for this relationship:

______________________________________.

4. An economist is hired to determine the relationship between real estate value and proximity to the waterfront in a Manitoba lake shore resort community. The table below gives selling prices for undeveloped building lots sold in 1995.

(a) On the graph provided, plot the lot prices on the vertical axis and the distance to shore on the horizontal axis.

Lot	Distance to Shore	Price
A	200 metres	$ 9,000
B	0	18,000
C	50	16.000
D	100	15,000
E	50	17,000
F	150	10,000
G	200	7.000
H	125	12,000

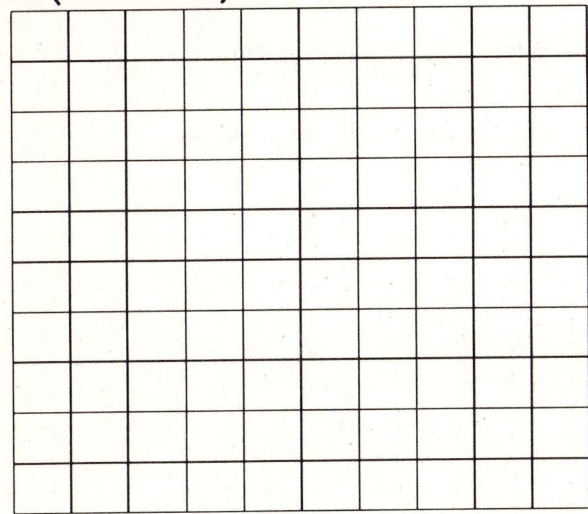

(b) The scatter diagram suggests that lots prices are (directly, inversely, not) __________ related to their proximity to the waterfront.

(c) With a ruler, draw in what appears to be the "best-fitting" line through these data points.

(d) The value of the vertical intercept is __________. This value indicates price for a lot that is ____________.

(e) The value of the slope is __________. This value indicates that price (falls, rises) by $__________ for each 100 metres from the waterfront.

5. This question is based on the graph below.

(a) The function has a negative slope between the X values of ________ and ________. Over this range the relationship between X and Y is (direct, inverse) __________.

(b) Find the slope of the curve at the following points:

A: __________, B: ___________, C: __________

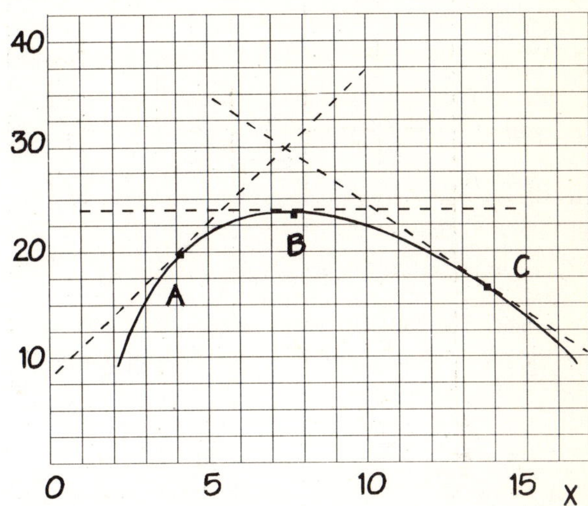

True-False

Circle the T if the statement is true; the F if it is false.

1. Graphs provide a visual representation of the relationship between two variables. **T F**

2. If the straight line on a two-variable graph is upward sloping to the right, then there is a positive relationship between the two variables. **T F**

3. A variable that changes as a consequence of a change in another variable is considered to be a dependent variable. **T F**

4. *Ceteris paribus* means that the value of all other variables is set equal to 0. **T F**

5. In the ratio for the calculation of the slope of a straight line, the horizontal change is divided by the vertical change. **T F**

6. If the slope of the linear relationship between consumption (on the vertical axis) and income (on the horizontal axis) is 0.90, then it tells us that for every $1 increase in income there will be a $0.90 increase in

consumption. **T F**

7. The slope of a straight line is 0. **T F**

8. If a linear equation is $y = 10 + 5x$, the vertical intercept is 10. **T F**

9. A function with a constant slope becomes steeper as the independent variable increases. **T F**

10. If the slope of a straight line on a two-variable (x, y) graph is 2 and the vertical intercept was 6, then if the value for x is 10, the value for y is 22. **T F**

11. A slope of 4 for a straight line in a two-variable graph indicates that there is an inverse relationship between the two variables. **T F**

12. If there is an inverse relation between price and quantity demanded, the graph of this function will be downward sloping. **T F**

13. In the relationship between rainfall and demand for umbrellas, rainfall is the dependent variable. **T F**

14. An upward slope for a straight line that is tangent to a nonlinear curve would indicate that the slope of the curve is positive at that point. **T F**

15. If two points described by the (x, y) combinations of (13, 10) and (8, 20) lie on a straight line on a graph with x on the horizontal axis and y on the vertical axis, then the slope would be 2. **T F**

16. In a linear equation of $y = -2 + 6x$, when the value of x is 3, the value calculated for y would be 16. **T F**

Multiple-Choice

Circle the letter that corresponds to the best answer.

1. If an increase in one variable is associated with a decrease in another variable, then we can conclude that the variables are:
(a) nonlinear
(b) directly related
(c) inversely related
(d) positively related

2. Economists:
(a) always put the independent variable on the vertical axis
(b) always put the independent variable on the horizontal axis
(c) sometimes put the dependent variable on the horizontal axis
(d) use only linear functions

3. If the curve in a two-variable graph shifts, what does this indicate?
(a) the two variables are positively related
(b) the two variables are negatively related
(c) the relationship between the two variables must be nonlinear
(d) some third variable must have changed

4. If y is plotted on the vertical axis and x is on the horizontal axis, which of the following is a false statement regarding the equation $y = 100 + 0.4\,x$?
(a) the vertical intercept is 100
(b) the slope is 0.4
(c) when x is 20, y is 108
(d) the graph is nonlinear

5. If a straight line drawn tangent to a nonlinear curve has a slope of zero, then at the point of tangency the curve is:
(a) vertical
(b) horizontal
(c) upward sloping
(d) downward sloping

6. Assume a household has the following relationship between consumption (C) and income (Y): C=100+.75Y. At what level of income will consumption and income be equal?
(a) Y=0
(b) Y=100
(c) Y=200
(d) Y=300
(e) Y=400

Answer questions 7 through 10 on the basis of the following diagram.

7. The graph indicates that price and quantity supplied

are:
(a) positively related
(b) negatively related
(c) indirectly related
(d) nonlinear

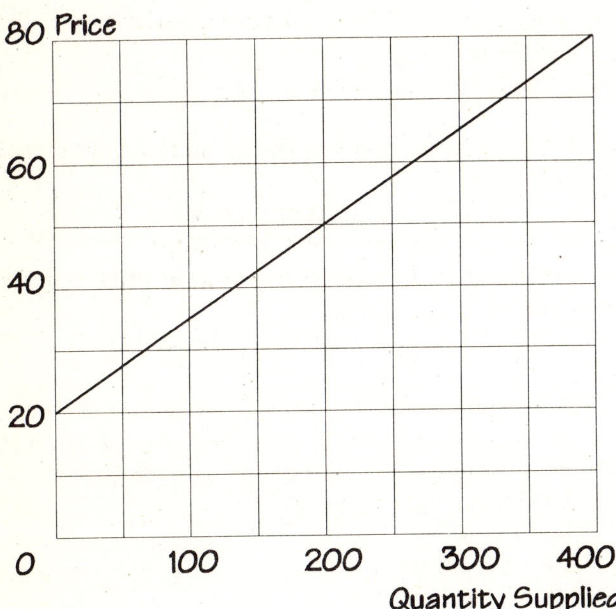

8. The slope of the line is:
(a) 0.15
(b) 0.20
(c) 1.50
(d) 6.67

9. The vertical intercept is:
(a) 0
(b) 10
(c) 20
(d) 80

10. The linear equation for the function is:
(a) $p = 20 + 0.15q$
(b) $q = 20 + 6.67p$
(c) $p = 20 + 6.67q$
(d) $q = 20 + 0.15p$

11. Which of the following statements is true?
(a) a vertical line has a slope of zero
(b) a horizontal line has a slope of infinity
(c) a nonlinear curve has different slopes at different points
(d) the slope of an upward sloping line is negative

Discussion Questions

1. Why do economists use graphs in their work? Give two examples of a graph that illustrates the relationship between two economic variables.

2. If the vertical intercept increases in value but the slope of a straight line stays the same, what happens to the graph of the line? If the vertical intercept decreases in value, what will happen to the line?

3. When you know that the price and quantity of a product are inversely related, what does this tell you about the slope of a line showing the relationship between these two variables? What do you know about the slope when the two variables are positively related?

4. Which variable is the dependent and which is the independent in the following economic statement: "A decrease in business taxes had a positive effect on investment spending." How do you tell the difference between a dependent and independent variable when examining economic relationships?

5. Why is an assumption made that all other variables are held constant when we construct a two-variable graph of the price and quantity of a product?

6. If you were to plot a two-variable graph of the price of gasoline versus per capita use of gasoline, using the data for a variety of nations, what sort of graph would you expect, and what sort of relationship would this represent? In all likelihood the data points would be somewhat scattered, rather than consistently located along a precise line or curve. Give some examples of reasons that the data points might be somewhat scattered.

7. How do mathematicians and economists differ at times in the way they construct two-dimensional graphs? Give an example.

8. How do the slopes of a straight line and a nonlinear curve differ? How do you estimate the slope of a nonlinear curve?

Answers

Fill-in questions

1. (a) independent, dependent; dependent, independent; economics (b) scales, ranges (c) held constant; held constant

2. an inverse; direct; direct, inverse

3. vertical, horizontal; positive, negative; vertical intercept

4. (a) intercept, slope (b) dependent, independent; (c) 22; 30; 14

5. straight line, nonlinear, tangent

Problems and projects

1. (a) housing starts; mortgage interest rates; (d) inverse; down; (b) and (c):

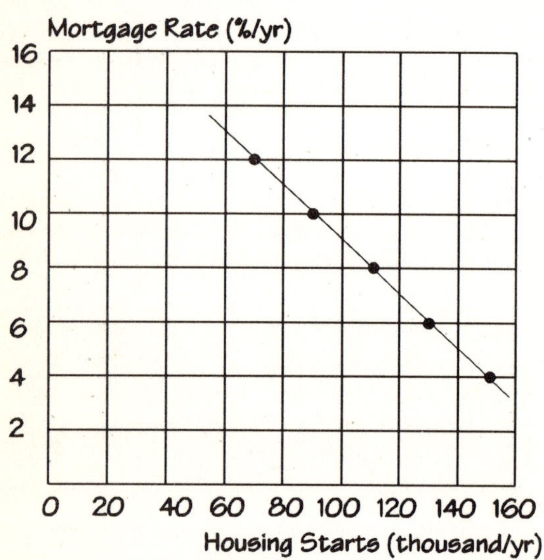

2. (a) reduction of 10,000 units; (b) more; more; rightward; shift of; (c) less; less; leftward; shift of.

3. (a) see table
(b) CD sales; performances; (d) 10; (e) 4; (f) CD Sales = 10 + 4 Performances; (c) see graph

Performances	CD Sales
0	10
5	30
10	50
15	70
20	90

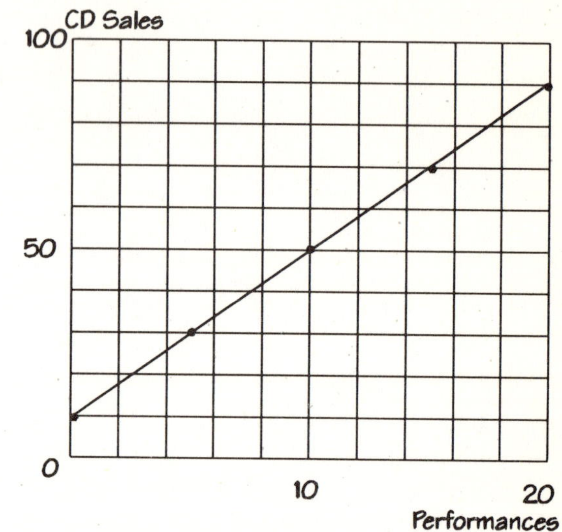

4. (a) see graph; (b) inversely; (c) see graph; (d) about \$19,000; on the waterfront; (e) about -55; falls; about \$5500.

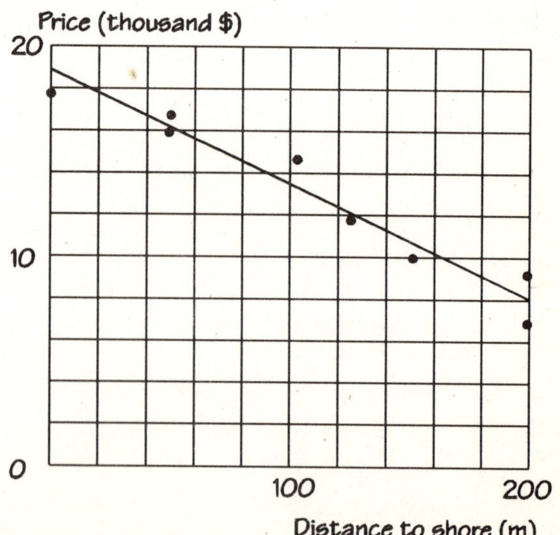

5. (a) 8; 16; inverse; (b) 3.0; 0; -2.1.

True-False

1. T **2.** T **3.** T **4.** F **5.** F **6.** T
7. F **8.** T **9.** F **10.** F **11.** F **12.** T
13. F **14.** T **15.** T **16.** T

Multiple-choice

1. (c) **2.** (c) **3.** (d) **4.** (d) **5.** (b) **6.** (e)
7. (a) **8.** (a) **9.** (c) **10.** (a) **11.** (c)

CHAPTER 2

The Economizing Problem: Scarcity, Wants and Choices

The central problem of economics is that resources--the ultimate means of satisfying material wants--are scarce *relative* to the insatiable wants of society. The main categories of resources are land, labour, capital and entrepreneurial ability. Resources are found in nature, such as land, or are manufactured, such as capital. The science of economics is the study of how society should allocate its scarce resources to produce the particular array of goods and services that achieves maximum satisfaction from fulfilling some of society's unlimited wants.

Given the condition of scarcity, satisfaction can only be maximized if all resources are fully employed and used efficiently. Efficiency has two elements: allocative efficiency is achieved if resources are used to produce those goods society wants most, and productive efficiency is achieved if resources are used in the least cost manner.

The production possibilities table and curve are used to illustrate the meaning of many concepts in this chapter--especially scarcity, choice, the law of increasing opportunity cost, allocative and productive efficiency, unemployment and economic growth. The production possibilities model can be applied to many economic questions in the real world. It is both one of the most basic and one of the most important economic models that you will study.

Every economy is faced with the problem of scarcity and has to find ways to allocate resources for the production of different goods and services. No two economies arrive at exactly the same systems for addressing their fundamental economic problems. Between the extremes of pure (or *laissez-faire*) capitalism and the command economy (or communism) are various economic systems; all of these systems are different methods of organization for finding solutions to the problem of scarcity in the face of unlimited wants.

The circular flow of income model illustrates how businesses and households interact in market-based economies. They interact in resource markets where households sell and businesses buy, and in product markets where households buy and businesses sell.

Checklist

When you have studied this chapter, you should be able to:

- ☐ Write a definition of economics that incorporates the relationship between scarce resources and unlimited wants.
- ☐ Explain why choices are necessary.
- ☐ Identify the four categories of economic resources and the type of income associated with each.
- ☐ Distinguish between full employment and full production and explain why both are necessary for efficient use of resources.
- ☐ State the four assumptions made when a production possibilities table or curve is constructed.
- ☐ Construct a production possibilities curve when you are given the appropriate data.
- ☐ Define opportunity cost.
- ☐ Calculate opportunity cost from a production possibilities table or curve.
- ☐ State the law of increasing opportunity costs and present the economic rationale for this law.
- ☐ Use a production possibilities curve to illustrate expanding resource supplies, technical change, and underemployment of resources.
- ☐ Define productive and allocative efficiency and indicate their relationship to the production possibilities curve.

- ☐ Come up with your own examples of applications of the production possibilities model.
- ☐ Describe some economic characteristics of pure capitalism, the command economy, and a mixed economic system.
- ☐ Draw the circular flow diagram; and label the real and money flows and the two major types of markets.

Chapter Outline

1. The study of economics rests on two facts:
(a) Society's material wants are unlimited.
(b) The economic resources that are the ultimate means of satisfying these wants are scarce in relation to the wants.
(1) Economic resources are classified as land, capital, labour, and entrepreneurial ability.
(2) The payments received by those who provide the economy with these four resources are rental income, interest income, wage, and profits, respectively.
(3) Because these resources are scarce (or limited), the output the economy is able to produce is also limited.

2. Economics, then, is the study of how society's scarce resources are used (allocated) to obtain the greatest possible satisfaction of its material wants. To achieve this goal society must use its resources efficiently, achieving both full employment and full production.

3. Full production implies both:
(a) allocative efficiency--meaning that resources are devoted to those goods most wanted by society; and
(b) productive efficiency--meaning that goods are produced in the least cost way.

4. The production possibilities table indicates the alternative combinations of goods and services an economy is capable of producing when it has achieved productive efficiency.

5. Four assumptions are made when constructing a production possibilities table.
(a) productive efficiency
(b) fixed resources
(c) fixed technology
(d) two products

6. The data contained in the production possibilities table can be plotted on a graph to obtain a production possibilities curve.

7. If the economy is productively efficient, every point on the production possibilities curve can be attained. Society must choose one point representing one particular combination of goods. If the chosen combination provides the greatest satisfaction the economy is said to be allocatively efficient.

8. Which of the different attainable combinations of goods is selected depends upon the choice mechanism utilized by society to reflect preferences.

9. The production possibilities curve illustrates the concepts of scarcity, choice, and opportunity cost.

10. Given full employment and full production, increasing the production of one good necessitates decreasing the production of the other good. This foregone output is termed the opportunity cost and arises because resources must be shifted from producing one good to producing the other.

11. The opportunity cost of producing additional units of a product usually increases as more of that product is produced. This generalization is the law of increasing opportunity costs.
(a) Increasing opportunity costs are assumed to arise because resources are not perfectly adaptable from one production use to another.
(b) Increasing opportunity cost is reflected in a production possibilities curve that is concave (bowed out from the origin).

12. The optimal production level for any good is where the marginal benefit received from the last unit equals its marginal cost (representing the opportunity cost of the resources used in its production).
(a) This optimal production level corresponds to the point of allocative efficiency.
(b) Marginal benefit falls as more is produced.
(c) Marginal cost rises as more is produced.

13. Relaxing the assumptions underlying the production possibilities model gives some additional results.
(a) The failure to achieve full employment and full production reduces the output of the economy.

Production is occurring inside the production possibilities curve.
(b) Improvements in technology and increased amounts of resources expand the output the economy is capable of producing. The production possibilities curve shifts to the right.
(c) The production choices made today help to determine production possibilities in the future. By using its resources for the production of capital today society increases tomorrow's productive capacity.

14. Many contemporary events and problems can be analyzed with the production possibilities model. These include: personal budgeting, discrimination, productivity slowdown, environmentalism, growth, international trade, famine in Africa, and problems of central planning in Cuba.

15. Different societies use different economic systems for addressing the fundamental economic problem of scarcity.
(a) At one extreme is pure capitalism, which relies upon the private ownership of its economic resources, the profit motive, and the market system.
(b) At the other extreme, the command economy uses public ownership of its resources and central planning.
(c) Economies in the real world lie between these two extremes and are hybrid systems.
(d) Some less developed nations have traditional (or customary) economies which are directed by the customs and traditions of the society.

16. Canada has a "mixed" economy with varying degrees of private control and governmental regulation in different sectors.

17. The circular flow model illustrates the interaction between businesses and households in resource markets and product markets. In exchange for resources that households supply to firms, firms pay incomes that households in turn use to demand goods and services produced by firms.

Terms and Concepts

allocative efficiency
authoritarian capitalism
capital goods
circular flow
command economy
consumer goods
economic growth
economizing problem
economic resources
full employment
full production
investment
land, capital, labour, and entrepreneurial ability
law of increasing opportunity costs
market socialism
opportunity cost
production possibilities table (curve)
productive efficiency
product market
pure or laissez-faire capitalism
traditional or customary economies
utility

Hints and Tips

1. It is nearly impossible to overemphasize the importance of the concept of opportunity cost. The same can be said for the definition of the optimum point where the marginal benefit of a product equals the marginal cost of a product. These are concepts that you will encounter repeatedly in the chapters to come.

2. The production possibilities model is the first instance where graphing skills are needed. If you have serious difficulty mastering the graphical analysis of this model you may have a general weakness in graphing that you should address immediately. Graphs are used constantly in the chapters that follow. Spend extra time on the graphical questions in this study guide, the relevant sections of the chapter, and with Appendix 1A of this study guide. Your instructor may also have additional resources or advice for you.

3. A movement from one point on the production possibilities curve to another point on the same curve indicates a change in what combination of products society *chooses*. In contrast, a shift of the whole production possibilities curve indicates a change in the *set of choices* available to society.

4. Many students initially confuse the coordinates of a

point on the production possibilities curve with the intercepts of the curve. The intercepts indicate the *maximum*, or *potential*, production for each good, whereas the coordinates of the production point show *actual* production for each good.

Fill-In Questions

1. The two fundamental facts that provide the foundation of economics are:

(a) ______________________________

(b) ______________________________

2. The four types of resources are:

(1) ______________________

(2) ______________________

(3) ______________________

(4) ______________________

3. The four types of incomes that individuals receive from supplying the resources listed above are, respectively:

(1) ______________________

(2) ______________________

(3) ______________________

(4) ______________________

4. Consumer goods satisfy human wants (directly, indirectly) __________ and capital goods satisfy these wants __________.

5. Economics can be defined as: ______________________________.

6. Economic efficiency requires that there be both full __________ of resources and full __________.

7. When a production possibilities table or curve is constructed, four assumptions are made. These assumptions are:

(a) ______________________________

(b) ______________________________

(c) ______________________________

(d) ______________________________

8. Below is a production possibilities curve for tractors and suits of clothing.

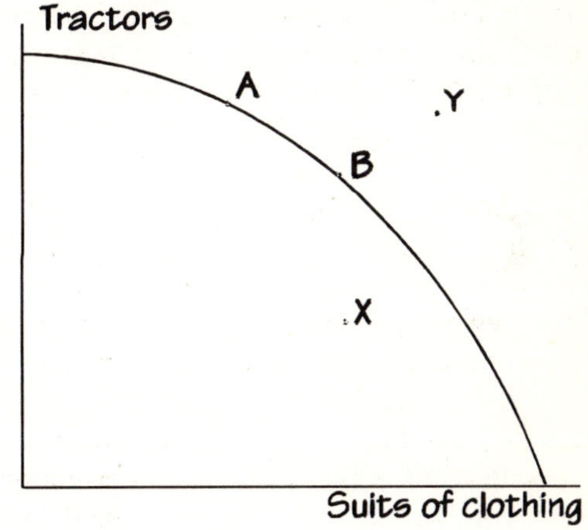

(a) If the economy moves from point *A* to point *B*, it will produce (more, fewer) __________ tractors and (more, fewer) __________ suits.

(b) If the economy is producing at point *X*, some of the resources of the economy are either __________ or __________.

(c) If the economy moves from point *X* to point *B* (more, fewer) __________ tractors and (more, fewer) __________ suits will be produced.

(d) If the economy is to produce at point *Y*, it must either __________ or __________.

9. The quantity of other goods and services an economy must go without in order to produce more low-cost housing is the __________ of producing the additional low-cost housing.

10. If Canada attempts to expand her apple industry, the opportunity cost per apple produced will tend to increase because ____________________. This is an example of the generalization known as ____________________.

11. For each situation below, indicate whether there is overallocation, underallocation, or optimal allocation of resources to the production of the good in question.

(a) marginal benefit is greater than marginal cost at the current output level __________

(b) marginal benefit is less than marginal cost at the current output level __________

(c) marginal benefit equals marginal cost at the current output level __________

12. The more an economy consumes of its current output, the (more, less) __________ it will be capable of producing in future years if other things are equal.

13. If some available resources are unemployed, productive efficiency (is, is not) __________ met, and the economy is (to the right of, to the left of, on) __________ its production possibilities curve.

14. Productive efficiency means that the __________ production techniques are used in the production of wanted goods and services.

15. Production is allocatively efficient when, given the distribution of resources, the economy produces that combination of goods __________ by society.

16. All points on the production possibilities curve are __________ efficient but some points are not __________ efficient.

17. Full production implies that two kinds of efficiency, __________ and __________, are achieved.

18. Improvements in technology would shift the production possibilities curve to the (right, left) __________. Depletion of forest resources would shift the production possibilities curve to the __________.

19. In pure capitalism property resources are (publicly, privately) __________ owned; in a command economy resources are __________ owned.

20. The term "laissez-faire" can be roughly translated as __________ and means a __________ role for government in the economy.

21. The Canadian economy leans toward __________ but the government plays an active role in some sectors.

Problems and Projects

1. Below is a list of resources. Indicate in the space to the right of each whether the resource is land (Ld), capital (K), labour (L), or entrepreneurial ability (EA) or some combination of these.

(a) fishing grounds in the North Atlantic _____

(b) a farmer's inventory of wheat _____

(c) an irrigation ditch in Saskatchewan _____

(d) the Saddledome in Calgary _____

(e) the work performed by the late Henry Ford _____

(f) the oxygen breathed by human beings _____

(g) Cavendish beach in Prince Edward Island _____

(h) Stelco's steel plant in Hamilton, Ontario _____

(i) the tasks accomplished in making the Apple Computer a commercial success _____

(j) the work done by a welder on an assembly line _____

2. An economy produces two products, timber (T) and fish (F), according to the production possibilities table below. The usual assumptions apply.

(a) Plot the data from the production possibilities table on the graph provided. Place T on the vertical axis and F on the horizontal axis.

(b) Can the economy produce 4 of F and 22 of T? __________ If not, why? __________ What is the maximum amount of T that can be produced in combination with 4 of F?__________

Combination	Timber	Fish
a	0	6
b	7	5
c	13	4
d	18	3
e	22	2
f	25	1
g	27	0

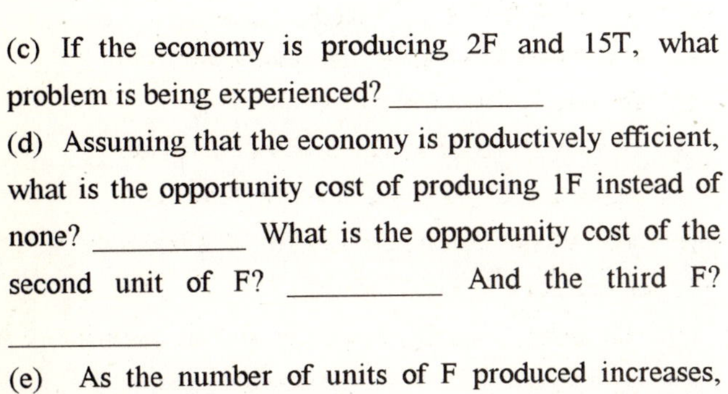

(c) If the economy is producing 2F and 15T, what problem is being experienced? __________

(d) Assuming that the economy is productively efficient, what is the opportunity cost of producing 1F instead of none? __________ What is the opportunity cost of the second unit of F? __________ And the third F? __________

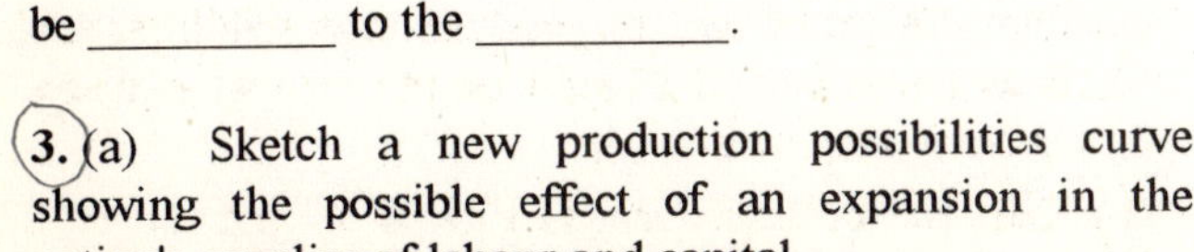

(e) As the number of units of F produced increases, what is the trend in the number of units of T that must be given up to get the extra F? __________. Because of this trend, the shape of the production possibilities curve will be __________ to the __________.

3. (a) Sketch a new production possibilities curve showing the possible effect of an expansion in the nation's supplies of labour and capital

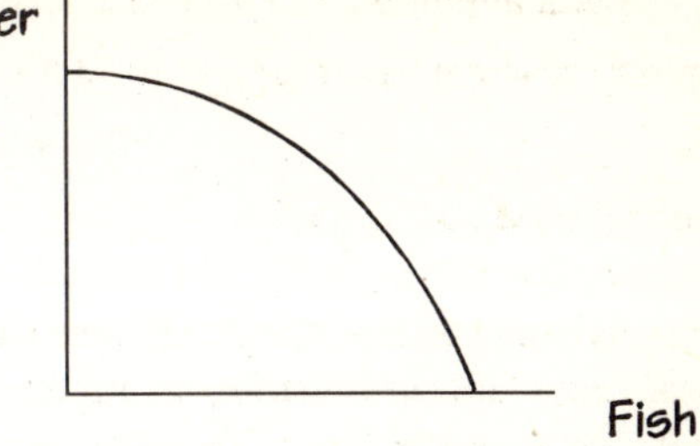

(b) Sketch a new production possibilities curve showing what might happen to this production possibilities curve if new silviculture techniques improve growth rates in tree plantations.

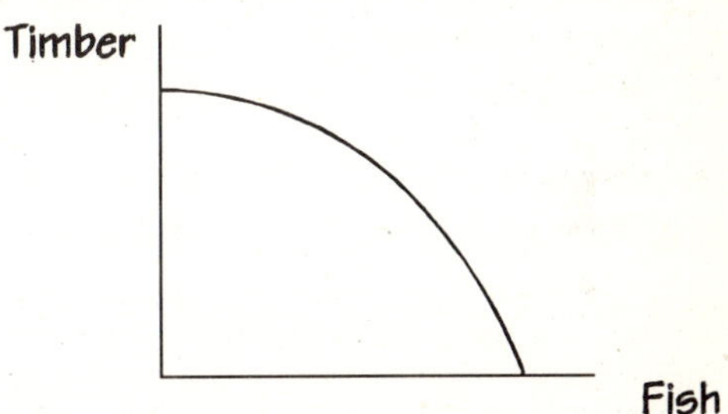

(c) Sketch a new production possibilities curve showing the possible effect of an ecological disaster that wipes out a large part of the fish stocks.

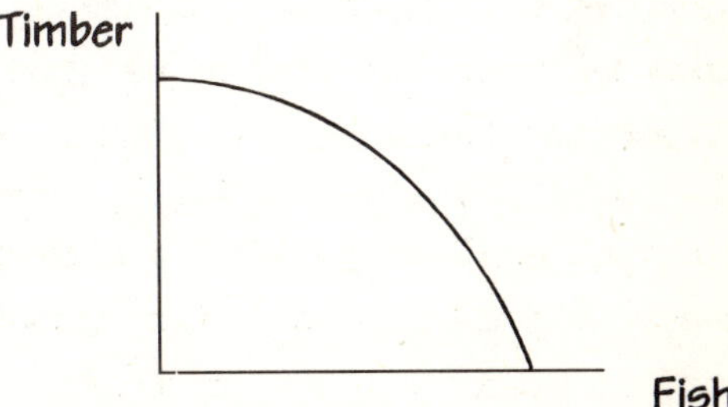

4. An economy is allocatively efficient, producing a combination of only two goods: automobiles and food. Now a technological advance occurs which enables this economy to produce automobiles with fewer resources than previously. How is it possible for the society to consume more automobiles *and* more food as a result? Illustrate below with a production possibilities diagram.

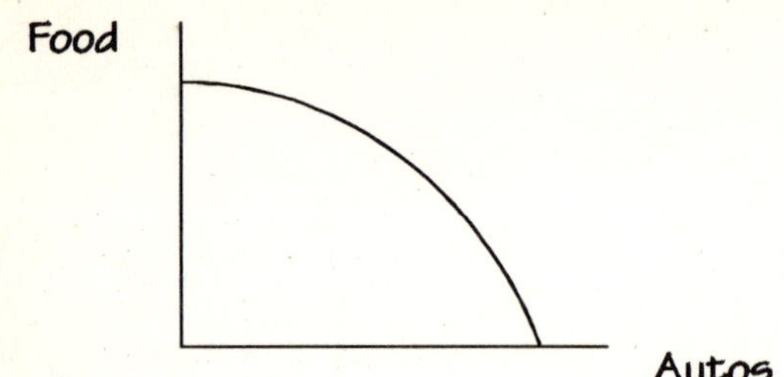

5. Below is a list of economic goods. Indicate in the space beside each whether the good is a consumer good (C), a capital good (K), or that it depends (D) upon who is using it and for what purpose.
(a) a dairy cow ____
(b) a tractor ____
(c) a shopping mall parking lot ____
(d) a telephone pole ____
(e) a telephone ____
(f) your refrigerator ____
(g) a refrigerator in a restaurant ____

6. A department store is installing video cameras to reduce shoplifting. The marginal costs and marginal benefits of additional cameras are:

Camera	MB ($/month)	MC ($/month)
1	300	100
2	250	125
3	160	150
4	50	175

(a) If the store must choose one of the numbers shown in the table, the optimal number of cameras is _____.
(b) How much better off is the store with the optimal number than with one camera fewer? _____
(c) How much better off is the store with the optimal number than with one camera more? _____

True-False

Circle T if the statement is true, F if it is false.

1. If standing in line for six hours gives you a seat at a free concert by the Tragically Hip, there is no opportunity cost to you for seeing the concert. **T F**

2. Money is a resource and is classified as "capital." **T F**

3. A Canada Savings Bond is classified as a capital good. **T F**

4. Profit is the reward paid to those who provide the economy with capital. **T F**

5. The payment to Quebec Hydro for electricity service by a resident of Montreal is a rent payment. **T F**

6. The main opportunity cost of going to college is the foregone earnings. **T F**

7. Other things being equal university enrolment should increase during periods of high unemployment. **T F**

8. The opportunity cost of producing a good tends to increase as more of it is produced because resources less suitable to its production must be employed. **T F**

9. Drawing a production possibilities curve concave to the origin is the geometric way of stating the law of increasing opportunity costs. **T F**

10. An economy cannot produce outside its production possibilities curve because resources are limited. **T F**

11. The problem of scarcity is likely to be solved by technological progress. **T F**

12. Every person in a society would prefer any point on the production possibilities curve to every point off the curve. **T F**

13. An economy that is employing the least cost productive methods has achieved allocative efficiency. **T F**

14. Given full employment and full production, it is not possible for an economy that can produce only two goods to increase its production of both. **T F**

15. Economic growth can be represented by a shift of the production possibilities curve to the right. **T F**

16. The more capital goods an economy produces today, the greater will be its ability to produce all goods in the future, *ceteris paribus*. **T F**

17. The marginal cost curve for a product rises because of increasing satisfaction from the consumption of the product. **T F**

18. Most economies are arrayed between the extremes of pure capitalism and the command economy. **T F**

19. In a command economy most resources are privately owned and are allocated by the market system. **T F**

20. In the circular flow model, households function on the demand side of the resource and product markets. **T F**

Multiple-Choice

Circle the letter that corresponds to the best answer.

1. An "innovator" is defined as an entrepreneur who:
(a) makes basic policy decisions in a business firm
(b) combines factors of production to produce a good or service
(c) invents a new product or production process
(d) introduces new products on the market or employs a new method to produce a product

2. An economy is efficient when it has achieved:
(a) full employment
(b) full production
(c) either full employment or full production
(d) both full employment and full production

3. When a production possibilities schedule is written (or a production possibilities curve is drawn), four assumptions are made. Which of the following is *not* one of those assumptions?
(a) only two goods are produced
(b) wants are unlimited
(c) the economy has both full employment and full production
(d) the quantities of all resources available to the economy are fixed

Answer the next four questions on the basis of the following diagram.

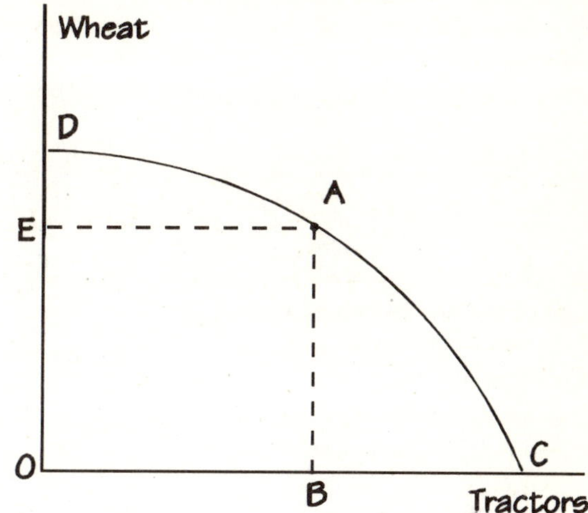

4. At point *A* on the production possibilities curve:
(a) less wheat than tractors is being produced
(b) fewer tractors than wheat are being produced
(c) the economy is employing all its resources
(d) the economy is not employing all its resources

5. The opportunity cost of producing 0*B* of tractors is:
(a) 0*D* of wheat
(b) 0*E* of wheat
(c) E*D* of wheat
(d) 0*C* of tractors

6. If there occurred a technological improvement in the production of tractors but not wheat:
(a) point *D* would remain fixed and point *C* shift to the left
(b) point *C* would remain fixed and point *D* shift upward
(c) point *D* would remain fixed and point *C* shift to the right
(d) point *C* would remain fixed and point *D* shift inward

7. The production possibilities curve is:
(a) concave
(b) convex
(c) linear
(d) positive

8. For a movement along a production possibilities curve:
(a) resources remain fixed but are reallocated between the production of the two goods
(b) resources are increased and are reallocated between the two goods
(c) resources are increased and production of both goods increased
(d) idle resources are put to work to increase the production of one good

9. A production possibilities curve that displays constant opportunity costs will be
(a) concave to the origin
(b) convex to the origin
(c) a downward sloping straight line
(d) parallel to the horizontal axis

10. Which of the following would cause a nation's production possibilities curve to shift inward toward the origin?
(a) increase in the labour force
(b) increased international trade
(c) increased employment
(d) not replacing the capital stock as it wears out

11. Which of the following will cause the movement of the Canadian production possibilities curve to the right to slow down?
(a) increasing rate of technological change
(b) increased immigration
(c) decrease in the birth rate
(d) decreased impediments to the interprovincial flow of goods and services

12. The opportunity cost of providing a governmentally financed stadium for the city's baseball team is:
(a) the interest on the money borrowed to finance the stadium
(b) the future tax increase the public will be forced to contribute to pay for the stadium
(c) there is no opportunity cost since Ottawa will finance the stadium under a regional development program
(d) the other goods and services that must be sacrificed so that resources can be used for stadium construction.

13. Private ownership of property resources, use of the market system to direct and coordinate economic activity and the presence of the profit motive are characteristic of:
(a) pure capitalism
(b) the command economy
(c) market socialism
(d) the traditional economy

14. An economy with some public ownership and numerous governmental regulations together with an emphasis on private ownership, profit motive, and market determined prices can be described as a:
(a) pure capitalistic system
(b) market socialism
(c) mixed capitalistic system
(d) command economy

15. Public ownership of property resources and use of a market system to direct and coordinate economic activity are characteristic of:
(a) authoritarian capitalism
(b) the command economy
(c) market socialism
(d) pure capitalism

16. Productive efficiency is attained when:
(a) resources are all employed
(b) output is produced at least possible cost
(c) there is no government involvement in the economy
(d) the production possibilities curve is concave

17. The term "laissez faire" refers to:
(a) the absence of government intervention in markets
(b) the absence of monopoly
(c) the absence of competition in markets
(d) efficient use of employed resources

Discussion Questions

1. Explain what is meant by the "economizing problem." Why are resources scarce?

2. In what sense are wants satiable, and in what sense are they insatiable?

3. When is a society economically efficient? What is meant by "full production," and how does it differ from "full employment"?

4. What four assumptions are made in drawing a

production possibilities curve or schedule? How do technological progress and an increased supply of resources in the economy affect the curve schedule?

5. Why cannot an economist determine which combination in the production possibilities table is "best"? What determines the optimum product-mix?

6. What is opportunity cost? What is the law of increasing cost? Why do costs increase?

7. Would the economic problem disappear if the affluent countries offered to pay more for the products of the Third World countries? Explain.

8. Would the economic problem disappear if every country abolished all trade restrictions? If your answer is "no," then explain why so much emphasis was placed on the Canada-U.S. Free Trade Agreement. Answer using the economic concepts from this chapter.

9. Suppose resources in an economy are fully employed. What would be the effect on living standards if the government decided to increase the output of capital? Explain using the production possibilities curve introduced in this chapter.

10. Explain why you agree or disagree with the statement: "The opportunity cost of increased production during a recession is different from the opportunity cost during a period of full employment."

11. Explain the difference between productive and allocative efficiency.

12. How is the "what to produce" question solved under the pure capitalistic system as compared to a mixed capitalistic system?

13. What are the roles of households and of businesses in the resource market and the product market?

Answers

Fill-in questions

1. (a) material wants are unlimited; (b) economic resources are scarce (or limited in relation to these wants)

2. (1) land or raw materials, (2) capital, (3) labour, (2) entrepreneurial ability

3. (1) rent, (2) interest, (3) wages, (4) profits

4. directly; indirectly

5. a social science concerned with the problem of allocating scarce resources to attain maximum satisfaction from fulfilling some of society's unlimited wants

6. employment, production

7. (a) full employment; (b) fixed factor supplies; (c) fixed technology; (d) two goods are produced

8. (a) fewer, more;. (b) unemployed, underemployed; (c) more, more; (d) increase resource supplies, improve technology

9. opportunity cost

10. resources are not perfectly substitutable in the production of various goods; the law of increasing opportunity costs

11. (a) underallocation; (b) overallocation; (c) optimal allocation

12. less

13. is not; to the left of

14. least costly

15. most wanted

16. productively, allocatively

17. productive, allocative

18. right; left

19. privately, publicly

20. let it be, limited

21. pure capitalism

Problems and projects

1. (a) Ld; (b) K; (c) K; (d) K; (e) EA; (f) Ld; (g) Ld; (h) K; (i) EA; (j) L

2. (b) No; this combination lies outside the production possibilities curve; (c) productive inefficiency (unemployment or underemployment); (d) 2T, 3T, 4T; (e) increasing, concave, origin

3. (a) Both T and F intercepts shift out; (b) T intercept shifts out, F intercept is unchanged; (c) F intercepts shifts in, T intercept is unchanged

4. More automobiles can now be produced with a given amount of resources, so the automobiles intercept shifts out. By moving some resources (such as labour or raw materials) from autos to food, the society can produce more food and more automobiles. On your diagram this is indicated by a shift of the production possibilities curve, followed by a movement to a new point, with the new point being northwest of the original point.

5. (a) K, (b) K, (c) K, (d) K, (e) D, (f) C, (g) K

6. (a) 3 cameras; (b) $10/month is the net benefit for the 3rd camera; (c) $125/month is the net loss for the 4th camera

True-False

1. F	**2.** F	**3.** F	**4.** F	**5.** F	**6.** T
7. T	**8.** T	**9.** T	**10.** T	**11.** F	**12.** F
13. F	**14.** T	**15.** T	**16.** T	**17.** F	**18.** T
19. F	**20.** F				

Multiple-choice

1. (d)	**2.** (d)	**3.** (b)	**4.** (c)	**5.** (c)	**6.** (c)
7. (a)	**8.** (a)	**9.** (c)	**10.** (d)	**11.** (c)	**12.** (d)
13. (a)	**14.** (c)	**15.** (c)	**16.** (b)	**17.** (a)	

CHAPTER 3

Overview of the Market System

Chapter 2 outlined the central economic problem faced by every economy. The nature of the problem is reflected in five basic questions that must be answered: how much will be produced; what will be produced; how will it be produced; to whom will it be distributed; and how can the system can be made to adapt to changes. To answer these questions Canada uses a mixed system--depending mainly on the market system, but also using elements of the command system. This chapter begins to describe our economy, starting with the model of an idealized market system, also called pure capitalism. In later chapters, more aspects and details are added to the model so the system that finally emerges at the close of the course does represent the present-day Canadian economy.

The pure market system has six key characteristics: the institution of private property; freedom of choice for consumers and freedom of enterprise for suppliers; the pursuit of self-interest; competition or economic rivalry; reliance on markets; and a very limited role for government. Households exercise choice over how to supply the resources that they own. Households spend the incomes from their resources on those goods and services that will best satisfy their wants. Firms use the resources that they employ to produce goods that seem to them likely to yield the greatest profit. The interaction of these demand and supply decisions determines prices in the market economy. These prices provide incentives and signals to consumers and producers--thereby serving as a coordinating mechanism that determines the allocation of society's resources. Prices are influenced by consumers and producers, and in turn influence their actions.

Competitive forces lead society to produce at some point on the production possibilities curve where productive and allocative efficiency are realized. In the market system self-interest of the individual, through the discipline of competition, is led to work for the well-being of society. It is as though the participants are led by an "invisible hand" to promote society's interest even though each individual is concerned solely with his/her own profit. Forced by unending competition to produce at least cost, the producer uses a minimum of society's scarce resources. Productive and allocative efficiency are met so society is obtaining maximum satisfaction from its scarce resources. The system automatically responds to changes in consumers' tastes, technology, or resource supplies.

All modern economies have three other features that contribute to greater efficiency and productivity. Use of advanced technologies usually depends on roundabout production techniques, implying extensive use of capital goods. There is a high degree of specialization among individual workers, and among regions and nations. Market economies invariably develop a system of money to facilitate the vast amount of exchange required when workers are highly specialized. Without a system of money, exchange would be done by barter, requiring a coincidence of wants between transactors. This would generally be so inconvenient as to impede exchange, and therefore impede the gains society can realize from extensive specialization.

Checklist

When you have studied this chapter, you should be able to:

- ☐ Identify and explain the six important institutional characteristics of market economies.
- ☐ List the Five Fundamental Questions every economy must answer and explain how the answers are determined in a market economy.

- ☐ Identify and explain the three other characteristics of all modern economies.
- ☐ Explain why specialization is beneficial.
- ☐ Explain why specialization leads to trade, which in turn results in the formation of markets and the determination of prices.
- ☐ Explain how the use of money facilitates trade.
- ☐ Explain the case for the market system.

Chapter Outline

1. The market system, or capitalism, is defined as an economic system having the characteristics of: private property, freedom of enterprise and choice, self-interest, competition, reliance upon markets, and a limited role for government.
(a) Under private property, resources are owned by households, firms, and other institutions, rather than by government; these owners are free to obtain, control, employ and dispose of their property as they see fit.
(b) Freedom of enterprise means that firms are free to choose what resources to employ, how to use the resources, what goods to produce, and where to sell these goods. Freedom of choice means that consumers can spend their incomes on whatever goods they want, and resource owners can supply their land, labour, etc. as they see fit.
(c) Self-interest is assumed to be the driving force. For example, consumers try to maximize their satisfaction, and entrepreneurs try to maximize their firms' profits.
(d) There is pervasive competition, or economic rivalry, meaning that each market has many independent buyers and sellers, all of whom have freedom to enter or exit the market.
(e) Decisions by buyers and sellers for both products and resources are coordinated in markets, through the price mechanism.
(f) Markets create a sufficiently self-regulating, self-adjusting and efficient allocation of resources that there is little economic role for the government to play.

2. All modern economies, not just market economies, have three other main characteristics:
(a) The use of latest technologies, which requires extensive use of capital goods: goods that are produced in order to produce more efficiently the goods that consumers ultimately want. This is known as roundabout production.
(b) Specialization prevails at all levels. Each individual produces only a very narrow range of goods, and relies on the existence of markets and prices to be able to trade what they produce for goods that others have specialized in producing. The same is true of regions and nations.
(c) In order to overcome the inconvenience and transactions costs of organizing barter transactions, some system of money emerges in every modern society. Anything that is generally acceptable by buyers and sellers in exchange is considered money.

3. Faced with unlimited wants and scarce resources, every economy must find answers for the Five Fundamental Questions: how much output to produce with our resources; what goods and services to produce; how to organize the production of these goods and services; how to divide this output among the citizens of society; and how to accommodate changes in tastes, resources, and technology.

4. The market system, or price mechanism, provides answers to the last four Fundamental Questions.
(a) Consumer demands for products and firms' desires for profits determine what and how much of each good is produced, and at what price.
(b) The desires of business firms to maximize profits by minimizing their production costs guide them to employ the most efficient techniques of production and determine their demands for and prices of the various resources; competition will drive them out of business unless they use the most efficient techniques.
(c) With resource prices determined, the money income of each household is determined; and with product prices determined, the quantity of goods and services which these money incomes can buy is determined.
(d) Changes in consumer tastes, technology, and resource supplies are signaled by price changes that give households and firms incentives to adjust their choices; thus the economy spontaneously accommodates changes.
(e) Competition in the economy compels firms and households acting in their own self-interest to promote (as though led by an "invisible hand") the best interest of society as a whole.

5. The market system has a number of merits. The two economic virtues of the system are the efficient allocation of resources and the incentives for productive efficiency in the use of resources. A noneconomic virtue is the personal freedom allowed in a market economy.

Terms and Concepts

bartering
coincidence of wants
competition
firms
Five Fundamental Questions
freedom of choice
freedom of enterprise
households
"invisible hand"
market economy
medium of exchange
money
private property
roundabout production
self-interest
specialization and division of labour

Hints and Tips

1. It is important to recognize that prices have a dual role: to provide both signals and incentives. An increase in the price of a product signals that for some reason this product has become relatively more scarce. The price increase gives consumers the incentive to reduce their consumption (as they ration their limited incomes) and gives producers the incentive to produce more (in order to maximize profits).

2. The spontaneous and decentralized manner in which households and firms respond to price changes is the essence of the market system. Nobody is in control of the whole economy; nobody has the responsibility to coordinate the allocation of resources. All economic agents contribute to this process as they respond to price signals and incentives. As if by an "invisible hand" these self-interested responses produce outcomes that are socially beneficial.

Fill-In Questions

1. The ownership of resources by private individuals and organizations is the institution of __________.

2. Two basic freedoms encountered in the market system are the freedoms of __________ and __________.

3. According to the assumption of self-interest each economic unit attempts to do what ______________.

4. Property rights entail the rights to __________, __________, and __________ of property.

5. Competition is present if two conditions prevail; these two conditions are

(a) ______________________________

(b) ______________________________

6. Market prices of products are determined by the demand from (firms, households)__________ and the supply from __________. Market prices of resources are determined by the demand from __________ and the supply from __________.

7. In a market system, an increase in the scarcity of a product is signaled by a(n) (increase, decrease) __________ in the __________ of the product. This change gives consumers and producers the incentive to revise their choices in furthering their own __________.

8. The concept of the pure market system as a self-regulating economy precludes any significant role for __________.

9. List the six characteristics of the market system.

(a) ____________________________

(b) ____________________________

(c) ____________________________

(d) ____________________________

(e) ____________________________

(f) ____________________________

10. Economic units seeking to further their own self-interest and operating within the capitalistic system will simultaneously, as though directed by an __________, promote the __________ interest.

11. Firms are forced by competition to use the __________ production methods.

12. List the Five Fundamental Questions to which every society must respond.

(a) ______________________________

(b) ______________________________

(c) ______________________________

(d) ______________________________

(e) ______________________________

13. Changes in consumer __________ cause competitive markets to __________ resources.

14. The three practices or institutions common to modern economies are:

(a) ______________________________

(b) ______________________________

(c) ______________________________

15. Specialization tends to (decrease, increase) __________ productive efficiency.

16. If an economy engages in extensive specialization, the individuals living in the economy are extremely (independent, interdependent) __________ and if these individuals are to enjoy the benefits of specialization there must be __________ among them.

17. Bartering refers to trading __________ for __________.

18. Exchange by barter requires a __________ of wants.

19. Money is a social invention for __________ exchange.

20. For an item to serve as money it needs to pass only one test: __________.

Problems and Projects

1. Consider a college with fewer parking spots than students who would like to drive to school. At present the college offers free parking on a first-come-first-served basis. They are considering charging for parking, setting the price high enough that there would always be a few spots open.
(a) Why would the system of charging for parking change the allocation of parking spots?
(b) Why would some students be in favour of the change while others would not?
(c) What socially beneficial incentives would be created by the proposed charge for parking?

2. Suppose that a firm can produce 100 units of product X by combining labour, land, capital, and entrepreneurial ability in three different ways as shown in the table below. It can hire labour at $2 per unit, land at $3 per unit, capital at $5 per unit, and entrepreneurial ability at $10 per unit.

	Method		
Resource	1	2	3
Labour	8	13	10
Land	4	3	3
Capital	4	2	4
Entrepreneurial ability	1	1	1

(a) Which is the least cost method of producing 100 units of X? _____

(b) If the price of labour should rise from $2 to $3 per unit, which is the least cost method of producing 100 units of X? _____

(c) If the firm produces 100 X, the increase in the price of labour gives the firm the incentive to (increase, decrease) its use of labour from _____ units to _____ units.

3. Under Canada's supply management system the right to produce some agricultural products is limited and is allocated to existing industry producers on some agreed-on basis. Generally the rights are marketable and tend to command a high price. To what extent are these rights a form of private property? Suppose you had a yearly quota or production right of 50,000 dozen eggs. What would happen to the value of your production right if supply management was abolished and anyone could produce and sell eggs?

True-False

Circle T if the statement is true, F if it is false.

1. The Canadian economy can be classified as "pure capitalism." **T F**

2. The United States economy can be classified as "pure capitalism." **T F**

3. In the real world there are usually legal limits placed on the rights of private property. **T F**

4. A price system is used only in capitalistic economies. **T F**

5. In the market system prices are set by a governmental agency. **T F**

6. If property rights did not exist for intellectual property, individuals would have less incentive to create music, books and computer programs. **T F**

7. In the market system prices serve as signals for the allocation of resources. **T F**

8. The market system promotes productive efficiency. **T F**

9. Because the market system is efficient in resource use, it follows that every individuai is better off under this form of economic organization than any alternative. **T F**

10. The distribution of output in the market economy depends upon the distribution of resources. **T F**

11. In a purely capitalistic economy, firms make the ultimate decisions about what to produce. **T F**

12. Competition serves to regulate self-interest for the benefit of society in the market model. **T F**

13. The employment of capital to produce goods and services implies that there will be roundabout means of production. **T F**

14. Roundabout means of production are used because they are more efficient than direct production. **T F**

15. Specialization allows for a more efficient use of resources. **T F**

16. Money is a device for facilitating the exchange of goods and services. **T F**

17. The only real money is gold. **T F**

18. "Coincidence of wants" means that two persons desire to acquire the same good or service. **T F**

19. The market system ensures that all households will receive an equitable share of the economy's output of goods and services. **T F**

20. The "invisible hand" refers to government intervention in the market. **T F**

Multiple-Choice

Choose the letter that corresponds to the best answer.

1. Which of the following is not one of the six characteristics of capitalism?
(a) competition
(b) freedom of enterprise and choice
(c) self-interest
(d) private property
(e) central economic planning

2. In the market system the price of a good in the output market does all of the following except:
(a) provides information on prospective profits and therefore affects resource allocation
(b) reflects the intensity of the desire for the good by consumers and the supply offered by sellers
(c) indicates the least cost combination of resources used in the production of the good
(d) is a determinant of the price that will be paid to the resources used in the production of that good

3. To decide how to use its scarce resources to satisfy human wants, laissez faire capitalism relies on:
(a) central planning
(b) roundabout production
(c) a price system together with the profit motive
(d) the coincidence of wants

4. The "invisible hand" is used to explain how in the market system:
(a) property rights are defined
(b) resources are allocated
(c) the self-interest of individuals is harnessed for the benefit of society
(d) allocative efficiency is achieved

5. In the market system a decrease in the demand for a good should result in all but:
(a) an increase in the price of the resources producing the good
(b) a decrease in the profitability of producing the good
(c) a movement of resources out of the production of the good
(d) a decrease in the price of the good

6. Roundabout production refers to:
(a) the use of resources by government
(b) the use of resources to produce consumer goods directly
(c) the use of resources to produce services
(d) the use of resources to produce capital goods that in turn are used to produce other goods

7. The basis for competition, or economic rivalry, entails all but:
(a) the presence of a large number of buyers
(b) the freedom to enter or leave a particular market
(c) the presence of a large number of sellers
(d) a fair price determined by a public agency
(e) (c) and (d)

8. Specialization in production is more efficient because:
(a) increasing opportunity costs reduce the resources used in the production of an extra unit of output
(b) barter transactions are rendered unnecessary
(c) regions and individuals possess unique resources and talents
(d) experience or "learning-by-doing" results in increased output
(e) (c) and (d)

9. Which of the following is not a necessary consequence of specialization?
(a) people will use money
(b) people will engage in trade
(c) people will be dependent upon each other
(d) people will produce more of one thing than they would produce in the absence of specialization

10. Barter:
(a) is the major method of trading in capitalistic economies
(b) is the main method of trading in socialist economies
(c) is the exchange of a good for money
(d) is the exchange of a good for a good

11. One of the following is not a disadvantage of specialization:
(a) increased interdependence among economic units
(b) the performance of repetitive and boring tasks
(c) increased production
(d) need for exchange

12. One of the following is not a virtue of the market system:
(a) allocative efficiency
(b) productive efficiency
(c) fair distribution of income
(d) ability to adapt to changes in tastes, technologies and resource supplies

13. The term "division of labour" means the same as:
(a) specialization
(b) barter
(c) economies of scale
(d) coincidence of wants

14. All modern economies have the following characteristics except for:
(a) specialization
(b) limited government interference
(c) use of money
(d) roundabout means of production

Discussion Questions

1. List the Five Fundamental Questions that all economies must answer. Explain how the market system determines the answers to these questions.

2. How does the pursuit of self-interest by all economic units in the market system model ultimately benefit society? Is self-interest synonymous with selfishness?

3. If the basic decisions are not made in a capitalist economy by a central authority, how are they made?

4. At one time the world price of oil was expected to hit $100 a barrel by the 1990s. If so, the Canadian economy would presumably have allocated more resources to oil production. How would market forces have produced such a result? How would market forces have changed the gasoline consumption habits of Canadian households?

5. If housing prices are rising in Vancouver and falling in Burnaby, what does this signal? What incentives do these price changes create?

6. What are the advantages of "indirect" or "roundabout" production?

7. In order for a market to be competitive, why must there be many buyers and many sellers? What might be some consequences of a lack of large numbers of buyers or sellers?

8. How does an economy benefit from specialization and division of labour?

9. What is money? What important function does it perform? Explain how money performs this function and how it overcomes the disadvantages associated with barter. Why are people willing to accept paper money in exchange for goods and services they have to sell?

Answers

Fill-in questions

1. private property

2. enterprise, choice

3. is best for itself

4. own, use, dispose

5. (a) large number of buyers and sellers; (b) freedom of exit from and entry to any market

6. households, firms; firms, households

7. increase, price, self-interest

8. government

9. (a) private property; (b) freedom of enterprise and choice; (c) self-interest; (d) markets and prices; (e) competition; (f) limited government

10. "invisible hand," social (or public)

11. least cost

12. (a) How much is to be produced?; (b) What is to be produced?; (c) How is the output to be produced?; (d) Who is to receive the output?; (e) How can the system adapt to change to remain efficient?

13. tastes, reallocate

14. (a) specialization; (b) use of money; (c) roundabout production

15. increase

16. interdependent, trade

17. good, good

18. coincidence

19. facilitating

20. generally acceptable by buyer and seller

Problems and projects

1. (a) Some students willing and able to arrive early enough, or to spent time hunting for a spot may be unwilling to spend the money for a spot, whereas others may be more willing and able to spend the money; (b) differences in availability of money and time; (c) those who place a low value on parking would have incentive to walk, bus, carpool; firms seeking profit would have more incentive to provide near campus parking for a fee.

2. (a) 2 at $55; (b) 1 at $66; (c) decrease, 13, 8.

True-False

1. F **2.** F **3.** T **4.** F **5.** F **6.** T
7. T **8.** T **9.** F **10.** T **11.** F **12.** T
13. T **14.** T **15.** T **16.** T **17.** F **18.** F
19. T **20.** F

Multiple-Choice

1. (e) **2.** (c) **3.** (c) **4.** (c) **5.** (a) **6.** (d)
7. (d) **8.** (e) **9.** (a) **10.** (d) **11.** (c) **12.** (c)
13. (a) **14.** (b)

CHAPTER 4

Understanding Individual Markets: Supply and Demand

Chapter 4 is an introduction to the most fundamental model of economic analysis: the demand and supply model. This model permits us to analyze how various forces and factors affect the market price and quantities traded in competitive markets. Although many real world markets do not exactly correspond to the assumptions of the basic demand and supply model, the predictions derived from the model have proven to be correct in a wide variety of situations. Therefore, it is the model most often used by economists to predict changes in market prices and quantities.

Demand and supply are simply "boxes" or categories into which we can sort all the forces and factors that affect the price and the quantity of a good bought and sold in a competitive market. To focus on the price and quantity variables which are of central interest, we apply the *ceteris paribus* assumption. We hold constant all factors (independent variables), other than its own price, that affect the quantity taken off the market by demanders or placed on the market by profit-maximizing firms. With this assumption in effect, we can represent demand and supply using two-dimensional diagrams with price and quantity on the axes. Demand is an inverse relationship between price and quantity demanded, *ceteris paribus*. Supply is a positve relationship between price and quantity supplied, *ceteris paribus*. The demand and supply relationships can be expressed in the form of algebraic equations, schedules placed in tables, or in graphs.

Many students never understand how to apply the model because they never learn to define demand and supply exactly and because they never learn: (1) what is meant by an increase or decrease in demand or supply; (2) the important distinctions between "demand" and "quantity demanded" and between "supply" and "quantity supplied". Your work with the graphical model of demand and supply will greatly help clarify these concepts.

Holding constant all the nonprice factors affecting demand and supply, there is only one price at which the quantity demanded by consumers exactly equals the quantity supplied by sellers. This is the equilibrium price, or market clearing price. The equilibrium quantity is the quantity demanded and supplied at the equilibrium price. If you can determine the equilibrium price and quantity under one set of demand and supply conditions, you can determine them under any other set, and so will be able to analyse the effects of changes in the nonprice factors on the equilibrium price and quantity.

Starting from an initial equilibrium, a change in any nonprice factor that determines demand or supply will shift one of the two curves, and throw the market out of equilibrium--creating either a shortage or a surplus. To eliminate a shortage (or surplus) the price must rise (or fall) to restore the balance between how much consumers are willing and able to buy and producers are willing and able to sell.

The demand and supply model has so many applications that it is the single most important tool in economics. Success in economics is impossible without a solid grasp of this model.

Checklist

When you have studied this chapter, you should be able to:

- ☐ Define a market.
- ☐ Define demand and state the law of demand.
- ☐ Graph a demand curve from a demand schedule.
- ☐ Derive a market demand from individual demands.
- ☐ List the major nonprice determinants of demand and explain how each one shifts the demand curve.
- ☐ Distinguish between a change in demand and a change in quantity demanded.

- ☐ Define supply and state the law of supply.
- ☐ Graph a supply curve from a supply schedule.
- ☐ List the major nonprice determinants of supply and explain how each one shifts the supply curve.
- ☐ Distinguish between a change in supply and a change in quantity supplied.
- ☐ Explain the concept of equilibrium.
- ☐ Determine, when you are given the demand for and the supply of a good, what the equilibrium price and the equilibrium quantity will be.
- ☐ Explain, when there is a shortage or a surplus, the underlying actions of consumers and business firms that bring about an equilibrium price.
- ☐ Predict the effects of changes in demand and supply on equilibrium price and equilibrium quantity; and on the prices of substitute and complementary goods.
- ☐ Explain the meaning of the rationing function of prices.

Chapter Outline

1. A market is any institution or mechanism that brings together the buyers and the sellers of a particular good or service. In this chapter it is assumed that markets are purely competitive.

2. Demand is the relationship between the price of a product and the amount of that product the consumer is willing and able to purchase in a specific time period.
(a) The market demand is derived by "adding up" the individual demands of all consumers in the market.
(b) The law of demand states that, other things being equal, there is an inverse relationship between price and quantity demanded.
(c) The law of demand holds because of the:
1) substitution effect--consumers buy more of goods that become cheaper relative to substitute goods;
2) income effect--lower prices increase the buying power of consumers' fixed money incomes, enabling them to buy more goods.

3. The demand curve is a graphic representation of demand and the law of demand.
(a) The graph has price on the vertical axis, and quantity demanded on the horizontal axis.
(b) A change in price leads to a movement along the demand curve. This is termed a change in quantity demanded.

4. The nonprice factors that determine demand are: 1) tastes, 2) number of buyers, 3) income, 4) prices of related goods (substitutes and complements), 5) expectations.
(a) A change in any of the nonprice determinants will shift demand to the left or right, creating an entirely different demand curve. This is termed a change in demand.
(b) A change in demand and a change in the quantity demanded are not the same thing.

5. If the demand for one good increases as a result of an increase in the price of another good, then the two goods are termed substitutes. If the demand for one good decreases as a result of an increase in the price of another good, then the two goods are termed complements.

6. If the demand for a good increases as a result of an increase in income, the good is termed a normal good. If the demand decreases due to an increase in income, then the good is termed an inferior good.

7. Supply is the relationship between the price of a product and the amount of that product that suppliers will offer to sell in a specific time period. The law of supply states that, other things being equal, there is a positive relationship between price and quantity supplied.

8. The supply curve is a graphic representation of supply and the law of supply.
(a) The graph has price on the vertical axis, and quantity supplied on the horizontal axis.
(b) A change in price leads to a movement along the supply curve. This is termed a change in quantity supplied.

9. The nonprice factors that determine supply are: 1) resource prices, 2) technology, 3) taxes and subsidies, 4) prices of other goods, 5) expectations, 6) number of sellers.
(a) A change in any of the nonprice determinants will shift supply to the left or right, creating an entirely different supply curve. This is termed a change in supply.
(b) A change in supply and a change in the quantity supplied are not the same thing.

10. The market or equilibrium price of a commodity is that price at which quantity demanded and quantity supplied are equal; and the quantity exchanged in the

market (the equilibrium quantity) is equal to the quantity demanded and supplied at the equilibrium price.
(a) At any price above the equilibrium, there is a surplus (quantity demanded is less than quantity supplied) which will cause the price to fall.
(b) At any price below the equilibrium, there is a shortage (quantity demanded is greater than quantity supplied) which will cause the price to rise.
(c) The rationing function of price is the elimination of shortages and surpluses of the commodity.

11. A change in a nonprice determinant will cause a shift in the demand curve or the supply curve, and result in a new equilibrium price and quantity.
(a) Most changes shift only one of the two curves.
(b) Given the supply curve, there is a direct relationship between a change in demand and the resulting change in equilibrium price and quantity.
(c) Given the demand curve, there is an inverse relationship between a change in supply and the resulting change in equilibrium price, and a direct relationship between a change in supply and the resulting change in equilibrium quantity.
(d) In situations where both supply determinants and demand determinants change, both curves will shift; the direction of price change or quantity change will be predictable, the other will be indeterminate.

12. In resource markets, suppliers are households and demanders are business firms, and in product markets, suppliers are business firms and demanders are households. Supply and demand are useful in the analysis of prices and quantities exchanged in both types of markets.

Terms and Concepts

change in demand (supply) versus change in the quantity demanded (supplied)
complementary goods
demand
demand schedule
diminishing marginal utility
equilibrium price and quantity
income and substitution effects
inferior goods
law of demand
law of supply
market
normal (superior) good
rationing function of prices
shortage
substitute goods
supply
supply schedule
surplus

Hints and Tips

1. This chapter is the most important one in the book. Be sure to spend extra time on it, and to return to it for review of the fundamentals if you run into difficulties when studying later chapters.

2. You have not mastered the chapter until you can clearly distinguish between a change in demand and a change in quantity demanded; the same for supply. You should be able to articulate the difference verbally, and using a graph.

3. More than any of the previous chapters, this chapter requires active practice. Pick up your pencil and draw graphs. Begin by plotting demand and supply schedules onto graphs. Study carefully the examples in the text and study guide to learn the appropriate labels for such graphs. Read off the equilibrium price and quantity. Go to other prices and determine the size of the shortage or surplus.

4. Once you are confident of working with graphs with concrete numbers, go to the next step of drawing abstract graphs where numbers are implied, but not explicitly given, on the price and quantity axes. Work through many hypothetical scenarios.

Fill-In Questions

1. (a) A market is the institution or mechanism that brings together the __________ and the __________ of a particular good or service.
(b) In resource markets, prices are determined by the

demand decisions of (business firms, households) __________ and the supply decisions of __________.

(c) In the product markets, prices are determined by the demand decisions of __________ and the supply decisions of __________.

2. The demand schedule reflects a (positive, negative) __________ relationship between price and quantity demanded. The supply schedule reflects a __________ relationship between price and quantity supplied.

3. "Demand is a schedule that shows the units of a product consumers are willing and able to purchase at each specific price during a specific period of time, all other things being equal." The "all other things" are __________, __________, __________, __________, and __________. They are sometimes referred to as the __________ determinants.

4. When demand or supply is graphed, price is placed on the __________ axis and quantity on the __________ axis.

5. The graph of the demand schedule is called the demand __________ and according to the law of demand is __________ sloped.

6. A change in price causes a change in (demand, quantity demanded) __________, and results in a (movement along, shift in) __________ the demand curve. A change in consumer incomes causes a change in (demand, quantity demanded) __________, and results in a (movement along, shift in) __________ the demand curve.

7. A consumer tends to buy more of a product as its price falls because:

(a) the purchasing power of the consumer is increased and the consumer can buy more of this and other products; this is called the __________ effect.

(b) the product becomes less expensive relative to similar products and the consumer tends to buy more of this and less of the other products; and this is called the __________ effect.

8. Along a given demand curve for sandwiches the price of other goods stays __________. Suppose the price of coffee is fixed at $1.00 and the price of a sandwich changes from $3.00 to $4.00. At a price of $3.00, a sandwich is __________ times as expensive as a coffee; while at a price of $4.00, a sandwich is __________ times as expensive as a coffee. The price of sandwiches as compared to or relative to the price of coffee has __________. Moving down the demand curve for sandwiches the relative price of sandwiches __________.

9. The fundamental factors that determine the supply of any product are:

(a) __________

(b) __________

(c) __________

(d) __________

(e) __________

(f) __________

(g) __________

10. A change in price causes a change in (supply, quantity supplied) __________, and results in a (movement along, shift in) __________ the supply curve. A change in resource costs causes a change in (supply, quantity supplied) __________, and results in a (movement along, shift in) __________ the supply curve.

11. A change in supply is the result of a change in the __________ factors. An increase in supply is shown by a shift of the entire supply curve to the __________. A decrease in supply is shown by a shift of the entire supply curve to the __________.

12. The equilibrium price of a commodity is the price at which __________ equals __________.

13. If quantity demanded exceeds quantity supplied, price is (above, below) __________ the equilibrium price; and the (shortage, surplus) __________ will cause the price to (rise, fall) __________.

14. Consider the market for wine. In the space after each of the following, indicate whether the demand (D) or the supply (S) is shifted, whether it is an increase (+) or decrease (-) in the curve.

(a) Increase in the price of grapes __________

(b) Increase in population of consumers __________

(c) Increase in the price of cheese __________

(d) Improvement in production technology __________

(e) New subsidies for wine production __________

(f) Increase in the price of beer __________

(g) Consumers expect new sales taxes on alcohol products __________

15. In the spaces provided, indicate the effect [increase (+), decrease (-), or indeterminate (?)] upon the equilibrium price and equilibrium quantity of each of these changes in demand and/or supply.

(a) Increase in demand, supply constant
P:_____ Q:_____

(b) Increase in supply, demand constant
P:_____ Q:_____

(c) Decrease in demand, supply constant
P:_____ Q:_____

(d) Decrease in supply, demand constant
P:_____ Q:_____

(e) Increase in demand, increase in supply
P:_____ Q:_____

(f) Increase in demand, decrease in supply
P:_____ Q:_____

(g) Decrease in demand, decrease in supply
P:_____ Q:_____

(h) Decrease in demand, increase in supply
P:_____ Q:_____

16. If supply and demand establish a price for a good such that there is no shortage or surplus of the good, then price is successfully performing its __________ function.

Problems and Projects

1. (a) Plot the demand and supply schedule below on the graph provided. Indicate on the graph the equilibrium price and quantity by drawing lines from the intersection of the demand and supply curves to the price and quantity axes, and label the values P* and Q*.

Price per Unit	Quantity Demanded	Quantity Supplied
$13	18	54
12	21	48
11	24	42
10	27	36
9	30	30
8	33	24
7	36	18
6	39	12

(b) At equilibrium, P* = _____, and Q* = _____.

(c) A price of $13 is not the equilibrium price because a __________ exists.

(d) A surplus of 18 units would exist if the price was

__________.

(e) The government puts in place a fixed price of $6. At this price the quantity demanded will be __________; the quantity supplied will be __________. At this price there will be a (surplus, shortage) __________ of __________ units. Indicate the fixed price, the quantity demanded and quantity supplied, and shortage on the graph.

2. Three individuals' demand schedules for bread are shown below. Assuming these three are the only buyers in the market, fill in the total or market demand schedule for bread.

Price (per loaf)	Quantity Demanded (loaves of bread per month)			
	Doug	Leslie	Chong	Total
$1.20	10	6	8	_____
1.10	12	8	10	_____
1.00	15	11	12	_____
0.90	19	15	14	_____
0.80	24	18	16	_____

3. The table below records for four consecutive months what Dustin's income was, what prices he faced for goods X and Y, and what quantities he purchased of each good. Based on these data, answer the questions that follow.

Period	Income	P_X	Q_X	P_Y	Q_Y
May	$600	$10	20 units	$8	9 units
June	600	10	24	11	7
July	600	13	14	11	8
August	800	13	18	11	7

(a) Between which two months is there a movement along Dustin's demand curve for X? __________ and __________.

(b) From May to June, Dustin's purchases of good X (increase, decrease) __________ as the price of good _____ (increases, decreases) __________, while income is __________. This indicates that he regards X and Y as (complements, substitutes) __________.

(c) Dustin treats good X as (normal, inferior) __________ because from the month of __________ to the month of __________ consumption of X __________ as income __________, *ceteris paribus*. Dustin treats good Y as __________.

(d) Dustin's demand curve for X shifts to the right between the months of __________ and __________, and again between __________ and __________.

4. Suppose that the demand and supply model is applicable to the Canadian beef market. For each of the following occurrences, sketch a demand and supply graph that shows the effect on the equilibrium price and quantity of beef in Canada.

(a) A popular singer remarks that red meat in the diet may be a contributing factor in heart and circulatory diseases.

(b) The East coast fishery is closed due to failure of the fish stock.

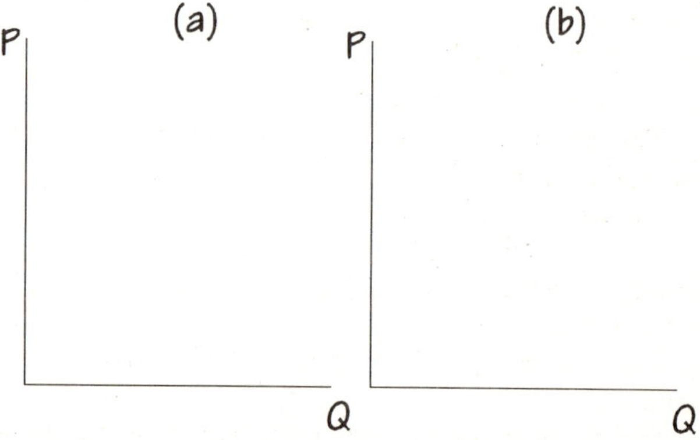

(c) The United States government lifts an embargo that has until now prevented the importation of beef from Canada.

(d) The price of livestock feed grains falls sharply due to a record harvest.

(e) Agriculture Canada discovers a new growth hormone that will increase the weight of beef cattle by 20% with the same feed intake.

(f) Most people that work in outlets that serve beef receive the minimum wage. The governments of all Canadian provinces declare a 50% increase in the minimum wage.

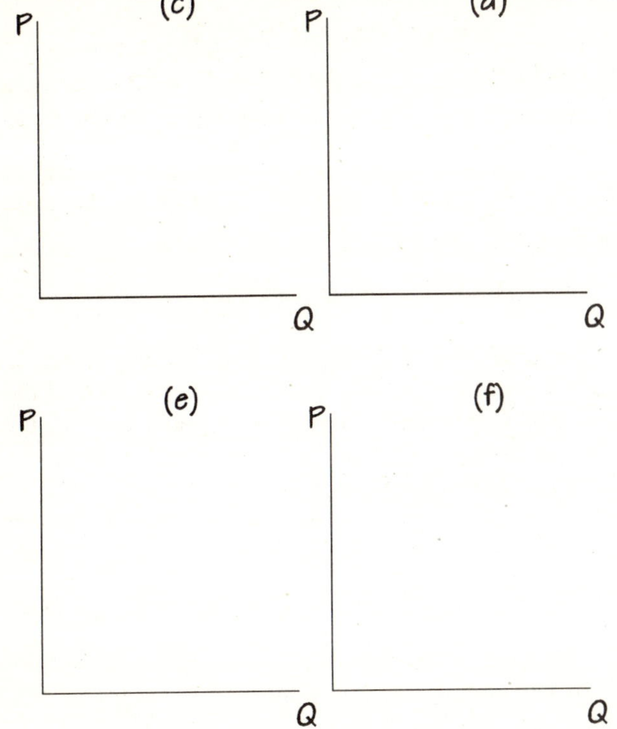

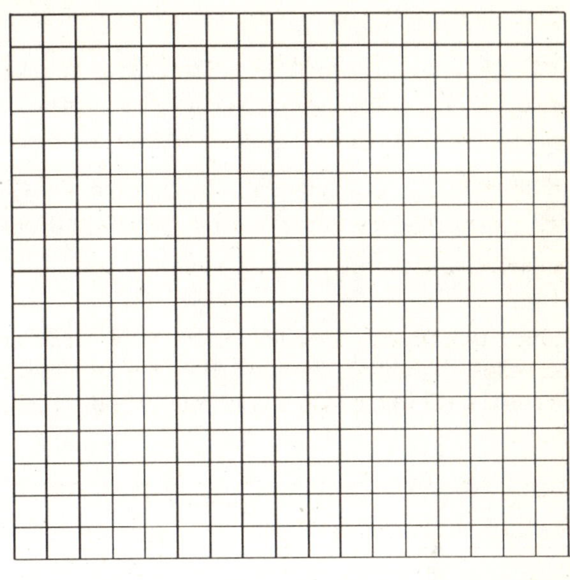

5. This question uses algebraic expressions of demand and supply. Suppose the market demand for roofing nails is given by: $Q_d = 1600\text{-}400P$. The market supply is given by $Q_s = 500P\text{-}200$. Q_d is quantity demanded, Q_s is quantity supplied (both in kilograms), and P is the price (in $ per kilogram).

(a) Use algebra to find the equilibrium price and quantity.

(b) Plot the demand and the supply on the next graph to confirm the answer you found by algebra.

6. Over the last thirty years airfares from Canada to Europe have increased substantially. Yet, over the same period, the number of people flying from Canada to Europe has increased substantially. This observation (is, is not) __________ a violation of the law of demand. Three reasons for this conclusion are:

(a) ______________________________

(b) ______________________________

(c) ______________________________

7. The graph below shows the demand and supply for daily parking spots in the centre of a major city.

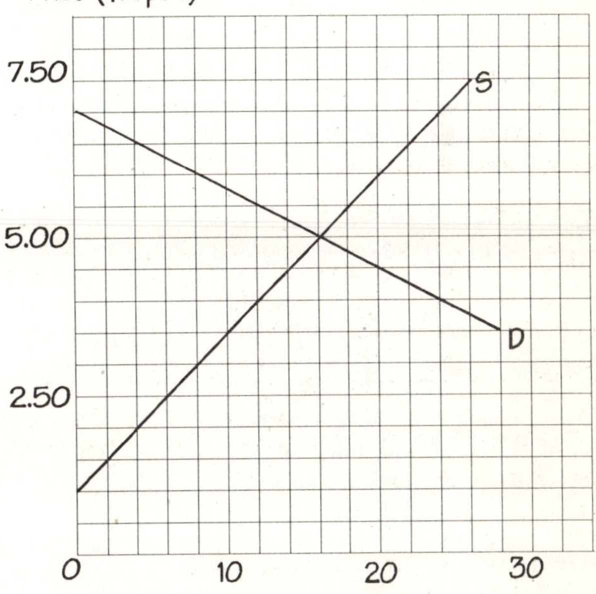

(a) The current equilibrium price is _____ per spot, and _____ spots are rented each day.

(b) Suppose that the city government levies a new tax on

parking lot operators in order to raise revenue to pay for a rapid transit system. The tax is set at $1 per spot rented. If the consumer pays $6, the supplier gets to keep $6-$1=$5. If the consumer pays $5, the supplier gets to keep _____.

(c) Show the new supply curve reflecting the tax. (The supply curve will shift upward by the amount of the tax because producers require this much extra in order to be willing to maintain the same supply as before).

(d) The new equilibrium price is _____ per spot, and _____ spots are rented each day. Accordingly, the price consumers pay for one spot has (fallen, risen) __________ by $_____, and the price that suppliers get to keep has __________ by $_____. Therefore, the consumers' burden of the tax is _____ percent, and the suppliers' burden is _____ percent.

8. The table below shows the demand and supply schedules for firewood in two small towns, Eastwick and Westwood. Initially each town has a perfectly competitive market apart from the other town because there is no passage across the river that separates them.

	Eastwick		Westwood		Total	
Price	Qd	Qs	Qd	Qs	Qd	Qs
225	80	100	45	105	____	____
200	90	90	55	95	____	____
175	100	80	65	85	____	____
150	110	70	75	75	____	____
125	120	60	85	65	____	____

(a) In Eastwick the equilibrium price is _____ per cord, and the equilibrium quantity is _____ cords per year.

(b) In Westwood the equilibrium price is _____ per cord, and the equilibrium quantity is _____ cords per year.

Now a bridge is built across the river, turning Eastwick and Westwood into one combined market.

(c) Fill in the market demand and supply schedules.

(d) The new equilibrium price is _____ per cord. This represents an increase in (Westwood, Eastwick) __________ and a decrease in __________.

(e) In Westwood quantity demanded is now _____ cords per year, and quantity supplied is now _____ cords per year. In Eastwick quantity demanded is now _____ cords per year, and quantity supplied is now _____ cords per year. At the new price, if there was no trade between the two towns, in Westwood there would be a (shortage, surplus) __________ of _____ cords per year. In Eastwick there would be a (shortage, surplus) __________ of _____ cords per year.

True-False

Circle T if the statement is true, F if it is false.

1. A market is any arrangement that brings together the buyers and sellers of a particular good or service. **T F**

2. Demand is the amount of a commodity or service a buyer will purchase at a particular price. **T F**

3. The law of demand states that as price increases, the quantity of the product demanded increases. **T F**

4. The law of demand states that as price increases, the demand for the product decreases, *ceteris paribus*. **T F**

5. In graphing supply and demand schedules, supply is put on the horizontal axis and demand on the vertical axis. **T F**

6. A fall in the price of a good will cause the demand for goods that are substitutes for it to decrease. **T F**

7. If two goods are complements, such as film and cameras, an increase in the price of one will cause the demand for the other to decrease. **T F**

8. A change in buyers' tastes will cause the demand curve to shift. **T F**

9. An increase in income increases the demand for normal goods. **T F**

10. An inferior good is a lower quality good that is consumed by the bottom income group in society. **T F**

11. Diminishing marginal utility refers to the phenomenon that the consumer gets less additional satisfaction from one more unit of a product the more of the product he already has. **T F**

12. Since the amount purchased must equal the amount sold then demand and supply must always equal each other. **T F**

Questions 13-15 are based on the accompanying graph.

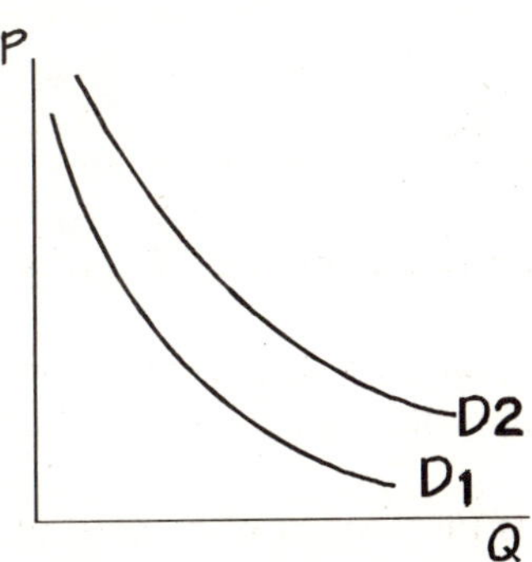

13. If the demand curve moves from D_1 to D_2 demand has increased. **T F**

14. The shift of the demand curve from D_1 to D_2 could be caused by a decrease in the price of complements. **T F**

15. The shift of the demand curve from D_1 to D_2 could be caused by a decrease in supply. **T F**

16. A normal good is also termed a superior good. **T F**

17. A decrease in quantity supplied is caused by an increase in production costs. **T F**

18. A shift to the right of the supply curve is called a decrease in supply. **T F**

19. If the market price of a commodity is momentarily below its equilibrium, the price will tend to rise because demand will decrease and supply will increase. **T F**

20. When quantity demanded exceeds quantity supplied, the market price will tend to fall. **T F**

21. When a surplus exists, the market price will tend to fall. **T F**

22. The rationing function of prices is the elimination of shortages and surpluses. **T F**

23. A change in demand alters both equilibrium price and equilibrium quantity in the opposite direction to the change in demand. **T F**

24. There is an inverse relationship between a change in supply and the resulting change in equilibrium price. **T F**

Multiple-Choice

Circle the letter that corresponds to the best answer.

1. An increase in the quantity demanded of oranges can be caused by:
(a) a shift to the left of the supply curve of oranges
(b) a shift to the right of the supply curve of oranges
(c) a decline in the demand for orange juice
(d) a rise in the demand for orange juice
(e) a decrease in the price of salt

2. A decrease in the quantity demanded:
(a) shifts the demand curve to the left
(b) shifts the demand curve to the right
(c) is a movement down along the demand curve
(d) is a movement up along the demand curve

3. If two goods are substitutes for each other, an increase in the price of one will necessarily:
(a) decrease the demand for the other
(b) increase the demand for the other
(c) decrease the quantity demanded of the other
(d) increase the quantity demanded of the other

4. Which pair of goods would most consumers regard as complementary goods?
(a) coffee and tea
(b) tennis balls and tennis racquets
(c) hamburger meat and bus rides
(d) books and televisions

5. Which of the following is **not** among the determinants of demand?
(a) consumer incomes

(b) consumer expectations of future prices
(c) number of consumers
(d) prices of substitute goods
(e) cost of resources

6. If an increase in income causes the demand for a particular good to decrease, then that good is:
(a) normal
(b) inferior
(c) substitute
(d) complement

7. According to the law of supply:
(a) equilibrium quantity will always increase when equilibrium price increases
(b) equilibrium quantity will always decrease when equilibrium price increases
(c) the supply curve has a negative slope
(d) other things remaining the same the quantity supplied increases whenever price increases

8. A supply curve indicates:
(a) the profit-maximizing quantities sellers place on the market at alternative prices
(b) the minimum quantities sellers place on the market at alternative prices
(c) the maximum quantities sellers will place on the market at different prices for inputs
(d) the quantities sellers place on the market in order to meet consumer demand at that price

9. The supply curve of the firm slopes upward in the short run because:
(a) the increased production requires the use of inferior inputs
(b) hiring more inputs for the extra production requires the payment of higher input prices
(c) the increased technology to produce more output is expensive
(d) productive efficiency declines because certain productive resources cannot be expanded in a short period of time

10. A movement along a supply curve for a good would be caused by:
(a) an improvement in the technology of production
(b) an increase in the price of the good
(c) an increase in the number of suppliers of the good
(d) a change in expectations

11. Which of the following would increase the supply of books?
(a) an increase in the demand for books
(b) an increase in the price of books
(c) an increase in the cost of paper
(d) a decrease in the wages paid to printers

12. A market is in equilibrium when:
(a) inventories of the good are not rising
(b) suppliers can sell all of the good they decide to produce at the prevailing price
(c) quantity demanded equals quantity supplied
(d) demanders can purchase all of the good they want at the prevailing price

13. An increase in the demand for potatoes is expected this year. The demand-supply model predicts, other things being equal:
(a) an increase in the supply of potatoes
(b) a decrease in the quantity exchanged of potatoes
(c) an increase in equilibrium price and a decrease in equilibrium quantity
(d) an increase in the equilibrium price of potatoes

Questions 14 to 17 are based on this diagram.

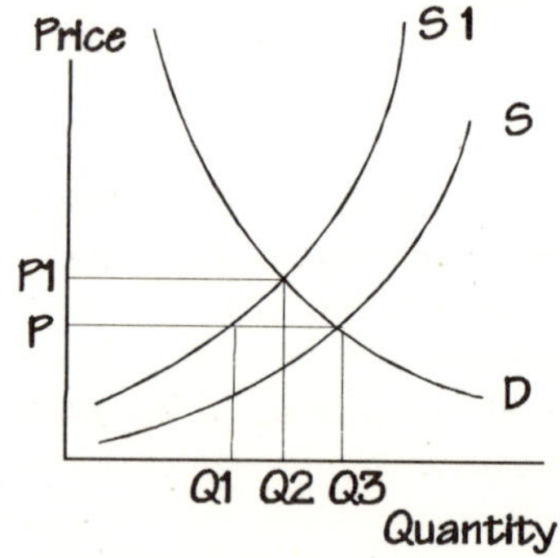

14. Given the original demand and supply curves are D and S:
(a) the equilibrium price and quantity were P and Q_1
(b) the equilibrium price and quantity were P and P_1
(c) the equilibrium price and quantity were P_1 and Q_1
(d) the equilibrium price and quantity were P_1 and Q_2
(e) the equilibrium price and quantity were P and Q_3

15. The shift of the supply curve from S to S_1 is termed:
(a) an increase in supply
(b) an increase in quantity supplied
(c) a decrease in supply

(d) a decrease in quantity supplied

16. The shift in the supply curve from S to S_1 could be caused by:
(a) an increase in the price of the good
(b) a technological improvement in the production of the good
(c) a decrease in demand
(d) an increase in the cost of the resources used in the production of the good

17. If the price was prevented from adjusting when the supply shifted from S to S_1 the result would be:
(a) a surplus of $Q_3 - Q_1$
(b) a shortage of $Q_2 - Q_1$
(c) a shortage of $Q_3 - Q_1$
(d) a surplus of $Q_3 - Q_2$

18. An increase in supply and an increase in demand will:
(a) increase price and increase the quantity exchanged
(b) decrease price and increase the quantity exchanged
(c) affect price in an indeterminate way and decrease the quantity exchanged
(d) affect price in an indeterminate way and increase the quantity exchanged

19. A decrease in supply and an increase in demand will:
(a) increase price and increase the quantity exchanged
(b) decrease price and increase the quantity exchanged
(c) affect quantity exchanged in an indeterminate way and decrease the price
(d) affect quantity exchanged in an indeterminate way and increase the price

Discussion Questions

1. What is a market? For what kinds of goods does a laundromat bulletin board, or classified pages in a student newspaper, often serve as a market?

2. Carefully state the law of demand and explain the two reasons put forth in this chapter to justify downward sloping demand curves.

3. The last time OPEC succeeded in sharply increasing the price of oil, drivers reacted by significantly reducing their gasoline consumption. Explain this in terms of the income effect and substitution effect.

4. Explain the difference between an increase in demand and an increase in quantity demanded. What are the factors that cause a change in demand?

5. Define supply and explain why supply curves are upward sloping.

6. Explain the differences between a change in supply and a change in quantity supplied. What are the factors that cause a change in supply?

7. Neither demand nor supply remains constant for long. Economic circumstances are always changing so the actual prices we see are not equilibrium prices. Why then do economists spend so much time trying to determine the equilibrium price and quantity if these magnitudes change so frequently?

8. How are normal, inferior, substitute, complementary, and independent goods defined? During a recession, who would fare better, firms that sell normal goods, or firms that sell inferior goods?

9. Given the demand for and the supply of a commodity, what price will be the equilibrium price of this commodity? Explain why this price will tend to prevail in the market and why higher (lower) prices, if they do exist temporarily, will tend to fall (rise).

10. Analyse the following quotation and explain the fallacies contained in it. "An increase in demand will cause price to rise; with a rise in price, supply will increase and the increase in supply will push price down. Therefore, an increase in demand may or may not result in a price increase."

Answers

Fill-in questions

1. (a) buyers (demanders), sellers (suppliers) (either order); (b) business firm, households; (c) households, business firms

2. negative, direct

3. 1) tastes, 2) income, 3) prices of related goods, 4) expectations, 5) number of buyers; nonprice

4. vertical, horizontal

5. curve, downward (negative)

6. quantity demanded, movement along; demand, shift in

7. (a) income; (b) substitution

8. fixed; 3; 4; increased; decreased

9. (a) price of the product, (b) resource prices, (c) technology, (d) taxes and subsidies, (e) prices of other goods, (f) expectations, (g) number of sellers

10. quantity supplied, movement along; supply, shift in

11. nonprice; right; left

12. quantity demanded, quantity supplied

13. below; shortage, rise

14. (a) S-; (b) D+; (c) D- (complements); (d) S+; (e) S+; (f) D+ (substitutes); (g) D+

15. (a) +, +; (b) -,+; (c) -,-; (d) +,-; (e) ?,+; (f) +,?; (g) ?,-; (h) -,?

16. rationing

Problems and Projects

1. (b) $9, 30; (c) surplus; (d) $11; (e) 39, 12; shortage, 27.

2. 24, 30, 38, 48, 58

3. (a) June, July; (b) increase, Y, increases, constant; substitutes; (c) normal, July, August, increases, increases; inferior; (d) May, June, July, August.

4. (a) D shifts left: P -, Q -; (b) D shifts right: P +, Q +; (c) S shifts left: P +, Q -; (d) S shifts right: P -, Q +; (e) same as (d); (f) same as (c).

5. (a) set Qd = Qs. Solving yields P* = 2, Q* = 800.

6. is not; (a) population growth, (b) increased incomes, (c) increased prices for substitutes, etc.

7. (a) $5.00, 16,000; (b) $4.00; (d) about 5.30, 13,000, risen, 0.30, fallen, 0.70, 30, 70.

8. (a) 200, 90; (b) 150, 75; (c) Qd = 125, 145, 165, 185, 205; Qs = 205, 185, 165, 145, 125; (d) 175, Westwood, Eastwick; (e) 65, 85; 100, 80; surplus, 20, shortage, 20.

True-False

1. T	**2.** F	**3.** F	**4.** F	**5.** F	**6.** T
7. T	**8.** T	**9.** T	**10.** F	**11.** T	**12.** F
13. T	**14.**T	**15.** F	**16.** T	**17.** F	**18.** F
19. F	**20.** F	**21.**T	**22.** T	**23.** F	**24.** T

Multiple-Choice

1. (b)	**2.** (d)	**3.** (b)	**4.** (b)	**5.** (e)	**6.** (b)
7. (d)	**8.** (a)	**9.** (d)	**10.** (b)	**11.** (d)	**12.** (c)
13. (d)	**14.** (e)	**15.** (c)	**16.** (d)	**17.** (c)	**18.** (d)
19. (d)					

CHAPTER 5

The Public Sector

This chapter investigates the possible economic functions of the public sector in a mixed economy which is dominated by the market system. Even though, in most respects, the market mechanism allocates resources very efficiently and responsively, there are crucial roles for government:

(a) Government must provide a legal framework within which people can live and businesses can operate. In order to facilitate production, specialization and exchange, government must establish the legal status of businesses, contracts, property rights, etc. Government must also provide police services, a system of weights and measures, and a monetary system.

(b) Because a market system is not centrally controlled, we depend on competition to ensure that product and resource suppliers are subject to the dictates of consumer sovereignty. In some markets government intervention is needed to maintain competition instead of allowing monopoly to occur. In other cases, the best solution is government regulation of a monopoly, or even public ownership, to prevent misallocation of resources and abuse of power that unregulated private monopoly may create.

(c) The market system does not necessarily distribute its output equally, or according to need. Because distribution strictly according to market forces would leave many people with unacceptably low incomes, there is a role for government to redistribute incomes. This may be accomplished through transfer payments, taxes, price controls and other market interventions.

(d) Competitive markets may, under a variety of circumstances, fail to produce an efficient allocation of resources. When spillovers or externalities exist, some of the costs or benefits of production or consumption of a good affect someone other than the immediate producer or consumer; therefore they ignore these costs or benefits, leading to too much or too little production or consumption of the good. Goods which everyone can benefit from collectively, and which non-payers cannot be excluded from enjoying, are called public goods. Users' incentives to "free ride" rather than pay may make it impossible for private firms to supply such goods. Inefficiencies of externalities and public goods may be solved by taxes, subsidies, regulations, or direct government involvement in providing the good.

(e) Adjustments in an economy do not occur instantaneously or painlessly as they do in a classroom discussion. Governments can act to stabilize the economy or to adopt programs that help the reallocation of resources that must accompany structural change.

The chapter returns to the circular flow model first presented in Chapter 2. The model has now been modified to include governments along with businesses and households. The addition of government changes the real and monetary flows in the model. The twelve linkages among the household, business, and government sectors in the model are presented.

The next section describes the size of government and the nature of the respective roles of the federal, provincial, and municipal governments in Canada. Government expenditures involve both government purchases (which are "exhaustive" in the sense of directly absorbing or employing resources) and transfer payments (which are "non-exhaustive" because they do not directly absorb resources). By almost any measure, the government sector has grown massively as a proportion of the nation's economy since World War II. Governments' expenditures have grown faster than their revenues, which has created persistent and growing deficits. From the early 1970s to the early 1990s the major changes in the allocation of government spending have been a rise from 10% to 20% in the portion spent on interest payments on government debt, and a drop from 19% to 12% in the portion spent on education. The federal government gets almost half of its revenues from income taxes, and more than half of its spending is on transfer payments to persons and businesses, and debt charges. Provinces raise the bulk of their revenues from a variety of taxes, and spend two thirds of their revenues on health, education and social services. For municipal governments, property taxes are the biggest revenue source, and education is the biggest expenditure category.

The last part of the chapter mentions the current debate over the proper size of government: a debate provoked largely by ballooning government debt. Those on the political right question the effectiveness to date of government solutions to social problems, and advocate cuts to government programs and transfer payments. Those on the left believe that social problems would be worse if government involvement is much reduced, and argue that debt problems should be solved through higher taxes on corporations and higher income households.

Checklist

When you have studied this chapter, you should be able to:

- ☐ Briefly explain why Canada is a mixed economy rather than a pure market economy.
- ☐ List the five economic functions of government in Canada.
- ☐ Give specific examples of what institutions and services government must maintain under the general heading of a "legal and social framework."
- ☐ Define monopoly and explain why government wishes to prevent monopoly and to preserve competition in the economy.
- ☐ Explain why government believes it should redistribute income; and list the three principal policies it employs for this purpose.
- ☐ Define a spillover cost and a spillover benefit; explain why a competitive market fails to allocate resources efficiently when there are spillovers; and list the things government may do to reduce spillovers and improve the allocation of resources.
- ☐ Define a public good and a private good and explain how government goes about reallocating resources from the production of private goods to the production of public goods.
- ☐ Draw a circular flow diagram that includes businesses, households, and government; label all the flows in the diagram; and use the diagram to explain how government alters the distribution of income, the allocation of resources, and the level of activity in the economy.
- ☐ Explain the differences between government purchases and transfer payments and the effect of each of these two kinds of expenditures on the composition of national output.
- ☐ Identify the largest revenue source and the largest expenditure category for each of the three levels of government in Canada: federal, provincial, municipal.
- ☐ Summarize the views of those in favour of cutting the size of government and the views of those in favour of maintaining the size of government.

Chapter Outline

1. The Canadian economy is neither a pure market economy nor a purely planned economy. It is an example of mixed capitalism, in which government affects the operation of the economy in important ways.

2. Government in the Canadian economy performs five economic functions.
(a) the provision of a legal and social framework that makes the effective operation of the market system possible.
(b) the maintenance of competition and the regulation of monopoly.
(c) the redistribution of income to reduce income inequality.
(d) the reallocation of resources to take account of spillover costs or benefits, and of public goods.
(e) the stabilization of the price level and the maintenance of full-employment.

3. By providing a legal and social framework government sets the "rules of the game" governing the relationships between consumers, businesses, and resource suppliers. That economic relationships are refereed gives market participants greater confidence in market transactions and lowers their costs of making these transactions. Therefore, the volume of trade expands.

4. When a market is monopolized, the seller has the incentive to raise price higher than is in the social interest. Trade is restricted and inefficient allocation of resources may result. When a market is competitive, each seller has the incentive to offer lower prices in order to attract more consumers. Thus, competition diminishes the influence of any individual seller. In order to prevent monopolization, Canada has established anti-combines laws prohibiting certain business behaviours. Secondly, in the case of natural monopoly (where monopoly is justified on cost grounds) government may either regulate or itself own the firm.

5. The market system yields high incomes to some and low incomes to others. This unequal distribution of income leads to poverty and other unacceptable results. Government redistributes income by transfer payments, income taxes and other taxes, and by direct market interventions such as price controls.

6. Market failure can arise from externalities or spillovers, where a third party incurs a cost or benefit resulting from the consumption or production of a good or service. The parties to a transaction ignore the presence of externalities since they neither bear the externally imposed cost nor benefit.
(a) In the presence of spillover costs (or, negative externalities) resources are overallocated to production. In the environmental pollution example, the misallocation can be corrected by legislation that prohibits or limits the pollution, or by specific taxes that give polluters the incentive to choose to reduce pollution to the optimal level.
(b) In the presence of spillover benefits (or, positive externalities) there is an underallocation of resources. In the education example, the misallocation can be corrected by government subsidization that increases the demand or the supply, or by direct government provision.

7. The market system fails to provide an optimal allocation of resources to the production of public goods. A public good, such as national defence, is indivisible and not subject to exclusion - once it is provided for one person it is available for all. It is in the self-interest of consumers to conceal their preferences for such goods, since the benefits of the good will be obtained if someone else pays for its production. Because of this free-rider problem, it will be unprofitable for firms to supply public goods. The public sector must provide public goods, and finance them through compulsory taxes.

8. In a democracy, the quantity of public goods to be produced is a collective choice, determined by the political process. The resources for public goods are diverted from the private sector by taxes which diminish the private demand for goods and services.

9. The most recently recognized function of government is to stabilize the economy at full employment, and at a stable price level. Without government intervention, the level of aggregate expenditures on the nation's output may be too high or too low. If demand for goods exceeds the economy's capacity to produce, inflation will result. If demand is below capacity, there will be unemployment among workers and other resources. Government can use its power to spend and to tax to manipulate the level of aggregate expenditures.

10. A circular flow diagram that includes the private sector (households and firms) and the public sector (governments) reveals that government purchases public goods from private businesses, collects taxes from and makes transfer payments to these firms, purchases labour services from households, and collects taxes from and makes transfer payments to these households. As well, government can alter the distribution of income, reallocate resources, and change the level of economic activity by affecting the six flows in the diagram.

11. Government expenditures include: (a) purchases of goods and services--which are "exhaustive" because they use up resources and produce output, and (b) transfer payments--which are "non-exhaustive" because they merely transfer households, firms, and governments the power to purchases resources. Total government expenditures in Canada have risen to over 45% of the annual production of the country. As proportions of the total, the most significant changes have been a rise in debt interest payments and a drop in education spending.

12. Federal expenditures fall into three key areas: social services, protection of persons and property, and interest on the public debt. The federal government's main revenue source is personal income taxes; corporate income taxes, the GST, and unemployment insurance contributions are also important.

13. Provincial governments spend more on health than anything else; education and social services are the next largest categories. Like the federal government, the provinces' main source of revenues is income tax. General sales taxes and transfer from the federal government are also important.

14. Municipal governments' top spending category is education. Their revenue sources are mainly property taxes and transfers from other levels of government.

15. In Canada the right wing is critical of many elements of government intervention, and believes that the government sector must be cut in order to reduce the government deficit. The left wing believes that cutting government will worsen our social problems, and that higher taxes are the solution to the deficit.

Terms and Concepts

corporate income tax
exclusion principle
free-rider problem
government purchases
monopoly
personal income tax
property taxes
public good
sales and excise tax
spillover costs and spillover benefits
transfer payments

Hints and Tips

1. The key thing to get out of this chapter is an understanding of the various failures of the market system which create a role for government.

2. You should be able to construct from memory the circular flow diagram with households, firms and the government sector. To help fix it in your mind, try to think of a concrete example for each of the twelve types of flows. For example, to remember the flow from resource markets to the government sector, you might think of school teachers' labour.

Fill-In Questions

1. All actual economies are "mixed" because they combine elements of a __________ economy and a __________ economy.

2. List the five economic functions of government:

(a) ______________________________

(b) ______________________________

(c) ______________________________

(d) ______________________________

(e) ______________________________

3. To control monopoly in Canada, government has: (a) created commissions to __________ the prices and the services of __________ monopolies; (b) enacted __________ laws to maintain competition.

4. The market economy has certain __________ and __________ that make it necessary for government to supplement and modify its operation.

5. The market system, because it is an impersonal mechanism, results in an (equal, unequal) __________ distribution of income. To redistribute income from the upper-to the lower-income groups, the federal government has used a variety of programs including __________ payments; market __________; and an __________ tax system that takes a __________ percentage of the incomes of the rich than the poor.

6. Government frequently reallocates resources when it finds instances of __________ failure. The two major cases of such failure of the competitive market involve __________ and __________ goods.

7. Spillovers occur when benefits or costs associated with the production or consumption of a good are incurred by a __________ party. Spillovers are also called __________.

8. Governments can resolve the problem of spillover costs through the use of __________ or __________.

9. If spillover benefits accompany the production of a good, then resources will be __________ to the production of that good by the market economy.

10. Governments can resolve the problem of spillover benefits through __________ that increase the __________ or the __________ for the good. Direct government __________ is another solution.

11. Public goods are not subject to the __________ principle. Once a public good is produced, the benefits from the good cannot be confined to the purchaser and result in a __________ effect. Therefore, private firms cannot make __________ by supplying these goods.

12. To reallocate resources from the production of private to the production of public goods, government reduces the demand for private goods by __________ consumers and firms and then __________ the production of public goods.

13. To stabilize the economy, government must:

(a) when there is less than full employment (increase, decrease) __________ aggregate expenditures by (increasing, decreasing) __________ its expenditures for goods and services and by (increasing, decreasing) __________ taxes.

(b) when there are inflationary pressures __________ aggregate expenditures by __________ its expenditures for goods and services and by __________ taxes.

14. In the expanded circular flow model, the net tax flow is obtained by subtracting all government __________ to firms and __________ to individuals from the taxes paid by firms and individuals.

Problems and Projects

1. The circular flow diagram below includes business firms, households, and government (the public sector). Also shown are the product and resource markets.

(a) Identify the sector that corresponds to each box:

a: __________

b: __________

c: __________

d: __________

e: __________

(b) Supply a label or an explanation for each of the twelve flows in the model:

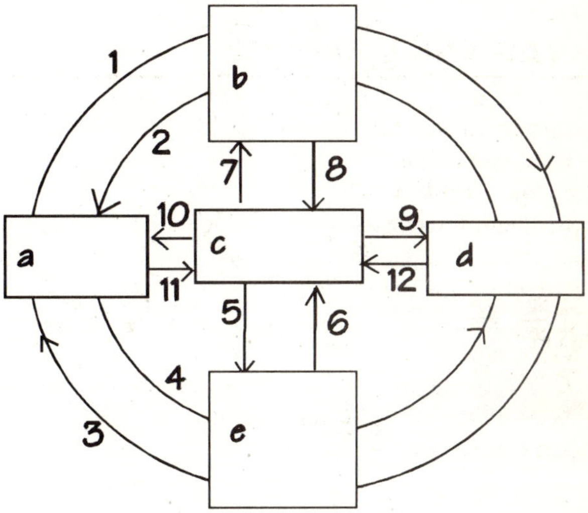

1: ____________________

2: ____________________

3: ____________________

4: ____________________

5: ____________________

6: ____________________

7: ____________________

8: ____________________

9: ____________________

10: ____________________

11: ____________________

12: ____________________

(c) If government wished to:

(1) increase the production of public goods and decrease the production of private goods in the economy, it would increase flows _____ and _____ or _____;

(2) redistribute income from high-income to low-income households, it would (increase, decrease) __________ the

net taxes (taxes minus transfers) paid by the former and __________ the net taxes paid by the latter in flows _____ and _____.

2. Below is a list of various government activities. Indicate in the space provided into which of the five classes of government functions the activity falls. If the activity falls under more than one of the five functions, indicate this.

(a) Maintaining an army. __________

(b) Providing for a system of unemployment-insurance benefits. __________

(c) Establishing the Bank of Canada. __________

(d) Providing equalization payments to the poorer provinces in Canada. __________

(e) Barring a merger of two large grocery store chains. __________

(f) Providing drought relief payments to farmers. __________

(g) Cutting income taxes during a recession. __________

(h) Taxing whiskey and other spirits. __________

(i) Regulating organized stock, bond, and commodity markets. __________

(j) Setting tax rates higher for large incomes than for smaller ones. __________

(k) Developing environmental programs to fight the greenhouse effect. __________

True-False

Circle T if the statement is true, F if it is false.

1. The only function of government is to facilitate and strengthen the operation of the market system. **T F**

2. Among governments in Canada it is only the policies and programs of the federal government that affect resource allocation. **T F**

3. When the federal government provides for a monetary system, it is functioning to provide the economy with public goods and services. **T F**

4. An economy in which strong and effective competition is maintained may need programs designed to redistribute income. **T F**

5. Competitive product and input markets do not always ensure an optimal allocation of an economy's resources. **T F**

6. The biases and shortcomings of the market system are always self-correcting. **T F**

7. In the short term the market system reacts so that aggregate expenditure leads to full employment. **T F**

8. A spillover or externality is a cost or benefit that is imposed upon an individual or group external to the market transaction. **T F**

9 Internalization of a spillover cost means that the party imposing the externality must bear the resulting cost. **T F**

10. The market system will overallocate resources to the production of goods that confer spillover benefits. **T F**

11. Pollution is a cause of market failure because the price of the polluting product does not reflect all the resource costs used in its production. **T F**

12. A government subsidy could be used to correct the misallocation of resources that results when spillover benefits are present. **T F**

13. Taxes imposed on products that create pollution will lower the marginal cost of production and increase supply. **T F**

14. A public good is any good or service that is provided free by the government. **T F**

15. For public goods the free-rider problem occurs when people can receive benefits without contributing to the cost of providing the good. **T F**

16. Governments provide environmental protection services because these services have social benefits and

private producers of environmental protection services would encounter the free-rider problem. **T F**

17. A government purchase of a snowplow truck is "non-exhaustive" while a government transfer payment to single parents is "exhaustive." **T F**

18. Over the last several decades, government expenditures and government revenues in Canada have grown at almost the same rate. **T F**

19. Canada's public debt has grown quickly, but not as quickly as the average for OECD countries. **T F**

Multiple-Choice

Circle the letter that corresponds to the best answer.

1. The functions of government include all of the following except:
(a) maintaining competition
(b) redistributing wealth and income
(c) promoting growth and stabilizing the economy
(d) determining the least cost method of production

2. Which of the following is not one of the methods utilized by government to control monopoly?
(a) the imposition of special taxes on monopolists
(b) government ownership of monopolies
(c) government regulation of monopolies
(d) anti-combines laws

3. One of the following is not presently employed by government to redistribute income. Which one?
(a) the negative income tax
(b) direct market intervention
(c) income taxes that take a larger part of the incomes of the rich than the poor
(d) transfer payments

4. A spillover cost exists when:
(a) a part of the cost of a transaction is suffered by an uninvolved third party
(b) a part of the cost of a transaction is paid for by the government
(c) the private and social costs of production are equal
(d) all of the above

5. If external benefits accompany the production of a good:
(a) resources will be overallocated to the production of the good
(b) resources will be underallocated to the production of the good
(c) a tax on the production of the good will result in the optimum production of the good
(d) the good is exported to foreign countries

6. The government could promote the optimal output when the production of a good results in spillover costs by:
(a) applying the provisions of the Competition Act
(b) a tax on the production of the good
(c) a subsidy to consumers of the good
(d) a subsidy to producers of the good

7. Which of the following is an example of government provision of a legal and social framework:
(a) police enforcement of speed limits on the Trans-Canada Highway
(b) establishment of regulations for product packaging
(c) inspection of pumps at gas stations and scales at butcher shops
(d) all of the above

8. Which of the following is a good example of a good or service providing spillover benefits?
(a) a video game
(b) landscaping
(c) a sofa
(d) an oil change for a car

9. Suppose that in order to relieve traffic congestion, user charges are imposed on drivers using urban expressways. This would be a response to what economic problem?
(a) spillover benefits
(b) spillover costs
(c) the free-rider problem
(d) inequitable income distribution

10. Public goods differ from private goods in that public goods are:
(a) divisible
(b) subject to the exclusion principle
(c) not subject to the free-rider problem
(d) *not* divisible and *not* subject to the exclusion principle

11. Quasi-public goods are goods and services:
(a) to which the exclusion principle could be applied
(b) which have large spillover benefits
(c) which would be produced by private producers through the market system
(d) which are indivisible

12. If the market system tends to overallocate resources to the production of good X:
(a) good X is a public good
(b) good X involves spillover benefits
(c) good X involves spillover costs
(d) good X is prone to the free-rider problem

13. Including government expenditures, taxes, and transfer payments in the circular flow affects:
(a) the distribution of income
(b) the allocation of resources
(c) the level of economic activity
(d) all of the above

14. Property taxes are the largest source of revenue for which level of government in Canada?
(a) federal
(b) provincial
(c) municipal
(d) no level of government

15. Unemployment insurance contributions are a revenue source for which level of government in Canada?
(a) federal
(b) provincial
(c) municipal
(d) no level of government

16. The largest expenditures category for provincial governments in Canada is:
(a) education
(b) highways
(c) social services
(d) health care

17. The largest expenditures category for Canada's municipal governments is:
(a) debt interest
(b) education
(c) social services
(d) police

Discussion Questions

1. What are the five economic functions of government in Canada's mixed economy? Explain what the performance of each of these functions requires government to do.

2. Would you like to live in an economy in which government undertook only the first two functions listed in the text? What would be the advantages and disadvantages of living in such an economy?

3. What is "market failure" and what are the two major kinds of such failures?

4. What are externalities and spillovers? Give examples of positive externalities and negative externalities.

5. (a) Should the government intervene in the externality dispute between two dormitory residents over the volume of one resident's music? Or between two property owners over the use of one party's land?
(b) Should the government intervene in an air pollution dispute beween the city residents and the firms that operate pulp mills in Prince George, B.C.?
(c) If your answers in (a) and (b) differ, explain why the two cases are to be treated differently.

6. What principles from this chapter seem relevant to understanding the Internet?

7. What characteristics differ as between private and public goods? Why does there tend to be underallocation of resources to public goods in the absence of government intervention?

8. What basic method does government employ in Canada to reallocate resources away from the production of private goods and toward the production of public goods?

9. What are the some of the key trends in expenditures and revenues for federal, provincial and municipal governments in Canada? What are some of the most contentious issues?

Answers

Fill-In questions

1. market, centrally planned (either order)

2. (a) provide legal and social framework; (b) maintain competition; (c) redistribute income; (d) reallocate resources; (e) stabilize the economy

3. (a) regulate, natural; (b) anti-combines

4. biases, shortcomings

5. unequal; transfer, intervention; income tax, larger

6. market; spillovers (or externalities), public

7. third; externalities

8. specific taxes, regulations or controls (either order)

9. underallocated

10. subsidies, demand, supply (either order), provision

11. exclusion; free-rider; profit

12. taxing, subsidizing

13. (a) increase, increasing, decreasing; (b) decrease, decreasing, increasing

14. subsidies, transfer payments

Problems and projects

1. (a) a: business firms, b: resource markets, c: government, d: households, e: product markets; (b) 1: businesses pay costs for resources that become money income for households, 2: households provide resources to businesses, 3: household expenditures become receipts for businesses, 4: businesses provide goods and services to households, 5: government spends money in product market, 6: government receives goods and services from product market, 7: government spends money in resource market, 8: government receives resources from resource market, 9: government provides goods and services to households, 10: government provides goods and services to businesses, 11: businesses pay net taxes to government, 12: households pay net taxes to government; (c) (1) 9, 10, 11 (either order); (2) increase, decrease, 11, 12

2. (a) reallocates resources; (b) redistributes income; (c) provides a legal foundation and social environment and stabilizes the economy; (d) redistributes income and wealth; (e) maintains competition; (f) redistributes income; (g) stabilizes the economy; (h) reallocates resources; (i) provides a legal foundation and social environment; (j) redistributes income and wealth; (k) reallocates resources.

True-False

1. F **2.** F **3.** F **4.** T **5.** T **6.** F
7. F **8.** T **9.** T **10.** F **11.** T **12.** T
13. F **14.** F **15.** T **16.** T **17.** F **18.** F
19. F

Multiple-Choice

1. (d) **2.** (a) **3.** (a) **4.** (a) **5.** (b) **6.** (b)
7. (d) **8.** (b) **9.** (b) **10.** (d) **11.** (b) **12.**(c)
13. (d) **14.** (c) **15.** (a) **16.** (d) **17.** (b)

CHAPTER 6

Canada in the Global Economy

International trade has grown dramatically in recent years, causing so-called "globalization" of markets with nations' economic fortunes becoming more intertwined than ever before. Canada's exports and imports are each equal to about one quarter of our national income. We depend almost exclusively on imports for many important products. Likewise, many of our producers rely mainly on customers in export markets. The United States is our most important trading partner, and most of our trade is with industrialized countries. An important trend on the world scene is the growth of the newly industrializing "Asian tigers" (Hong Kong, Singapore, South Korea and Taiwan).

Next, the circular flow model is revised to add the global economy ("rest of the world") to the produce market. The model now shows export flows paid for by foreign expenditures, and import flows paid for by expenditures from the domestic economy.

Then we turn to the basic question of why nations trade. According to the principle of comparative advantage, a nation will specialize in the production of those products for which their domestic opportunity costs are lower than their trading partners'. They then trade some of this output for the products their trading partners have specialized in. By trading for goods at a lower opportunity cost than they would incur by producing the goods themselves, a nation can ultimately consume combinations of goods that lie outside their production possibilities curve. Perhaps surprisingly, these benefits are available to all nations that trade, even nations that are absolutely less productive than their trading partners.

In reality, nations usually do not barter goods with one another, as represented in the simplified scenario of the comparative advantage model. Instead, international trade is conducted through monetary transactions between households and firms in different countries acting as buyers and sellers. Such transactions require a foreign exchange market where currencies may be traded. For instance, Canadian car importers may sell dollars in exchange for yen in order to purchase cars from Japanese manufacturers. The exchange rate, or equilibrium price of a currency, is determined by the supply and the demand for the currency. The basic principles of supply and demand that you studied in Chapter 4 apply to foreign exchange markets also. Shifts in the supply or demand for a currency will change its price. If the currency's price rises (falls) in terms of another currency it has appreciated (depreciated) relative to the other currency.

Despite the important benefits from specialization and international trade, many nations employ policies to limit trade. The major protectionist policies are: (1) protective tariffs, (2) import quotas, (3) nontariff barriers, and (4) export subsidies. But why do governments seek to reduce imports and/or increase exports? One reason may be the mistaken yet widely held belief that exports are beneficial because they create jobs, whereas imports are harmful because they destroy jobs at home. Another explanation is found by examining who gains and who loses from policies that limit trade. Domestic firms facing tough competition from imports often lobby governments to impose tariffs or quotas. Domestic consumers would lose from the resulting higher prices. However, even if the benefits of protection for the domestic firms are less than the harm done to domestic consumers, the harm is obscure and dispersed. Therefore, government may receive better political payoffs by imposing tariffs and quotas than by supporting free trade.

Protectionist measures taken by one nation may lead other nations that lose exports to retaliate with protectionist measures of their own. Such a "trade war" contributed to the spread of the Great Depression throughout the industrialized world.

In the interest of preventing such conflicts and reducing existing trade barriers, various agreements and institutions have evolved. The General Agreement on Tariffs and Trade (GATT) signed by Canada and over a hundred other nations has resulted in numerous multilateral reductions in trade barriers. Another institution is the regional free trade zone or trade bloc: such as the European Union (EU) and NAFTA. Members of such trade blocs enjoy freer trade with other nations in their bloc. Conversely, nonmember countries may continue to be disadvantaged by tariffs and other barriers to the point that they actually trade less with bloc countries.

Public reaction to Canada's membership in NAFTA has been mixed. Many support NAFTA as a way to further our specialization according to comparative advantage and to provide access to larger markets. Others fear that many Canadian firms will not be able to compete, and that jobs will move to Mexico, where wages and working conditions are much below Canadian levels.

Checklist

When you have studied this chapter, you should be able to:

- ☐ Explain the importance of international trade to the Canadian economy in terms of volume, dependence, trade patterns, and financial linkages.
- ☐ Describe four factors that have facilitated growth in world trade since World War II.
- ☐ Identify some of the world's key trading nations, and nations whose importance is growing.
- ☐ Draw the circular flow diagram including the international trade dimension.
- ☐ Explain the basic principle of comparative advantage.
- ☐ Compute the comparative costs of production from a numerical example with data on production possibilities for two goods for two producers.
- ☐ Determine from the example which producer has the comparative advantage in each good.
- ☐ Indicate the range in which the terms of trade will be found in the example.
- ☐ Compute the gains from specialization and trade in the example.
- ☐ Describe the main characteristics of the foreign exchange market.
- ☐ Draw a graph showing how the principles of supply and demand apply to the foreign exchange market.
- ☐ Distinguish between appreciation and depreciation of a currency.
- ☐ Identify four types of government interferences with free trade.
- ☐ Discuss two reasons why governments intervene in international trade.
- ☐ Explain the lesson of Bastiat's Petition of the Candlemakers.
- ☐ Describe the nature and purpose of GATT, and list some of the highlights of the Uruguay round provisions.
- ☐ Describe the history, goals and results of the European Union.
- ☐ Describe the features of NAFTA, including the arguments for and against Canada's participation.
- ☐ Discuss the ability of Canadian firms to compete in the global economy.

Chapter Outline

1. The volume of international trade is now so large, and national economies so interdependent, that the world can be thought of as a "global economy."

2. Compared to most other nations, Canada relies relatively heavily on trade.
(a) Exports equal 27% of our GDP, and imports equal 24% of our GDP, up substantially over the last few decades.
(b) The bulk of Canada's trade is with other industrialized nations, particularly the United States.
(c) Canada's major exports include automotive products, machinery and equipment, industrial goods and materials, forest and energy products, agricultural and fish products. Our major imports include machinery and equipment, automotive products, industrial goods and materials, consumer goods, agricultural and fishing products, and energy.

3. Several factors have facilitated rapid growth of trade since World War II:
(a) improved transportation technology, (b) improved communications technology, (c) general decline in tariffs, (d) peace in most industrialized nations.

4. In sheer volume of trade, the world's major players

are the United States, Japan, and Western Europe. The fastest growing participants are the newly industrializing "Asian tigers": Hong Kong, Singapore, South Korea and Taiwan. China is an emerging trading power, and the Eastern European nations are expected to grow in importance.

5. The circular flow model can be expanded to include the international trade dimension by adding the "rest of the world" box to the model. This box is connected to the Canadian product market through flows of imports and exports, and the Canadian and foreign expenditures on these goods.

6. Specialization and trade among economic units (individuals, firms, provinces, regions, or nations) are based on the principle of comparative advantage, articulated by David Ricardo in the early 1800s. Specialization and trade increase productivity and output.

7. The basic principle of comparative advantage can be illustrated with an example of two individuals able to do two jobs, or with an example of two nations producing two goods.
(a) An accountant needing her house painted can paint it herself, or can hire a house painter. The accountant will seek to minimize her opportunity cost. By the law of comparative advantage, even if the accountant can do the painting in less time than the painter can, if the accountant incurs a lower opportunity cost by hiring the painter, the accountant will specialize in accounting. Likewise, the painter will specialize in painting, and hire an accountant to prepare his tax return, if this minimizes his opportunity costs.
(b) Mexico and Canada both can produce corn and soybeans. Assuming that each nation has a straight line production possibilities curve (or constant cost ratio), each nation has the lower opportunity cost--and therefore comparative advantage--in producing one of the two goods.
(c) By specializing in producing one good, the nation can trade for the other good. The terms of trade--the ratio at which one good is traded for another--lies between the cost ratios for the two nations.
(d) Specialization and trade according to comparative advantage allow a nation to consume a combination of goods outside their domestic production possibilities curve; in effect the scarcity constraint is relaxed to a degree.

8. National currencies are traded in the foreign exchange market. This market is competitive and establishes the exchange rate of a domestic currency for foreign currency. The price of a domestic currency, or its exchange rate, is the amount of domestic currency that must be exchanged to acquire one unit of foreign currency. Exchange rates link all domestic prices with all foreign prices.

9. Supply and demand determine the exchange rate. Supply and demand shifts cause exchange rate appreciation or depreciation.
(a) Increased demand or decreased supply for the domestic currency will decrease the exchange rate, or price of a unit of foreign currency. The domestic currency appreciates.
(b) Decreased demand or increased supply for the domestic currency will increase the exchange rate, or price of a unit of foreign currency. The domestic currency depreciates.

10. Governments implement policies that reduce trade between nations:
(a) Such policies include protective tariffs, import quotas, nontariff barriers, and export subsidies.
(b) Trade restrictions may be imposed because governments do not understand the nature of the gains from trade, or because they are responding to political incentives by protecting domestic businesses or groups against international competition.
(c) Regardless of governments' motives, restrictive trade policies impose costs that outweigh the benefits. Consumers pay higher prices, exporters have less access to foreign markets, and the nation makes less efficient use of its resources.

11. When one nation imposes import barriers, other nations that lose exports may retaliate with their own import barriers. In a "trade war" tariffs escalate and trade shrinks. Such policies contributed to the spread of the Great Depression throughout the industrialized world.

12. To prevent protectionism and to promote trade, various national policies and international institutional arrangements have evolved. Nations have signed bilateral agreements extending tariff reductions to one another through most-favoured-nation clauses.

13. More comprehensively, the General Agreement on

Tariffs and Trade (GATT) is a forum to reduce tariffs on a multilateral basis among over a hundred nations. Over the last several decades GATT has been the vehicle for eight rounds of negotiations to reduce trade barriers.

14. As a result of the recent Uruguay round, many major changes will be phased in between 1995 and 2005: thousands of tariff reductions, inclusion of services, cuts to agricultural subsidies, protection of intellectual property, reduced quotas on textiles and apparel, and the establishment of a World Trade Organization.

15. The European Union (EU) is a regional free trade zone or trade bloc. It has abolished tariffs between its member countries and developed some common economic policies (such as tariffs that will apply to nonmember countries). The EU has produced freer trade and increased efficiency of production in member nations, but has also created frictions with nonmember nations including Canada.

16. In 1989 Canada and the United States signed the Free Trade Agreement (FTA). In 1993 the bloc formed by the FTA was extended to include Mexico under the terms of the North American Free Trade Agreement (NAFTA). Critics fear that Canada will lose jobs to Mexico where wages are low and the workplace is less regulated than Canada. Proponents argue that the typical advantages from freer trade outweigh any drawbacks.

17. Globalization of trade intensifies competition for Canadian producers. Some have succeeded in lowering production costs, using new technology, and offering superior products to retain market shares in Canada and capture new markets abroad. Other firms have been unable to compete, and have lost market share or even folded. Many of the unsuccessful firms previously enjoyed long periods of protection from imports via tariffs or quotas. These observed results of globalization are consistent with the principle of comparative advantage: with freer trade Canada expands output where its producers have a comparative advantage, and shrinks output where they have a comparative disadvantage.

Terms and Concepts

appreciation
"Asian tigers"
Canada-U.S. Free Trade Agreement (FTA)
comparative advantage
depreciation
European Union (EU)
export subsidies
foreign exchange market
General Agreement on Tariffs and Trade (GATT)
import quotas
most-favoured nation clauses
multinational corporations
nontariff barriers
North American Free Trade Agreement (NAFTA)
protective tariffs
terms of trade
trade bloc

Hints and Tips

1. Finding which producer has the comparative advantage for a given good depends on being able to compare opportunity costs across producers. If the data on production possibilities, reflects constant costs, opportunity costs can be found easily by dividing a producer's maximum outputs of each of the two goods. For example, suppose Norway's maximum outputs are 100 fish or 20 tables. What is the cost of 1 table? Divide the number of tables into the number of fish: 100 fish/20 tables = 5 fish per table. What is the cost of 1 fish? Divide the number of fish into the number of tables: 20 tables/100 fish = 1/5 table per fish.

2. Foreign exchange rates are confusing because they can be expressed in two ways. Is Canada's exchange rate the amount of foreign currency that one Canadian dollar can buy, or the amount of Canadian dollars that it takes to buy one unit of foreign currency? In fact, either form is correct. For example, our exchange rate with Mexico could be 4 pesos for $1, or $0.25 for 1 peso. These are reciprocal expressions of exactly the same rate! Always be careful which form of the exchange rates you are using.

Fill-In Questions

1. A nation is more likely to rely on international trade the more (diversified, limited) __________ its resource base is and the (larger, smaller) __________ its domestic market is.

2. In recent decades Canada's trade has (increased, decreased) __________ in absolute terms, and __________ as a percentage of our national income. Canada trades mainly with (developing, developed) __________ nations. Our major trading partner is __________.

3. Factors that have facilitated growth in trade since World War II include improvements in __________ and __________ technology, a general decline in __________, and __________ between the major trading nations in the world.

4. The major "players" in international trade include __________, __________ and the nations of Western Europe. These nations are home to the headquarters of most __________ corporations. The so-called "Asian tigers" are the growing and newly industrializing nations of __________, __________, __________ and __________.

5. In the circular flow model, imports and exports are added as flows to the __________ market. Canadian expenditures pay for (exports, imports) __________, and foreign expenditures pay for __________.

6. If Nigeria can produce 10 kg of coffee at a cost of 1 barrel of oil, and Kenya can produce 25 kg of coffee at a cost of 1 barrel of oil, then __________ has the lower cost for producing oil, and __________ has the lower cost of producing coffee. The comparative advantage for oil lies with __________ and for coffee lies with __________.

7. The amount of one product that a nation must export in order to import one unit of another of product is the __________.

8. When the dollar price of foreign currency increases, the dollar has (appreciated, depreciated) __________, while foreign currency has __________.

9. In the market for Japanese yen, an increase in the (demand for, supply of) __________ yen will decrease the dollar price of yen, while an increase in the __________ yen will increase the dollar price of yen. If the dollar price of yen increases, then Japanese goods imported into Canada will be (more, less) __________ expensive to Canadians, while Canadian goods exported to Japan will be __________ expensive for Japanese.

10. The major government policies that restrict trade include protective __________, import __________, __________ barriers, and __________ subsidies.

11. Governments may mistakenly intervene in trade with other nations because they mistakenly think of (exports, imports) __________ as helpful, and __________ as harmful for their own economy. In fact, there are important gains from trade. Trade makes it possible to obtain __________ at a lower cost than would be the case of they were produced domestically, and the earnings from __________ help a nation pay for these lower cost __________.

12. Another reason why governments interfere with free trade is based on __________ considerations. Groups or industries seek protection from foreign competition through __________, import __________, or other kinds of trade restrictions. The costs of trade protectionism are (clear to, hidden from) __________ consumers in the price of the protected product.

13. Tariffs and quotas (benefit, cost) __________

domestic firms and their employees in the protected industries but __________ domestic consumers of their products in the form of (lower, higher) __________ prices than would exist if there were free trade.

14. The three cardinal principles established in the GATT are:

(a) __________ treatment for all member nations;

(b) reduction of __________ by multilateral negotiations; and

(c) the elimination of import __________.

15. The major provisions of the Uruguay round of GATT negotiations include __________ reductions, coverage of __________ by GATT, cuts in subsidies to __________ producers, protection of __________ property, phased reduction of __________ on textiles and apparel, and the formation of a __________ Organization.

16. The trade bloc first formed as the Common Market in 1958 is now known as the __________. The specific aims of the Common Market were to abolish tariffs and __________ among member nations, to establish common tariffs on goods imported from __________ nations, to permit free movement of capital and __________ within the Common Market nations, and to adopt common policies on other matters.

17. Canada's first participation in a trade bloc came in 1989 with the FTA formed with the __________. In 1993, this was extended to the NAFTA, which brought __________ into the bloc.

Problems and Projects

1. Julius and Murray are tailors. Their production possibilities tables for trousers and jackets are given below. Julius chooses production alternative D, while Murray chooses E from his alternatives.

JULIUS: Production Possibilities Table

	Production Alternative					
Product	A	B	C	D	E	F
Trousers	75	60	45	30	15	0
Jackets	0	10	20	30	40	50

MURRAY: Production Possibilities Table

	Production Alternative						
Product	A	B	C	D	E	F	G
Trousers	60	50	40	30	20	10	0
Jackets	0	5	10	15	20	25	30

(a) For Julius 1 pair of trousers costs _____ jackets, and 1 jacket costs _____ pairs of trousers.

(b) For Murray 1 pair of trousers costs _____ jackets, and 1 jacket costs _____ pairs of trousers.

(c) The comparative advantage in making trousers lies with __________ because his opportunity cost is (lower, higher) __________. The comparative advantage in making jackets lies with ____________ because his opportunity cost is (lower, higher) __________.

(d) If Julius and Murray form a partnership, Julius should specialize in making the __________, and Murray should specialize in making the __________.

(e) Working independently Julius and Murray would produce a total of 50 pairs of trousers and 50 jackets. If each specializes fully, their combined output will be _____ pairs of trousers, and _____ jackets. Thus, the gain from specialization is _____ pairs of trousers and _____ jackets.

2. The nations of Venezuela and Costa Rica have the production possibility tables shown below.

(a) Find the opportunity costs as follows:

Venezuela: 1 apple costs __________

1 banana costs __________

Costa Rica: 1 apple costs __________

1 banana costs __________

(b) Determine which country has the comparative advantage in each good:

Apples: __________

Bananas: __________

VENEZUELA: Production Possibilities Table

Product	A	B	C	D	E	F
	Production Alternative					
Apples	40	32	24	16	8	0
Bananas	0	4	8	12	16	20

COSTA RICA: Production Possibilities Table

Product	A	B	C	D	E	F
	Production Alternative					
Apples	75	60	45	30	15	0
Bananas	0	5	10	15	20	25

(c) The information in the question is not sufficient to determine specifically what the terms of trade will be. However, the terms of trade must be greater than _____ apples per banana, and less than _____ apples per banana.

(d) Suppose that each nation would choose production alternative C if specialization and trade were impossible. The combined production in the two countries would be _____ apples and _____ bananas.

(e) If each nation specializes completely according to comparative advantage, their combined production will be _____ apples and _____ bananas.

(f) Their combined gains from specialization will be _____ apples and _____ bananas.

(g) Suppose that the nations specialize and then agree to trade 25 apples for 10 bananas. This trade will leave Venezuela consuming _____ apples and _____ bananas. Costa Rica will consume _____ apples and _____ bananas.

(h) Compared to production alternative C, this leaves Venezuela with a gain of _____ apples and _____ bananas. Compared to production alternative C, this leaves Costa Rica with a gain of _____ apples and _____ bananas.

3. The table below shows four different currencies and how much of each can be purchased with 1 Canadian dollar.

(a) In the blanks indicate whether the Canadian dollar appreciated (A) or depreciated (D) against these currencies from Year 1 to Year 2.

Country	Currency	Currency per Canadian $ Year 1	Year 2	A or D
France	Franc	4.9	4.8	_____
Germany	Deutschemark	1.40	1.44	_____
Kuwait	Dinar	.25	.20	_____
Japan	Yen	84	86	_____

(b) Compute the amount of Canadian currency one would have to exchange to get 100 units of each of the four foreign currencies. Use Year 1 exchange rates.

100 Francs = $ _____

100 Deutschemarks = $ _____

100 Dinar = $ _____

100 Yen = $ _____

True-False

Circle T if the statement is true, F if it is false.

1. Canada is completely dependent on other nations for many products that we do not produce domestically. **T F**

2. No nation in the world has a higher percentage of GDP represented by exports and imports than Canada does. **T F**

3. The principle of comparative advantage was first explained by David Ricardo. **T F**

4. The principle of comparative advantage applies just as well to individuals or regions as it does to nations. **T F**

5. If two nations produce only coal and lumber, one of the nations could have the comparative advantage over the other in both coal and lumber. **T F**

6. If two nations have identical cost conditions for producing two goods, neither nation will have a comparative advantage. **T F**

7. A nation that has resources that are more productive

in every good than another nation's resources will be unable to gain by trading with the less productive nation. **T F**

8. Specialization and trade according to comparative advantage allows a nation to have combinations of goods that lie outside the nation's production possibility curve. **T F**

9. In the foreign exchange market graph, if the British pound price of Japanese yen is plotted on the vertical axis, on the horizontal axis must be the quantity of British pounds. **T F**

10. An increase in incomes of Canadian households would tend to increase the supply of Canadian dollars in the exchange market. **T F**

11. If the supply of Canadian dollars in the foreign exchange market increases, the Canadian dollar will appreciate relative to foreign currencies, *ceteris paribus*. **T F**

12. If the U.S. dollar price of the Canadian dollar is $0.80, then the Canadian dollar price of the U.S. dollar must be $1.20. **T F**

13. An appreciation of the Canadian dollar will make our imports less expensive to Canadian consumers, and our exports more expensive to foreign consumers. **T F**

14. Export subsidies are government payments to domestic producers to encourage them to export more. **T F**

15. Bastiat's purpose in the Petition of the Candlemakers was to satirize the arguments of producers who seek protection from competition. **T F**

16. The formation of a trade bloc encourages efficiency in production because access to larger markets enables producers to benefit from large-scale production. **T F**

17. The 1989 Free Trade Agreement has benefitted some Canadian firms and has harmed others. **T F**

18. NAFTA includes Canada, the United States, Mexico and some Central American nations. **T F**

Multiple-Choice

Circle the letter that corresponds to the best answer.

1. As of the 1990s, our imports and exports amount to approximately what fraction of Canada's GDP?
(a) 1/10
(b) 1/6
(c) 1/4
(d) 1/3

2. In 1994, which sector represented the largest percentage of Canadian exports?
(a) agricultural products
(b) automotive products
(c) energy products
(d) forest products

3. In 1994, which sector represented the largest percentage of Canadian imports?
(a) agricultural products
(b) automotive products
(c) consumer products
(d) machinery and equipment

Questions 4 through 7 are based on the data in the table which shows maximum productions levels for the regions of Heath and Cliff, both of which have constant costs of production, and are able to trade with one another.

Heath		Cliff	
Wool	Peat	Wool	Peat
100	20	120	40

4. In Heath, the comparative cost of:
(a) 1 wool is 5 peat
(b) 1 wool is 1/5 peat
(c) 1 wool is 1.2 wool
(d) 1 peat is 1/5 wool

5. In Cliff, the comparative cost of:
(a) 1 peat is 3 wool
(b) 1 peat is 2 peat
(c) 1 wool is 3 peat
(d) 1 peat is 1/3 wool

6. Which of the following statements is **not** true?
(a) Heath has the comparative advantage in wool
(b) Cliff should specialize in peat

(c) both Heath and Cliff could gain from trading with one another
(d) Heath has the comparative advantage in both wool and peat

7. The terms of trade will be:
(a) more than 3 wool for 1 peat
(b) less than 5 wool for 1 peat
(c) between 3 and 5 wool for 1 peat
(d) not between 3 and 5 wool for 1 peat

8. The foreign exchange market is a market for:
(a) imports
(b) exports
(c) shares in multinational corporations
(d) bonds sold by foreign government
(e) currencies

9. If the equilibrium exchange rate changes so that the dollar price of Japanese yen increases:
(a) the dollar has appreciated
(b) the yen has depreciated
(c) Canadians will be able to buy more Japanese goods
(d) Japanese will be able to buy more Canadian goods

10. If the United States begins to demand more Mexican goods:
(a) the demand for the peso will increase, causing the peso to appreciate
(b) the demand for the peso will increase, causing the peso to depreciate
(c) the supply of U.S. dollars will decrease, causing the dollar to appreciate
(d) the supply of U.S. dollars will decrease, causing the dollar to depreciate

11. Which of the following is designed to restrict trade?
(a) export subsidies
(b) NAFTA
(c) GATT
(d) import quotas

12. Why do governments often restrict international trade?
(a) to expand their nation's production possibilities
(b) to protect domestic industries from foreign competition
(c) to encourage efficiency in production
(d) to benefit consumers

13. One important outcome of the Uruguay round of GATT was:
(a) elimination of services from the agreement
(b) greater restrictions on patents and copyrights
(c) increasing tariffs on manufactured products
(d) reductions in agricultural subsidies

14. Which of the following was a contributing factor to the Great Depression?
(a) the formation of free trade zones
(b) retaliatory tariffs
(c) GATT
(d) most-favoured-nation clauses
(e) voluntary export restraints

15. The European Common Market:
(a) helped to abolish tariffs and import quotas among its members
(b) aimed for the eventual free movement of capital and labour within the member nations
(c) imposed common tariffs on products imported from countries outside the Common Market
(d) did all of the above

16. One potential problem with the European Union is that:
(a) a free flow of labour and capital within the EU is likely to create mass unemployment
(b) economies of large-scale production will result in higher consumer prices
(c) trade with nonmember nations may diminish
(d) all of the above

17. A trade bloc is the same thing as a:
(a) nontariff barrier
(b) import quota
(c) free-trade zone
(d) trade restriction

18. For Canada, one advantage of NAFTA is:
(a) higher prices for consumer goods
(b) access for Canadian producers to larger markets
(c) the opportunity to reduce our reliance on imports
(d) more low wage job opportunities for Canadians

19. What is Mercsur?
(a) a South American free-trade zone
(b) the controlling body of the EU
(c) the world's largest multi-national corporation
(d) a body that adjudicates international trade disputes

Discussion Questions

1. What are Canada's principal exports and imports? Why does Canada trade so much with the United States? Why does international trade represent a bigger part of Canada's economy than of the U.S. economy?

2. What are some factors contributing to the growth in international trade since World War II?

3. Who are the major players in international trade? Which nations are growing rapidly in their relative influence?

4. Sketch how the international trade component can be built into the circular flow model.

5. Explain how comparative costs determine which producer has the comparative advantage. What determines the terms of trade? What is the gain that results from specialization and trade according to comparative advantage?

6. Suppose that Dr. Ocula is an outstanding eye surgeon with good enough hand-eye coordination that he keyboards faster than anyone else in town. Use the principle of comparative advantage to explain why he hires someone else to do the word-processing in his office, instead of doing it faster himself.

7. How might an appreciation of the value of the Canadian dollar relative to the American dollar depress the Canadian economy? Which Canadians would be harmed, and which would benefit?

8. What are the major types of trade impediments, and how do they work to restrict international trade?

9. Hypothetically, suppose that Canada has a 20% import tariff on shoelaces. Further suppose that there are only about twenty Canadian manufacturers of shoelaces. If the tariff raises shoelace prices in Canada by 25 to 50 cents a pair, estimate the annual cost of this tariff to you. Estimate the annual benefit of the tariff to each Canadian manufacturer. Do you know whether in fact there is a shoelace tariff? Do you think that Canadian shoelace manufacturers know? How do you explain the difference in the knowledge, and how does this help explain why the government might have implemented this tariff?

10. What does Canada gain from participating in GATT? Which kinds of Canadian industries would be most likely to support the GATT initiatives? And which would be most likely to oppose them?

11. Is it possible that both Canada and the United States can gain from the FTA? If so, how?

12. What concerns do free trade critics have with the 1993 NAFTA as compared with the 1989 FTA? What are the rebuttals to these concerns?

13. "Canadian firms cannot compete in the global economy because wages are too high in Canada." Discuss this assertion.

Answers

Fill-in questions

1. limited, smaller

2. increased; increased; developed; United States

3. transportation, communications, tariffs (trade barriers), peace

4. U.S., Japan; multinational; Hong Kong, Singapore, South Korea, Taiwan

5. product; imports, exports

6. Nigeria, Kenya; Nigeria, Kenya

7. terms of trade

8. depreciated, appreciated

9. supply of, demand for; more, less

10. tariffs, quotas, nontariff, export

11. exports, imports; imports, exports, imports

12. political; tariff, quotas; hidden from

13. benefit, harm, higher

14. equal or non-discriminatory; tariffs; quotas

15. tariff, services, agricultural, intellectual, quotas, World Trade

16. European Union; quotas, nonmember, labour

17. United States; Mexico

Problems and projects

1. (a) 2/3, 1 1/2; (b) 1/2, 2; (c) Murray, lower, Julius, lower; (d) jackets, trousers; (e) 60, 50; 10, 0.

2. (a) 1/2 banana, 2 apples, 1/3 banana, 3 apples; (b) Costa Rica, Venezuela; (c) 2, 3; (d) 69, 18; (e) 75, 20; (f) 6, 2; (g) 25, 10, 50, 10; (h) 1, 2, 5, 0.

3. (a) D,A,D,A; (b) 20.83, 69.44, 400, 1.19

True-False

1. T	**2.** F	**3.** T	**4.** T	**5.** F	**6.** T
7. F	**8.** T	**9.** F	**10.** T	**11.** F	**12.** F
13. T	**14.** T	**15.** T	**16.** T	**17.** T	**18.** F

Multiple-choice

1. (c)	**2.** (b)	**3.** (d)	**4.** (b)	**5.** (a)	**6.** (d)
7. (c)	**8.** (e)	**9.** (d)	**10.** (a)	**11.** (d)	**12.** (b)
13. (d)	**14.** (b)	**15.** (d)	**16.** (c)	**17.** (c)	**18.** (b)
19. (a)					

PART

The Economics of Consumption, Production, and Cost

CHAPTER 7

Demand and Supply: Elasticities and Applications

Chapter 7 is a continuation of Chapter 4, as you may have guessed from the title. In this chapter we add to the basic tools presented in Chapter 4, and look at some examples of how demand and supply analysis can shed light on important public issues. If you feel less than confident with the material from Chapter 4, you should review that chapter now.

The law of demand tells us that when price rises, quantity demanded will fall, *ceteris paribus*. But by how much? The concept of price elasticity of demand gives us a numerical measure of the degree of responsiveness of quantity demanded to price changes. With respect to the concept of price elasticity of demand, it is essential for you to understand (1) what elasticity measures; (2) how the price-elasticity formula is applied to measure the elasticity of demand; (3) the difference between elastic, inelastic, and unitary elastic demand; (4) how total revenue varies in each of these three cases; (5) the meaning of perfect elasticity and perfect inelasticity; (6) the major determinants of this elasticity; and (7) how to apply the concept to economic questions.

Most of the discussion of elasticity deals with price elasticity of demand. When you are thoroughly acquainted with this elasticity you will have little trouble understanding other elasticities. Any elasticity is a measure of responsiveness of some dependent variable to changes in an independent variable, and as such is computed as the ratio of the percentage change in the dependent variable over the percentage change in the independent variable.

Price elasticity of supply measures the responsiveness of quantity supplied to price changes. Again, it is important to distinguish between elastic and inelastic, and to understand the role of time in determining the elasticity. The responsiveness of quantity demanded to changes in income is termed income elasticity of demand. The sign of this elasticity indicates whether the good is normal or inferior. The responsiveness of quantity demanded to a change in the price of *another* good is called the cross elasticity of demand. The sign of the cross elasticity shows whether the two goods are substitutes or complements.

The remainder of the chapter is devoted to applications. The first is the analysis of the incidence of an excise tax on producers. We find that the burden is incurred by both the producers and the consumers: producers receive a lower price, and consumers pay a higher price. The incidence, or sharing of the burden, depends on the price elasticity of the demand and of the supply. The second application is the analysis of price ceilings and price floors. Such controls prevent the market mechanism from establishing the equilibrium price; therefore a rationing problem results. Price ceilings create shortages, and price floors create surpluses. However, both create a host of unintended side effects, including black market transactions, because disappointed or frustrated market participants try to minimize the effect of the price control on themselves.

Checklist

When you have studied this chapter, you should be able to:

- ☐ Define price elasticity of demand and compute the coefficient of elasticity when you are given data on demand.
- ☐ State two reasons why percentages--not absolute amounts--are used in the elasticity formula.
- ☐ Illustrate why the midpoints formula is preferred for elasticity calculations.
- ☐ Explain the meaning of elastic, inelastic, and unitary price elasticity of demand.

- ☐ Define and illustrate graphically the concepts of perfectly elastic and perfectly inelastic demand.
- ☐ Apply the total-revenue test to determine whether demand is elastic, inelastic, or unitary elastic.
- ☐ Illustrate graphically the relationship between price elasticity of demand and total revenue.
- ☐ List the four major determinants of the elasticity of demand and explain how each one affects elasticity.
- ☐ Define elasticity of supply and compute the coefficient of the elasticity of supply from data.
- ☐ Differentiate between the market period, the short run, and the long run; explain how time affects the elasticity of supply.
- ☐ Define cross elasticity of demand, compute its coefficient from data, and interpret from the coefficient whether two goods are complements, substitutes, or independent.
- ☐ Define income elasticity of demand, compute its coefficient from data, and interpret from the coefficient whether a good is normal or inferior.
- ☐ From a graph showing an excise production tax, determine the consumer's burden and the producer's burden.
- ☐ Illustrate how the consumer's tax burden and the producer's tax burden are changed when demand or supply becomes extremely elastic or inelastic.
- ☐ Define price ceilings and price floors, and identify examples of each.
- ☐ Explain and illustrate the effects of price ceilings and price floors.

Chapter Outline

1. Price elasticity of demand is a measure of the responsiveness or sensitivity of quantity demanded to changes in the price of the product. Elasticity is measured as a number that can be computed from the data contained in a demand (whether expressed as a schedule, a curve, or an algebraic function).

(a) The formula for price elasticity of demand is:

$$E_d = \frac{\text{\% change in quantity demanded}}{\text{\% change in price.}}$$

(b) In the elasticity formula quantity demanded is the dependent variable, price is the independent variable, and the measurement is taken for movements along a demand curve.

(c) The changes in quantity demanded and in price are measured in percentages so that the elasticity coefficient is not affected by the choice of units employed to measure price and quantity. Use of percentages also facilitates comparisons between different goods.

(d) Because price and quantity demanded are inversely related, the price elasticity of demand coefficient is a negative number; but economists ignore the minus sign and focus their attention on the absolute value of the coefficient.

(e) Suppose a value of 3 is computed as the elasticity coefficient. This indicates that at this particular point on the demand curve a 1 percent change in price will result in a 3 percent change in quantity demanded. Remembering that price and quantity are inversely related, the price change and quantity change will be in opposite directions.

(f) The elasticity coefficient can range in (absolute) value from 0 to infinity. An elasticity coefficient of 0 indicates demand is perfectly inelastic, while a coefficient of infinity indicates demand is perfectly elastic. Demand is termed elastic (inelastic, unit elastic) when the elasticity coefficient is greater than (less than, equal to) 1.

(g) When calculating the percentage changes in quantity and in price between two points on a demand curve or demand schedule, the average of the two quantities and the average of the two prices are used as the reference points. The use of this midpoints formula avoids annoying ambiguity in the exact value of the elasticity coefficient.

(h) Elasticity is not the same as slope. For example, a straight line demand has constant slope at each point but a different elasticity at each point.

2. Suppliers' total revenue from a selling a good is the price per unit multiplied by the number of units sold. The way in which total revenue changes (increases, decreases, or remains constant) when price changes is related to the product's price elasticity of demand.

(a) With an elastic (inelastic) demand the change in price and the change in total revenue go in opposite (the same) directions.

(b) Where elasticity is one, total revenue is maximized. A price change will lead to no change in revenue because quantity demanded changes by the same percentage as price. The price and quantity changes have exactly offsetting effects on total revenue.

3. There are four key determinants of price elasticity of demand. Demand for a product is more price elastic the more good substitutes the product has, the greater the proportion of the consumer's budget is spent on the good, if the good is a luxury good rather than a necessity, and the longer the period of time under consideration.

4. Price elasticity of demand is of practical importance in matters of public policy and in the setting of prices by the individual business firm.
(a) Because demand for agricultural products is inelastic, bumper crops lead to huge price decreases and lower total revenues for producers.
(b) Technological change which reduces costs by reducing labour requirements may or may not create unemployment. The price of the product will fall, and if product demand is elastic, growth in quantity demanded may absorb all of the workers displaced because of automation.
(c) Governments seeking increased revenues through excise taxes will tend to tax commodities with inelastic demands.
(d) Because the demand for heroin is price inelastic, law enforcement attempts to reduce the supply drive the price up sharply. The drop in drug consumption is less than the rise in drug prices, so addicts' total expenditures on drugs are increased. This leads to more street crime as addicts try to increase their incomes.

5. Price elasticity of supply measures the sensitivity of quantity supplied to changes in the price of the product.

$$E_s = \frac{\text{\% change in quantity supplied}}{\text{\% change in price}}$$

The elasticity of supply is greater the more time sellers have to adjust to a price change. In this regard economists distinguish between elasticities in the market period, the short run, and the long run.

6. Income elasticity of demand is defined as:

$$E_i = \frac{\text{\% change in quantity demanded}}{\text{\% change in income}}$$

Unlike the case of price elasticity of demand, signs are not ignored. If the income elasticity coefficient is greater than 0 the good is called a normal good. An inferior good has a negative income elasticity.

7. Cross elasticity of demand is defined as:

$$E_{xy} = \frac{\text{\% change in quantity demanded of good X}}{\text{\% change in price of good Y}}$$

Signs are also important for cross elasticity. If the cross elasticity is: (a) greater than 0 the goods are called substitutes; (b) less than 0 the goods are called complements; (c) equal to 0 the goods are independent.

8. An excise tax shifts the supply curve up by the amount of the tax, creating a new equilibrium. The price including tax has increased by a portion of the tax. This increase is the consumer's burden. The net of tax price received by the producers has decreased by the remaining portion. This decrease is the producer's burden.
(a) Given the supply, the more inelastic the demand, the larger the portion of the tax shifted to consumers.
(b) Given the demand, the more inelastic the supply, the larger the portion of the tax borne by producers.

9. Sometimes governments impose price ceilings when prices seem unfairly high to buyers, or impose price floors when prices seem unfairly low to sellers. Such controls prevent market-clearing adjustments from performing the rationing function.
(a) A price ceiling is a maximum legal price. It results in a shortage of the commodity; may bring about formal rationing by the government and a black market; and causes a misallocation of resources.
(b) A price floor is a minimum legal price. It results in a surplus of the commodity; may induce government to take measures to restrict the supply, increase demand, or purchase the surplus; and causes a misallocation of resources.
(c) There are many examples in our economy of price controls. Cases of price ceilings include rent controls on apartments, proposals to regulate credit card interest rates, and pricing on rock concert tickets (even though no government intervention is involved in this case). Cases of price floors are agricultural price supports and minimum wage laws.

Terms and Concepts

cross elasticity of demand
elastic versus inelastic demand
income elasticity of demand
market period
perfectly elastic demand
perfectly inelastic demand
price elasticity of demand
price elasticity of supply
short run and long run

total-revenue test
unit elasticity

Hints and Tips

1. Do *not* judge elasticity from the slope of the demand curve (except in the case of horizontal and vertical demand curves). Remember that even a constant slope demand curve has a different elasticity at each point. It is also useful to know that on a straight line demand curve the price elasticity is one at the midpoint.

2. Master the total-revenue test for assessing price elasticity of demand. If all you need to determine is whether demand is elastic or inelastic, determining the direction of total revenue change can be easier than computing price elasticity from the midpoints formula. Also be aware that if you know whether elasticity is greater or less than one that you infer the direction of change in total revenue for a given price change.

3. All elasticities are ratios of percentage changes. The percentage change in the dependent variable is in the numerator, and the percentage change in the independent variable is in the denominator.

Fill-In Questions

1. Elasticity of demand is a measure of the __________ of quantity demanded to changes in the price of the good and can be computed from the formula: E_d = percentage change in __________/ percentage change in __________.

2. Suppose that when a golf course raises their green fees from $23 to $27 that the number of golfers falls from 105 per day to 95 per day. The change in quantity demanded is ____ golfers. The average of the two quantities is _____ golfers. Therefore the percentage change in quantity is (_____/_____) x 100% = _____%. The change in price is $_____. The average of the two prices is $_____. Therefore the percentage change in price is (_____/_____) x 100% = _____%. The elasticity coefficient is (_____%/_____%) = _____.

3. If a relatively large change in price results in a relatively small change in quantity demanded, demand is __________; if a relatively small change in price results in a relatively large change in quantity demanded, demand is __________.

4. The price elasticity formula uses __________ changes rather than __________ changes in order to avoid the problem of an arbitrary choice of units.

5. To avoid ambiguous results when computing elasticity of demand, one uses the __________ of the two quantities and the __________ of the two prices when calculating the percentage change in these two values.

6. If demand is elastic, price change and total revenue change are (directly, inversely) __________ related; if demand is inelastic, they are __________ related.

7. Complete the summary table.

If demand is:	The elasticity coefficient is	If P rises, TR will	If P falls, TR will
Elastic	______	______	______
Inelastic	______	______	______
Of unitary elasticity	______	______	______

8. If a change in price causes no change in quantity demanded, demand is perfectly (elastic, inelastic) __________ and the demand curve is (horizontal, vertical) __________. The elasticity coefficient at any point on this demand curve is __________. If an extremely small change in price results in an extremely large change in quantity demanded, demand is perfectly __________ and the demand curve is nearly

__________. The elasticity coefficient at any point on this demand curve is nearly __________.

9. If the price of a commodity declines:

(a) when demand is inelastic, the loss of revenue due to the lower price is (greater, less) __________ than the gain in revenue due to the greater quantity demanded;

(b) when demand is elastic, the loss of revenue due to the lower price is (greater, less) __________ than the gain in revenue due to the greater quantity demanded;

(c) when demand is of unitary elasticity, the loss of revenue due to the lower price is __________ the gain in revenue due to the greater quantity demanded.

10. For all straight line demand curves, demand tends to be more __________ in the upper-left portion than in the lower-right portion.

11. The slope of a straight line demand curve is __________, but the price elasticity __________ along such a demand curve.

12. List four determinants of price elasticity of demand.

(a) ______________________________

(b) ______________________________

(c) ______________________________

(d) ______________________________

13. Legislatures that want to maximize tax revenue from the imposition of excise taxes will place the taxes on products with (elastic, inelastic) __________ demands.

14. A demand elasticity coefficient of 2 indicates that for every __________ percent decrease in price there will be a __________ percent increase in __________.

15. If supply is elastic, a given percentage change in __________ will lead to a larger percentage change in __________.

16. If the supply curve is vertical then supply is infinitely __________. In this case a change in price causes __________ change in the quantity supplied.

17. A perfectly elastic supply curve is drawn as a __________ line.

18. The most important factor affecting the price elasticity of supply is __________. In the __________ period producers are unable to adjust to demand changes. This is reflected in a __________ supply curve. In the __________ run firms have enough time to use existing plants more intensively. This is reflected in an __________ supply curve. In the __________ run there is time for firms to __________ their plant capacities, and for the number of firms to __________. This is reflected in a supply curve that is __________ elastic than the __________ run supply curve.

19. A given increase in demand will result in a larger increase in the equilibrium price the more __________ the supply curve.

20. An inferior good has a (positive, negative) __________ income elasticity.

21. An income elasticity of 0.5 indicates that a 10% increase in __________ would result in a __________% increase in __________.

22. Substitute goods have a (positive, negative) __________ cross elasticity of demand. Complementary goods have a __________ cross elasticity.

23. Because cigarettes have few good substitutes, their demand is __________. If government increases the excise tax on cigarettes by $1.00 per package, the

__________ curve will shift __________ by the amount of the tax. If the equilibrium price increases by $0.75, the producers' tax burden is __________.

24. In order to be effective, a ceiling price must be set (above, below) __________ the equilibrium price, whereas a floor price must be set __________ the equilibrium.

25. A price ceiling prevents the market mechanism from performing its __________ function. Some other means must be found for allocating the available supply. Illegal means are called __________ market transactions.

Problems and Projects

1. Fill in the table below by computing total revenue at the seven price levels, the six price elasticity coefficients between these prices, and indicating whether the character of demand is elastic, inelastic, or of unitary elasticity between each pair of prices. (Each elasticity coefficient is entered between two prices because it is an "average" over that price interval.)

P	Qd	Total Revenue	Elasticity coefficient	Character of demand
10	300	_____		
			_______	_______
9	400	_____		
			_______	_______
8	500	_____		
			_______	_______
7	600	_____		
			_______	_______
6	700	_____		
			_______	_______
5	800	_____		
			_______	_______
4	900	_____		

2. This question uses the data in the previous question.
(a) Use the first graph below to plot the demand curve (price vs. quantity demanded). Using the same horizontal scale as on your first graph, use the second graph to plot the total revenue curve (total revenue vs. quantity demanded).

(b) Based on your answers in the previous question, the demand curve is price elastic between the prices _____ and _____. In this range the total revenue curve has a(n) __________ slope. The demand curve has unitary elasticity between the prices _____ and _____. In this vicinity the total curve has a(n) __________ slope. The demand curve is inelastic between the prices _____ and _____. Here the total revenue curve has a(n) __________ slope. These results illustrate that along a straight line demand curve, price elasticity __________ as price increases, and that total revenue is __________ at the point of __________ elasticity.

3. For each case below determine whether the demand is elastic, inelastic, or of unitary elasticity.
(a) When the Flin Flon Flyers cut prices by 10% they sold 20% more tickets to their roller hockey games.
(b) When the cablevision company increased their subscription rates by 15% their total revenues increased 3%.
(c) Momma's Deli finds that no matter whether they charge a little more or a little less for their bagels, their total revenue from bagels remains the same.

4. Using the supply data in the schedule shown below, complete the table by computing the four price elasticity of supply coefficients between each of the five prices, and indicate whether supply is elastic, or of unitary elasticity.

Price	Quantity supplied	Elasticity coefficient	Character of supply
$0.90	800		
		__________	__________
0.80	700		
		__________	__________
0.70	600		
		__________	__________
0.60	500		
		__________	__________
0.50	400		

5. On the following graph are three different supply curves (S_1, S_2, S_3) for a product bought and sold in a competitive market.
(a) The supply curve for the (1) market period is the one labelled _____; (2) short run is the one labelled _____; (3) long run is the one labelled _____.
(b) No matter what the period of time under consideration, if the demand for the product were D_1, the equilibrium price of the product would be __________ and the equilibrium quantity would be __________.
(c) Were demand to increase from D_1 to D_2, (1) in the market period, the equilibrium price would increase to __________ and the equilibrium quantity would be __________; (2) in the short run, the price of the product would increase to __________ and the quantity would increase to __________; (3) in the long run, the price of the product would be __________ and the quantity would be __________.

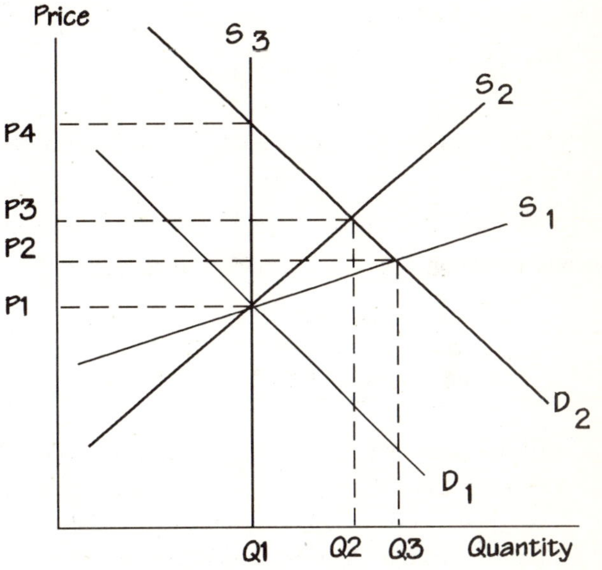

(d) The longer the period of time allowed to sellers to adjust their outputs, the (more, less) __________ elastic is the supply of their product.
(e) The more elastic the supply of a product, the (greater, less) __________ is the effect on equilibrium price, and the __________ is the effect on equilibrium quantity of an increase in demand.

6. Suppose you own the only bridge across a river. Also assume that there are no operating costs connected with the operation of the bridge. You want to maximize profit. How would you change the price you charge for using the bridge if you were told by an economist that you were currently operating:
(a) in the inelastic portion of the demand curve for bridge use.
(b) in the elastic portion of the demand curve for bridge use.
(c) where the elasticity of demand for bridge use is equal to one.

7. The graph below shows a supply curve and two hypothetical demand curves. Note that regardless of whether demand is initially represented by D_1 or by D_2 the equilibrium price and quantity are the same.

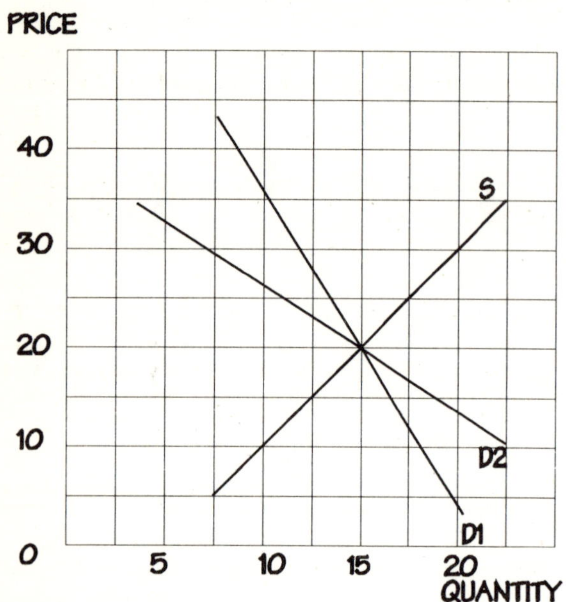

(a) Show the effect of a $10 per unit excise tax.

(b) If demand was initially D_1 the imposition of the tax raises price to _____. The equilibrium quantity falls to _____. The tax burden is a price increase of _____ for consumers, and a price decrease of _____ for producers.

(c) If demand was initially D_2 the imposition of the tax raises price to _____. The equilibrium quantity falls to _____. The tax burden is a price increase of _____ for consumers, and a price decrease of _____ for producers.

(d) The difference between the results in (b) and (c) illustrates the generalization that a tax will impose a greater burden on consumers, and a lesser burden on producers, the more (elastic, inelastic) __________ is the demand curve.

8. This problem uses algebra to express the demand and supply functions. Demand is represented by the straight line function $Q_d = 100 - 3P$ and supply by the straight line function $Q_s = 7P$. Price in $ is expressed by P, and quantity is represented by Q

(a) Equilibrium is found where quantity demanded equals quantity supplied. Therefore, by substitution, and solving: P = _____, and Q = _____.

(b) If government institutes a price floor of $11, Q_d = _____, Q_s = _____. Therefore, there is a (shortage, surplus) __________ of _____ units. To maintain the floor price government may be required to (buy, sell) __________ a quantity of _____ units for a total (expenditure, revenue) __________ of $_____.

9. In each case below, identify:
(1) which good is the central focus,
(2) which of the four types of elasticities studied in Chapter 7 is relevant,
(3) whether the speaker expects the elasticity to be negative (-) or positive (+), and
(4) whether the speaker is hoping for a large (L) or a small (S) elasticity.

(a) "Our company publishes crossword puzzle magazines. We expect that all of the layoffs and cutbacks people are suffering will actually help our sales." (1) __________ (2) __________ (3) _____ (4) _____

(b) "We have been having trouble attracting qualified machinists to work at this factory. Now we're going to try offering a higher wage rate." (1) __________ (2) __________ (3) _____ (4) _____

(c) "The frosts in the California orange groves have killed a big portion of their crop. Those of us growing apples in the Okanagan Valley should really benefit." (1) __________ (2) __________ (3) _____ (4) _____

(d) "The government really needs more revenue to fund social programs. That is why we have implemented this new tax on hotel rooms." (1) __________ (2) __________ (3) _____ (4) _____

True-False

Circle T if the statement is true, F if it is false.

1. If the relative change in price is greater than the relative change in quantity demanded, the price elasticity coefficient is greater than one. **T F**

2. Along a downward sloping linear demand curve demand tends to be elastic at higher prices and inelastic at lower prices. **T F**

3. If demand for wheat is inelastic, an increase in the harvest will reduce farm incomes from wheat sales. **T F**

4. If the quantity demanded of a product increases from 100 to 150 units when the price decreases from $14 to $10, demand is elastic in this price range. **T F**

5. If the elasticity coefficient is 3, this means that a one dollar decrease in price will lead to a three unit increase in quantity demanded. **T F**

6. If along a demand curve an increase in price results in no change in quantity demanded, the price elasticity of demand is equal to 0. **T F**

7. The demand for "necessities" tends to be inelastic, for "luxuries" elastic. **T F**

8. The price elasticity of demand will tend to be greater the larger the number of substitutes for the good. **T F**

9. If demand is elastic, an increase in price will result in an increase in total expenditure on the good. **T F**

10. Other things being equal, the larger the portion of one's income spent on a good the greater the elasticity of demand for that good. **T F**

11. The demand for a product tends to be more inelastic the longer the time period under consideration. **T F**

12. Because price and quantity supplied are directly related supply elasticity is usually positive. **T F**

13. In the market period the elasticity of supply is effectively zero. **T F**

14. If supply is perfectly inelastic, an increase in demand will result in price remaining the same. **T F**

15. The supply of a product tends to be more elastic the longer the time period under consideration. **T F**

16. A decrease in demand will not lower the price if supply is perfectly elastic. **T F**

17. The cross elasticity of demand between a pair of goods that are complements is negative. **T F**

18. A zero or near-zero coefficient for cross elasticity suggests that the two goods are unrelated or independent goods. **T F**

19. If the consumption of a good is inversely related to the income level of consumers, that good is a luxury good. **T F**

20. You collect empty beer bottles and sell them to a bottle depot for a set price of $2.80 a dozen. You face a demand curve for bottles that is perfectly elastic. **T F**

21. Scalping of hockey tickets outside the Montreal Forum arises from the same economic circumstances that lead to black markets under price ceilings. **T F**

22. Given the supply, the more inelastic is the demand, the greater is the producer's burden of a new excise tax. **T F**

23. Rent controls distort market signals so that resources are misallocated: too many resources are allocated to rental housing, too few to alternative uses. **T F**

24. When price floors are in place governments sometimes subsidise demand in order to eliminate surpluses. **T F**

25. If a natural gas company raises price and finds that in the short run their total revenues increase slightly, the price increase will likely increase their total revenues in the long run. **T F**

Multiple-Choice

Circle the letter that corresponds to the best answer.

1. The price elasticity of demand measures:
(a) the percentage change in quantity demanded as a result of a 1 percent change in supply
(b) the change in quantity demanded as the result of a 1

percent change in price
(c) the percentage change in quantity demanded as a result of a 1 percent change in price
(d) the slope of the demand curve

2. If, when the price of a product rises from $1.50 to $2.00, the quantity demanded of the product decreases from 1,000 to 900, the price elasticity of demand coefficient is:
(a) 3.00
(b) 2.71
(c) .37
(d) .33

3. If a 1 percent fall in the price of a commodity causes the quantity demanded of the commodity to increase 2 percent, demand is:
(a) inelastic
(b) elastic
(c) unit elastic
(d) perfectly elastic

4. Moving down a linear demand curve that has a slope of -2:
(a) the elasticity of demand coefficient is a constant equal to 2
(b) the elasticity of demand coefficient always equals 1
(c) the elasticity of demand coefficient declines from a number greater than 1 at high prices to a number less than 1 at low prices
(d) is largest at the intercept value on the quantity axis

5. If total expenditures are the same before and after a price decrease, then demand is:
(a) unit elastic
(b) inelastic
(c) elastic
(d) perfectly inelastic

6. For a downward sloping demand curve a price decrease results in an increase in total revenue whenever:
(a) demand is unit elastic
(b) demand is elastic
(c) demand is inelastic
(d) the good in question is a normal good

7. Suppose the only beer outlet in the town of Adanac increased the price of a liter of beer from $2.75 to $3.25. If the number of liters of beer sold decreased by 22 percent the elasticity of demand for beer is about:
(a) .67
(b) .90
(c) 1.0
(d) 1.32
(e) 1.64

8. Since bacon and eggs are complementary goods the cross elasticity of demand between them would be:
(a) greater than 1
(b) negative
(c) 1
(d) vary between -1 and +1

9. An increase in supply will lead to an increase in total expenditure on a good if:
(a) demand is elastic
(b) demand is unit elastic
(c) demand is inelastic
(d) none of the above

10. If demand is perfectly inelastic, a decrease in supply will result in:
(a) a decrease in the equilibrium price
(b) an increase in the equilibrium quantity
(c) a decrease in equilibrium quantity
(d) no change in equilibrium quantity

11. A perfectly elastic demand curve is:
(a) parallel to the quantity axis
(b) downward sloping with a slope of -1
(c) parallel to the price axis
(d) a "long-run" demand curve

12. If the price elasticity of demand for turnips is 2.0, what is the effect of an 8% decrease in the price?
(a) quantity demanded will fall by 16%
(b) quantity demanded will rise by 16%
(c) quantity demanded will rise by 4%
(d) there is not enough information to tell

13. Which of the following is not characteristic of a good for which the demand is price inelastic?
(a) the good has many good substitutes
(b) the buyer spends a small percentage of his/her total income on the good
(c) the good is regarded by consumers as a necessity
(d) the period of time for which demand is given is very short

14. Income elasticity indicates the responsiveness of consumer purchases to:
(a) a change in the price of the good
(b) a change in the price of a related good
(c) a change in income
(d) a change in tastes

15. Which of the following lists correctly ranks the products in descending order of price elasticity of demand (i.e. from most elastic to least elastic)?
(a) soft drinks, colas, Pepsi
(b) colas, soft drinks, Pepsi
(c) colas, Pepsi, soft drinks
(d) soft drinks, Pepsi, colas
(e) Pepsi, colas, soft drinks

16. The chief determinant of the price elasticity of supply of a product is:
(a) the number of good substitutes the product has
(b) the length of time sellers have to adjust to a change in price
(c) whether the product is a luxury or a necessity
(d) whether the product is durable or nondurable

17. Generally in the long run the supply curve:
(a) is less elastic than in the short run
(b) is more elastic than in the short run
(c) has the same elasticity as in the short run
(d) is perfectly elastic

18. Suppose the quantity available of a good is fixed. The elasticity of supply would:
(a) be fixed at some positive value
(b) be fixed at some negative value
(c) be zero
(d) change along the supply curve from a small value to a large value

19. If supply is perfectly elastic, an increase in demand will result in:
(a) an increase in the equilibrium price
(b) a decrease in the equilibrium price
(c) a decrease in the equilibrium quantity
(d) an increase in the equilibrium quantity
(e) no change in the equilibrium quantity

20. If an effective interest rate ceiling is imposed, the possible results will *not* include:
(a) increased numbers of credit cards issued to lower income individuals
(b) increased annual fees charged to cardholders
(c) increased merchandise prices in stores that issue credit cards to their customers
(d) card users charged a fee for each card transaction

Questions 21 through 23 refer to the graph below.

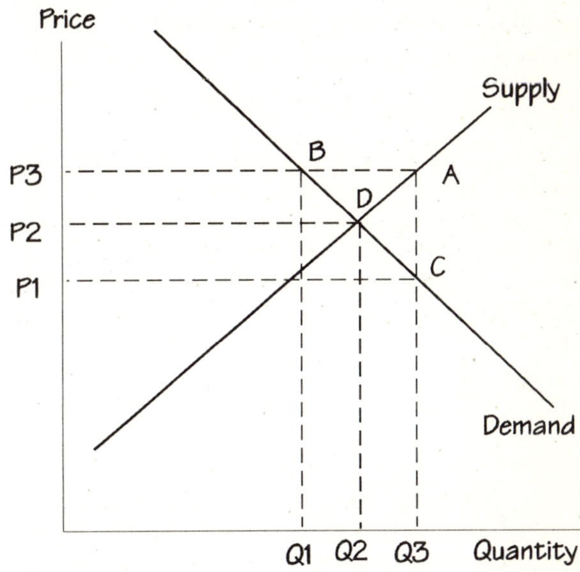

21. If a price floor of P_3 is imposed, the quantity demanded will be:
(a) Q_1B
(b) Q_3A
(c) Q_1
(d) Q_2
(e) Q_3

22. If a price floor of P_3 is imposed, the result will be:
(a) a surplus of AB
(b) a surplus of AC
(c) a shortage of AB
(d) a shortage of BD
(e) a surplus of AD

23. What is the result if the government announces a price support at P_3, guaranteeing producers this price by paying the difference between P_3 and what consumers are willing to pay?
(a) producers will produce Q_1 and the government will pay a price support of $P_3 - P_2$
(b) producers will produce Q_2 and the government will pay a price support of $P_2 - P_1$
(c) producers will produce Q_3 and the government will

pay a price support of $P_3 - P_1$
(d) producers will produce Q_2 and the government will pay a price support of $P_3 - P_2$

24. An effective minimum wage law can be expected to:
(a) increase incomes for all workers who previously worked for less than the minimum wage
(b) have no effect on teenage unemployment
(c) create more jobs for teenagers
(d) reduce employment among teenagers

25. If the government fixes apartment rents below their equilibrium level, there will occur in the long run:
(a) an increase in the supply of apartments
(b) a decrease in the demand for apartments
(c) conversion of condominiums into rental units
(d) a withdrawal of capital from the apartment market into other sectors of the economy

Discussion Questions

1. Define and explain the price elasticity of demand concept in terms of each of the following: (a) the relative sensitivity of quantity demanded to changes in price; (b) the behaviour of total revenue when price changes; (c) the elasticity coefficient; (d) the relationship between the relative (percentage) change in quantity demanded and the relative (percentage) change in price.

2. What is meant by perfectly elastic demand? By perfectly inelastic demand? What does the demand curve look like when demand is perfectly elastic? When it is perfectly inelastic?

3. In computing the price elasticity coefficient it usually makes a considerable difference whether the higher price and lower quantity or the lower price and higher quantity are used as a point of reference. How do we eliminate the confusion that would arise if the elasticity-of-demand coefficient varied and depended upon whether a price rise or price fall were being considered?

4. It is common to see many vacant seats at movie theaters. Presumably this is no surprise to the theater owners. Why don't the theater owners drop the price far enough to fill all of the seats? Give an explanation based on the concept of price elasticity of demand.

5. What is the relationship, if any, between the elasticity of demand and the slope of the demand curve?

6. What factors determine the price elasticity of demand for a product?

7. Of what practical importance is the price elasticity of demand? Cite examples of its importance to business firms, workers, farmers, and governments.

8. Explain what determines the elasticity of supply of a product.

9. Explain why, if you were the only seller of a product, you would never set the price in the inelastic portion of the demand curve.

10. What are some of the unintended consequences that normally result when a price ceiling is implemented? When a price floor is implemented?

11. Suppose that a college having financial difficulty has more students applying than they have spaces for, but is prevented by a government policy from raising tuition fees to a market clearing level. Based on the theory of price ceilings, what specific predictions can you make about how the college might respond?

Answers

Fill-in questions

1. sensitivity, quantity, price

2. 10; 100; 10, 100, 10; 4; 25; 4, 25, 16; 10, 16, 0.63.

3. inelastic, elastic

4. percentage, numerical or absolute

5. average, average

6. inversely, directly

7. Elastic: greater than 1, decrease, increase; Inelastic: less than 1, increase, decrease; Unit elastic: equal to 1, remain constant, remain constant

8. inelastic, vertical; zero; elastic, horizontal; infinity

9. (a) greater, (b) less, (c) equal to

10. elastic

11. constant; changes

12. (a) number of substitutes, (b) proportion of income spent on the good, (c) necessity or luxury, (d) time period under consideration

13. inelastic

14. 1, 2, quantity demanded

15. price, quantity supplied

16. inelastic; no

17. horizontal

18. time; market; vertical; short; upsloping; long, expand, increase; more, short

19. inelastic

20. negative

21. income, 5, quantity demanded

22. positive; negative

23. inelastic; supply, upward, $0.25.

24. below; above

25. rationing; black

Problems and projects

1. Total revenue: 3000, 3600, 4000, 4200, 4200, 4000, 3600; Elasticity coefficient: 2.71, 1.89, 1.36, 1.00, 0.73, 0.53; Character of demand; elastic, elastic, elastic, unit elastic, inelastic, inelastic

2. (b) 7, 10; positive; 6, 7; zero; 4, 6; negative; increases, maximized, unitary

3. (a) elastic, (b) inelastic, (c) unitary elasticity

4. Elasticity coefficient: 1.13, 1.15, 1.18, 1.22; Character of supply: elastic, elastic, elastic, elastic

5. (a) (1) S_3; (2) S_2; (3) S_1; (b) P_1, Q_1 (c)(1) P_4, Q_1; (2) P_3, Q_2, (3) P_2, Q_3; (d) more (e) less, greater

6. (a) increase, (b) decrease, (c) no change

7. (b) $27; 13; $7, $3; c) $24; 12; $4, $6; d) inelastic.

8. (a) 10, 70; (b) 67, 77; surplus, 10; buy, 10, expenditure, 110.

9. (a) crossword puzzle magazines, income elasticity, -, L; (b) machinists, elasticity of supply, +, L; (c) apples, cross price elasticity, +, L; (d) hotels, price elasticity of demand, -, S.

True-False

1. F	**2.** T	**3.** T	**4.** T	**5.** F	**6.** T
7. T	**8.** T	**9.** F	**10.** T	**11.** F	**12.** T
13. T	**14.** F	**15.** T	**16.** T	**17.** T	**18.** T
19. F	**20.** T	**21.** T	**22.** F	**23.** F	**24.** T
25. F					

Multiple-choice

1.(c)	**2.** (c)	**3.** (b)	**4.** (c)	**5.** (a)	**6.** (b)
7. (d)	**8.** (b)	**9.** (a)	**10.** (d)	**11.** (a)	**12.** (b)
13. (a)	**14.** (c)	**15.** (e)	**16.** (b)	**17.** (b)	**18.** (c)
19. (d)	**20.** (a)	**21.** (e)	**22.** (a)	**23.** (c)	**24.** (d)
25. (d)					

CHAPTER 8

Consumer Behaviour and Utility Maximization

The law of demand asserts that there is an inverse relationship between price and quantity demanded. Chapter 8 looks behind this basic proposition, and offers two complementary explanations for why consumers behave this way.

The first explanation, using concepts already introduced in Chapter 4, is a general and simple one that is based on income and substitution effects. From this perspective, if a product's price increases the consumer will buy less because the consumer now has less real income (or buying power) and because this product's opportunity cost has increased in terms of other products the consumer could buy.

The second explanation is based on the law of diminishing marginal utility. According to this theory, consumers get less additional utility or benefit from each additional unit that they consume of any given commodity. Therefore the price that consumers are willing to pay for each additional unit also decreases; hence the downsloping demand curve. The more sharply the marginal utility falls as the consumer has more of the good, the more inelastic the consumer's demand curve will be.

Diminishing marginal utility also provides a theory of how rational consumers allocate their limited incomes in an effort to maximize their utility. Given the consumer's subjective preferences, limited income, and the current market prices of goods, the consumer's income is allocated so that the last dollar spent on each product yields the same marginal utility. The numerical example used to illustrate this principle also illustrates that each point on a consumer's demand curve for a particular good corresponds to a utility maximizing allocation of the consumer's income. Economists do not claim that consumers actually perform such mental gymnastics before making purchases at the grocery store. However, to the extent that consumers behave "as if" they make such calculations, this model will permit us to make correct predictions about how consumer choices respond to price changes or income changes.

The final section of the chapter describes how the theory of consumer choice can be used to explain many economic events in the real world. The examples discussed are the growing dominance of compact discs over record albums, the diamond-water paradox, the value of time in consumption, and the effects of gifts in cash versus gifts in kind.

Checklist

When you have finished this chapter, you should be able to:

- ☐ Explain how the substitution effect and (for normal goods) the income effect generate a downward sloping demand curve.
- ☐ Define marginal utility, total utility, and state the law of diminishing marginal utility.
- ☐ Explain the relationship of the law of diminishing marginal utility to demand and to price elasticity of demand.
- ☐ List the four assumptions made in the theory of consumer behaviour.
- ☐ State the utility-maximizing rule and use some reasoning to justify it.
- ☐ Use the utility-maximizing rule to determine how the consumer would allocate a fixed income when utility and price data are given.
- ☐ Derive a consumer's demand schedule for a product from data on utility, income, and the product price.
- ☐ Give examples of how consumer theory can be used to explain such economic phenomena as the increased consumption of compact discs, the

diamond-water paradox, the value of time in consumption, the efficiency of cash gifts versus gifts in kind.

Chapter Outline

1. Both the income effect and the substitution effect can explain the law of demand.
(a) If the price of a good falls, the consumer's income can purchase more. In the case of a normal good, this income effect leads to increased purchases.
(b) If the price of a good falls, its relative price or opportunity cost measured in other goods falls. This leads the consumer to substitute in favour of buying more of this good.

2. Utility is a subjective measure of the satisfaction or benefit that a consumer receives from the consumption of a good or a service.
(a) We assume the consumer is able to measure utility in terms of units sometimes called "utils."
(b) Marginal utility is the extra satisfaction received from the consumption of an extra unit of a good. Total utility is the satisfaction received from the consumption of a specific number of units of a good.
(c) Under the law of diminishing marginal utility we assume that marginal utility decreases as the consumer has more of the good. For example, the extra utility received from the consumption of the fifth unit of a good is less than the marginal utility received from the fourth unit of the good.
(d) Diminishing marginal utility provides an explanation for the law of demand, and for differing price elasticities of demand. The more sharply a consumer's marginal utility for a good falls, the more inelastic is his or her demand for that good.

3. Diminishing marginal utility provides an explanation for how a consumer chooses what to buy. This theory relies on several assumptions:
(a) The consumer behaves rationally, attempting to maximize his or her utility;
(b) The consumer has well established preferences between various goods and services;
(c) The consumer has a budget constraint (a limited income);
(d) The consumer faces a given set of prices for the various goods and services.

4. The consumer spends his or her income so as to maximize the satisfaction received from consuming the goods. Given just two goods, A and B, the consumer will be maximizing utility when the marginal utility of A divided by the price of A just equals the marginal utility of B divided by the price of B. This is the utility-maximizing rule and can be summarized as $(MU_A/P_A) = (MU_B/P_B)$. When this condition is met the last dollar spent on either good yields the same amount of extra utility. If the rule is violated, utility is not maximized.

5. Suppose the consumer is presently consuming amounts of A and B such that the utility-maximizing rule is met. The price of A falls while income, tastes, and the price of B remain constant. At the previous consumption level the utility-maximizing rule will not be met. The consumer, in order to maximize utility at the new price for A, will purchase more of A until the utility-maximizing condition, is again fulfilled.

This yields two different prices of A and the two different utility-maximizing quantities of A the consumer will purchase, given that the price of B, income, and preferences are all fixed. Two entries in the demand schedule for A have been obtained and the full demand schedule can be computed by making further changes in the price of A and noting the quantities that fulfill the utility-maximizing rule.

6. There are many applications and extensions of consumer theory in the real world, four of which are discussed in this chapter.
(a) Compact discs now dominate the market for recorded music because of the change in consumer preferences and the fall in the price of CD players.
(b) Diamonds are high in price, but of limited usefulness, while water is low in price, but essential for life. This paradox is resolved by explaining the distinction between marginal and total utility. Because water is so abundant its price is very low, causing us to consume it up to the point that its marginal utility becomes nearly zero. Because diamonds are in very limited supply they are very expensive, and at our utility-maximizing consumption their marginal utility is still very high.
(c) Marginal utility theory recognizes the fact that consumption takes time, and time is a scarce resource. The full price of any consumer good or service is its market price plus the value of the time taken to consume it (i.e., the income that the consumer could have earned had that time been used for work).

(d) For recipients, gifts in kind are less efficient than cash transfers. A cash transfer allows the consumer to choose whatever goods he or she prefers, whereas with a gift in kind the choice is restricted.

Terms and Concepts

budget constraint
income effect
law of diminishing marginal utility
marginal utility
substitution effect
total utility
utility
utility-maximizing rule

Hints and Tips

1. Utility is an abstraction that is useful for explaining consumer behaviour. Do not be distracted by the fact that utility is not measurable. It is true that in advanced economics little use is made of this model precisely because of this problem; nevertheless the model is instructive because we can think of consumers making choices "as if" they are applying the utility-maximizing rule, whether or not utility is observable.

2. Master the difference between marginal and total utility. Think of consumers as allocating their incomes one dollar at a time; the next dollar always being allocated to the good that produces the highest marginal utility from one more dollar spent.

Fill-In Questions

1. The law of demand (which states that demand curves are __________ sloping) can be explained in terms of the __________ and __________ effects.

2. A fall in the price of a product tends to (increase, decrease) __________ the purchasing power of a consumer. This causes the __________ effect. A fall in price makes the product (more, less) __________ expensive *relative* to other goods. This causes the __________ effect.

3. Utility is a measure of the __________ obtained from the consumption of a good or service. The extra satisfaction obtained from consuming one more unit of the good is called __________ utility. The satisfaction obtained from some number of units of a product is called __________ utility. One can calculate __________ utility by summing the __________ figures.

4. Other things being equal, if the marginal utility falls sharply as successive units are consumed, we would expect demand to be (elastic, inelastic) __________. Modest declines in marginal utility as consumption increases imply an __________ demand.

5. The marginal utility theory of consumer behaviour assumes that the consumer is __________ and that the consumer has certain __________ for various goods.

6. Saying that all individuals make consumption decisions subject to a budget constraint means that for each individual's __________ is limited, and that goods have __________.

7. The utility-maximizing rule states that the last dollar spent on each product purchased should yield the same amount of __________. The utility-maximizing condition, for two goods, A and B, can be rewritten as: MU_A/P_A= __________.

8. Suppose the consumer is presently consuming where ($MU_A/P_A > MU_B/P_B$). The symbol > stands for "greater than". In order to increase utility the consumer should consume less of good __________ and use the money to purchase more of good __________.

9. In deriving a consumer's demand schedule for a particular good the two factors (other than consumer preferences) which are held constant are:

(a) __________

(b) __________

10. It is the __________ utility and not __________ utility that is relevant to the price people are willing to pay for a good.

11. In addition to the monetary price, the opportunity cost of consumption of most goods also includes the dollar value of __________ that is used.

12. Noncash gifts are (more, less) __________ efficient than cash gifts because they yield consumers (more, less) __________ utility.

Problems and Projects

1. Suppose that a consumer's utility levels from consuming goods A, B, and C are given in the table on this page. Assume that the level of utility from any one good is independent of how much is consumed of other goods. The utility of the consumer is calculated by adding together the utility obtained from each good. "U" denotes utility and "MU" denotes marginal utility.

Assume the consumer's income equals $17 and the three goods' prices are given by $P_A = \$1$, $P_B = \$2$, and $P_C = \$4$.

(a) Complete the table by computing the values for the marginal utility column and the marginal utility per dollar column.

(b) Consider the first unit purchased. The individual would take good _____ because the marginal utility per dollar spent for the first unit of _____ is _____ while it would be _____ for the first unit of good A and _____ for the first unit of good C.

(c) The consumer takes a unit of good B and now has $_____ left to spend.

(d) For the second unit purchased the consumer would take good _____ since the marginal utility per dollar spent on that unit of good _____ is _____ as compared to _____ for good _____ and _____ for good _____.

(e) The third unit purchased would be good _____ and the marginal utility per dollar spent to get that unit is _____.

(f) To maximize utility the consumer will buy _____ units of good A, _____ units of good B, and _____ units of good C. Total utility will be _____.

(g) The marginal utility of the last dollar spent on each good will be _____.

(h) The consumer could have purchased 2 units of C, 2 units of B, and 5 units of A, but did not. Why? __________

Good A				Good B				Good C			
Qa	Ua	MUa	MUa/Pa	Qb	Ub	MUb	MUb/Pb	Qc	Uc	MUc	MUc/Pc
1	6	6	___	1	36	___	___	1	22	___	___
2	11	5	___	2	64	___	___	2	38	___	___
3	15	___	___	3	72	___	___	3	50	___	___
4	18	___	___	4	76	___	___	4	54	___	___
5	20	___	___	5	79	___	___	5	56	___	___

2. Ms. Thompson has an income of $36 to spend each week. The only two goods she wants to purchase are D and E. The marginal utility schedules for these two goods are shown in the table on the next page.

The price of E is $4, and does not change from week to week. The marginal utility per dollar from good E at this price is also shown in the table. But the price of D varies from one week to the next. The marginal utility per dollar from good D when the price of D is $6. $4, $3, and $2 is shown in the table.

Complete the demand schedule in the table on the next page to show how much of good D Ms. Thompson will buy each week at each of these four possible prices of D.

	Good D					Good E	
Q	MU	MU/$6	MU/$4	MU/$3	MU/$2	MU	MU/$4
1	45	7.5	11.25	15	22.5	40	10
2	30	5	7.5	10	15	36	9
3	20	3.33	5	6.67	10	32	8
4	15	2.5	3.75	5	7.5	28	7
5	12	2	3	4	6	24	6
6	10	1.67	2.5	3.33	5	20	5
7	9	1.5	2.25	3	4.5	16	4
8	7.5	1.25	1.88	2.5	3.75	12	3

Price of D	Quantity of D demanded
$6	_____
$4	_____
$3	_____
$2	_____

3. This question uses a little algebra to obtain the consumer's utility-maximizing bundle. Suppose the individual consumes two goods, A and B, the prices of which are $4 and $1 respectively. Income is $32 and is all spent on the two goods. The consumer knows that the marginal utility obtained from consuming units of good A is: $MU_A = 24 - 2A$, where A is the number of units of A consumed. The marginal utility obtained from units of B is: $MU_B = 10 - B$, where B is the number of units of B consumed. Assuming that both A and B are divisible, how many units of A and B should be purchased to maximize utility?

One could proceed by constructing a marginal utility table like the ones in the problems above. An alternative procedure is to list the conditions that must be met to maximize utility. According to the utility-maximizing rule at the point of maximum satisfaction $MU_A/P_A = MU_B/P_B$. At the same time all income must be spent on the two goods or $P_AA + P_BB = \$32$ where P_AA gives the amount spent on A and P_BB the amount spent on B. Rewrite the two equations by substituting for MU_A and MU_B and P_A and P_B from the information given in the problem. This yields:

$(24 - 2A)/4 = (10 - B)/1$ and

$4A + 1B = 32$

Solve for B in terms of A in the second equation and substitute in the first equation. This will give:

$(24 - 2A)/4 = (10 - (32 - 4A))/1$

(a) Solve for A and B; A = ________________; B = ________________

Check to see if at the values you found for A and B that $MU_A/P_A = MU_B/P_B$ and income is exactly spent.

(b) Suppose the price of A decreases to $2, *ceteris paribus*. At the new equilibrium, purchases of good A = _____ and of good B = _____. At the lower price the total expenditure on good A = __________ Over the price range considered, when the price of A fell, the total expenditure on good A (fell, rose) __________. Therefore, the demand for good A is (elastic, inelastic) __________.

4. Assume that the only two goods a consumer can purchase are R (recreation) and M (material goods). The market price of R is $2 and the market price of M is $1. The consumer spends all her income in such a way that the marginal utility of the last unit of R bought is 12 and the marginal utility of the last unit of M bought is 6.

(a) If we ignore the time it takes to consume R and M, is the consumer maximizing the total utility she obtains from the two goods? __________

(b) Suppose that it takes 4 hours to consume each unit of R and 1 hour to consume one unit of M; and the consumer can earn $2 an hour by working.

1) The full price per unit of R is $__________.

2) The full price per unit of M is $ __________.

(c) If we can take into account the full price of each of the commodities, is the consumer maximizing total utility? _____

How do you know this? ____________________

(d) If the consumer is not maximizing utility, should she consume more of R or of M? _____

Why should she do this? ____________________

(e) Will she then use more or less time on R? _____

True-False

Circle T if the statement is true, F if it is false.

1. Utility and usefulness are synonymous. **T F**

2. Utility is a measure of the satisfaction received from the consumption of goods and services. **T F**

3. Marginal utility is the extra utility derived from consuming an extra unit of a good or service. **T F**

4. Decreasing marginal utility means that total utility falls when another unit of the good is consumed. **T F**

5. The theory of consumer behaviour assumes that the consumer acts to maximize utility while being constrained by a fixed income. **T F**

6. When a consumer is maximizing total utility, the marginal utilities of the last unit of every product bought are identical. **T F**

7. When a consumer is maximizing utility, the total utility received from the consumption of each good is equal. **T F**

8. When utility is maximized the consumer allocates money income so that the last dollar spent on each product purchased yields the same amount of extra utility. **T F**

9. At Farhan's current consumption levels of two goods A and B it is found that ($MU_A/P_A > MU_B/P_B$). Given that prices and income are fixed, Farhan should consume more of A and less of B in order to maximize utility. **T F**

10. In making the consumption decision the rational consumer will compare the extra utility from each product with its price. **T F**

11. If a good were offered free, consumption would be extended to the point where the marginal utility of the last unit equals zero. **T F**

12. A low market price for a good reflects the low total utility received from the good. **T F**

13. The price of water is low because the marginal utility received from water is low. **T F**

14. Because utility cannot actually be measured, the marginal utility theory cannot really explain how consumers will behave. **T F**

15. High labour productivity gives time a high market value. **T F**

16. The rise of the "fast food" industry is partly due to the increased value of time. **T F**

17. One reason for the shift from record albums to compact discs has been the reduction in price of CD players that are complements to CDs. **T F**

18. Government might be able to increase the utility of recipients of government subsidized education or housing by giving the recipients a cash subsidy less than the government's cost for the housing or education. **T F**

Multiple-Choice

Circle the letter that corresponds to the best answer.

1. Which of the following best expresses the law of diminishing marginal utility?
(a) the more a person consumes of a product, the smaller becomes the utility received from its consumption
(b) the more a person consumes of a product, the smaller becomes the utility received as a result of consuming an additional unit
(c) the less a person consumes of a product, the smaller becomes the utility received from its consumption
(d) the less a person consumes of a product, the smaller becomes the extra utility received as a result of consuming an additional unit of the product

2. Sabina Azula buys only two goods: food and clothing. Both are normal goods for Sabina. If the price of food decreases, Sabina's consumption of clothing will:
(a) decrease due to the income effect
(b) increase due to the income effect
(c) increase due to the substitution effect

(d) decrease due to the substitution effect
(e) both b and d

The table below shows total utility data for a consumer of chocolate bars. Questions 3 and 4 use these data.

Chocolate bars consumed	Total utility
0	0
1	9
2	19
3	27
4	35
5	42
6	42
7	40

3. This consumer begins experiencing diminishing marginal utility after he consumes the:
(a) first chocolate bar
(b) second chocolate bar
(c) sixth chocolate bar
(d) seventh chocolate bar

4. If this consumer can eat chocolate bars free of charge, how many will he eat?
(a) six or seven
(b) five or six
(c) two
(d) as many as possible

5. An individual consumes two products, A and B with price P_A, P_B. Utility is maximized when, if all income is spent, the following condition is met:
(a) $MU_A = MU_B$
(b) $MU_A < MU_B$
(c) $MU_A/P_A = MU_B/P_B$
(d) $MU_A/P_B = MU_B/P_A$

6. Suppose the price of A is $3, and the price of B is $2; that Diego is spending his entire income and buying 4 units of A and 6 units of B; and the marginal utility of both the 4th unit of A and the 6th unit of B is 6. It can be concluded that:
(a) Diego is in maximizing utility
(b) Diego should buy more of A and less of B
(c) Diego should buy less of A and more of B
(d) Diego should buy less of both A and B

7. Suppose that the prices of A and B are both $3 and the consumer is maximizing utility. The $MU_A = 7$. It can be concluded that:
(a) the utility received from good A must equal the utility received from good B
(b) the consumer must be purchasing an equal number of units of good A and good B
(c) the two goods are substitutes
(d) $MU_B = 7$

8. A decrease in the price of good X, other things remaining the same, will:
(a) increase marginal utility per dollar spent on X
(b) decrease marginal utility per dollar spent on X
(c) increase marginal utility for every unit of X consumed
(d) increase total utility for every unit of X consumed

Answer the next three questions on the basis of the following table. The price of good A is $4 and the price of good B is $5, and income is $35. Suppose the utility received from good A is independent of the number of units of good B consumed. Total utility from consumption is obtained by adding the utility from A to the utility from B.

Units of A	Total Utility	MU of A	Units of B	Total Utility	MU of B
1	32	32	1	20	20
2	60	28	2	35	15
3	72	12	3	40	5
4	80	8	4	43	3
5	84	4	5	45	2
6	86	2	6	46	1

9. What is the total utility for the consumer when the utility-maximizing combination of A and B is purchased?
(a) 120
(b) 124
(c) 126
(d) 118

10. How many units of A and B will be purchased?
(a) 5 of A and 3 of B
(b) 5 of A and 4 of B
(c) 5 of A and 5 of B
(d) 4 of A and 4 of B

11. If the consumer's income was reduced to $22, the consumer would maximize satisfaction by consuming:

(a) 2 of A and 2 of B
(b) 3 of A and 3 of B
(c) 2 of A and 3 of B
(d) 3 of A and 2 of B

12. Other things being equal, demand is likely to be inelastic if the marginal utility of the product:
(a) decreases rapidly as additional units are consumed
(b) decreases slowly as additional units are consumed
(c) increases rapidly as additional units are consumed
(d) increases slowly as additional units are consumed

13. The full price of a product to a consumer is:
(a) its market price
(b) its market price plus the value of its consumption time
(c) its market price less the value of its consumption time
(d) the value of its consumption time less its market price

14. If the opportunity cost of the time spent in consumption is added to the market price of a good when making a purchase decision, we can expect:
(a) the same combination of goods will be purchased as when time is ignored
(b) more of the time-intensive good will be purchased
(c) the consumer's demand curve for the good to be upward sloping
(d) none of the above

15. Compared to cash transfers, noncash transfers are:
(a) of greater total utility but of less marginal utility
(b) of less total utility but of greater marginal utility
(c) more efficient because they do not waste resources
(d) less efficient because they do not generally match recipients' preferences

Discussion Questions

1. Is it possible to compare the marginal utility received by John and Joe when each consumes a third lobster? How does the subjective nature of utility limit the practical usefulness of the marginal utility theory of consumer behaviour?

2. "The marginal utility of money or of the goods purchased with money declines. Therefore society's total utility will be increased by taking money from the rich and giving it to the poor." What is wrong with this argument?

3. What key element of consumer theory would be overturned if we allowed the marginal utility of one good to increase as more units are consumed?

4. What essential assumptions are made about consumers and the nature of goods and services in developing the marginal utility theory of consumer behaviour? What is meant by the "budget constraint"?

5. Mr. Ritz says "I don't clip cents-off coupons out of the paper--it's not worth it to me." Mr. Brown, who reads the same newspaper, shops at the same store, and buys the same goods, says "I save a lot of money by using the coupons from the paper." What concept discussed in this chapter might explain the difference in their behaviours?

6. Suppose you take two hours off work to go to the dentist's, including travel time and waiting time. The dentist charges you $360. What is your full price for this dental service?

7. My doctor always schedules patients 15 minutes apart, even though he knows that it takes more than 15 minutes of his time for most patients. The result is a crowded waiting room and long delays. Why doesn't the doctor schedule patients 20 or 30 minutes apart?

8. If you won a charity golf tournament and could choose between a $1000 cash prize and a new set of golf clubs with a retail value of $1000, which would you prefer? Why? What concept from the chapter is relevant?

Answers

Fill-in questions

1. down; income, substitution

2. increase; income; less; substitution

3. satisfaction (benefit); marginal; total; total; marginal

4. inelastic; elastic

5. rational, preferences (tastes)

6. income, prices

7. utility; MU_B/P_B

8. B, A

9. income, prices

10. marginal, total

11. time

12. less, less

Problems and projects

1. (a) MU_A: 6, 5, 4, 3, 2; (MU_A/P_A): 6, 5, 4, 3, 2; MU_B: 36, 28, 8, 4, 3; (MU_B/P_B): 18, 14, 4, 2, 1.5; MU_C: 22, 16, 12, 4, 2; (MU_C/P_C): 5.5, 4, 3, 1, 0.5; (b) B, B, 18, 6, 5.5; (c) $15; (d) B, B, 14, 6, A, 4.5, C (e) A, 6 (f) 3, 3, 2; 127 (g) 4 (h) utility would equal 122, which is less than the 127 received in (f).

2. 2, 3, 4, 6, 8

3. (a) 6.22, 7.11 (b) 11.33, 9.33, $22.67, inelastic; The price of A fell and the total expenditure on A fell.

4. (a) yes (b) (1)$10, (2)$3; (c) No; The marginal utility to price ratio is not the same for the two goods. (d) M; because its MU/P ratio is greater (e) less

True-False

1. F	**2.** T	**3.** T	**4.** F	**5.** T	**6.** F
7. F	**8.** T	**9.** T	**10.** T	**11.** T	**12.** F
13. T	**14.** F	**15.** T	**16.** T	**17.** T	**18.** T

Multiple-choice

1. (b)	**2.** (e)	**3.** (b)	**4.** (b)	**5.** (c)	**6.** (c)
7. (d)	**8.** (a)	**9.** (b)	**10.** (a)	**11.** (d)	**12.** (a)
13. (b)	**14.** (d)	**15.** (d)			

APPENDIX TO CHAPTER 8

Indifference Curve Analysis

This appendix outlines a third approach to the theory of consumer behaviour. Once again, consumers' choices depend upon their preferences for different goods and the constraints on what goods they can afford.

The consumer's constraints are his or her income and the prices of the goods the consumer has to choose between. These variables define the position of the budget line which represents the set of all combinations of goods available to this consumer. The consumer's preferences are represented in his or her indifference curves. These indifference curves can be constructed as long as the consumer is able to make preference rankings between different goods or combinations of goods. For example, if comparing a CD to a pizza, the consumer must be able to indicate one of three things: (1) "I prefer the CD," (2) "I prefer the pizza," or (3) "I am indifferent between the two." This is less restrictive than the marginal utility theory which requires that the consumer be able to quantify in "utils" how much satisfaction a CD gives and how much a pizza gives.

When the consumer's indifference curve map is superimposed on the budget line, we find the consumer's equilibrium point where the budget line is tangent to the highest attainable indifference curve. At this tangency the slope of the budget line (which is the opportunity cost of one good in terms of the other) is equal to the marginal rate of substitution (which is rate at which the consumer is willing to trade one good for the other while remaining equally satisfied).

If the price of a good falls, the budget line fans out, creating a new tangency point on a higher indifference curve. We can derive a demand curve by finding a series of such tangency points as we vary the price of one good.

Checklist

When you have studied this appendix, you should be able to:

- ☐ Define the budget line.
- ☐ Derive a budget line from given data on income and prices of two goods.
- ☐ Show the effect on the budget line of varying: (a) income only; (b) both prices only; (c) one price only.
- ☐ Define an indifference curve.
- ☐ State the two characteristics of an individual indifference curve.
- ☐ Explain the meaning of an indifference map.
- ☐ Given an indifference map, determine which indifference curves bring a consumer more or less total utility.
- ☐ Place both the indifference map and the budget line on a graph to show the combination of goods that maximizes the consumer's utility.
- ☐ Explain the utility-maximizing rule in terms of the slope of the indifference curve and the slope of the budget line.
- ☐ Derive the consumer's demand curve for a product using indifference curve analysis.
- ☐ Compare and contrast the marginal utility and the indifference curve analyses of consumer behaviour.

Appendix Outline

1. A budget line graphs the different combinations of two goods that a consumer can purchase at given prices, with a given money income. Because all the income is being spent, the consumer can only purchase more of one good by giving up some of the other good. Therefore the budget line is negatively sloped.

(a) An increase (decrease) in money income will shift the budget line to the right (left) in a parallel manner.

(b) A change in one of the prices will cause a slope change. The intercept will increase (decrease) on the axis showing the good whose price has decreased (increased). The intercept will remain unchanged for the good whose price has not changed.

(c) If the two goods are X and Y, with X on the horizontal axis and Y on the vertical axis, the slope of the budget line is written as (the negative of) P_X/P_Y.

2. An indifference curve shows graphically the various combinations of two goods that give the consumer the same total utility.
(a) An indifference curve is downward sloping; since both goods generate utility, if utility is to remain constant when the quantity of one good increases, the quantity of the other good must decrease.
(b) We assume indifference curves are convex to the origin: the more a consumer has of one product, the smaller is the quantity of the second product that he or she is willing to give up to obtain an additional unit of the first product.
(c) The consumer has an indifference curve for every level of total utility; the farther to the right on the graph the position of the indifference curve, the higher the level of utility obtained from the combinations on that curve.
(d) The slope of the indifference curve measures the marginal rate of substitution and shows the rate at which the consumer substitutes one good for another while maintaining a constant utility level.

3. At the point of maximum satisfaction the indifference curve is tangent to the budget line. This condition can be shown to be identical to the utility-maximizing rule in the marginal utility approach.

4. A demand curve for good X is derived by varying the price of X and noting the different quantities of X where the new budget lines are tangent to an indifference curve.

Terms and Concepts

budget line
equilibrium position
indifference curve
indifference map
marginal rate of substitution

Hints and Tips

1. Because each consumer has different preferences, one consumer's indifference curve map looks somewhat different from another consumer's. Nevertheless, their maps will share the common properties discussed in this appendix.

2. When a consumer moves from one indifference curve to another this indicates a change in utility *not* a change in preferences. If the consumer's preferences change each of the indifference curves in the consumer's map would change shape.

Fill-In Questions

1. A budget line shows the various combinations of two products that can be purchased with a given __________, holding constant the __________ of the two goods.

2. When the quantities of X are measured horizontally and the quantities of Y vertically, the budget line has a slope equal to the ratio of the __________ to the __________.

3. When the consumer's income increases, the budget line moves to the (right, left) __________, and its slope (does, does not) __________ change.

4. If quantity of X is measured horizontally and quantity of Y is measured vertically, an increase in the price of X will fan the budget line (inward, outward) __________ around a fixed point on the __________ axis. The budget line becomes (steeper, flatter) __________.

5. An indifference curve shows the different combinations of two goods that give the consumer the __________ level of total utility.

6. An indifference curve slopes (downward, upward) __________; and the slope of an indifference curve measures the marginal __________ of __________. The

indifference curve is (concave, convex) __________ to the origin.

7. As the consumer moves down along the indifference curve (from left to right) the indifference curve becomes (flatter, steeper) __________.

8. The farther from the origin an indifference curve lies, the (greater, smaller) __________ is the total utility obtained from the combination of products on that curve.

9. At the consumer's utility maximizing combination of goods, the budget line is __________ to the indifference curve. At this point, the __________ of the budget line and the __________ of the indifference curve are __________. At this point the consumer's marginal rate of substitution is equal to the __________ of the budget line.

10. If Oksana purchased a combination of two products that lies on her budget line, and at which point the budget line is steeper than the indifference curve intersecting that point, she could increase satisfaction by choosing a different combination (lower down, higher up) __________ the budget line.

11. The marginal utility approach to consumer behaviour requires that we assume utility (is, is not) __________ numerically measurable. The indifference curve approach (does, does not) __________ require that assumption.

Problems and Projects

1. Michelle spends all of her income of $200 on gasoline (G) and sandwiches (S). The prices per unit are: $P_G = \$0.50$ and $P_S = \$2$.

(a) The maximum amount of gasoline that Michelle can consume is _____.

(b) The maximum number of sandwiches that Michelle can consume is _____.

(c) Therefore the intercepts of Michelle's budget line are _____ G and _____ S.

(d) Graph Michelle's budget line on the following graph.

(e) Michelle (can, cannot) __________ afford to buy a combination of 200 G and 60 S because this combination of goods is located (outside, inside, on) __________ her budget line.

(f) The slope of this budget line is __________.

2. Some consumer's preferences between goods A and B are represented by the three indifference curves that are defined by the schedules given below.

Indifference Schedule 1		Indifference Schedule 2		Indifference Schedule 3	
A	B	A	B	A	B
0	28	0	36	0	45
1	21	1	28	1	36
2	15	2	21	2	28
3	10	3	15	3	21
4	6	4	10	4	15
5	3	5	6	5	10
6	1	6	3	6	6
7	0	7	1	7	3
		8	0	8	1
				9	0

(a) On the graph below, measure quantities of A along the horizontal axis (from 0 to 9) and quantities of B along the vertical axis (from 0 to 45). Then: (1) Plot the 8 combinations of A and B from Indifference Schedule 1, and draw through the 8 points a smooth curve. Label this curve IC^1.
(2) Similarly, use Indifference Schedule 2 to plot IC^2.
(3) Plot IC^3 using Indifference Schedule 3.

(b) Move down along Indifference Schedule 1 from the (0A, 28B) to (1A, 21B). The consumer will give up _____ of B to get ______ of A. Now look at the combinations (5A, 3B) and (6A, 1B). To get one more A the consumer will give up _____ of B. The amount of B the consumer will give up to get another A __________ as we move down along an indifference curve. This indifference curve will be __________ and the marginal rate of substitution __________.

(c) Assume the price of A is $12, the price of B is $2.40, and that the consumer has an income of $72.
(1) Complete the following table to show the quantities of A and B this consumer is able to purchase.
(2) Plot this budget line on the graph you completed in part (a) above.
(3) This budget has a slope equal to __________.

(d) To obtain the greatest satisfaction or utility from an income of $72 this consumer will purchase _____ units of A and _____ units of B. Expenditure on A will equal _____ and expenditure on B will be _____.

A	B
0	_____
1	_____
2	_____
3	_____
4	_____
5	_____
6	_____

3. The graph below has three indifference curves and three budget lines. The objective is to obtain a demand schedule for product C. The consumer has a fixed income of $60 and the price of good D is fixed at $3.

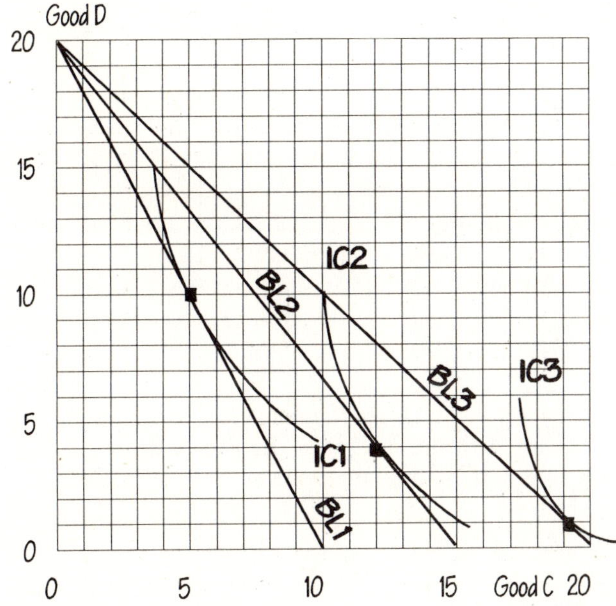

(a) When the price of C is $10.00, the consumer's budget line is BL1 because the maximum purchase of C is _____ units. At the utility maximum point the consumer purchases _____ of C and _____ of D and spends $ _____ on C and $ _____ on D.

(b) On the new budget line, BL2, the new price of C is _____, and the consumer purchases _____ of C.

(c) BL3 corresponds to a price of C of _____. At this price the consumer will purchase _____ of C.

(d) Based on your results in (a) through (c), fill in the following demand schedule for good C:

Price of C	Quantity Demanded of C
$6	_____
_____	_____
_____	_____

True-False

Circle T if the statement is true, F if it is false.

1. The slope of the budget line when good X is measured horizontally and good Y vertically is: (price of Y/price of X). **T F**

2. An increase in money income shifts the budget line to the right and causes it to become steeper. **T F**

3. If good Y is on the vertical axis and good X is on the horizontal axis, an increase in the price of X, *ceteris paribus*, will make the budget line become steeper. **T F**

4. A consumer is unable to purchase any of the combinations to the left of the budget line. **T F**

5. An indifference curve gives the various combinations of two goods that give the consumer the same level of total utility. **T F**

6. Along an indifference curve money income remains constant. **T F**

7. Indifference curves slope downward because in order to keep utility constant increases in the consumption of one good must be offset by decreases in the consumption of the second good. **T F**

8. The following combinations of goods X and Y could not lie on the same indifference curve: (3X and 5Y) and (6X and 7Y). **T F**

9. An indifference curve exists only for those combinations of goods the consumer can afford. **T F**

10. A change in tastes can change the slope of an indifference curve. **T F**

11. The closer to the origin an indifference curves lies, the smaller is the total utility the consumer obtains from the combinations of products on that indifference curve. **T F**

12. If several indifference curves are placed on the same graph, the resulting figure is called an indifference map. **T F**

13. A decrease in the price of the two goods moves the indifference curves closer to the origin. **T F**

14. A consumer maximizes utility for a given income at the combination of goods at which the indifference curve is tangent to the budget line. **T F**

15. If the prices of both goods double, and money income doubles, there is a parallel inward shift in the budget line. **T F**

16. A demand curve is derived by changing the consumer's income and noting the combinations of goods where the budget line and indifference curves are tangent. **T F**

17. If the price of cheese is $4 and the price of steak is $8, at the consumer's equilibrium his marginal rate of substitution is 2 cheese per 1 steak. **T F**

Multiple-Choice

Circle the letter that corresponds to the best answer.

1. Along a consumer's budget line:
(a) utility is constant
(b) the consumer's income is constant
(c) prices of the two goods are changing
(d) marginal rate of substitution is constant
(e) the consumer's choice of goods is constant

2. A decrease in income will:
(a) shift the budget line inward and increase its slope
(b) shift the budget line outward and increase its slope
(c) shift the budget line outward and have no effect on its slope
(d) shift the budget line inward and have no effect on its slope

3. If good Y is on the vertical axis and good X is on the horizontal axis, a lower price for X will, *ceteris paribus*:
(a) rotate the budget line outward around the intercept term on the Y axis
(b) rotate the budget line inward around the intercept term on the X axis
(c) shift the budget line outward in a parallel fashion
(d) shift the budget line inward in a parallel fashion

4. Suppose that a consumer has an income of $8, the price of R is $1 and the price of S is $0.50. Which of the following combinations is on the consumer's budget line?
(a) 8R and 1S
(b) 7R and 1S
(c) 6R and 6S
(d) 5R and 6S

5. If the consumer has an income of $200, if the price of good X is $10 and the price of good Y is $20, the budget line can be obtained by joining the intercept terms, which are:
(a) 10 on the X axis and 5 on the Y axis
(b) 20 on the X axis and 10 on the Y axis
(c) 20 on the X axis and 20 on the Y axis
(d) 10 on the X axis and 20 on the Y axis

6. When the income of the consumer is $20, the price of T is $5, the price of Z is $2, and the quantity of T is measured horizontally, the slope of the budget line is:
(a) 2/5
(b) 2.5
(c) 4.0
(d) 0.4

7. An indifference curve shows the different combinations of two goods that:
(a) give the consumer equal marginal utilities
(b) cost the same
(c) give a consumer equal total utility
(d) can be purchased with a given income

8. The amount of one good the consumer is willing to give up to get an additional unit of another good is called:
(a) cross elasticity of demand
(b) slope of the budget line
(c) the income constraint

(d) marginal rate of substitution
(e) relative price ratio

Use the following diagram to answer multiple-choice questions 9 to 14.

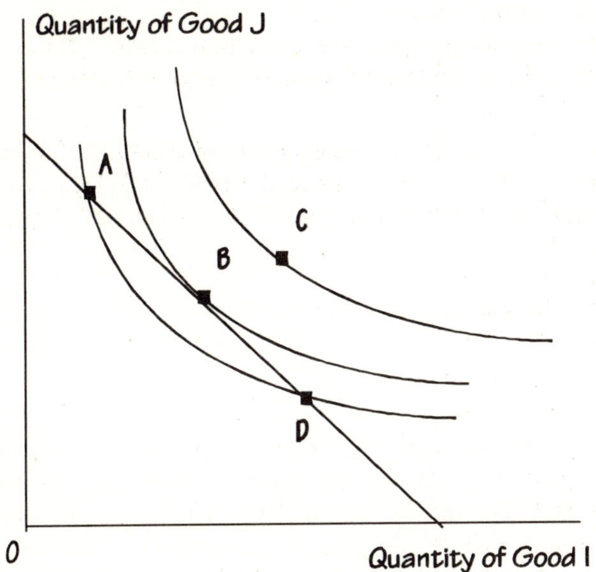

9. Which combination is unattainable?
(a) *A*
(b) *B*
(c) *C*
(d) *D*

10. For this consumer it can be said that:
(a) combination *A* is preferred to combination *D*
(b) combination *A* is preferred to combination *C*
(c) combination *B* is preferred to combination *C*
(d) combination *B* is preferred to combination *A*

11. The consumer will purchase combination:
(a) *A*
(b) *B*
(c) *C*
(d) *D*

12. Which of the following may allow the consumer to purchase combination *C*?
(a) a decrease in income
(b) an increase in the price of good I
(c) an increase in the price of good J
(d) a decrease in the price of good I

13. Suppose the price of I decreases. The budget line will fan:
(a) inward around a point on the J axis
(b) outward around a point on the J axis
(c) inward around a point on the I axis
(d) outward around a point on the I axis

14. To derive the demand for good I, the price of I is varied. Held constant is:
(a) money income of the consumer
(b) price of good J
(c) consumer's tastes
(d) all of the above

15. The fact that the marginal rate of substitution diminishes along an indifference curve is reflected in:
(a) the convexity of the indifference curve
(b) the negative slope of the indifference curve
(c) the fact that there are many indifference curves
(d) the negative slope of the budget line

Use the next diagram to answer multiple-choice questions 16 to 19.

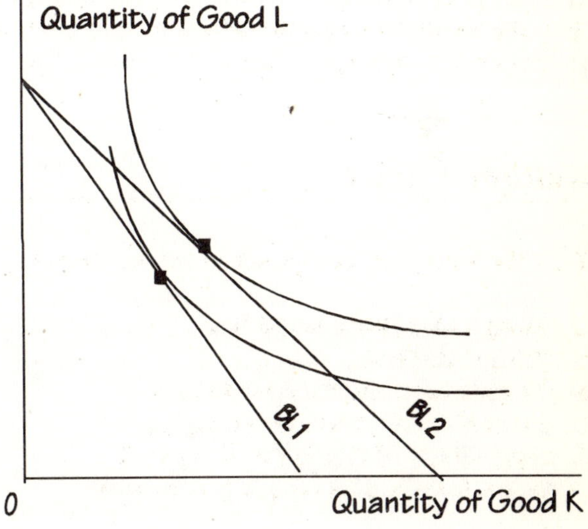

16. If the budget line shifts from BL1 to BL2, it is because:
(a) the price of K has increased
(b) the price of K has decreased
(c) the price of L has increased
(d) the price of L has decreased

17. The diagram shows that when the budget line shifts from BL1 to BL2, this consumer will:
(a) buy more of both K and L
(b) buy less of K and more of L
(c) buy less of both K and L
(d) buy more of K and less of L

18. Jamila is consuming at a point on her budget line where her marginal rate of substitution is 3 apples per 1 cappucino. The market prices are $0.50 for apples, and $2 for cappucino. Therefore:
(a) Jamila is in a utility-maximizing equilibrium
(b) Jamila can increase utility by purchasing more apples and less cappucino
(c) Jamila can increase utility by purchasing less apples and more cappucino
(d) Jamila can increase utility by purchasing more apples and more cappucino

Discussion Questions

1. Explain why the slope of the budget line is negative.

2. Explain why the slope of the indifference curve is negative, and why it is convex.

3. Explain why the budget line can be called "objective" whereas the indifference curve is "subjective."

4. Explain how the consumer's indifference map and budget lines are utilized to derive the consumer's demand for one of the products. In deriving demand what is varied and what is held constant?

5. Construct an indifference curve-budget line diagram to illustrate the case of a person buying a combination of goods where the indifference curve cuts down through the budget line. Is the individual spending all his/her income? Is the individual getting the maximum possible utility from their income? Draw in a new budget line to show that the individual could obtain the same level of utility now being enjoyed for a smaller outlay of money.

6. How can the indifference curve theory be useful in explaining consumer behaviour if we consumers do not actually work through such a model when we go shopping?

7. What is the "important difference between the marginal utility theory and the indifference curve theory of consumer demand"?

Answers

Fill-in questions

1. income, prices

2. price of X, price of Y

3. right, does not

4. inward, vertical; steeper

5. same

6. downward, rate, substitution; convex

7. flatter

8. greater

9. tangent; slope, slope, equal; slope

10. higher up

11. is; does not

Problems and projects

1. (a) 400; (b) 100; (c) 400, 100; (e) cannot, outside; (f) 4

2. (b) 7, 1; 2; decreases; convex, declines (c) (1) 30, 25, 20, 15, 10, 5, 0 (3) 5 (d) 3, 15, 36, 36

3. (a) 10, 5, 10; $30, $30; (b) $4, 12; (c) $3, 19; (d) price: $6, $4, $3; quantity demanded: 5, 12, 19.

True-False

1. F	**2.** F	**3.** T	**4.** F	**5.** T	**6.** F
7. T	**8.** T	**9.** F	**10.** T	**11.** T	**12.** T
13. F	**14.** T	**15.** F	**16.** F	**17.** T	

Multiple-choice

1. (b)	**2.** (d)	**3.** (a)	**4.** (d)	**5.** (b)	**6.** (b)
7. (c)	**8.** (d)	**9.** (c)	**10.** (d)	**11.** (b)	**12.** (d)
13. (b)	**14.** (d)	**15.** (a)	**16.** (b)	**17.** (a)	**18.** (c)

CHAPTER 9

The Organization and Costs of Production

In Chapter 8 we studied the consumption behaviour of households, acquiring a better understanding of the demand side of markets. Chapter 9 is the first of several chapters that examine the supply side of markets. This chapter begins by describing the general nature and organization of business firms in Canada.

We assume that the goal of all firms is to maximize profits. But firms differ drastically in form and size. The three major legal forms are the sole proprietorship, the partnership, and the corporation. Over 70% of all firms in Canada are proprietorships, yet corporations account for about 90% of all sales. The chapter discusses the advantages and disadvantages of each legal form. A key point is that the limited liability which corporations offer their owners has made the corporation the dominant form of business in industries where firms with large amounts of financial capital enjoy some advantage. Corporations raise capital by selling stocks and bonds.

Firms can also be grouped by industry. The Canadian economy is divided into twelve broad industry classes, each of which falls into one of three sectors: primary, secondary or tertiary. Over the last century the secondary and tertiary sectors have grown in relative importance while the primary sector (especially agriculture and forestry) has declined. Since 1960 the secondary sector has also been losing ground to the tertiary sector which includes the rapid-growing service industry. Many Canadian industries are largely under foreign ownership and control, and many are dominated by a few firms that control a large fraction of the market. The relative importance of different industries, as well as concentration trends, can change over time due to demand changes, improvements in productivity, and population characteristics. The forces of competition, now on a global scale, and the changing demand and supply conditions result in the demise of many businesses and the birth and growth of others. Such change is an integral part of a vibrant market economy.

Much of the chapter examines how one determines and interprets the production costs that firms incur in their pursuit of profits. In the next few chapters we will see how these costs determine firms' production choices in different market structure settings: what to produce, how much to produce, what price to charge, etc. Costs arise from the hiring of inputs used to produce output. Chapter 9 investigates how these input costs vary systematically with output levels. The underlying economic factors lead to somewhat different relationships between costs and output in the short run than in the long run. The behaviour of costs in the short run is the result of the law of diminishing returns and the behaviour of costs in the long run is the consequence of economies and diseconomies of scale. You will learn not only *how* the costs of the firms vary as their output varies, but also *why* the costs vary the way they do.

Understanding of this chapter is absolutely essential for understanding several chapters that follow. Because it is so important, and because so many new terms and concepts are introduced, you will have to spend a disproportionately long time on this chapter in order to master the material. Rest assured that it will pay off when you come to the next few chapters.

Checklist

When you have studied this chapter, you should be able to:

☐ Explain the difference between a plant, a firm, and

an industry.

- ☐ Describe the three legal forms of business enterprise and give the advantages and disadvantages of each form.
- ☐ Understand why limited liability is important for attracting financial capital for risky business ventures.
- ☐ Explain the difference between stocks and bonds as investment instruments.
- ☐ Describe the broad shifts that have occurred over time between the main sectors of Canada's economy.
- ☐ Discuss reasons for the extent of foreign ownership and control of the Canadian economy.
- ☐ Define economic cost and distinguish between explicit and implicit cost.
- ☐ Explain the difference between normal profit and economic profit; explain why the former is a cost and the latter is not a cost.
- ☐ Distinguish between an accounting profit and an economic profit.
- ☐ Explain the difference between the short and long run in production.
- ☐ State the law of diminishing returns and explain its rationale with examples.
- ☐ Compute the marginal and average product when you are given the necessary data; explain the relationship between marginal and average product.
- ☐ Explain the difference between fixed cost and variable cost, and between average cost and marginal cost.
- ☐ Compute and graph average fixed cost, average variable cost, average total cost, and marginal cost when you are given total cost data.
- ☐ Obtain cost data when you are given a graph of the various cost curves.
- ☐ State the relationship, in the short run, between average product and average variable cost, and between marginal product and marginal cost.
- ☐ Explain why cost curves might shift.
- ☐ Explain the difference between short-run costs and long-run costs.
- ☐ State why the long-run average-cost curve is expected to be U-shaped.
- ☐ Discuss the causes and relevance of the economies and the diseconomies of scale.
- ☐ Define constant returns to scale.
- ☐ Explain the concept of minimum efficient scale.
- ☐ Indicate the relationship between long-run average costs and the structure and competitiveness of an industry.

Chapter Outline

1. Regardless of the size or legal form of the firm, the main goal of the firm is to maximize profits. Profits are the difference between total revenues and total costs.

2. A plant is a physical establishment where production takes place (such as a factory, store, or mine). A firm is a business organization that typically owns one or more plants. Many firms also produce more than a single good.
(a) A vertical combination of plants operate at various stages of the production process, while being owned by the same firm.
(b) A horizontal combination of plants all operate at the same stage of production.
(c) A conglomerate is a firm that operates plants producing goods across a number of markets or industries.

3. An industry is composed of firms that produce the same or similar products. The Canadian economy consists of many imperfectly defined and overlapping industries.

4. The entrepreneur has three choices of legal forms under which to operate his or her firm: sole proprietorship, partnership, or corporation.
(a) The proprietorship is operated by the single owner and as such has the advantages of ease of organization, maximum freedom and individual incentive. Its drawbacks are a lack of financial resources, inability to divide and specialize in management functions, and unlimited liability for the owner.
(b) A partnership has two or more owners who pool their resources in order to mobilize more financial resources and take advantage of greater specialization. Partnerships can be hampered by disagreements in management, lack of continuity, and unlimited liability for each partner--even for the consequences of decisions made by their partners.
(c) A corporation is a legal entity, distinct and separate from the shareholders (or shareholders) who own it. Limited liability for investors enables corporations to attract large amounts of money capital, thus making possible mass-production technologies and specialization. Disadvantages of the corporation include bureaucracy and expense in organization, double taxation of income, and possible lack of incentive due to the separation of ownership and control.

5. Corporations finance their operations by accumulated profits, by loans from financial institutions, and by selling stocks and bonds.
(a) A stockholder is a part owner of the firm, and is entitled to share in the profits and to vote at elections of corporate officers.
(b) A bondholder is a lender to the firm, and is entitled to specified regular interest payments, and when the bond reaches maturity, the return of the original investment.

6. The Canadian economy can be characterised as follows:
(a) There are more proprietorships than other businesses of other forms, but the corporation accounts for the major portion of the economy's output.
(b) Over the years the broad industry groups known as the primary and secondary sectors have declined in relative importance as sources of employment, while the tertiary sector has grown.
(c) Large firms are a characteristic of the Canadian economy and many industries are dominated by a few firms.
(d) The Canadian economy has a higher degree of foreign ownership than most other industrialized economies.

7. Resources are scarce and may be used to produce many different products, so the economic cost of producing any one product is an opportunity cost: the amount of other products that could have been produced with the same resources.
(a) A firm must be willing to pay resource suppliers enough to attract their resources away from alternative production opportunities.
(b) These resource payments are called costs and may be either explicit or implicit. An explicit cost is a direct monetary outlay from a firm to an input supplier. An implicit cost is the opportunity cost of the firm's use of a self-owned and self-employed input. A key type of implicit cost is "normal profit". Unless the entrepreneur earns a return equal to what could be obtained by using his/her skills in an alternative industry, he/she will leave to seek the higher return available elsewhere. Normal profit is the minimum payment that the entrepreneur must receive for performing the entrepreneurial functions for the firm.
(c) Economic, or pure, profit is the revenue a firm receives in excess of all its explicit and implicit opportunity costs of all inputs used. In contrast, accounting profit is the firm's total revenue less only its explicit costs.
(c) The firm's economic costs vary as the firm's output varies; and how costs vary with output depends upon whether the firm is able to make short-run or long-run changes in the amount of resources it employs. The firm's plant is a fixed resource in the short run and a variable resource in the long run.

8. In the short run the firm cannot change the size of its plant and can vary its output only by changing the quantities of the variable resources it employs.
(a) The law of diminishing returns states that as successive units of a variable resource are added to a fixed resource, beyond some point the marginal product will decline. This law, together with the input prices, determines the manner in which the costs of the firm change as output varies in the short run.
(b) The total short-run costs of a firm are the sum of its fixed and variable costs. As output increases:
(1) the total fixed costs do not change;
(2) the total variable costs increase, at first at a decreasing and then at an increasing rate; and
(3) total costs at first increase at a decreasing and then at an increasing rate.
(c) Average fixed, average variable, and average total cost are equal, respectively, to the firm's fixed, variable, and total cost divided by the output of the firm. As output increases in the short run:
(1) average fixed cost decreases;
(2) average variable cost at first decreases and then increases; and
(3) average total cost also decreases at first and then increases.
(d) Marginal cost is the extra cost incurred in producing one additional unit of output.
(1) Because the marginal product of the variable resources increases and then decreases (according to the law of diminishing returns as more of the variable resource is employed to increase output), marginal cost decreases and then increases as output increases.
(2) At the output at which average variable cost is a minimum, average variable cost and marginal cost are equal; and at the output at which average total cost is a minimum, average total cost and marginal cost are equal.
(3) Given fixed input prices, the marginal cost and average cost curves are mirror images of the marginal product and average product curves respectively. On a graph, marginal cost will always intersect average variable cost and average total costs at their minimum points and from below.

9. Changes in either resource prices or technology will cause the cost curves to shift.

10. In the long run all resources employed by the firm are variable resources; therefore all its costs are variable costs.
(a) The long-run average total cost curve shows the least per-unit cost that can be achieved at each output level, given that the firm has had time to make all appropriate adjustments to its plant.
(b) As the firm expands its output by expanding its plant, average cost tends to fall at first because of the economies of large-scale production; but as this expansion continues, if it is taken far enough, average total cost will begin to rise because of the diseconomies of large-scale production.
(c) Economies of scale result from the greater specialization of labour and management possible in larger plants, more efficient capital equipment, and the use of by-products. Scale diseconomies are caused by managerial problems encountered in large firms.
(d) The economies and diseconomies encountered in the production of different goods are important influences on the structure and competitiveness of various industries.
(1) Minimum efficient scale (MES) is the smallest level of output at which a firm can minimize long-run average costs. This concept explains why relatively large and small firms could coexist in an industry and be viable when there is an extended range of constant returns to scale.
(2) In other industries the long-run average-cost curve will decline over a range of output. Given consumer demand, efficient production will be achieved only with a small number of large firms.
(3) When economies of scale extend beyond the market size, the conditions for a natural monopoly are produced, meaning that per-unit costs are minimized only if the product is produced by only a single firm.

Terms and Concepts

plant
firm
horizontal and vertical combinations
conglomerates
industry
sole proprietorship
partnership
corporation
limited liability
separation of ownership and control
double taxation
unlimited liability
foreign ownership
average fixed cost
average total cost
average variable cost
constant returns to scale
economic (opportunity) cost
economies and diseconomies of scale
explicit and implicit costs
fixed costs
law of diminishing returns
marginal cost
minimum efficient scale
natural monopoly
normal and economic profits
short run and long run
total cost
total, marginal, and average product
variable costs
primary, secondary, and tertiary sectors

Hints and Tips

1. Many different kinds of costs are described in this chapter. Make yourself a glossary to ensure that you know them all. Also know their abbreviated forms since they are often referred to this way.

2. Make sure that you clearly recognize the difference between *marginal* and *average* relationships. Marginal always refers to something incremental--i.e. for one unit more. Average is always a per unit measure calculated over a number of units.

3. You have not mastered the various concepts until you can correctly sketch from memory: (1) the productivity curves, (2) the short-run total cost curves, (3) the short-run average and marginal cost curves, and (4) the long-run cost curves. You should also be able to explain the relationship between the curves in each set that you draw.

4. In graphs and tables, marginal product and marginal cost are always treated as "in between". For example, the marginal cost value calculated from data at 10 units of output and 20 units of output should be graphed at 15 units of output.

Fill-In Questions

1. The firm's main goal is to maximize __________.

2. McDonald's is an example of a(n) __________. The McDonald's restaurant in Salmon Arm is an example of a(n) __________. McDonald's and all other fast food restaurants together represent a(n) __________.

3. A multi-plant firm would be a (vertical, horizontal) __________ combination of plants if each plant is at the same stage in the production process, and a __________ combination if each plant is at a different stage in the production process.

4. A firm that owns plants that operate across different markets and industries is termed a __________.

5. The main legal forms of business enterprise are: __________, __________ and __________.

6. Two advantages of the sole proprietorship are:
(a) ______________________________
(b) ______________________________

7. Three disadvantages of the sole proprietorship are:
(a) ______________________________
(b) ______________________________
(c) ______________________________

8. The advantages of the corporate form of business organization are:
(a) ______________________________
(b) ______________________________
(c) ______________________________
(d) ______________________________

9. Double taxation of corporate profit refers to the fact that corporate income is taxed twice: once as __________ and again, if paid out in dividends, as part of stockholders' __________.

10. The liability for business losses of a sole proprietor or of partners is __________, but the liability of stockholders for the debts of a corporation is __________.

11. Corporations can finance their activities through:
(a) ______________________________
(b) ______________________________
(c) ______________________________

12. A purchaser of a corporate (stock, bond) __________ owns a portion of the corporation, whereas a purchaser of a corporate __________ is simply lending to the corporation.

13. A bondholder earns periodic __________ payments until the __________ date of the bond, at which time the bondholder is repaid the __________ amount.

14. The relationship between bond prices and interest rates is (direct, inverse) __________. Therefore, an increase in interest rates causes the market price of existing bonds to __________.

15. Suppose you paid $1000 for a bond that pays interest of $50 yearly. For simplicity, assume the bond has no maturity date and lasts forever. You would be receiving a _____ percent return on your money. Suppose interest rates in the economy rose to 10 per cent. The market price of your bond would now be (greater than, less than) __________ $1000. In order to make the rate of return on your bond competitive with other investments, the price of your bond would (rise, fall) __________ to $_____.

16. Dividends cannot be paid to __________ until a corporation has made all __________ payments due to __________.

17. A separation of ownership and control can occur in a corporation when stockholders (do, do not) __________ exercise their right to vote.

18. Corporations dominate the economy because of their superior ability to raise __________.

19. The primary sector of the Canadian economy is made up of the following broad industry categories:
(a) ____________________
(b) ____________________
(c) ____________________
(d) ____________________

20. Since about the Second World War the secondary sector has been (contracting, expanding) __________ in terms of employment share in the Canadian economy, while the tertiary sector has been __________.

21. Among the reasons for Canada's high rates of foreign ownership are:
(a) ____________________
(b) ____________________
(c) ____________________

22. Costs exist because resources are __________. The value or worth of any resource is what it can earn in its best __________ and is called the __________ cost of that resource.

23. A monetary payment a firm makes to outside suppliers is called an (explicit, implicit) __________ cost. An __________ cost is the opportunity cost of self-owned, self-employed resources.

24. A normal profit is a return for performing the __________ function and is an __________ cost.

25. An economic profit is defined as total revenue less the __________ of all inputs. An economic profit is realized when total revenues __________ what is required to keep the entrepreneur in a particular line of production.

26. An accounting profit equals total revenues minus __________ costs.

27. In the short run the firm can change its output by changing the quantity of the (fixed, variable) __________ resources it employs; but it cannot change the quantity of the __________ resources. This means that the firm's plant capacity is fixed in the (short, long) __________ run and variable in the __________ run.

28. The change in output as a result of using one more unit of the variable input is called __________.

29. The marginal product may be positive, __________, or __________.

30. If marginal product is positive, it means that output __________ whenever one more unit of the variable input is employed.

31. The law of diminishing returns is that as successive units of a (fixed, variable) __________ resource are added to a __________ resource, beyond some point the (total, marginal) __________ product of the (fixed, variable) __________ resource will decrease. Marginal product ultimately diminishes because too much of the __________ resource is being used relative to the __________ resource.

32. When the total product:
(a) increases at an increasing rate, the marginal product is (rising, falling) __________;

(b) increases at a decreasing rate, the marginal product is (positive, negative, zero) __________, but (rising, falling) __________;
(c) is at a maximum, the marginal product is (positive, negative, zero) __________;
(d) decreases, the marginal product is (positive, negative, zero) __________.

33. Average product is defined as: (total output/units of __________).

34. Because both marginal and average products are related to __________ product, they are related to each other.

35. Suppose that the average weight of the Ajax Axemen football team was 85 kilograms. A new player weighing 106 kilograms was added to the team without anyone being dropped. The average weight of the team (increased, decreased) __________. This example indicates that when the marginal value is (greater, less) __________ than the average value, the average value will (rise, fall) __________.

36. When the marginal product of any input: (a) exceeds its average product, the average product is (rising, falling) __________; (b) is less than its average product, the average product is __________.

37. Variable costs come from hiring the __________ inputs, while fixed costs arise from the usage of the __________ inputs. In the long run, all inputs are variable so all costs are __________ costs. In the short run, production costs increase as output increases because more of the __________ input must be hired to produce the increased output.

Questions 38 to 42 are based on the table below:

38. The variable input is __________ and the fixed input is __________.

39. When production is 56 units of output, total variable cost is _____ and total fixed cost is _____.

40. The marginal product of the 4th unit of variable input is __________; the marginal product of the 6th unit of variable input is __________.

41. The law of diminishing returns (does, does not) __________ hold in this case because with one (fixed, variable) __________ input, the (average, marginal, total) __________ product of the __________ input (increases, decreases) __________.

42. In the table, as output goes from 10 to 27 units, total costs go from $_____ to $_____. Therefore marginal cost will be _____/_____ = _____.

43. The decreasing part of the marginal cost corresponds to (decreasing, increasing) __________ marginal product and the increasing section corresponds to __________ marginal product. The minimum point of marginal cost matches the __________ point of marginal product.

Units of Labour	Units of Capital	Total Product	Total Cost of Labour	Total Cost of Capital	Total Cost of Production
1	1	10	$15	$30	$45
2	1	27	30	30	60
3	1	40	45	30	75
4	1	50	60	30	90
5	1	56	75	30	105
6	1	58	90	30	120

44. Fill in the blanks in the cost definitions below:

(a) average total cost = (total cost/__________)

(b) average variable cost = (total ______ cost/output)

(c) average fixed cost = (total ________ cost/output)

(d) marginal cost = (change in total cost/change in _______)

45. In the table above:

(a) the average variable cost of 50 units of output is __________

(b) the average fixed cost of 50 units of output is __________

(c) the average total cost of 50 units of output is __________

46. If marginal cost is less than average variable cost, average variable cost will be (rising, falling, constant) __________.

47. The long-run average total cost curve shows the __________ per unit cost at which any output can be produced after the firm has had time to make all appropriate adjustments in its __________ .

48. Economies of scale explain the __________ -sloping part of the (long-run, short-run) __________ average total cost curve.

49. Factors that lead to lower average costs of production as plant size increases are:

(a) ____________________________

(b) ____________________________

(c) ____________________________

(d) ____________________________

50. The smallest level of output at which a firm can minimize long-run average cost is termed __________. Relatively large and small firms could coexist in this type of industry and be equally viable when there is an extended range of __________ returns to __________.

51. In some industries, the long-run average-cost curve will (increase, decrease) __________ over a long range of output and efficient production will be achieved with only a few (small, large) __________ firms. The conditions for a __________ are created when unit costs are minimized by having a single firm produce a product, so that (economies, diseconomies) __________ of scale extend beyond the market's size.

Problems and Projects

1. The Jack of Diamonds Trading Company reports the following results for 1996:

Total sales revenue	$2,000,000
Cost of labour and materials	1,650,000
Bond debt outstanding	2,500,000
Interest rate on bonds	8%
Shares outstanding	1,000,000

(a) The amount of interest payable to bondholders is __________.

(b) The total explicit costs are __________.

(c) The amount of accounting profit is __________.

(d) The firm's economic profit is less than this accounting profit because the accounting profit calculation overlooks the cost of __________.

(e) If the entire accounting profit is paid out to stockholders in the form of dividends, what is the dividend per share? __________

(f) If a stockholder bought her shares for $10 each, and their market value has remained unchanged, the dividend represents a rate of return of _____%.

2. (a) In September, 1995, a bond issued sometime previously by BC Gas with a face value of $1000 and a stated interest rate of 8.15% had a market price of $987.50. At the same time, another $1000 bond issued by the same firm but with a stated interest rate of 11.80% had a market price of $1258.80. Why was one price above face value and the other below?

(b) Would general increases in market interest rates cause the prices of BC Gas bonds to increase or to decrease?

3. The table below shows the daily production at Texas Style Textiles, a firm that manufactures jeans using labour, capital and materials. Capital is held constant in the short run.

Labour	Total Production	Average Product of Labour	Marginal Product of Labour
( )	( )	( )	( )
0	0	---	
			_____
1	80	_____	
			_____
2	200	_____	
			_____
3	330	_____	
			_____
4	400	_____	
			_____
5	450	_____	
			_____
6	480	_____	
			_____
7	490	_____	
			_____
8	480	_____	

(a) In the parentheses at the head of each column, indicate the units in which each variable is measured.
(b) Fill in the values for the average product column.
(c) Fill in the marginal product column.
(d) There are increasing returns to labour from the first to the _____ unit of labour, and diminishing returns from the _____ to the eighth unit.
(e) When total production is increasing, marginal product is (positive, negative) __________, and when total production is decreasing, marginal product is __________.
(f) When the marginal product is greater than the average product, the average product (increases, decreases) __________.
(g) Adding together the marginal product of the first two units of labour gives __________. This sum equals the total product of __________ units of labour.

4. Indicate, in the spaces to the right of each of the following, whether these business characteristics are associated with the proprietorship (PROP), partnership (PART), corporation (CORP), two of these, or all three of these legal forms.
(a) Much red tape and legal expense in beginning the firm _______
(b) Unlimited liability _______
(c) No specialized management _______
(d) Has a life independent of its owner(s) _______
(e) Its owners are called stockholders _______
(f) Greatest ability to acquire funds for the expansion of the firm _______
(g) Permits some but not a great degree of specialized management _______
(h) Possibility of an unresolved disagreement among owners over courses of action _______
(i) Businessperson can avoid responsibility for business losses _______
(j) Issues common shares with voting rights _______

5. Centurion Tax Services has a fixed amount of capital (office space and computer equipment). It varies its output of tax returns by varying the number of clerks it employs. The table below shows the relationships between the amount of labour employed, the output of the firm, the marginal product of labour, and the average product of labour.
(a) Assume there is a fixed cost of $200 for capital resources. Fill in the total fixed cost column.
(b) Assume each unit of labour costs $50. Compute the cost of labour, or total variable cost, for each quantity of labour that Century might employ, and enter these figures in the table.
(c) Fill in the average variable cost column.
(d) Fill in the marginal cost column.
(e) When the marginal product of labour (1) increases, the marginal cost of the firm's product (increases, decreases) __________; (2) decreases, the marginal cost of production (increases, decreases) __________.

(f) When the average product of labour (1) increases, the average variable cost of the output (increases, decreases) __________; (2) decreases, the average variable cost of the output (increases, decreases) __________.

(g) Fill in the average fixed cost column.

(h) Fill in the average total cost column.

(i) In this example average total cost falls and then rises. At the output level closest to the lowest value of average total cost, average fixed cost is (falling, rising) __________ and average variable cost is __________.

(j) Marginal cost has approximately the same value as average variable cost and average total cost in the vicinity of the __________ values for each of these.

Labour	Output	Marginal Product of Labour	Avg Product of Labour	Total Variable Cost	Marginal Cost	Avg Variable Cost	Total Fixed Cost	Avg Fixed Cost	Total Cost	Avg Total Cost
clerks	returns	returns/ clerk	returns/ clerk	$	$/return	$/return	$	$/return	$	$/return
0	0		---	___		---	___	---	---	---
		5			___					
1	5		5	___		___	___	___	___	___
		6			___					
2	11		5.5	___		___	___	___	___	___
		7			___					
3	18		6	___		___	___	___	___	___
		6			___					
4	24		6	___		___	___	___	___	___
		5			___					
5	29		5.8	___		___	___	___	___	___
		4			___					
6	33		5.5	___		___	___	___	___	___
		3			___					
7	36		5.1	___		___	___	___	___	___
		2			___					
8	38		4.8	___		___	___	___	___	___

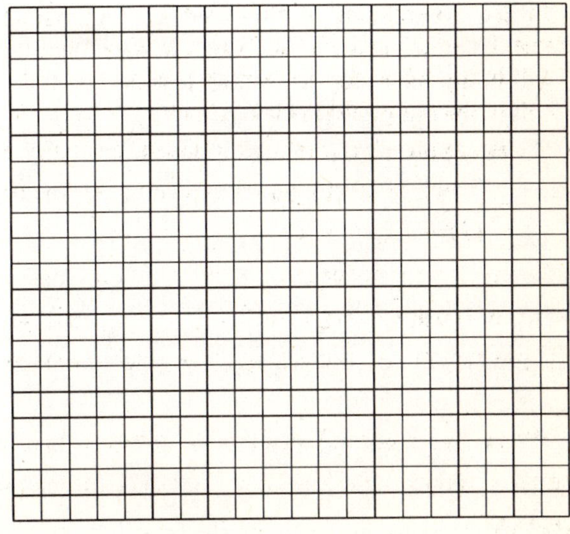

6. Using the graphs on the previous page, plot the data from question 5 as follows:
(a) In one graph plot total fixed cost, total variable cost, and total cost.
(b) In the other graph plot average fixed cost, average variable cost, average total cost, and marginal cost.

7. An economic historian has recovered the following table of costs from a 19th century coal mine. The document is crumbling with age, so many of the entries are illegible (marked as blanks). Use your knowledge of cost relationships to fill in the blank values.

	Q = 1	Q = 2	Q = 3	Q = 4	Q = 5
TFC	____	____	____	____	____
TVC	____	____	9.00	____	____
TC	____	25.00	____	____	____
AFC	____	____	____	____	4.00
AVC	3.00	____	____	____	4.00
ATC	____	____	____	8.50	____

8. The diagram below shows the short-run average-total-cost schedules for three different plant sizes. Assume that these are the only possible plant sizes that a firm might build.

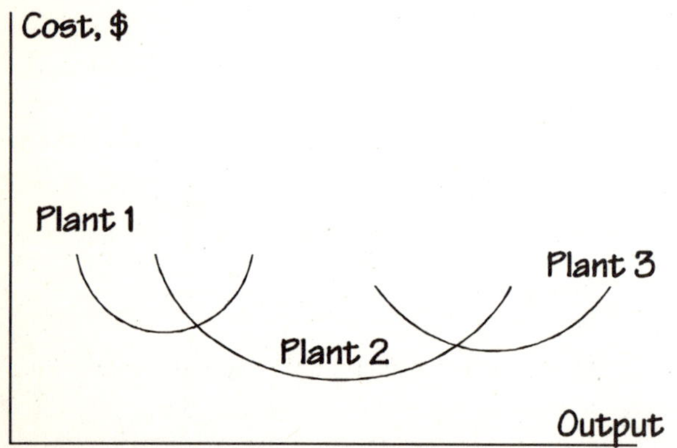

(a) Draw the firm's long-run average cost curve in this diagram.
(b) On the output axis, indicate the range of production levels for which Plant 1 is most efficient, the range for which Plant 2 is most efficient, and the range for which Plant 3 is the most efficient.

9. Suppose last year you went into business buying and selling used textbooks. It cost you $10,000 to buy used books from students at the end of the term. The purchase was financed by a bank loan that has been repaid with an interest cost of $665. In addition, paid part-time help cost $7000 for the year. You operated your business out of your garage and paid utility expenses of $500 annually. You bought a cash register, bookshelves, etc. with $1200 from your savings account. Your part-time help happened to be an accounting student who told you that you should make an allowance of $200/year for the wear and tear on the $1200 of equipment you bought.

You estimate that you worked 500 hours in your store but did not take any wage payment. The previous year you had worked in the campus book store and were paid $5 per hour. You used to rent your garage for $20 per month. Your savings were earning 10% interest.
(a) List the explicit and the implicit costs.

(b) Suppose you sold all the purchased books for $21,600. (1) Did you make an accounting profit? (yes, no) ______; how much? __________;

(2) an economic profit? (yes, no); _______; how much? _________

(c) If you could sell your equipment for $1000 and rent the garage for $20/month would you continue in business for another year? _____.

True-False

Circle T if the statement is true, F if it is false.

1. Economists assume that the main goal of the firm is to maximize the revenue generated from the sale of goods or services. **T F**

2. A plant is defined as a group of firms under a single management. **T F**

3. A firm that operates a number of plants at the same stage in the productive process would be termed a horizontal combination. **T F**

4. Canadian Pacific Investments would be a conglomerate because it owns plants in a number of different provinces. **T F**

5. Imperial Oil Ltd. would be a horizontal combination since it owns some plants that refine crude oil and other plants that sell the refined product. **T F**

6. General Motors of Canada is an example of a subsidiary that is foreign owned. **T F**

7. The sole proprietorship form of business organization is subject to unlimited liability. **T F**

8. The partnership form of business organization allows for greater specialization in management than the sole proprietorship form. **T F**

9. The death of a partner usually leads to dissolution and complete reorganization of the firm. **T F**

10. A corporation is a legal entity, distinct and separate from its owners. **T F**

11. The owners of a corporation are called bondholders. **T F**

12. When a person purchases a common stock he/she becomes a part owner of the corporation. **T F**

13. The return paid to shareholders by the corporation is called an interest payment. **T F**

14. A dividend is automatically paid to shareholders whenever the corporation has made a profit. **T F**

15. A shareholder is liable for the unpaid debts of the corporation he/she owns. **T F**

16. As compared to bondholders, stockholders have a "legal prior claim" to corporate income. **T F**

17. A bond is an I.O.U. or a promise to pay. **T F**

18. Bonds are typically issued by all forms of business organizations. **T F**

19. A bondholder is not an owner but a lender or creditor. **T F**

20. The purchase of a corporate bond provides a risk-free investment since the bond can always be sold for its initial purchase price. **T F**

21. A capital gain can be realized on the purchase and sale of corporate bonds. **T F**

22. The price of an existing bond varies inversely with the rate of interest. **T F**

23. The service sector now dominates the Canadian economy in terms of its share of domestic output. **T F**

24. The primary sector has experienced an almost continuous decline in terms of GDP share over the last 75 years. **T F**

25. Canadian industries tend to be less concentrated than comparable industries in the United States. **T F**

26. Relatively high Canadian tariffs have historically been one of the causes of the high level of foreign investment in Canada. **T F**

27. The economic costs of a firm are the payments it must make to resource owners to attract their resources from alternative employments. **T F**

28. Economic or pure profit is a return over and above the alternative cost of all inputs. **T F**

29. Normal profit is an implicit cost of production. **T F**

30. Accounting profits are the firm's total revenues minus its explicit costs. **T F**

31. It is possible for a firm to report an accounting profit but to suffer an economic loss at the same time. **T F**

32. In the short run all factors of production are variable. **T F**

33. In the short run, the reason that marginal product declines is that variable inputs of inferior quality are hired last and produce less. **T F**

34. If marginal product is negative, total output decreases when an extra unit of the variable input is utilized in production. **T F**

35. The law of diminishing returns states that as successive amounts of a variable resource are added to a fixed resource, beyond some point the marginal product of the variable resource will decline. **T F**

36. The larger the output of the firm, the smaller is the firm's total fixed cost. **T F**

37. Marginal cost is the extra cost incurred by hiring one more unit of input. **T F**

38. Minimum efficient scale occurs at the largest level of output at which a firm can minimize long-run average costs. **T F**

39. In the short run the change in total cost and the change in total variable cost associated with each additional unit of output are always the same. **T F**

40. With constant input prices, when the marginal product of an input increases, the marginal cost of producing an extra unit of output decreases. **T F**

41. The average cost curve intersects the marginal cost curve at the lowest point of the marginal cost curve. **T F**

42. One explanation of why the long-run average cost curve of a firm rises after some level of output has been reached is the law of diminishing returns. **T F**

43. A firm that is experiencing constant returns to scale can double output by doubling its employment of all inputs. **T F**

44. If a firm has constant returns to scale in the long run, the average total cost of production does not change when it expands or contracts its output. **T F**

45. Diseconomies of scale are caused by problems of coordination and communication that arise in large firms. **T F**

Multiple-Choice

Circle the letter that corresponds to the best answer.

1. A group of three plants that is owned and operated by a single firm and consists of a farm growing wheat, a flour-milling plant, and a plant that bakes and sells bakery products, is an example of:
(a) a horizontal combination
(b) a vertical combination
(c) a conglomerate combination
(d) a corporation

2. Limited liability is associated with:
(a) only proprietorships
(b) only partnerships
(c) only corporations
(d) both proprietorships and partnerships

3. Which of the following forms of business organization can most effectively raise money capital?
(a) corporation
(b) partnership
(c) proprietorship
(d) vertical combination

4. Double taxation of corporate profits arises because:
(a) personal income tax must be paid on dividends but not on interest earned
(b) both the federal government and the provinces in Canada levy a corporation profits tax
(c) United States-owned corporations in Canada are taxed by both the Canadian and American governments
(d) a corporation pays a corporate profits tax and a shareholder also pays a personal income tax on any dividends received from the corporation

5. Corporations pay dividends:
(a) only when a profit is made
(b) before bondholders receive any interest payments
(c) only if profits are greater than corporate profits tax
(d) whenever a dividend has been declared by the Board of Directors

6. A reason why bonds are less risky than stocks is:
(a) bond interest is not taxed in the hands of investors, while dividends are subject to tax
(b) bondholders have a "legal prior claim" on corporate income
(c) bond prices do not vary, while stock prices may decrease
(d) bondholders can vote at meetings of the Board of Directors

7. If company A has effective control of company B then company B is called a:
(a) vertical combination
(b) subsidiary
(c) conglomerate

(d) horizontal combination

8. The separation of ownership and control in corporations raises questions concerning:
(a) accountability of corporate managers to corporate stockholders
(b) dividend policy
(c) managerial benefits
(d) all of the above

9. From the viewpoint of the purchaser of shares which one of the following is false?
(a) shares allow an individual to obtain some of the monetary rewards of successful businesses without having to take an active part in management
(b) shares allow an individual to diversify risk
(c) paying dividends to shareholders is a legal obligation of the corporation
(d) shares can be readily bought and sold

10. Over time in Canada there has occurred:
(a) an increasing percentage of employment generated by the agricultural industry
(b) an increasing percentage of employment generated by the whole primary sector
(c) an increasing percentage of employment generated by manufacturing industries
(d) an increasing percentage of employment generated by the tertiary sector

11. All of the factors listed below have led to increased foreign ownership of the Canadian economy with the exception of:
(a) the corporate form of business organization
(b) Canadian patent policy
(c) proximity to the United States
(d) relatively high Canadian tariffs

12. Normal profit is defined as the cost of obtaining the services of:
(a) management
(b) entrepreneurs
(c) capital
(d) land

13. The revenues of a firm less its explicit costs are defined as the firm's:
(a) normal profit
(b) accounting profit
(c) economic profit
(d) economic rent

Questions 14 through 16 refer to the following table. Assume that labour is the only variable resource, and that as more labour is used, the output of the firm changes as shown.

Amount of Labour	Amount of Output
1	3
2	8
3	12
4	15
5	17
6	18
7	17

14. The marginal product of the fourth unit of labour is:
(a) 2 units of output
(b) 3 units of output
(c) 4 units of output
(d) 5 units of output

15. When the firm hires four units of labour, the average product of labour is:
(a) 3 units of output
(b) 3.75 units of output
(c) 4 units of output
(d) 15 units of output

16. Diminishing returns becomes operative when:
(a) the second unit of labour is employed
(b) the third unit of labour is employed
(c) the fifth unit of labour is employed
(d) the seventh unit of labour is employed

17. Because the average product of a variable resource initially increases and later decreases as a firm increases its output:
(a) average variable cost decreases at first and then increases
(b) average fixed cost declines as the output of the firm expands
(c) variable cost at first increases by increasing amounts and then increases by decreasing amounts
(d) marginal cost at first increases and then decreases

18. Because the marginal product of a resource at first increases and then decreases as the output of the firm increases:

(a) average fixed cost declines as the output of the firm increases
(b) average variable cost at first increases and then decreases
(c) variable cost at first increases by increasing amounts and then increases by decreasing amounts
(d) marginal cost at first decreases and then increases

19. Average total cost equals:
(a) average fixed cost plus marginal cost
(b) average variable cost plus marginal cost
(c) average variable cost plus average fixed cost
(d) average variable cost minus average fixed cost

The table below refers to a firm with a fixed cost of $500, and variable costs as indicated in the table. Questions 20 through 22 use the given data.

Output	Total Variable Cost
1	$ 200
2	360
3	500
4	700
5	1,000
6	1,800

20. The average variable cost when the firm produces 4 units of output is:
(a) $175
(b) $200
(c) $300
(d) $700

21. The average total cost of 4 units of output is:
(a) $175
(b) $200
(c) $300
(d) $700

22. The marginal cost of the sixth unit of output is:
(a) $200
(b) $300
(c) $700
(d) $800

23. Marginal cost and average variable cost are equal at the output at which:
(a) marginal cost is a minimum
(b) marginal product is a maximum
(c) average variable cost is a minimum
(d) average variable cost is a maximum

Questions 24 through 29 are based on the diagram below.

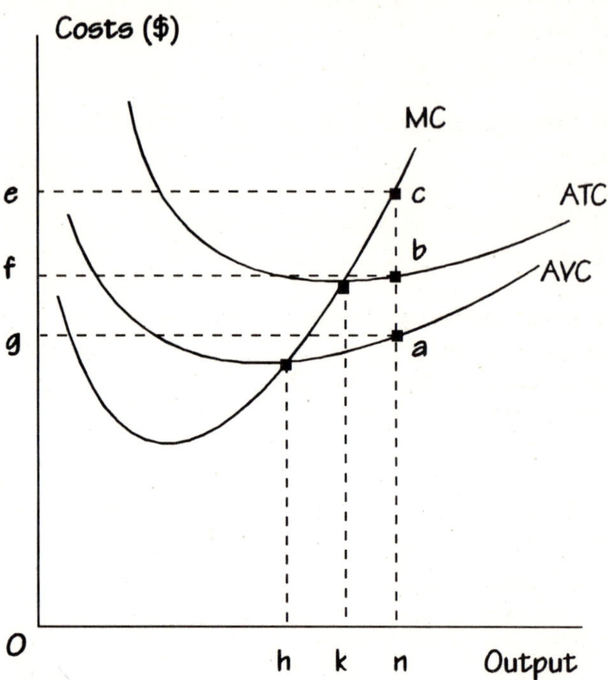

24. The marginal cost of the *n*th unit of output is distance:
(a) 0*e*
(b) 0*f*
(c) 0*g*
(d) 0*h*

25. The average fixed cost at output 0*n* is distance:
(a) 0*e*
(b) 0*f*
(c) *gf*
(d) 0*g*

26. Total fixed cost for 0*n* units of output is area:
(a) *ecfb*
(b) 0*fbn*
(c) 0*gan*
(d) *fgab*

27. Total variable cost of 0*n* units of output is area:
(a) 0*nag*
(b) 0*nfb*
(c) 0*nec*

(d) *fbec*

28. Total cost of 0*n* units of output is area:
(a) 0*nag*
(b) 0*nbf*
(c) 0*nce*
(d) *fbce*

29. Average total cost is at a minimum at output:
(a) 0*k*
(b) 0*h*
(c) 0*n*
(d) *nc*

30. In the following table, three short-run cost schedules are given for three plants of different sizes that a firm might build in the long run. What is the long-run average cost of producing 30 units of output?
(a) $7
(b) $8
(c) $9
(d) $10

Plant 1		Plant 2		Plant 3	
Output	ATC	Output	ATC	Output	ATC
10	$10	10	$12	10	$14
20	9	20	10	20	11
30	8	30	9	30	9
40	9	40	8	40	7
50	10	50	9	50	9

31. Using the table above, at what output is long-run average cost at a minimum?
(a) 20
(b) 30
(c) 40
(d) 50

32. The minimum efficient scale of plant is:
(a) the size of plant where average fixed cost is a minimum
(b) the size of plant where average variable cost is falling
(c) the smallest level of output at which a firm can minimize long-run costs
(d) the smallest level of output at which a firm can minimize long-run average cost

33. The long-run average costs of producing a particular product is one of the factors that determines:
(a) the competition among firms producing the product
(b) the number of firms in the industry producing the product
(c) the size of each of the firms in the industry producing the product
(d) all of the above

34. In the short run, which of the following curves will not shift as a result of an increase in the price of labour?
(a) average fixed cost
(b) average variable cost
(c) average total cost
(d) marginal cost

Discussion Questions

1. What is the difference between a plant and a firm? Between a firm and an industry? Which of these three concepts is the most difficult to apply in practice? Why? Distinguish between a horizontal, a vertical, and a conglomerate combination.

2. What are the principal advantages and disadvantages of each of the three legal forms of business organization? Which of the disadvantages of the proprietorship and partnership account for the employment of the corporate form among the big businesses of the Canadian economy?

3. Explain what "separation of ownership and control" of the modern corporation means. What problems does this separation create for stockholders and the economy?

4. What are the advantages and disadvantages to the corporation of obtaining money capital through selling shares rather than bonds. What are the advantages and disadvantages to the investor of bonds versus stocks?

5. Explain the meaning of the opportunity cost of producing a product, and the difference between an explicit and an implicit cost. How would you determine the implicit cost of a resource?

6. What is the difference between normal and economic profit? Why is the former an economic cost? How do you define accounting profit?

7. What type of adjustments can a firm make in the long run that it cannot make in the short run? What adjustments can it make in the short run? How long is the short run?

8. Why is the distinction between the short run and the long run important?

9. State precisely the law of diminishing returns. Is this a short run or a long run phenomenon? Why?

10. Distinguish between a fixed cost and a variable cost. Why are short-run total costs partly fixed and partly variable costs, and why are long-run costs entirely variable?

11. Construct a graph to illustrate the way in which short-run average fixed cost, average variable cost, average total cost, and marginal cost vary as the output of the firm increases.

12. Given that the price of inputs is fixed, what is the connection between marginal product and marginal cost and between average product and average variable cost? What is the precise relationship between marginal cost and minimum average variable cost? Between marginal cost and minimum average total cost? Why are these relationships necessarily true?

13. What happens to the average total cost, average variable cost, average fixed cost, and marginal cost curves when the price of a variable input increases or decreases? Describe what other factor can cause short-run cost curves to shift.

14. What does the long-run average-cost curve of a firm show? What relationship is there between long-run average-cost and the short-run average-total-cost schedules of the different-sized plants a firm might build?

15. Why is the long-run average-cost curve of a firm U-shaped? What is meant by and what are some causes of economies of large scale? What is meant by and what causes diseconomies of large scale?

16. Why are the economies and diseconomies of scale of great significance? How do they influence the size of firms in an industry and the number of firms in an industry?

Answers

Fill-in questions

1. profits

2. firm; plant; industry

3. horizontal; vertical

4. conglomerate

5. sole proprietorship, partnership, corporation

6. ease of organization; freedom of action

7. limited financial resources; limited specialization in management; unlimited liability

8. ability to raise money capital; limited liability; ability to benefit from specialization; an independent life

9. corporate profits, personal incomes

10. unlimited, limited

11. undistributed profits; borrowings from financial institutions; selling stocks and bonds to investors

12. stock, bond

13. interest, maturity, principal

14. inverse, decrease.

15. 5%; less than; fall, $500

16. shareholders, interest, bondholders

17. do not

18. money capital

19. (a) agriculture, (b) forestry, (c) fishing and trapping, (d) mining, quarrying and oil wells

20. contracting, expanding

21. (a) tariffs, (b) patent policy, (c) shared border

22. scarce; alternative use, opportunity

23. explicit; implicit

24. entrepreneurial, implicit

25. opportunity costs; exceed

26. explicit

27. variable, fixed; short, long

28. marginal product

29. zero, negative

30. increases

31. variable, fixed, marginal, variable; variable, fixed

32. (a) rising, (b) positive, falling (c) zero, (d) negative

33. variable input

34. total

35. increased; greater, rise

36. (a) rising; (b) fallling

37. variable, fixed; variable; variable

38. labour, capital

39. $75, $30

40. 10; 2

41. does, fixed, marginal, variable, decreases

42. $45, $60; $15/17, $0.88

43. increasing, decreasing; maximum

44. (a) output, (b) variable, (c) fixed, (d) output

45. (a) $1.20, (b) $0.60, (c) $1.80

46. falling

47. lowest, plant size

48. downward, long-run

49. labour specialization, managerial specialization, efficient capital, by-products

50. minimum efficient scale; constant; scale

51. decrease, large; natural monopoly, economies

Problems and projects

1. (a) $200,000, (b) $1,850,000, (c) $150,000, (d) owners' capital, (e) $0.15, (f) 1.5%

2. (a) these prices equalize the rates of return on these bonds in relation to today's interest rates; (b) fall

3. (a) L = workers/day, Q = jeans/day, AP and MP = jeans/worker; (b) AP = 80, 100, 110, 100, 90, 80, 70, 60; (c) MP = 80, 120, 130, 70, 50, 30, 10, -10; (d) third, fourth; (e) positive, negative (f) increases (g) 200, two

4. (a) CORP; (b) PROP and PART; (c) PROP; (d) CORP; (e) CORP; (f) CORP; (g) PART; (h) PART; (i) CORP; (j) CORP

5. (a) TFC = $200 at all output levels; (b) TVC = $0, $50, $100, $150, $200, $250, $300, $350, $400; (c) $10, $9.09,$8.33, $8.33, $8.62, $9.09, $9.72, $10.53; (d) MC = $10, $8.33, $7.15, $8.33, $10, $12.50, $16.67, $25.00; (e) decreases, increases; (f) decreases, increases; (g) $40, $18.18, $11.11, $8.33, $6.90, $6.06, $5.55, $5.26; (h) ATC = $50, $27.27, $19.44, $16.66, $15.52, $15.15, $15.27, $15.79; (i) falling, rising; (j) minimum

7. TFC = $20, $20, $20, $20, $20; TVC = $3, $5, $9, $14, $20; TC = $23, $25, $29, $34, $40; AFC = $20, $10, $6.67, $5, $4; AVC = $3, $2.5, $3, $3.5, $4; ATC = $23, $12.5, $9.67, $8.5, $8

9. (a) Explicit costs: book purchase $10,000, interest payment $665, wages for part-time help $7000, utility $500. Implicit costs: own wage $2500, garage rent $240, saving account interest $120, depreciation $200 (b) (1) yes, $3435 (Accounting recognizes depreciation as an explicit cost so the $3435 would be reduced by that amount) (2) yes, $375 (c) An economic profit was realized so you should stay in this business.

True-False

1. F	2. F	3. T	4. F	5. F	6. T
7. T	8. T	9. T	10. T	11. F	12. T
13. F	14. F	15. F	16. F	17. T	18. F
19. T	20. F	21. T	22. T	23. T	24. T
25. F	26. T	27. T	28. T	29. T	30. T
31. T	32. F	33. F	34. T	35. T	36. F
37. F	38. F	39. T	40. T	41. F	42. F
43. T	44. T	45. T			

Multiple-choice

1. (b)	2. (c)	3. (a)	4. (d)	5. (d)	6. (b)
7. (b)	8. (d)	9. (c)	10. (d)	11. (a)	12. (b)
13. (b)	14. (b)	15. (b)	16. (b)	17. (a)	18. (d)
19. (c)	20. (a)	21. (c)	22. (d)	23. (c)	24. (a)
25. (c)	26. (d)	27. (a)	28. (b)	29. (a)	30. (b)
31. (c)	32. (d)	33. (d)	34. (a)		

PART

3

Markets, Prices, and Resource Allocation

CHAPTER 10

Price and Output Determination: Pure Competition

Chapter 10 is the first of four chapters which bring together the demand for a product and the costs of producing the product. The goal of any firm is to maximize profit, which is the difference between revenues and costs. The theory of costs developed in Chapter 9 applies essentially to all firms. But the revenue or demand side of the profit equation depends on the type of market structure that the firm exists in. Therefore the choices that the firm makes regarding how much output to produce and what price to charge is dependent on market structure. In Chapter 10 we study the firm's choices under the market structure known as pure competition. The market structures of monopoly, monopolistic competition and oligopoly are studied in the next three chapters.

The questions which are analysed and for which we want both short-run and long-run answers are the following:

(1) What amount of output should the firm produce to maximize profits?

(2) What will be the market price of the product?

(3) What will be the output of the entire industry?

(4) What is the relationship between price, average total cost, and marginal cost?

For each market structure the answers are somewhat different because they are obtained by applying logic to a different set of assumptions. It is important, therefore, to note exactly what the assumptions are for each market structure model.

The important differences in the models which account for the differing answers involve market characteristics such as the number of sellers, the ease of entry into and exodus from the market, product differentiation, and nonprice competition.

The chapter derives results for the purely competitive market structure in both a numerical and geometric fashion. Also, both a "total approach" and a "marginal approach" are presented as alternative routes for arriving at the same destination--the profit-maximizing output level. The last section of Chapter 10 considers the efficiency of resource use in a competitive economy.

Chapter 3 asserted that a competitive system would place society on the production possibilities curve where productive and allocative efficiency are met. The last part of Chapter 10 explains--subject to several exceptions--how profit-maximization by purely competitive firms assures that these conditions are met. In the next three chapters, it will be found that in imperfectly competitive market structures resource allocation is less than ideal. You, therefore, should pay special attention in Chapter 10 to what is meant by an ideal allocation of resources and why pure competition results in this perfect allocation.

Checklist

When you have studied this chapter, you should be able to:

- ☐ List the four basic market models and the five predominant characteristics of each.
- ☐ Explain why a purely competitive firm is a "price taker."
- ☐ Describe the firm's view of the demand for its product and the marginal revenue from the sale of additional units.
- ☐ Compute average, total, and marginal revenue for various output levels when you are given the price

faced by a purely competitive firm.

- ☐ Use both the total-revenue and total-cost and the marginal-revenue and marginal-cost approaches to determine the profit-maximizing output the purely competitive firm will produce in the short run, and to explain why this output level is optimal.
- ☐ Explain the conditions under which a competitive firm may continue to operate in the short run even though a loss is being realized.
- ☐ Find the firm's short-run supply schedule and supply curve from its short-run cost schedules.
- ☐ Find the industry's short-run supply curve (or schedule) from the short-run supply schedule of the various firms.
- ☐ Determine under short-run conditions, the price at which the product will sell, the output of the industry, and the output of the individual firm.
- ☐ Determine under long-run conditions, the price at which the product will sell, the output of the industry, and the output of the individual firm.
- ☐ Explain the role of profits or losses and entry or exit of firms in reaching the long-run equilibrium.
- ☐ Define a constant-cost, decreasing-cost, and an increasing-cost industry; explain how to obtain the long-run industry supply curve in these industries.
- ☐ Explain how a competitive price system determines what will be produced.
- ☐ Explain the difference between constant cost, increasing cost, and decreasing cost industry, and the implications for the long-run industry supply curve.
- ☐ Predict how permanent shifts in demand will affect the price, output, and number of firms in an industry, depending on the long run supply curve.
- ☐ Explain the significance of MR (= P) = MC = minimum ATC in the long run.
- ☐ Distinguish between productive and allocative efficiency.
- ☐ Identify four types of problems that may prevent a competitive market from achieving allocative and productive efficiency.

Chapter Outline

1. The goal of the firm is to maximize profits. The profit-maximizing price and output level for the firm's product depend not only on the demand for the product, and the costs of producing it, but also on the character (or structure) of the industry (market) in which the firm sells the product.

2. The key characteristics that define market structure are: number of firms in the industry, product type (differentiated or standardized), control over price, conditions of entry, and degree of nonprice competition.

3. Four different market models based on variations of the above characteristics receive the most attention in microeconomics: pure competition, monopoly, monopolistic competition, and oligopoly.

4. Pure competition is a situation in which a large number of independent firms, no one of which is able by itself to influence market price, sell a standardized product in a market that firms are free to enter and to leave in the long run. Although pure competition is rare in practice, there are at least three good reasons for studying this model.

5. A purely competitive firm sells only a minute part of the industry output of a standardized good. Therefore the firm cannot influence the selling price of the product. Therefore such a firm is called a "price taker."
(a) The demand for its product is, therefore, perfectly elastic.
(b) Total revenue increases at a constant rate as the firm increases its output. On a graph the total revenue will be a straight line from the origin with a positive slope dependent on the price.
(c) Price (or average revenue) and marginal revenue are equal and constant at the fixed market price. On a graph all three appear as the identical horizontal line when plotted against output.

6. There are two complementary approaches to the analysis of the output that the purely competitive firm will produce in the short run.
(a) In the total-revenue and total-cost approach, the firm will produce the output at which total economic profit is the greatest or total loss is the least, provided that the loss is less than the firm's fixed costs (that is, provided that total revenue is greater than total variable cost). If the firm's loss is greater than its fixed cost, it will minimize its loss by closing down and producing no output.
(b) In the marginal-revenue and marginal-cost approach, the firm will produce the output at which marginal revenue (or price) and marginal cost are equal,

provided price is greater than average variable cost. If price is less than average variable cost, the firm's loss would be greater than its fixed costs; so to minimize the loss it will close down.

7. The rules for determining output lead us directly to supply curves:
(a) The short-run supply curve of the individual firm is that part of its short-run marginal cost curve that is above average variable cost.
(b) A short-run supply curve of the industry is found by summing horizontally the supply curves of the individual firms.
(c) The short-run supply curve of the industry and the total demand for the product determine the short-run equilibrium price and equilibrium output of the industry. At this short-run equilibrium firms may be either enjoying profits or suffering losses.

8. The presence of an economic profit will attract firms seeking the extra return, while losses will lead to an exodus of firms seeking higher returns in alternative industries. The analysis changes from short run to long run.

9. If economic profits exist, new firms will enter in the long run, increasing the total industry supply, and reducing the equilibrium price until it equals the minimum average total cost at which firms can supply the product. The adjustments continue until the firms in the industry make only normal profits (or, zero economic profits).

10. If losses are being suffered, some firms will leave the industry in the long run (seeking to avoid losses), reducing total industry supply, resulting in a price increase until the remaining firms will earn enough revenue to cover their opportunity costs, making normal profits but no economic profits. At that point, price and minimum average cost are equal.

11. When firms enter and leave the industry, the demands for the inputs used in the industry increase or decrease. Depending on how these demand shifts change the prices of the inputs, we define increasing cost, decreasing cost, and constant cost industries. The slope of the industry's long-run supply curve is dependent upon whether the industry is of the increasing-cost, decreasing-cost, or constant-cost variety.
(a) In a constant-cost industry, the entry of new firms does not affect input prices, so the average-total-cost curves of firms in the industry are unchanged. Therefore, the price that firms need to sell their products for in order to recoup their opportunity costs is unchanged. An increase in demand for the industry's product results in no change in the long-run equilibrium price, and the industry can supply larger quantities at a constant price. The long-run supply curve is horizontal at the price level equal to the minimum average total cost and is perfectly elastic.
(b) In an increasing-cost industry, the entry of new firms pushes input prices upwards, and so increases firms' average-total-cost curves. The minimum price that firms need to sell their products for is increased. An increase in demand, therefore, will raise the long-run equilibrium price, and the industry can supply larger quantities only at a higher prices. The long-run industry supply curve is upward sloping.
(c) In a decreasing-cost industry, an increase in demand causes a decrease in input prices and, hence, a decrease in long-run average cost. The long-run equilibrium price will fall and the industry will supply larger outputs at lower prices. The long-run supply curve will be downward sloping.

12. Productive efficiency is achieved when the average total cost of producing goods is at a minimum. In the long run, competition forces the firm to produce the output where price, marginal cost, and average total cost are equal and average total cost is a minimum. Competition assures that only the most efficient will be able to stay in business.

13. Allocative efficiency is achieved when goods are produced in such quantities that the total satisfaction obtained from the economy's resources is a maximum; or when the price of each good--which also reflects its marginal benefit to consumers--is equal to its marginal cost.

14. Competition in the economy drives firms who seek only their own interests to promote the best interest of society: an allocation of resources dictated by consumer wants and production by the most efficient means, resulting in the lowest possible unit cost. Competition results in an economy being on its production possibilities curve at a point determined by consumers.

15. Even in a purely competitive market economy the allocation of resources may not, for at least four reasons, be the most efficient.

(a) The competitive market system may distribute incomes unequally, and create distortions in allocation of resources and the production of goods and services.

(b) Spillover costs and benefits and the production of public goods may not be taken into account in allocating resources in the competitive market model.

(c) The rate of technological advance may be slower and use of the best-known productive techniques may be less widespread in purely competitive industries.

(d) The range of consumer choice and the development of new products may be restricted in a purely competitive economy.

Terms and Concepts

allocative efficiency
average, total, and marginal revenue
break-even point
close-down case
constant-cost industry
decreasing-cost industry
exclusion principle
external costs and benefits
imperfect competition
increasing-cost industries
long-run supply curve
loss-minimizing case
market failure
monopolistic competition
MR (= P) = MC rule
oligopoly
price taker
productive efficiency
profit-maximizing case
public goods
pure competition
pure monopoly
short-run supply curve
spillover costs and benefits

Hints and Tips

1. The purely competitive model is the standard against which other market models--pure monopoly, monopolistic competition, and oligopoly--are compared for economic efficiency. Therefore you should have a thorough understanding of this chapter before you tackle any of the next three chapters.

2. You can think of the firm as making its short-run output decision in two steps: (1) find the output where MC = MR (= P); (2) produce this output if P > AVC, otherwise produce zero output (and close down).

3. Consider the case of a firm suffering losses. A very common mistake is to believe that the firm continues to produce in the short run only if it earns enough revenue to cover fixed costs. It is variable costs that must be covered to justify continued operation. Fixed costs, after all, are unavoidable so should not affect the decision.

4. The triple equality of MR (= P) = MC = minimum ATC is crucial because it allows us to judge the allocative and productive efficiency of a purely competitive economy. Check your understanding of this equality by explaining what happens to productive efficiency if P > minimum ATC, or to allocative efficiency if P < MC or P > MC.

Fill-In Questions

1. The four basic market models examined in this and the next three chapters are:

(a) ____________________

(b) ____________________

(c) ____________________

(d) ____________________

2. The basic market models or market structures differ in terms of the __________ of firms; type of __________; control over __________; conditions of __________ and __________ competition.

3. The four distinct characteristics of pure competition are:

(a) ____

(b) ____

(c) ____

(d) ____

4. A pure monopolist has no close rivals or competitors because there are __________ to entry into the industry.

5. Monopolistic competition is characterized by a relatively large number of __________ producing __________ products.

6. The individual firm in a purely competitive industry finds that the demand for its product is perfectly (elastic, inelastic) __________, and that marginal revenue is (less than, greater than, equal to) __________ the price of the product.

7. Economic profit is calculated as __________ minus __________.

8. The two approaches that may be used to determine the most profitable output for any firm are the __________ approach and the __________ approach.

9. The demand curve faced by the individual firm in a purely competitive industry is perfectly __________, while the market or industry demand curve is __________ sloping.

10. A firm should produce in the short run only if it can obtain a __________ or suffer a loss no greater than its __________. Provided it produces any output at all: (a) it will produce that output at which its profit is a (maximum, minimum) __________ or its loss is a __________ (b) or, said another way, the output at which marginal __________ and marginal __________ are equal.

11. In the short run the firm is suffering a loss if price is below __________, but should continue to produce if price is higher than __________.

12. The short-run supply curve of the firm is that part of the __________ curve that lies above its __________ curve. The short-run market supply curve is the __________ of the individual firms' supply curves.

13. In the short run there is a fixed number of __________ in the industry, each with a __________ size of __________.

14. If firms in an industry are obtaining economic profits, firms will (enter, leave) __________ the industry, the price of the industry's product will (rise, fall) __________, the industry will employ (more, fewer) __________ resources, produce a (larger, smaller) __________ output, and the industry's economic profits will (increase, decrease) __________ until they are equal to __________.

15. When a purely competitive industry is in long-run equilibrium, the price that the firm receives for its product is equal not only to marginal revenue but to __________ cost and to __________ cost; and average cost is a (maximum, minimum) __________.

16. If the entry of new firms into an industry tends to raise the costs of all firms in the industry, the industry is a(n) (constant-, increasing-, decreasing-) __________ cost industry; and its long-run supply curve is (horizontal, downsloping, upsloping) __________.

17. The long-run supply curve of a constant-cost industry is (perfectly elastic, perfectly inelastic, unit elastic) __________.

18. The supply curve in a decreasing-cost industry has a (positive, negative, zero) __________ slope because an increase in industry output causes the prices of industry inputs to (increase, decrease. stay the same) __________.

19. If an economy is to make the best use of its scarce resources it is necessary that it achieve both __________ and __________ efficiency.

20. The purely competitive industry achieves allocative efficiency where price and __________ are equal. It will achieve productive efficiency where price and __________ are equal and the latter is at a (minimum, maximum) __________.

21. A competitive economy may not achieve allocative efficiency because of these four factors:

(a) ______________________________

(b) ______________________________

(c) ______________________________

(d) ______________________________

22. The __________ principle, which means that the good is consumed only by those who pay for the good, applies to (private, public) __________ goods, but does not apply to __________ goods. Therefore, once a __________ good is produced, it can be enjoyed by all members of society.

23. An __________ or a __________ occurs when a benefit or cost of production or consumption of a good is incurred by a party other than the producer or consumer.

Problems and Projects

1. Employing the following set of terms, complete the table at the bottom of this page by inserting the appropriate letter or letters in the blanks.

a. one
b. few
c. many
d. a very large number
e. standardized
f. differentiated
g. some
h. considerable
i. very easy
j. blocked
k. fairly easy
l. fairly difficult
m. none
n. unique

2. The table below shows data for Blue Lite, a match maker, who sells their product in a purely competitive market.

Output (boxes/yr)	Total Cost ($/yr)	Total Revenue ($/yr)	Profit ($/yr)
0	200	______	______
1000	250	______	______
2000	275	______	______
3000	325	______	______
4000	400	______	______
5000	500	______	______
6000	625	______	______
7000	775	______	______
8000	950	______	______

(a) Assume that the market price for matches is $0.16 per box. Fill in the total revenue column using based on this price.
(b) Fill in the values in the profit column.
(c) What level of output maximizes profits for Blue Lite? _____
(d) At the top of the next page, in the TR1 and Profit 1 columns, recompute the results for Blue Lite assuming that the price of matches is now $0.09 per box.

	Market Structure Model			
Market characteristics	Pure Competition	Monopoly	Monopolistic Competition	Oligopoly
Number of firms	________	________	________	________
Type of product	________	________	________	________
Control over price	________	________	________	________
Conditions of entry	________	________	________	________
Nonprice competition	________	________	________	________

Output	TC	TR 1	Profit 1	TR 2	Profit 2
0	$200	$___	$____	$___	$____
1000	250	____	____	____	____
2000	275	____	____	____	____
3000	325	____	____	____	____
4000	400	____	____	____	____
5000	500	____	____	____	____
6000	625	____	____	____	____
7000	775	____	____	____	____
8000	950	____	____	____	____

(e) If Blue Lite does produce at this price, they would produce _____ boxes/year. Their loss at this output is $_____ per year. Because Blue Lite's total fixed cost is $_____ per year, they (should, should not) __________ continue in the short run to produce matches at a price of $0.09. Their loss by continuing to produce is $_____ per year (less than, more than) __________ their loss if they close down and incur only their total fixed cost.

(f) Recompute the results in the TR2 and Profit 2 columns assuming that the price of matches is now $0.03 per box.

(g) If Blue Lite does produce at this price, they would produce _____ boxes/year. Blue Lite (should, should not) __________ continue in the short run to produce matches at this price. Their loss by producing at this price is $_____ per year, compared to a total fixed cost of $_____ per year.

3. A perfectly competitive firm faces the following demand schedule and marginal cost schedule.

(a) Compute the average revenue (AR) and marginal revenue (MR) schedules from the demand schedule data.

(b) If the P, AR, and MR schedules were graphed as a function of Qd, all three would be the same (horizontal, vertical) __________ line at price = $_____.

(c) Given the marginal cost and marginal revenue data, the profit maximizing quantity of output is _____. The last unit produced adds $_____ to revenues and adds $_____ to costs. Therefore, it adds $_____ to profits. If one more unit would be produced it would add $_____ to revenues, and $_____ to costs, therefore reducing profits by $_____. Therefore, at the optimum, every unit has been produced that can contribute anything to profit.

Q d	P	AR	MR	MC
1	$10	$____	$____	$4
2	10	____	____	3
3	10	____	____	4
4	10	____	____	6
5	10	____	____	9
6	10	____	____	13
7	10	____	____	18

4. The pumpkin industry is purely competitive, and is comprised of 100 identical firms, each with costs as shown in the schedule below.

Output	ATC	MC
20	$6.00	
		$2.00
40	4.50	
		3.00
60	4.00	
		4.00
80	4.00	
		5.00
100	4.20	
		6.00
120	4.50	

(a) Plot the average total costs and marginal costs for a typical firm on the left hand panel of the following graphs. Remember to plot MC at the midpoints of the output ranges. (For example, plot $3 at quantity = 50).

(b) Suppose that the minimum average variable cost for this producer is $1.00. Based on this, the firm's supply curve is its __________ curve above $1.

(c) On the right hand panel is shown the market demand for pumpkins. Derive and plot the short-run market supply (knowing that there are 100 firms with supply curves identical to the one shown in your left hand graph).

(d) From the short-run equilibrium now shown in the industry graph, the market price is $_____, and the market quantity is _____.

(e) Based on the market price from the industry graph, and the individual firm's supply curve, the firm will maximize profits (or minimize losses) by producing an output of_____.

(f) We can check the consistency of the industry result and the firm result by multiplying the firm's output by the number of firms. This gives _____ (which should equal the industry output).

(g) On the diagram show the area that represents their short-run profit (or loss) at this equilibrium.

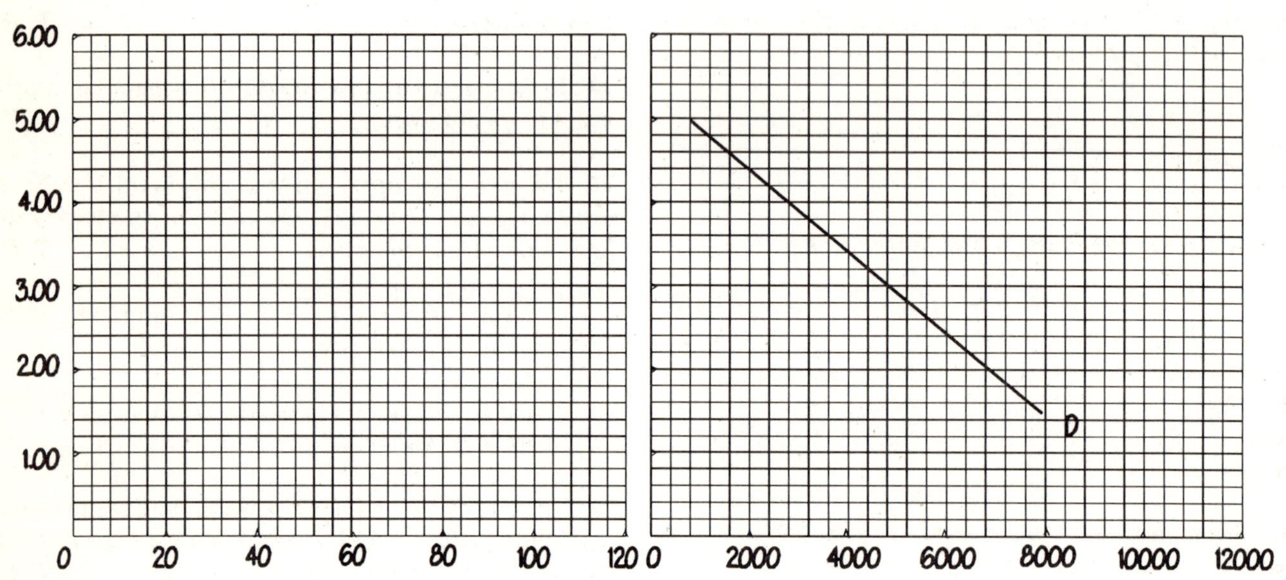

5. This question makes use of the graphs of the pumpkin market in the previous question. Assume that the short-run average total cost and marginal cost data also represent long-run ATC and MC. Also assume that pumpkins are produced in a constant-cost industry.

(a) Since each firm is suffering losses at the short-run equilibrium, there is an incentive for (entry, exodus) __________.

(b) The long-run equilibrium price is found at the __________ point of the ATC, which is where ATC = _____.

(c) At the industry level, this long-run equilibrium price will result only if the market supply curve intersects the existing market demand curve at a quantity of_____.

(d) At this long-run equilibrium price, the firm will produce a quantity of_____.

(e) Given the equilibrium quantity at the industry (or market) level, and the optimum quantity for the firm, the long run equilibrium number of firms is approximately _____ (divide the two). Therefore, about _____ firms must leave the industry.

(f) Draw in the new short-run industry supply curve after the number of firms has changed.

(g) Because this is a constant-cost industry, the long-run industry supply is a __________ line, which is located at a price equal to the individual firm's minimum ATC. Draw in this supply curve.

6. Suppose that you are a Canadian wheat producer operating in a purely competitive industry. Use the average and marginal diagram to indicate the short-run effect on output and profit of:

(a) a decrease in fertilizer prices: Q:_____, Profit: _____

(b) an increase in Asian demand for Canadian wheat: Q:_____, Profit: _____

(c) an increase in freight rates for shipping grain to market: Q:_____, Profit: _____

7. Skeena Mills and Stikine Forest Products are hypothetical firms in a purely competitive lumber market. They have somewhat different cost structures. At normal price ranges for lumber they produce the same quantity of lumber, but Stikine makes a larger short-run profit than Skeena does. However, when lumber prices fall temporarily, Stikine closes down temporarily, while Skeena continues producing. Sketch a pair of diagrams showing ATC, AVC and MC for each firm consistent with the facts presented.

True-False

Circle T if the statement is true, F if it is false.

1. There are no barriers to industry entry or exodus in the purely competitive model. **T F**

2. The presence of extensive advertising and dealer rebates indicates that the automotive industry is purely competitive. **T F**

3. Purely competitive producers compete mainly on the basis of product quality. **T F**

4. If an industry has many firms it must be purely competitive. **T F**

5. The demand curve for the single competitive producer is horizontal at the prevailing price. **T F**

6. Purely competitive producers cannot make economic profits in the short run. **T F**

7. In the short run a purely competitive firm maximizes profits by producing where price equals average total cost. **T F**

8. The competitive firm will shut down in the short run if fixed costs cannot be met at all possible output levels. **T F**

9. The break-even point is found in the short run where the firm's total revenue equals total costs. **T F**

10. In the long run the competitive firm that spends most on research and development will earn economic profits. **T F**

11. When a purely competitive firm is in a long-run equilibrium, product price will be exactly equal to the firm's minimum average total cost. **T F**

12. Given sufficient time for entry or exodus, the economic profits in a purely competitive industry will tend to disappear. **T F**

13. In an increasing-cost industry the long-run supply curve is upward sloping. **T F**

14. The long-run supply curve is downward sloping in decreasing-cost industries because of technological improvements in production. **T F**

15. In constant-cost industries the long-run supply curve has an elasticity value of one. **T F**

16. A purely competitive economy tends to produce a very equal income distribution. **T F**

17. When there are spillover benefits from a product, a purely competitive industry tend to produce more of the product than is optimal for society. **T F**

18. If the technology of an industry is such that, at the point of minimum average total cost, output is so large that one plant could supply the whole market, then a natural monopoly is said to exist. **T F**

19. Economists believe the competitive system provides for the widest possible range of product choice. **T F**

20. There is greater incentive for firms to develop new technologies under pure competition than under any other market structure. **T F**

Multiple-Choice

Circle the letter that corresponds to the best answer.

1. The four market structure models differ in their assumptions concerning:
(a) the number of firms in the industry
(b) how easy or difficult it is for new firms to enter the

industry
(c) whether the product is standardized or differentiated
(d) all of the above

2. Which of the following is not one of the four market models?
(a) pure competition
(b) monopoly
(c) monopolistic competition
(d) imperfect competition

3. All of the four market models are characterized by nonprice competition except:
(a) pure competition
(b) monopoly
(c) monopolistic competition
(d) oligopoly

4. In which of the following market models is the seller of a product a "price taker"?
(a) pure competition
(b) monopoly
(c) monopolistic competition
(d) oligopoly

5. Entry is blocked in:
(a) pure competition
(b) monopoly
(c) monopolistic competition
(d) oligopoly

6. Examples of oligopolistic industries in Canada would include all but:
(a) commercial banking
(b) steel
(c) airlines
(d) wheat farming

7. The market model in which there is considerable interdependence among firms is:
(a) pure competition
(b) monopoly
(c) monopolistic competition
(d) oligopoly

8. Which of the following is not characteristic of pure competition?
(a) large number of sellers
(b) advertising by individual sellers
(c) easy entry
(d) standardized products

9. The demand schedule or curve confronted by the individual purely competitive firm is:
(a) perfectly inelastic
(b) inelastic but not perfectly inelastic
(c) perfectly elastic
(d) unit elastic

10. For the purely competitive firm, price equals:
(a) marginal revenue
(b) average revenue
(c) both marginal revenue and average revenue
(d) none of the above

11. Using the total-revenue and total-cost approach the competitive firm should produce, given total variable costs are covered, the level of output where:
(a) total revenue is a maximum
(b) total revenue equals total cost
(c) a normal profit is realized
(d) the difference between total revenue and total cost is maximized

12. Using the marginal-revenue and marginal-cost approach the competitive firm chooses the level of output where:
(a) average cost equals price
(b) average variable cost equals price
(c) marginal cost equals price
(d) marginal cost equals average variable cost

13. The competitive firm would be earning an economic profit in the short run if it is producing the quantity where marginal cost equals price and:
(a) average fixed cost is less than price
(b) average variable cost is greater than price
(c) average total cost is greater than price
(d) average total cost is less than price

14. A firm will be willing to operate at a loss in the short run if:
(a) the loss is no greater than its average fixed costs
(b) the loss is no greater than its total fixed costs
(c) the loss is no greater than its total variable costs
(d) the loss is no greater than its average variable costs

15. Suppose at the present rate of output a competitive firm finds that marginal cost is less than price. To maximize profits this firm should:

(a) close down
(b) reduce output
(c) increase output
(d) reduce the price

Questions 16 through 20 are based on the following cost data for a firm that sells in a purely competitive market.

Output	AFC	AVC	ATC	MC
1	$300	$100	$400	$100
2	150	75	225	50
3	100	70	170	60
4	75	73	148	80
5	60	80	140	110
6	50	90	140	140
7	43	103	146	180
8	38	119	157	230

16. If the market price for the product is $140, this firm will produce:
(a) 0 units
(b) 6 units
(c) 7 units
(d) 8 units

17. If the market price for the firm's product is $180, the firm's maximum profit in the short run will be:
(a) an economic profit of $238
(b) an economic profit of $592
(c) an economic profit of $1,071
(d) an economic profit of $0

18. If the market price is $60, this firm will:
(a) produce 3 units and lose $330
(b) produce 3 units and lose $300
(c) produce 5 units and break even
(d) close down and lose $300

19. If the market price is $110, this competitive firm will
(a) close down
(b) produce 5 units at a loss of $150
(c) produce 5 units at a profit of $150
(d) produce 7 units and break even

20. The total fixed costs are
(a) $100
(b) $200
(c) $300
(d) $400

Answer questions 21 through 27 on the basis of the following diagram that represents the short-run costs of a purely competitive firm.

21. Given that the price is 0*e* the profit-maximizing competitive firm should produce:
(a) *cn* units
(b) 0*n* units
(c) 0*k* units
(d) 0*h* units

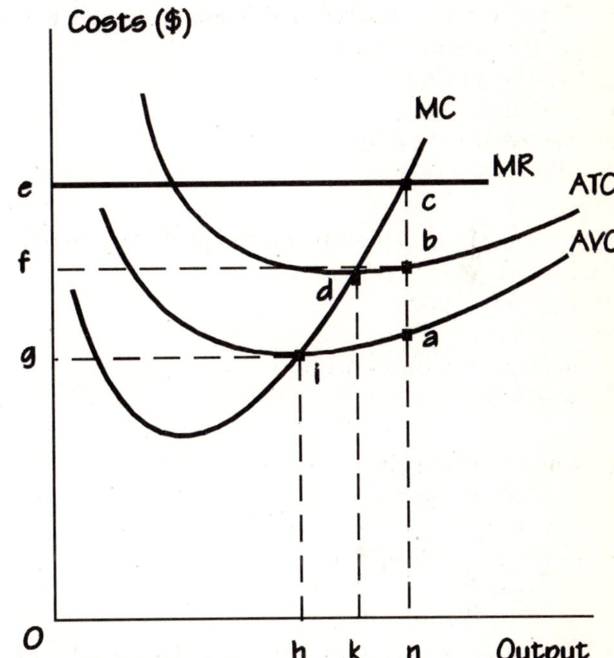

22. The marginal cost at the profit-maximizing rate of output is:
(a) *an* dollars
(b) *nb* dollars
(c) 0*f* dollars
(d) 0*e* dollars

23. Total revenue at the profit-maximizing rate of output is given by the area
(a) 0*nbf*
(b) 0*ecn*
(c) 0*gan*
(d) *efab*

24. Total cost at the profit-maximizing rate of output is given by the area:
(a) *ec*0*n*

(b) 0*gan*
(c) *fbag*
(d) *fbn*0

25. Economic profit is given by the area:
(a) *ecbf*
(b) *fbag*
(c) *ecag*
(d) *ecdf*

26. The firm's short run supply curve is represented by:
(a) the ATC curve above point *d*
(b) the AVC curve above point *i*
(c) the MC curve above *i*
(d) the MR curve

27. The lowest price at which this firm will continue to produce output in the short run is:
(a) 0*e*
(b) 0*f*
(c) 0*g*
(d) the firm will produce at any price

28. In a competitive firm, technological progress that increases the productivity of labour would:
(a) shift the marginal-cost downward
(b) shift the marginal-cost curve upward
(c) shift the average-fixed-cost curve downward
(d) reduce the profit-maximizing output level

29. Assume that the market for macaroni is purely competitive. Currently, each firm making macaroni is experiencing economic losses. In the long run we can expect:
(a) the market supply curve to shift to the right
(b) the demand curve to increase
(c) the market supply curve to shift to the left
(d) the demand curve to decrease

30. The long-run supply curve under pure competition is upward sloping when increased product demand leads to:
(a) more firms entering the market
(b) firms building bigger plants
(c) input price increases
(d) economies of scale

31. Productive efficiency is achieved in the long run in a competitive industry because competition forces the firm to produce where:
(a) marginal cost equals price
(b) fixed cost is zero
(c) economic profits are positive
(d) price equals lowest long-run average total cost

32. An economy is producing the goods most wanted by society when for each and every good:
(a) price and average cost are equal
(b) price and marginal cost are equal
(c) economic profit is positive
(d) the amount sold equals the amount produced

33. When spillover costs exist, market forces in a purely competitive industry will, from society's point of view, lead to:
(a) an industry output that is too low
(b) an industry price that is too high
(c) exodus from the industry
(d) an overallocation of resources to the industry

34. With respect to public goods, purely competitive industries will:
(a) underproduce these goods
(b) underprice these goods
(c) not minimize costs of producing these goods
(d) produce the socially optimal amount of these goods

Discussion Questions

1. Explain why all firms in a purely competitive market must charge exactly the same price.

2. If pure competition is so rare in practice, why are students of economics asked to study it?

3. How can it be claimed that in a market characterized by a downward sloping demand curve the individual producer faces a horizontal or perfectly elastic demand curve?

4. Why is the firm willing to produce at a loss in the short run if the loss is no greater than fixed costs? At what point does a firm drop out of the industry? Would all firms drop out of the industry at the same time?

5. Explain how the short-run supply of an individual firm and of the purely competitive industry are determined.

6. What determines the equilibrium price and output of a purely competitive industry in the short run? Will economic profits in the industry be positive or negative?

7. Why do the MC = MR rule and the MC = P rule mean the same thing under conditions of pure competition? Where does this rule come from?

8. What are the important distinctions between the short run and long run? Between equilibrium in the short run and in the long run in a competitive industry?

9. Why must economic profits be zero in long-run equilibrium for a purely competitive industry? What forces the purely competitive firm into this position?

10. If economic profits end up at zero in long-run equilibrium, why should entrepreneurs bother starting up businesses in purely competitive industries?

11. What is a constant-cost industry? What is an increasing-cost industry? Under what economic conditions is each likely to be found? What will be the nature of the long-run supply curve in each of these industries?

12. What two kinds of efficiency are necessary if the economy is to make the most efficient use of its resources?

13. What roles do freedom of entry and existence of economic profits play in the long run reallocation of resources towards new industries?

14. What is Schumpeter's view of competition in his theory of "creative destruction"?

15. Even a purely competitive economy may not achieve allocative and productive efficiency in all circumstances. Why? Give several examples of how a competitive market system would fail to meet the efficiency criteria from the viewpoint of the whole of society.

16. For a course project you are asked to identify a declining industry in Canada. Based on the discussion on the long-run adjustments in this chapter, what criteria would you use to identify such an industry?

Answers

Fill-in questions

1. (a) pure competition; (b) monopoly; (c) monopolistic competition; (d) oligopoly

2. number, product, price, entry, nonprice

3. (a) a large number of independent sellers; (b) no single firm supplies enough to influence the market price; (c) standardized product; (d) no obstacles to the entry of new firms or the exit of old firms

4. barriers

5. sellers, differentiated

6. elastic, equal to

7. total revenue, total cost

8. total-revenue and total-cost; marginal-revenue and marginal-cost

9. elastic, downward

10. profit, fixed costs; (a) maximum, minimum (b) revenue, cost

11. ATC, AVC

12. MC, AVC, horizontal summation

13. firms, fixed, plant

14. enter, fall, more, larger, decrease, zero

15. average total, marginal, minimum

16. increasing, upsloping

17. perfectly elastic

18. negative, decrease

19. productive, allocative

20. MC; ATC, minimum

21. (a) income distribution problem; (b) market failure due to externalities and public goods; (c) the competitive system may result in a slow rate of technological change; (d) the range of consumer choice may be limited

22. exclusion, private, public; public

23. externality, spillover

Problems and projects

1. Number of firms: d, a, c, b; Type of product: e, n, f, e/f; Control over price: m, h, g, g; Conditions of entry; i, j, k, l; Nonprice competition: m, g, h, g/h

2. (a) 0, 160, 320, 480,.640, 800, 960, 1120, 1280; (b) -200, -90, 45, 155, 240, 300, 335, 345, 330; (c) 7000; (d) TR1 = 0, 90, 180, 270, 360, 450, 540, 630, 720; Profit 1 = -200, -160, -95, -55, -40, -50, -85, -145, -230; (e) 4000, 40, 200; should, 160, less than; (f) TR2 = 0, 30, 60, 90, 120, 150, 180, 210, 240; Profit 2 = -200, -220, -215, -235, -280, -350, -445, -565, -710; (g) 1000; should not; 220, 200

3. (a) AR and MR both $10 at all Q values; (b) horizontal, $10; (c) 5; 10, 9; 1; 10, 13, 3

4. (b) MC; (d) about $3, about 5000; (e) 50; (f) 5000; (g) rectangle = $62 loss

5. (a) exodus; (b) minimum, $4.00; (c) 2400; (d) 70; (e) 34; 66; (g) horizontal

6. (a) output +, profit +; (b) output +, profit +; (c) output -, profit -

7. Skeena's ATC is higher than Stikine's, whereas Stikine's AVC is higher than Skeena's.

True-False

1. T	**2.** F	**3.** F	**4.** F	**5.** T	**6.** F
7. F	**8.** F	**9.** T	**10.** F	**11.** T	**12.** T
13. T	**14.** F	**15.** F	**16.** F	**17.** F	**18.** T
19. F	**20.** F				

Multiple-Choice

1. (d)	**2.** (d)	**3.** (a)	**4.** (a)	**5.** (b)	**6.** (d)
7. (d)	**8.** (b)	**9.** (c)	**10.** (c)	**11.** (d)	**12.** (c)
13. (d)	**14.** (b)	**15.** (c)	**16.** (b)	**17.** (a)	**18.** (d)
19. (b)	**20.** (c)	**21.** (b)	**22.** (d)	**23.** (b)	**24.** (d)
25. (a)	**26.** (c)	**27.** (c)	**28.** (a)	**29.** (c)	**30.** (c)
31. (d)	**32.** (b)	**33.** (d)	**34.** (a)		

CHAPTER 11

Price and Output Determination: Pure Monopoly

Chapter 11 is the second of four chapters that deal with specific market models; it is concerned with monopoly--the market structure characterized by only one seller of a product that has no close substitutes. Like pure competition, pure monopoly is rarely found in the Canadian economy, and then mainly as the result of governmental action. But there are many markets that are very close to being pure monopolies. Also, an understanding of pure monopoly is helpful in understanding the more realistic situation of oligopoly.

After an introduction to monopoly, Chapter 11 turns to a description of the more important types of barriers to entry. Pure monopoly, approximations of pure monopoly, and oligopoly can exist only if something prevents new firms from entering the industry in the long run. Barriers stem from scale economies, legal protection, or exclusive ownership of key resources, Not only do barriers make it possible for monopoly to exist; they also explain why so many markets are oligopolies (Chapter 13 is devoted to oligopoly).

Chapter 11 answers similar questions for monopoly firms as Chapter 10 did for purely competitive firms. These include: how much output will the firm produce; what price will it charge; how much profit will it receive; and what will be the efficiency implications (in terms of the relationship between price and marginal cost)? As we address these questions for the monopoly firm, and compare pure competition and monopoly, you should note the following:

1. Both the competitive and monopoly firm maximize profits by setting output where marginal cost and marginal revenue are equal.

2. The individual competitor sees a perfectly elastic demand for its product at the going market price because it is only one of many firms in the industry; therefore they need only decide on output. Because the monopolist is the whole industry, the monopolist faces a downward sloping market demand and must therefore make a simultaneous price/output decision.

3. When demand is perfectly elastic, price is equal to marginal revenue and is constant; but when demand is less than perfectly elastic, marginal revenue is less than price and both decrease as the output of the firm increases.

4. Because entry to a monopolistic industry is blocked, economic profits will not be eroded by entry of new firms as would occur under conditions of pure competition.

In addition to exploring the monopolist's price and output decision, Chapter 11 has three other objectives. The first is to compare the economic effects and efficiency of monopoly with those of pure competition. The second is to explain what price discrimination is, under what conditions it can occur, and what its consequences are. Finally, the chapter looks at government regulation of a monopolist's prices.

Checklist

When you have studied this chapter, you should be able to:

- ☐ Define pure monopoly and list its four characteristics.
- ☐ List the three types of barriers to entry and explain how each of them can prevent or deter the entry of new firms.
- ☐ Describe the demand curve or schedule for the pure monopolist's product.
- ☐ Cite three implications of the monopolist's demand curve.
- ☐ Define marginal revenue and compute marginal revenue from data on demand for the monopolist's product.
- ☐ Explain why marginal revenue is less than price for a downward sloping demand curve.
- ☐ Explain why producing where marginal revenue equals marginal cost maximizes profit.
- ☐ Determine the profit-maximizing output and price levels when given data on demand and costs.

- ☐ Explain why the monopolist has no supply curve.
- ☐ Discuss three common misconceptions about monopoly pricing.
- ☐ Compare the price, output, and allocative efficiency results under monopoly with those achieved under pure competition.
- ☐ Explain how economies of scale, X-inefficiency, rent-seeking expenditures, and incentives for technological improvements complicate the comparison of costs in the competitive and monopoly model.
- ☐ Describe the effects of monopoly on the distribution of income in the economy.
- ☐ Define price discrimination, list the three necessary conditions for price discrimination to be used, and explain the two economic consequences of price discrimination.
- ☐ Identify, for the regulated monopoly (a public utility), the optimal social and the fair-return price; and explain the regulatory agency's dilemma.

Chapter Outline

1. Pure monopoly is a market structure in which a single firm sells a product for which there are no close substitutes. A monopoly is a "price-maker." While monopoly is rare in practice, its study provides an understanding of firms that are "almost" monopolies, and is useful in understanding monopolistic competition and oligopoly.

2. Pure monopoly (and oligopoly) can exist in the long run only if barriers exist to prevent potential competitors from entering the industry.
(a) There are three types of entry barriers: economies of scale, legal barriers (patents and licences), and ownership of essential resources.
(b) Barriers are seldom perfect in preventing entry of new firms, so long-run existence of a particular monopoly is usually the result of governmental policy. This often occurs in the case of natural monopoly where cost conditions dictate that efficiency can only be achieved if only one firm serves the market.

3. The monopolist is the industry so its demand curve is the downward sloping industry demand curve. This implies that:
(a) Sales can only be increased by reducing price. Marginal revenue will be less than price for every level of output except for the first unit.
(b) The monopolist chooses some price-quantity point along the industry demand curve and is a "price maker."
(c) The monopolist will not set price in the inelastic part of the demand curve since in that range an increase in price will raise total revenue and reduce total costs (because less output needs to be produced). Therefore, profits cannot be maximized unless price is set in the elastic part of the demand curve.

4. The monopolist selects the combination of price and output that maximizes the difference between revenues and costs.
(a) We assume that a monopolist hires inputs in a competitive market and utilizes the same technology as a competitive firm, as described in Chapter 10.
(b) The monopolist produces that output at which the marginal cost and marginal revenue are equal, and charges the highest price at which this output can be sold (as indicated by the demand schedule or demand curve).
(c) The monopolist does not have a supply curve because no unique relationship exists between price and quantity supplied. Depending on the position and shape of the demand curve, a particular price can be associated with various output levels.
(d) Three common misconceptions about monopolists are that they charge as high a price as possible, that they seek the maximum profit ***per unit*** of output, and that they always make economic profits.

5. The existence of pure monopoly has significant effects on the economy as a whole.
(a) Because it produces less output and sets a higher price than would result under conditions of pure competition, and because price is above both minimum average total and marginal cost, monopoly misallocates resources (results in neither productive nor allocative efficiency).
(b) As compared to a purely competitive system, monopoly transfers income from consumers to the owners of the firm, and adds to inequality of incomes.
(c) As compared to a pure competitor producing the same product, a monopolist may have lower or higher average costs.
(1) If there are economies of scale in production, the monopolist can produce at a lower long-run average cost than a large number of small pure competitors.
(2) Lack of competition can result in the monopolist being more susceptible to X-inefficiency than a purely

competitive firm; its long-run average cost at every level of output is higher than that of a purely competitive firm.
(3) Firms may incur rent-seeking expenditures (such as lobbying fees, and public relations expenditures), to gain or preserve monopoly position. These expenditures increase costs but add nothing to society's output.
(d) Dynamic efficiency may be better served by monopoly or pure competition. It depends on which market structure is more efficient over time in developing new lower-cost techniques of producing existing products and in developing new products.

6. To increase profits, a pure monopolist may engage in price discrimination by charging different prices to different buyers of the same product (when the price differences do not represent differences in the costs of producing the product).
(a) To discriminate, the seller must have some monopoly power, be capable of separating buyers into groups that have different elasticities of demand, and be able to prevent the resale of the product.
(b) The seller charges the group with the more inelastic demand the higher price. Price discrimination increases not only the profits but also the output of the monopolist.
(c) Price discrimination is common in Canada.

7. The prices charged for the products of natural monopolies are often regulated by governments to reduce the misallocation of resources.
(a) A ceiling price determined by the intersection of the marginal-cost and demand schedules is the optimal social price, and it improves the allocation of resources compared to the unregulated monopoly outcome.
(b) Because this ceiling price may force the firm to produce at a loss, government may set the ceiling at a level where the average total cost and demand intersect, thus allowing the monopolist a fair return.
(c) The dilemma of regulation is that the optimal social price may cause losses for the monopolist, and that a fair-return price results in a less efficient resource allocation.

Terms and Concepts

barriers to entry
dilemma of regulation
dynamic efficiency
"fair-return" price
natural monopoly
optimal social price
price discrimination
price maker
pure monopoly
rent-seeking behaviour
X-inefficiency

Hints and Tips

1. Do not fall into the trap of thinking that monopoly and monopolistic competition are the same. They are two distinct market structures.

2. In a monopoly, the demand and marginal revenue curves are separate. The MR curve is twice as steep as the demand curve, so the MR curve lies, at all points, halfway between the demand and the price axis.

3. The monopolist's price is ***on the demand curve***. First locate the monopolist's profit-maximizing output where MR = MC. Then go up to the demand curve to find the maximum price that consumers are willing to pay for this quantity.

4. Intuitively, it should be clear that how narrowly or broadly a market is defined will affect whether or not a firm might have a monopoly in that market. Canada Post may be the only firm selling door-to-door delivery of written messages at a very low price. It is not the only firm delivering messages; couriers and the telephone company also do this. Therefore, while Canada Post is a monopoly, the degree of their monopoly power depends on the degree to which their customers are willing to substitute these other services if Canada Post raises price.

Fill-In Questions

1. Pure monopoly is a market structure in which a single firm is the sole producer of a product for which there are no (substitutes, close substitutes) __________ and into which entry in the long run is (easy, difficult, blocked) __________.

2. The characteristics of the monopoly market model are:

(a) ______________________

(b) ______________________

(c) ______________________

(d) ______________________

3. The three most important types of barriers to entry are:

(a) ______________________

(b) ______________________

(c) ______________________

4. An industry in which the long-run average cost declines over the range of possible demand levels would be termed a __________ monopoly.

5. Public utility companies tend to be __________ monopolies, and they receive their franchises from and are __________ by governments.

6. The demand schedule confronting the pure monopolist is __________ sloping; this means that marginal revenue is (greater, less) __________ than price and that both marginal revenue and price (increase, decrease) __________ as output increases.

7. The profit-maximizing monopolist will always want to avoid the __________ segment of its demand curve in favour of a price-quantity combination somewhere in the __________ segment.

8. When the economic profits of a monopolist are being maximized, marginal revenue is equal to __________ cost.

9. If (at the output level where marginal revenue equals marginal cost) the price is greater than average variable cost but less than average cost, the monopolist is making a(n) __________ and will __________ the industry in the long run.

10. Given the same costs, the monopolist will find it profitable to sell (more, less) __________ output and to charge a (higher, lower) __________ price than would a competitive producer.

11. If the firm's costs exceed their minimum possible costs of production at their current output level, the firm experiences __________. Compared to purely competitive firms, monopolies are (more, less) __________ likely to have this problem because monopolies do not face the discipline of competition.

12. A firm that spends money on lobbying or public relations in effort to gain protection from competition is said to be engaging in __________ behaviour.

13. Monopolists are more __________ efficient than purely competitive firms if monopolists improve the __________ of producing existing products (thereby lowering the __________ of producing them), or develop new __________ over time more rapidly than pure competitors do.

14. There is price discrimination whenever a product is sold at different __________ and these differences are not because of differences in the __________ of supplying the product.

15. Price discrimination is possible only when the following three conditions are found:

(a) ______________________________

(b) ______________________________

(c) ______________________________

16. In order to increase profits by charging different prices in segmented markets the __________ of demand must be different in both markets.

17. The two economic consequences of price discrimination are a(n) (increase, decrease) __________ in the profits and a(n) __________ in the output of the monopolist.

18. The misallocation of resources that results from monopoly can be eliminated if a ceiling price for the monopolist's product is set equal to __________. However, such a price is often __________ than average total cost, meaning that the regulation will cause the monopolist to suffer a loss.

19. If a regulated monopolist is allowed to earn a fair return, the ceiling price for the product is set equal to __________; such a price reduces but does not eliminate the __________ of resources caused by monopoly.

Problems and Projects

1. The demand schedule and total cost schedule for the product produced by a monopolist are given in the table the follows.

(a) Complete the table by computing total revenue, marginal revenue, and marginal cost.

(b) This monopolist would never produce more than 5 units no matter what the level of costs. Why?

(c) Using the marginal-revenue and marginal-cost approach find the profit-maximizing output. (In numerical examples it can happen that there is no output level where marginal revenue and marginal cost are equal. In that case the extra unit should be produced as long as marginal revenue is greater than marginal cost.)

(d) What price will the monopolist charge?

(e) What will be the economic profit?

(f) Place price, marginal revenue, marginal cost, and average cost on the blank graph on the next page. (Remember to plot MR and MC at the "midpoints" of the quantity ranges over which they are calculated)

(g) Indicate on the graph the monopoly output, price and total profit.

Qd	P	TR	MR	TC	MC
0	$10	$___	- -	$4.00	- -
1	9	___	$9	4.25	$0.25
2	8	___	___	5.00	___
3	7	___	___	6.25	___
4	6	___	___	8.00	___
5	5	___	___	10.25	___
6	4	___	___	13.00	___
7	3	___	___	16.25	___

(h) Assume this monopolist is able to engage in price discrimination and to sell each unit of the product at a price equal to the maximum price the buyer of that unit of the product would be willing to pay.

(1) Complete the following table by computing total revenue at each quantity and the marginal revenue this discriminating monopolist obtains for each additional unit sold. [The total and marginal revenue will not be the same as in the table in part (a).]

Qd	P	TR	MR
0	$10	$___	- -
1	9	___	$9
2	8	___	___
3	7	___	___
4	6	___	___
5	5	___	___
6	4	___	___
7	3	___	___

(2) The table shows that the marginal revenue the discriminating monopolist obtains from the sale of an additional unit is equal to the __________.

(3) Using the original table of costs, the discriminating monopolist would produce __________ units, charge the buyer of the last unit of produced a price of $__________, and obtain a total economic profit of $__________.

(4) Compared to the situation where the monopolist charges each buyer the same price, when the monopolist is able to engage in price discrimination, its profits will be (larger, smaller, the same) __________ and it will produce (less, more) __________ output.

2. The demand for bridge crossings to an island in the Gulf of St. Lawrence is estimated by the following function: $Q_x = 30 - P_x$ where Q_x is the number of crossings and P_x is the price charged per crossing. There are no variable costs connected with operating the bridge, but the bridge will cost $100 to build and will last only one market period. The $100 figure includes all implicit costs. You are offered monopoly control if you should build the bridge. As a profit-maximizing monopolist would you build the bridge, and if you were to build the bridge, what price per crossing would you charge? Your answer for this question should include all the calculations you completed to come to a decision.

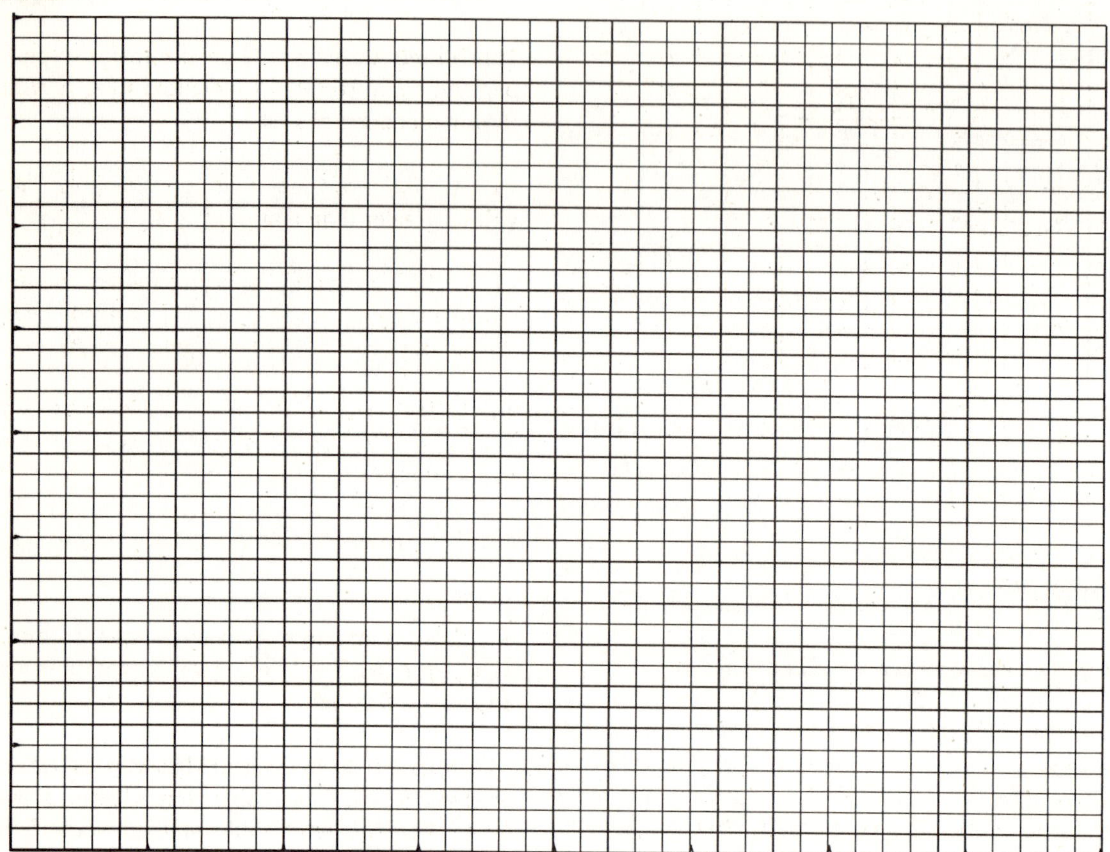

3. One-Eyed Jack's is the only saloon in Dry Gulch. The demand for Jack's whiskey is given by: $Q = 100 - P$ where Q is the number of shots sold per day, and P is the price in cents per shot. Jack's only variable costs are for the whiskey itself, and this cost is a constant 20 cents per shot. (Therefore the MC and AVC curves are horizontal at 20 cents). Jack's fixed costs are $12 per day for building rental and wages for himself, the barmaid and the piano player. There are no other costs.

(a) To maximize profits, how much whiskey should One-Eyed Jack's sell per day?

(b) What price will be charged?

(c) What is the total daily profit?

4. Answer the following questions based on interpretation of the following graph that depicts a pure monopolist that seeks to maximize profits.

(a) output ___________

(b) marginal revenue at this output ___________

(c) marginal cost at this output ___________

(d) price at this output ___________

(e) total revenue at this output ___________

(f) average cost at this output ___________

(g) total cost of this output ___________

(h) profit per unit of output ___________

(i) total profit ___________

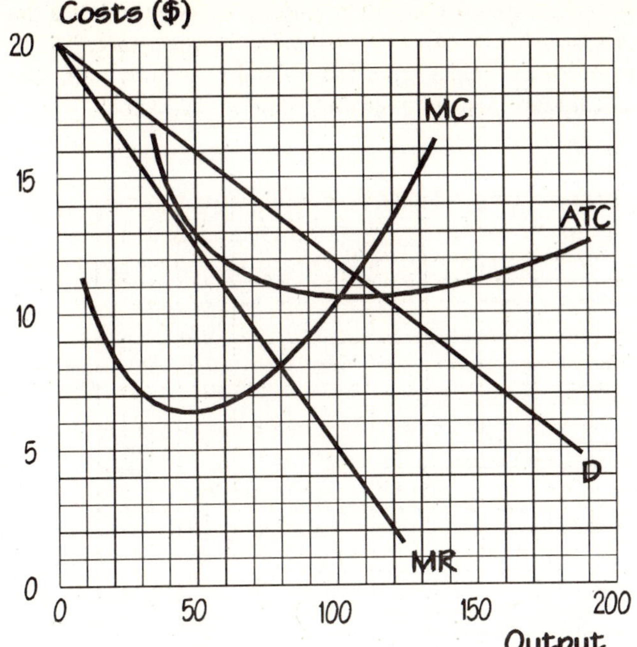

True-False

Circle T if the statement is true, F if it is false.

1. In the monopoly model the firm and the industry are one and the same. **T F**

2. Barriers to entry are not normally able to prevent entry in the long run. **T F**

3. A natural monopoly is a defined to be a firm that government has granted a monopoly franchise. **T F**

4. A purely competitive firm is a price taker, but a monopolist is a price maker. **T F**

5. On a graph the marginal revenue curve is half as steep as the demand curve. **T F**

6. Marginal revenue is less than price for downward sloping demand curves because in order to sell an extra unit the firm must lower the price of all previous units sold. **T F**

7. In Canada a patent usually gives an inventor 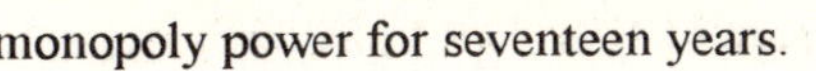
monopoly power for seventeen years. **T F**

8. Monopolists always make economic profits. **T F**

9. If a monopolistic firm is losing money, it can always make a profit by raising the price of its product. **T F**

10. Selling an extra unit in the inelastic portion of the demand curve results in increased total revenue, so may lead to increased profits. **T F**

11. At the profit-maximizing monopoly output, price will be greater than marginal cost. **T F**

12. If the monopolist is losing money in the short run where marginal revenue equals marginal cost, then at this point price must be less than average cost. **T F**

13. When a monopolist is maximizing its total profit, it is also producing that output at which its per unit (or average) profit is a maximum. **T F**

14. The monopolist has an upward sloping supply curve. **T F**

15. Since a monopoly sets price equal to marginal cost, at the profit-maximizing rate of output, resources are allocated efficiently. **T F**

16. When there are substantial economies of scale in production, the monopolist may charge a price that is lower than the price that would prevail if the product were produced by a purely competitive industry. **T F**

17. Rent-seeking behaviour adds to the inefficiency of monopoly. **T F**

18. The inefficiencies of monopoly may be somewhat offset by economies of scale and technological progress. **T F**

19. Whenever the same product is sold at two or more different prices, then price discrimination occurs. **T F**

20. Price discrimination is fairly unusual in Canada. **T F**

21. If a movie theatre sells tickets to college students at 25% less than the regular adult price, this is an example of price discrimination, assuming the cost of serving students equals the cost of serving other adults. **T F**

22. The price that achieves allocative efficiency is called the optimal social price. **T F**

23. A regulated utility is likely to make economic profit when price is set to achieve the most efficient allocation of resources. **T F**

24. A "fair-return" price for a regulated utility would have price set equal to average cost. **T F**

Multiple-Choice

Circle the letter that corresponds to the best answer.

1. Which of the following is the best example of a pure monopoly?
(a) a neighbourhood grocer in Saskatoon
(b) the only cable T.V. company in a small city
(c) the manufacturer of Crest toothpaste
(d) a bank in downtown Winnipeg

2. For the monopolist:
(a) price equals marginal revenue
(b) price is greater than marginal revenue
(c) price is less than marginal revenue
(d) price and marginal revenue are unrelated

3. In order to maximize profits the monopolist should operate at the level of output where:
(a) price equals marginal cost
(b) price equals average cost
(c) marginal revenue equals marginal cost
(d) marginal revenue equals average cost

4. Reasons for the existence of monopoly include all but:
(a) patents
(b) declining long-run average costs over a large range of output relative to industry demand
(c) control of a raw material
(d) inelastic demand for the product

5. Which of the following is the key characteristic of a natural monopoly?
(a) economies of scale throughout the range of market demand
(b) it is a public utility
(c) it has low fixed costs
(d) profits are large

6. Because the monopolist is the sole producer in the industry:
(a) the demand curve for the monopolist is the industry demand curve
(b) the monopolist's demand curve will be inelastic
(c) the monopolist will not lose sales when price is raised
(d) the marginal revenue will be greater than price at all levels of output

7. At its present output a monopolist determines that its marginal cost is $18 and its marginal revenue is $21. The monopolist will maximize profits or minimize losses by:
(a) increasing price while keeping output constant
(b) decreasing price and increasing output
(c) decreasing both price and output
(d) increasing both price and output

8. If a monopolist had no costs, it would produce the output where:
(a) price equals zero
(b) marginal revenue equals zero
(c) economic profit equals zero
(d) the demand curve cuts the price axis

Answer questions 9 through 11 on the basis of the demand and cost data for a monopolist given in the following table.

Output	Price	Total Cost
0	$80	$50
1	70	60
2	60	72
3	50	86
4	40	102
5	30	120

9. The marginal revenue of the third unit of output is:
(a) $10
(b) $20
(c) $30
(d) $40

10. The profit-maximizing monopolist would produce:
(a) 1 unit
(b) 2 units
(c) 3 units
(d) 4 units

11. The profit-maximzing monopolist would set its price at:
(a) $20
(b) $30
(c) $40
(d) $50

Use the diagram that follows to answer questions 12 through 14.

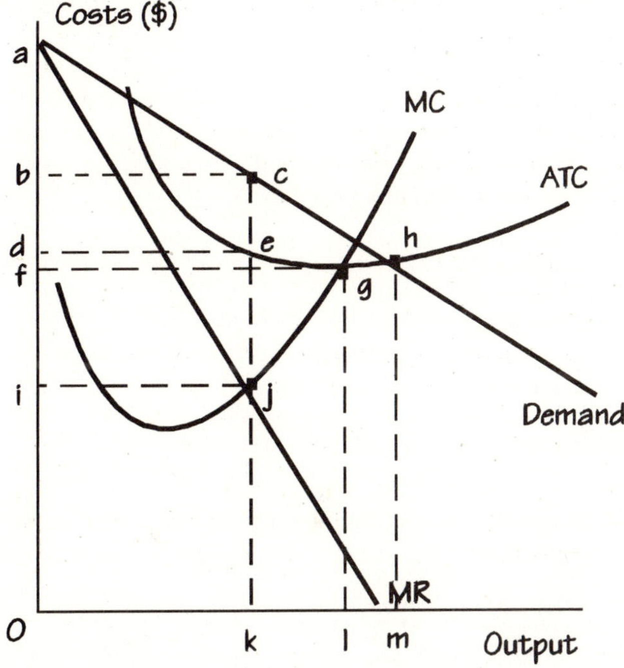

12. The profit-maximizing monopolist would produce:
(a) 0*k* units
(b) 0*l* units
(c) 0*m* units
(d) zero units

13. The profit-maximizing monopolist would set a price of:
(a) 0*a*
(b) 0*b*
(c) 0*f*
(d) 0*i*

14. The profit-maximizing monopolist would earn an economic profit of:
(a) *deji*
(b) *bck*0
(c) *abc*
(d) *bced*

15. At the output where marginal revenue equals marginal cost the rule for productive efficiency may not be met because:
(a) the average total cost of producing is not a minimum
(b) the marginal cost of producing the last unit is less than its price
(c) marginal cost may not be at its minimum value
(d) average revenue exceeds the cost of producing an extra unit of output

16. Which of the following is probably not an example of price discrimination?
(a) an airline charging higher prices for travellers who do not book ahead
(b) a taxicab charging more for longer trips
(c) a university charging higher tuition for an evening class in the executive MBA program than for a day class of the same course
(d) a ski hill charging different lift fees for local residents than for tourists

17. For which of the following goods would price discrimination be most workable?
(a) automobiles in the retail market
(b) textbooks at your school
(c) cosmetic surgery in a city with one surgeon
(d) wheat at the farm level

18. Which is not one of the conditions that must be realized before a seller finds price discrimination is workable?
(a) the buyer must be unable to resell the product
(b) the product must be a service
(c) the seller must have some degree of monopoly power
(d) the seller must be able to segment the market

19. If a monopolist engages in price discrimination rather than charging all buyers the same price, its:
(a) profits and its output are greater
(b) profits and its output are smaller
(c) profits are greater and its output is smaller
(d) profits are smaller and its output is greater

20. As compared to a competitive industry with the same costs, a monopolized industry will have:
(a) larger output and a higher price
(b) larger output and a lower price
(c) smaller output and a lower price
(d) smaller output and a higher price

Questions 21 through 25 are based on this graph.

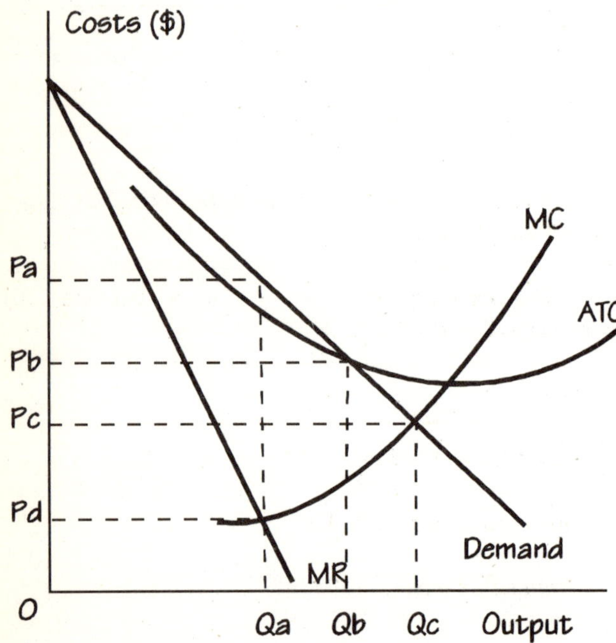

21. The monopoly depicted is:
(a) a natural monopoly because the demand curve is downward sloping
(b) a natural monopoly because ATC is still falling where it intersects demand
(c) a natural monopoly because MR and MC intersect at an output level below the social optimum
(d) not a natural monopoly

22. If unregulated, which price and output combination would this monopolist choose?
(a) *Pa* and *Qa*
(b) *Pd* and *Qa*
(c) *Pb* and *Qb*
(d) *Pc* and *Qc*

23. If the government regulates this monopolist so as to avoid allocative inefficiency, the price and output combination should be:
(a) *Pa* and *Qa*
(b) *Pd* and *Qa*
(c) *Pb* and *Qb*
(d) *Pc* and *Qc*

24. The problem with the regulated solution found in question 23 is that:
(a) the monopolist incurs a loss
(b) the monopolist still earns excessive profits
(c) the monopolist produces too little output
(d) the monopolist produces too much output

25. A regulatory compromise is to charge a price that allows the monopolist a "fair return" but also results in an output level close to the social optimum. Such a price and output combination is:
(a) *Pa* and *Qa*
(b) *Pd* and *Qa*
(c) *Pb* and *Qb*
(d) *Pc* and *Qc*

Discussion Questions

1. Describe the characteristics of the purely monopolistic market structure. Why is it included in the text if it is fairly rare in practice?

2. What is meant by a barrier to entry? What are the different kinds of barriers to entry? How important are they in pure competition, pure monopoly, monopolistic competition, and oligopoly?

3. For each type of barrier to entry, give an example of a firm in your community that has some monopoly power by virtue of this type of barrier.

4. Why are most natural monopolies also public utilities? What does government hope to achieve by granting exclusive franchises to and regulating such natural monopolies?

5. If you owned a National Hockey League franchise in Charlottetown, you would have more of a monopoly than if you owned the New York Rangers NHL franchise. Why? Would you have a natural monopoly in Charlottetown? Would you be able to make a profit?

6. If there is only one movie theatre in Jasper, Alberta, this theatre presumably has some monopoly power. What factors limit this monopoly power?

7. How do patent laws contribute to monopoly power? The federal government recently increased the duration of exclusive production for pharmaceutical patents. How could such an increase in the duration of a patent be justified when this chapter concludes that monopoly leads to allocative and productive inefficiency?

8. Compare the pure monopolist and the individual pure competitor with respect to:
(a) the demand schedule
(b) the marginal-revenue schedule
(c) the relationship between marginal revenue and the price
(d) the condition that must be met at the profit-maximizing output
(e) the ability to set price
(f) long-run economic profits
(g) long-run efficiency

9. Explain why marginal revenue is always less than price (or average revenue) when demand curves are downward sloping.

10. Suppose you are a pure monopolist and discover you are producing and selling an output at a point on the demand curve where demand for the product is inelastic. Explain why a decrease in output accompanied by a price increase must improve your profits.

11. What are the three complications that may result in a monopolist having lower or higher average costs than a competitive firm?

12. Does monopoly, when compared with pure competition, result in more or less dynamic efficiency (technological progress)? What are the arguments on both sides of this question?

13. What is meant by price discrimination and what conditions must be realized before it is workable?

14. How does price discrimination affect the profits and the output of the monopolist? How does it affect consumers?

15. How do public utility regulatory agencies attempt to eliminate the misallocation of resources that results from monopoly? Explain the dilemma that almost invariably confronts the agency in this endeavour; and explain why a fair-return price only reduces but does not eliminate misallocation.

Answers

Fill-in questions

1. close substitutes, blocked

2. (a) single seller; (b) no close substitutes; (c) "price maker"; (d) blocked entry

3. (a) economies of scale; (b) legal barriers; (c) ownership of essential inputs

4. natural

5. natural, regulated

6. downward, less, decrease

7. inelastic, elastic

8. marginal

9. loss, exit

10. less, higher

11. X-inefficiency, more

12. rent-seeking

13. dynamically, technology, cost, products

14. prices, cost

15. (a) monopoly power; (b) market segregation; (c) no resales

16. elasticity of demand

17. increase, increase

18. marginal cost; less

19. average total cost; misallocation

Problems and projects

1. (a) Total revenue: $0, 9, 16, 21, 24, 25, 24, 21; Marginal revenue: $9, 7, 5, 3, 1, -1, -3; Marginal cost: $.25, .75, 1.25, 1.75, 2.25, 2.75, 3.25; (b) Total revenue falls after 5 units so it would never pay to place a 6th unit on the market; (c) 4 units; (d) $6; (e) $16; (h) (1) Total revenue: $0, 9, 17, 24, 30, 35, 39, 42. Marginal revenue: $9, 8, 7, 6, 5, 4, 3. (2) price; (3) 6, $4, $36; (4) larger, larger

2. Yes, build the bridge and charge $15 for a crossing, because this is where MC = MR.

3. (a) 40 (b) $0.60 (c) $4.

4. (a) 80 (b) $8.00 (c) $8.00 (d) $13.50 (e) $1080 (f) $11.00 (g) $880 (h) $2.50 (i) $200

True-False

1. T	**2.** T	**3.** F	**4.** T	**5.** F	**6.** T
7. T	**8.** F	**9.** F	**10.** F	**11.** T	**12.** T
13. F	**14.** F	**15.** F	**16.** T	**17.** T	**18.** T
19. F	**20.** F	**21.** T	**22.** T	**23.** F	**24.** F

Multiple-choice

1. (b)	**2.** (b)	**3.** (c)	**4.** (d)	**5.** (a)	**6.** (a)
7. (b)	**8.** (b)	**9.** (c)	**10.** (c)	**11.** (d)	**12.** (a)
13. (b)	**14.** (d)	**15.** (a)	**16.** (b)	**17.** (c)	**18.** (b)
19. (a)	**20.** (d)	**21.** (b)	**22.** (a)	**23.** (d)	**24.** (a)
25. (c)					

CHAPTER 12

Price and Output Determination: Monopolistic Competition

Chapter 12 is the third of four chapters that deal with specific market structures. As its name implies, monopolistic competition is a blend of pure competition and pure monopoly. One reason for studying those relatively unrealistic market structures was to prepare you for the study of more realistic market structures. The monopolistic competition model realistically represents quite a number of Canadian industries. So does the oligopoly model of Chapter 13. Your study of monopolistic competition in this chapter will help you to understand that price competition is not the only method of competition; and that the welfare implications of the various forms of competition that prevail under monopolistic competition are complex. In combination with Chapter 13, Chapter 12 will also help you to understand why oligopoly is prevalent in the Canadian economy, and how oligopoly differs from monopolistic competition.

The first task is to learn exactly what is meant by monopolistic competition. Then you will be able to make sense of the demand curve the monopolistically competitive firm sees for its product, and of why it differs from the purely competitive firm's demand curve and the monopolist's demand curve. In this connection, you should also see that as the individual firm changes the characteristics of its product or changes the extent to which it advertises its product, both the costs of the firm and the demand for its product will shift. These results occur because of product differentiation between different firms' versions of the product. Each seller has some price making power, but not very much because other sellers produce goods which are close substitutes, and because potential new entrants could produce goods with similar characteristics.

To maximize their profits, monopolistically competitive firms try to choose an optimal combination of product quality, product promotion, and price. Given the product quality and level of advertising, the price-output analysis of the monopolistic competitors is straightforward. In the short run the analysis is identical to that outlined in Chapter 11 for the pure monopolist. In the long run the competition element makes itself apparent: the entry (or exit) of firms that produce close substitutes shifts the firm's demand curve and the price the firm charges towards the level of average cost, thus eroding economic profits (or losses). Where the price tends to stabilize is not equal either to minimum average cost or to marginal cost; and consequently monopolistic competition, on these two scores, can be considered less efficient than pure competition.

Much of Chapter 12 deals with nonprice competition because in monopolistically competitive industries firms compete as much by product differentiation, new product development, and advertising, as they do by price competition. Evaluating the welfare effects of monopolistic competition is more complicated than merely criticizing the productive inefficiency and allocative inefficiency as compared to the ideal standard achieved under pure competition. There are also socially beneficial and detrimental aspects to product differentiation, development, and advertising that have no counterpart in pure competition. Whether the shortcomings are offset by the advantages is a question economists have been unable to answer. Certainly, a central idea of Chapter 12 is that monopolistic competition cannot be compared with pure competition only on the basis of prices charged at any given time; it must also be judged on whether it results over time in better products, a wider variety of products, and better-informed consumers.

Checklist

When you have studied this chapter, you should be able to:

- ☐ List the three distinguishing characteristics of monopolistic competition.
- ☐ Describe four main forms of product differentiation.
- ☐ Compare the demand curve perceived by the monopolistic competitor with that faced by the pure competitor or that faced by the monopolist.
- ☐ Determine the price and output levels set by a monopolistic competitor (producing a given product and engaged in a given amount of promotional expenditures) in the short run when you are given the cost and demand data.
- ☐ Explain why the monopolistic competitor will tend to earn only normal profits in the long run (price tending to equal average total cost).
- ☐ Show graphically how excess capacity occurs, and why neither productive nor allocative efficiency are realized under monopolistic competition.
- ☐ Identify the two principal types of nonprice competition.
- ☐ Present the major arguments in the cases for and against advertising.
- ☐ Explain why monopolistic competition is more complex in practice than is suggested by the graphical analysis represented in the chapter.

Chapter Outline

1. A monopolistically competitive industry is one in which a fairly large number of independent firms produce differentiated products, in which both price and various forms of nonprice competition occur, and into which entry is relatively easy in the long run. Many Canadian industries approximate monopolistic competition.

2. Assume that firms in the industry produce products of given quality and characteristics, and are engaged in given amounts of promotional activity.
(a) The demand curve facing each firm is highly, but not perfectly, elastic. Because each firm sells a unique product, the firm has price making power; but this power is limited by the presence of close substitutes and many rival producers. The firm's demand is less elastic than a pure competitor's, but more elastic than a pure monopolist's.
(b) In the short run, the individual firm will produce the output at which marginal cost and marginal revenue are equal and charge the price at which the output can be sold; either profits or losses may result in the short run.
(c) If short run profits exist, entry of new firms in the long run will *tend* to decrease the demand curve for the product of the individual firm until economic profits are eliminated (price and average cost are made equal to each other). If short run losses exist, exodus of firms will *tend* to increase the demand curves of surviving firms until economic profits are once again zero.

3. In monopolistic competition firms end up with excess capacity, and neither allocative nor productive efficiency is reached. Because the industry is overcrowded with firms, no firm produces up to the point where price equals marginal cost, so allocative efficiency is not achieved. Although the average cost of each firm is equal to its price, the firm does not achieve productive efficiency because their output is less than the amount needed to reach the minimum attainable average cost.

4. Firms will attempt to use nonprice competition to improve on the normal profit that they will tend to earn in long-run equilibrium. Nonprice competition techniques include product differentiation and advertising. To the extent that they are successful, these strategies shift the demand curve to the right and make it more inelastic.

5. To the extent that nonprice competition leads to greater product selection, and results in product developments and improvements that consumers value, the wastes of monopolistic competition may be offset.

6. Whether the advertising of differentiated products results in economic waste or in greater economic efficiency is debatable; there are good arguments on both sides of this question and there is no clear answer to it.
(a) The arguments focus on opposing viewpoints in three areas:
1) whether advertising manipulates consumers' tastes or provides information

2) whether advertising promotes concentration or competition in the market
3) whether advertising is a waste of scarce resources or promotes efficiency.
(b) Empirical evidence on the economic effects of advertising has produced two schools of thought:
1) The traditional view argues and presents evidence in support of the hypothesis that advertising reduces competition among existing firms and serves as a barrier to entry to new firms. Higher prices to consumers and enhanced profits for existing firms result.
2) In the new perspective the logic and the evidence indicate that advertising acts as a relatively inexpensive way to communicate information to consumers, thus increasing competition by facilitating the entry of new firms selling substitute brands or new products.

7. Our graphical analysis cannot fully represent the adjustments and choices made within a monopolistically competitive industry. The firm tries to adjust its price, its product, and its promotion of the product so that the amount by which the firm's total revenue exceeds the total cost of producing and promoting its product is at a maximum. A longer term view suggests the benefits flowing from a greater variety of goods, product development, and increased consumer information offset some or all of the economic inefficiencies that characterize this market structure.

Terms and Concepts

excess capacity
monopolistic competition
nonprice competition
product differentiation
traditional and new perspective on advertising

Hints and Tips

1. Monopoly and monopolistic competition are two distinct market structures. Many students confuse the two, whether by careless reading, or from confusion of the concepts. Review Table 10-1 on the four basic market structure models for a summary of how monopolistic competition differs from monopoly (and other market structure models).

2. A monopolistic competitor sets profit-maximizing output and price in the same way that the monopolist does: by using the MC = MR rule.

3. A grasp of the conclusions drawn from Figure 12-2 is necessary to fully understand the inefficiencies associated with monopolistic competition.

4. If you have trouble seeing why monopolistic competition ***must*** result in excess capacity in the long-run equilibrium, try to sketch a diagram that shows all of the following: 1) a downward sloping demand, 2) output set where MC = MR, 3) this output also at the minimum of ATC, *and* 4) losses being incurred at every other possible output level. Such a diagram is impossible to draw.

Fill-In Questions

1. In a monopolistically competitive market, a (few, relatively large number of) __________ producers sell (standardized, differentiated) __________ products; these producers (do, do not) __________ collude; and they engage in both __________ and __________ competition. In the long run, entry into the industry is (difficult, fairly easy) __________.

2. Because monopolistically competitive firms sell differentiated products each firm has (no, limited, complete) __________ control over its product price.

3. List the four forms of product differentiation:
(a) ____________________
(b) ____________________
(c) ____________________
(d) ____________________

4. Given the product being produced and the extent to which that product is being promoted, in the short run:
(a) the demand curve confronting the monopolistically competitive firm will be (more, less) __________ elastic than that facing a monopolist and (more, less) __________ elastic than that facing a pure competitor;

(b) the elasticity of this demand curve will depend upon the number of __________ and the degree of __________.

5. The monopolistically competitive firm sets output at the level where __________ equals __________. Price is set according to the __________ curve at this output level.

6. In the long run, the entry of new firms into a monopolistically competitive industry will (expand, reduce) __________ the demand for the product produced by each firm in the industry and (increase, decrease) __________ the elasticity of that demand.

7. In the long run, given the product and the amount of product promotion, the price charged by the individual firm will tend to equal __________, its economic profits will tend to equal __________, and its average cost will be (less than, equal to, greater than) __________ the minimum average cost of producing and promoting the product.

8. The representative firm in a monopolistically competitive market *tends* to earn __________ profits in the long run, but complications may cause economic profits to persist for an extended period of time. These complications include:

(a) Some firms may be able to achieve a measure of product __________ that cannot be duplicated by rivals.

(b) There may be __________ to entry that prevent penetration of the market by new firms.

(c) Because they enjoy the "way of life", some entrepreneurs may accept a return that is (less than, more than) __________ a normal profit.

9. Economic efficiency requires the triple equality of __________, __________, and __________.

10. In monopolistic competition, allocative efficiency is not achieved because __________ is (less than, equal to, greater than) __________ marginal cost. Productive efficiency is not achieved because production does not take place at the minimum point of the __________ curve.

11. Monopolistic competition can be considered wasteful because it leads to __________ plants and higher than __________ prices.

12. In the long run, the monopolistic competitor attempts to protect and increase profits by various forms of nonprice competition including product __________, product __________, and __________.

13. To the extent that nonprice competition affords consumers the benefits of a wider __________ of goods and an improved __________ of goods over a period of time, the wastes of monopolistic competition may be offset.

14. The reason that a monopolistically competitive firm advertises is to shift the firm's demand curve __________ and simultaneously __________ its elasticity of demand.

15. The traditional view stresses the socially (positive, negative) __________ aspects of advertising, while the new perspective stresses the __________ aspects.

16. The debate between the *traditional view* and the *new perspective* focuses on three areas:

(a) __________ or __________

(b) __________ or __________

(c) __________ or __________

17. If advertising establishes "brand loyalty," it increases the firm's market __________, and results in increased

industrial __________, according to the __________ view.

18. According to the new perspective, the ability of advertising to provide consumers with __________ about new products, increases the ability of new firms to enter markets, thereby (increasing, decreasing) __________ the price-making power of incumbent firms.

Problems and Projects

1. Listed below are descriptions of several market situations. For each case, determine whether or not the monopolistic competition model fits. Consider not only the three main characteristics of this market structure, but also the sub-characteristics discussed in the chapter.
(a) Grocery Stores: A town of 5000 inhabitants is served by two food stores. Each store features some of the same brands, but also some different brands. They tend to have slightly different prices on specific items, but discount their prices at the same times.
(b) Tourist Accommodations: About one hundred hotels, motels, and lodges compete for tourists seeking accommodation in a resort town in the Rockies. Most of these firms advertise widely. All are required by local regulations to belong to the Tourist Bureau which does some collective advertising and promotional work for all members. Each year there is some turnover in the group of firms operating in this market.
(c) Barber Shops: In a city of about 200,000, the price of haircuts is "suggested" by the union to which all barbers belong. Attempts to establish nonunion barbershops failed on three separate occasions in recent years, even though prices charged were only half of those charged in the unionized shops.
(d) Fast Food: "Hell-Hot" Barbecued Turkey Wings are only available at franchised outlets, which are limited to one per 150,000 of population and must be 10 kilometres apart. The recipe for the sauce used to coat the turkey wings before barbecuing is "secret" and, although there have been attempts, no one has come close to producing its special taste and aroma.

2. Roma Pizza is a restaurant operating as a monopolistic competitor in the neighborhood of a Canadian university. Their most popular pizza now sells for a price of $12, and is being produced for an average total cost of $10. If Roma could sell enough pizzas, they could reduce this average total cost to $8.
(a) Sketch Roma's short run situation on a graph like those used in this chapter.
(b) How and why is Roma's demand curve likely to change in the long run?
(c) What will be the effect of this demand change on Roma's profits if the restaurant continues to produce the same pizzas and engage in their current promotional activities?
(d) What happens to Roma's demand curve and average total cost curve if Roma introduces new varieties of pizzas, or higher quality pizzas, or if Roma increases advertising? Will these measures necessarily improve Roma's profits?
(e) Will Roma ever be able to sell enough pizzas to push average total cost down to $8?

True-False

Circle T if the statement is true, F if it is false.

1. Monopolistic competitors have no control over the price of their products. **T F**

2. The publisher of this study guide is a monopolistic competitor. **T F**

3. In monopolistic competition each firm determines its policies after considering the possible reactions of rival firms. **T F**

4. Like the perfect competitor, the monopolistically competitive firm faces a perfectly elastic demand curve. **T F**

5. The smaller the number of firms in an industry and the greater the extent of product differentiation, the greater will be the elasticity of the individual seller's demand curve. **T F**

6. The firm in monopolistic competition will operate, in the short run, where price equals marginal cost. **T F**

7. In the short run, firms that are monopolistically competitive may earn economic profits or losses. **T F**

8. In the long run, barriers to entry in monopolistically competitive industries usually result in sustained economic profits for the firm. **T F**

9. Productive efficiency is achieved in the long run in a monopolistically competitive industry since economic profits tend to zero for the firm. **T F**

10. In long-run equilibrium the monopolistically competitive firm operates where its long-run average cost is tangent to its demand curve. **T F**

11. Monopolistically competitive industries tend to be overcrowded with firms, each of which is under-utilized. **T F**

12. One reason why monopolistic competition is wasteful, given the products the firms produce and the extent to which they promote them, is that the average cost of production is higher than the minimum attainable level. **T F**

13. Technological innovation and product improvement are often the result of product competition in monopolistically competitive industries. **T F**

14. Through product development and advertising expenditures, a monopolistically competitive firm strives to increase revenue from the sale of its product more than nonprice competition increases its costs. **T F**

15. Advertising is a mechanism through which the firm seeks to shift its demand curve to the right and make it more elastic. **T F**

16. There is consensus among economists that from society's perspective the positive effects of advertising outweigh the negative effects. **T F**

17. One pro-competitive view of advertising is that advertising increases knowledge of available products so that consumers are more aware of substitutes. **T F**

18. Those who contend that advertising contributes to the growth of monopoly argue that the advertising by established firms makes entry more difficult for new firms. **T F**

19. Both the pure competition and monopolistic competition models predict that a process of entry or exodus will result in economic profits tending towards zero in the long run. **T F**

20. Differences between individual firms' products have economic significance whether the differences are real or merely imagined by consumers. **T F**

21. In both the pure competition and monopolistic competition models, production takes place in the long run at the minimum point of the average cost curve. **T F**

Multiple-Choice

Circle the letter that corresponds to the best answer.

1. Which of the following is not characteristic of monopolistic competition?
(a) product differentiation
(b) a relatively large number of firms
(c) collusive agreements among firms
(d) relatively easy industry entry in the long run

2. Which of the following is not a form of product differentiation used in the clothing industry?
(a) quality
(b) warranties
(c) advertising
(d) pricing

3. A similarity between a monopoly firm and a monopolistically competitive firm is that they both:
(a) earn economic profits in the long run
(b) operate where price equals marginal cost in the short run
(c) operate at the minimum point of their long-run average cost in the long run
(d) face downward sloping demand curves
(e) both produce at minimum average total cost

4. In the short run, a monopolistically competitive firm:
(a) obtains an economic profit
(b) breaks even
(c) suffers an economic loss
(d) may have an economic profit or loss or break even

5. A monopolistically competitive firm is producing at an output level in the short run where average total cost

is $3.50, price is $3.00, marginal revenue is $1.50, and marginal cost is $1.50. This firm is operating:
(a) with a loss
(b) with a profit
(c) at the break-even level of output
(d) where its demand curve is tangent to its average cost curve.

Questions 6 through 9 are based on the following graph showing a monopolistically competitive firm in short-run equilibrium. The firm is part of an increasing-cost industry.

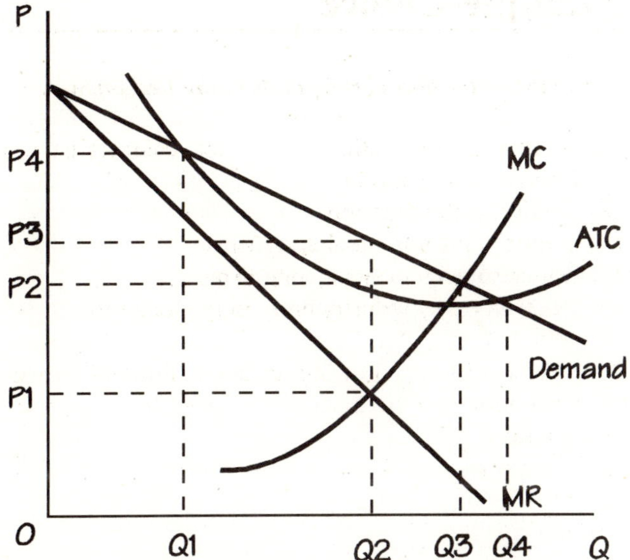

6. The equilibrium output for this firm will be:
(a) *Q1*
(b) *Q2*
(c) *Q3*
(d) *Q4*

7. The firm's profit-maximizing price will be:
(a) *P1*
(b) *P2*
(c) *P3*
(d) *P4*

8. At this equilibrium the firm will:
(a) realize an economic profit and remain in business
(b) suffer an economic loss and eventually exit
(c) suffer an economic loss and remain in business
(d) break even and eventually exit

9. If firms enter this industry in the long run:
(a) the ATC curve will shift up and demand will decrease
(b) the ATC curve will shift up and demand will increase
(c) the MR curve will shift up and demand will decrease
(d) the MR curve will shift up and demand will increase

10. For the monopolistic competitor who is enjoying an economic profit, given the product the firm is producing and the extent to which the firm is promoting it, in the long run:
(a) the firm will produce that output at which marginal cost and price are equal
(b) the elasticity of demand for the firm's product will be less than it was in the short run
(c) the number of firms in the industry will be less than they were in the short run
(d) the economic profits being earned by the firms in the industry will tend to equal zero

Questions 11 through 15 are based on the following diagram showing a monopolistic competitor in long-run equilibrium.

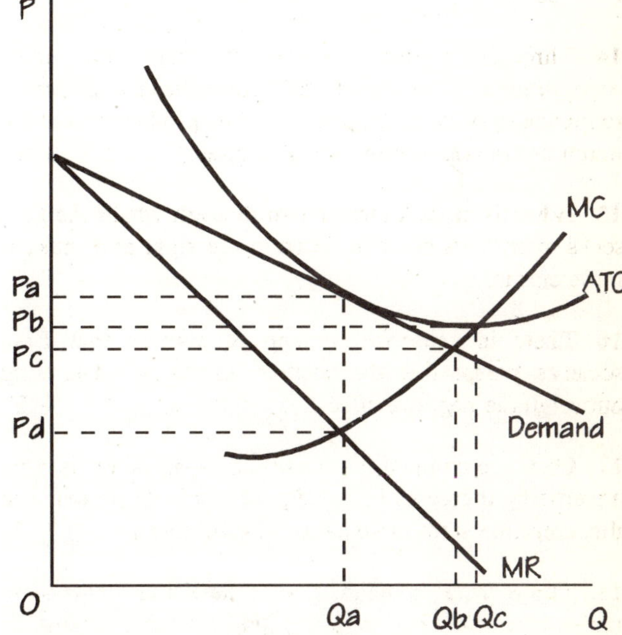

11. Long-run equilibrium output will be:
(a) *Qa*
(b) *Qb*
(c) *Qc*
(d) 0

12. Long-run equilibrium price will be:
(a) *Pa*
(b) *Pb*
(c) *Pc*
(d) *Pd*

13. This firm is:
(a) earning an economic profit
(b) covering its explicit costs but not its implicit costs
(c) earning a normal profit
(d) operating at the minimum average total cost of production

14. In order to meet the productive efficiency criterion this firm would have to produce an output of:
(a) *Qa*
(b) *Qb*
(c) *Qc*
(d) above *Qc*

15. The amount of excess capacity in this firm is:
(a) *Qb-Qa*
(b) *Qc-Qb*
(c) *Qc-Qa*
(d) there is no excess capacity in long-run equilibrium

16. The goal of advertising, according to the traditional viewpoint, is to:
(a) shift the firm's demand curve to the right and make it more elastic
(b) increase consumer awareness of substitute products
(c) increase demand in order to use up the excess capacity that exists at the long-run equilibrium price
(d) shift the demand curve to the right and make it more inelastic

17. According to the new perspective, advertising does all of the following with the exception of:
(a) providing a low-cost source of consumer information
(b) promoting economic power and concentration
(c) diminishing monopoly power by calling attention to an array of substitute goods or services
(d) facilitating the introduction of new products and, hence, enabling technological progress

18. Those who argue that advertising is inefficient are likely to think that:
(a) advertising has no effect on costs or output
(b) advertising lowers both costs and output
(c) advertising raises costs but leaves output unaffected because advertising by a number of competing firms is self-cancelling
(d) advertising raises costs but raises output substantially

19. Which of the following is not one of the features of monopolistic competition that may offset the wastes associated with such a market structure?
(a) a wider variety of products is offered to consumers
(b) much advertising is self-cancelling
(c) the quality of products improves over time
(d) consumers are better informed of the availability of substitute products

20. Even though prices may be higher under monopolistic competition than pure competition, consumers benefit from:
(a) lower prices than in the purely competitive model
(b) greater output than in the purely competitive model
(c) greater product variety than in the purely competitive model
(d) less advertising expenses than in the purely competitive model

Discussion Questions

1. What are the three chief characteristics of monopolistic competition? In what sense is there competition and in what sense is there monopoly in such a market?

2. What is meant by product differentiation? By what methods can products be differentiated? What methods are used in the markets for breakfast cereals, perfumes, rock music, and clothing?

3. "Product differentiation injects both an element of competition and an element of monopoly into a market." Evaluate this claim.

4. What is the difference between the elasticity of the demand curve faced by the monopolistically competitive firm and the purely competitive firm? What two factors determine just how elastic that demand curve will be?

5. What output will the monopolistic competitor produce in the short run, and what price will it charge for its product? Illustrate these results with a graph. What determines whether the firm will earn profits or suffer losses in the short run?

6. In the long run, what level of economic profits will the individual monopolistically competitive firm tend to receive? Why is this just a tendency? What forces economic profits toward this level?

7. Why will the firm produce a long-run output smaller than the most "efficient" output? In answering this question, assume that the firm is producing a given product and selling it with a given amount of promotional activity.

8. Using a graph that includes the average total cost curve and the demand curve, show why it is impossible for a monopolistic competitor who is both maximizing profit and making zero economic profit to also be producing at the minimum point on the average total cost curve.

9. What methods, other than price cutting, can an individual monopolistic competitor employ to attempt to protect and increase its profits in the long run?

10. How do product differentiation and product development tend to offset the "wastes" associated with monopolistic competition?

11. Does advertising result in a waste of resources, or does it promote a more efficient utilization of resources? What arguments can be presented to support the contention that it is wasteful and detrimental, and what claims are made to support the view that it is beneficial to the economy? What empirical evidence is there?

12. How is it possible for consumers to get a lower price with advertising than they would in the absence of advertising?

13. How is it possible that advertising efforts of firms may be offsetting and lead to higher prices for consumers?

14. When is a monopolistic competitor in long-run equilibrium, with respect to the price it is charging, the product it is producing, and the extent to which it is promoting its product?

15. Why does it make sense for a monopolistic competitor to advertise whereas it does not make sense for a perfect competitor?

Answers

Fill-in questions

1. relatively large number of, differentiated; do not; price, nonprice; fairly easy

2. limited

3. product quality, services, location, promotion and packaging

4. (a) more, less (b) rival firms, product differentiation

5. marginal cost, marginal revenue; demand

6. reduce, increase

7. average cost, zero, greater than

8. zero; (a) differentiation; (b) financial barriers; (c) less than

9. price, marginal cost, average total cost

10. price, greater than; average total cost

11. under-utilized, competitive

12. differentiation, development, advertising

13. variety, quality

14. to the right, decrease

15. negative, positive

16. (a) persuasion, information; (b) concentration, competition; (c) wastefulness, efficiency

17. share, concentration, traditional

18. information, decreasing

Problems and projects

2. (b) Economic profits will attract new firms, shifting Roma's demand curve to the left as their market share falls, and making it more elastic as the number of substitutes increases; (c) Roma's profits will tend towards zero; (d) If these nonprice competition strategies are successful, Roma's demand curve will decrease less than otherwise (or could even increase). Their demand will not become as elastic is otherwise. The average total cost curve will also increase, so Roma's profits may not improve; (e) No; entry of competitors will prevent Roma from gaining market share, and in long run equilibrium Roma's output will have excess capacity.

True-False

1. F	**2.** T	**3.** F	**4.** F	**5.** F	**6.** F
7. T	**8.** F	**9.** F	**10.** T	**11.** T	**12.** T
13. T	**14.** T	**15.** F	**16.** F	**17.** T	**18.** T
19. T	**20.** T	**21.** F			

Multiple-Choice

1. (c)	**2.** (d)	**3.** (d)	**4.** (d)	**5.** (a)	**6.** (b)
7. (c)	**8.** (a)	**9.** (a)	**10.** (d)	**11.** (a)	**12.** (a)
13. (c)	**14.** (c)	**15.** (c)	**16.** (d)	**17.** (b)	**18.** (c)
19. (b)	**20.** (c)				

CHAPTER 13

Price and Output Determination: Oligopoly

This is the last of four chapters on market structures, and in some ways it is the most difficult. To date, economics offers less definite answers on the topic of oligopoly than on the topics of pure competition, pure monopoly, or monopolistic competition. The reason for this is that under the umbrella of oligopoly are classified a wide variety of market situations that lead to a wide variety of businesses behaviours. Oligopoly may be the type of market structure most prevalent--or at least, most important--in the Canadian economy.

The basic concept of oligopoly is easy to grasp--a few firms that are mutually interdependent and that dominate the market for their product. They may sell either differentiated or homogeneous products. The degree to which a few firms dominate a market can be measured using a concentration ratio or the Herfindahl index. The small number of firms is due to entry barriers. Firms are mutually interdependent because each firm holds a large market share; if one firm sells more by cutting price, advertising more, or developing new products, their rivals will lose sales, and might respond with some competitive strategies of their own. A firm considering initiating a competitive action is well aware of this, and will choose its actions with such reactions in mind.

A demand curve shows the quantity demanded at various prices. But for the oligopolist a unique demand curve does not exist because any time the firm changes its price rival firms may react, which in turn affects quantity demanded. Since the reaction is unknown the oligopolist cannot be certain what effect its price change will have on its own sales. What economists have done in formulating oligopoly models is to make specific assumptions about how rivals react to changes in another firm's marketing strategy. This allows a demand curve for a firm to be obtained, but any conclusions on price and output hold only if the specific assumption on rivals' reactions hold. For every different assumption of a rival's reaction there is another demand schedule, another oligopoly model, and different specific conclusions.

To stress the strategic element of oligopoly, the overview of the theory portion of this chapter is built around a simple game theory example using a two firm industry. Analysis of the payoff matrix for the two firms reveals their mutual interdependence, their incentives to collude or cooperate, and their incentives to cheat on a collusive agreement.

Four specific oligopoly models are presented briefly in Chapter 13. The first one is the kinked demand curve model, which assumes no collusion, and different reactions from rivals depending on whether the firm raises or lowers price. The firm expects that rivals will match price cuts, but will not respond to price increases. The kinked demand curve model explains why prices may be relatively inflexible in an oligopoly, but it does not explain where oligopolists set prices in the first place.

The second model assumes that there is collusion between oligopolists: whether overt as in a cartel agreement, or covert as in a "gentlemen's agreement." In either case, the collusion model (or cartel model) results in price and output results at the industry level which correspond to the pure monopoly outcome. Though OPEC provides an example of a successful cartel, the many obstacles to effective collusion usually make cartels difficult to establish and even more difficult to sustain.

In the dominant firm model or price leadership model, the largest firm--or sometimes the most efficient firm--takes the initiative in setting prices and other firms tend to follow the leader. There is no overt collusion in setting prices, but unspoken acceptance of this industry-wide pricing convention eliminates price competition. Such a practice is also described as "tacit collusion".

For some firms it is difficult to get accurate

information on demand. In such cases it is difficult determine the profit-maximizing price, so managers may simply set prices by marking up costs by some percentage which allows the firm to achieve an acceptable return on invested capital. This fourth model is often referred to as "cost-plus pricing."

In the short run there is likely some degree of allocative and productive inefficiency in oligopolistic industries. The situation in the long run is more contentious. The Schumpeter-Galbraith view is that the market power and the kind of rivalry that typify oligopoly are conducive to technological advances. An opposing view is that oligopolists may exploit their market power to impede innovation.

The final section of the chapter is an extended examination of a classic oligopoly: the North American automobile industry. Until the 1970s, three firms dominated an industry characterized by high barriers to entry, price leadership, and nonprice competition. Then the forces of foreign competition, particularly from Japanese firms, overwhelmed the North American producers and broke their domination of the auto market.

Checklist

When you have studied this chapter, you should be able to:

- ☐ Define oligopoly and distinguish between homogeneous and differentiated oligopolies.
- ☐ Calculate a concentration ratio from given data and describe the shortcomings of this measure.
- ☐ Calculate a Herfindahl index and use it to assess the distribution of market power among dominant firms in an oligopoly.
- ☐ Explain how mutual interdependence among oligopolists makes it difficult to predict how price and quantity will be determined in oligopoly.
- ☐ Identify the most significant causes of oligopoly and explain how each of these tends to result in oligopolistic industries.
- ☐ Construct a profits-payoff matrix and explain how it illustrates three characteristics of oligopoly.
- ☐ Employ the kinked demand curve model to explain why oligopoly prices tend to be inflexible.
- ☐ Give two criticisms of the kinked demand curve model.
- ☐ Explain how price and quantity would be set by colluding oligopolists who produce a homogeneous good, and who have identical cost and demand curves.
- ☐ State three forms that collusion may take, and five obstacles to collusion.
- ☐ Provide examples of how oligopolists may practice covert and overt collusion.
- ☐ Use the history of OPEC to illustrate how the cartel has worked to benefit oil producers and how obstacles to collusion eventually weakened OPEC.
- ☐ Describe how a firm employs cost-plus pricing to determine the price of its product.
- ☐ Explain the role played by nonprice competition in oligopolistic industries, and two reasons oligopolists emphasize nonprice competition.
- ☐ Compare oligopoly with the other three market models with respect to productive and allocative efficiency.
- ☐ Compare the Schumpeter-Galbraith view of oligopolistic industries as engines of economic change with the traditional view of oligopoly and explain whether the empirical evidence supports either viewpoint.
- ☐ Describe the North American automobile industry in terms of the number of sellers and their market shares, the height and kinds of barriers to entry, the method employed to set prices, the types of nonprice competition, the level of profits, the rate of technological progress, and the evolution of import competition.

Chapter Outline

1. Oligopoly is a common industry structure in the Canadian economy. An oligopoly is an industry that is dominated by a few firms. The industry may sell a product that is homogeneous across firms or differentiated.

2. The degree of domination by large firms can be measured by calculating either a concentration ratio or the Herfindahl Index. One standard for defining oligopoly is a 40% four firm concentration ratio (that is, 40% of the market is held by the largest four firms). Any numerical measure of industry concentration is subject to a number of problems relating to ambiguities in how the relevant market is defined.

3. The existence of oligopoly is usually the result of economies of scale, other barriers to entry, and the advantages of merger.

4. Applying a simple game theory model yields insights into the determination of a specific strategy by an oligopolist. Through an example of two rival producers, each having to decide whether to set price high or low, this game theory approach leads to three conclusions.
(a) The number of firms is small enough in oligopoly that any one firm's actions will change their rivals' sales and profits enough that they must anticipate their rivals' reactions, and choose their own actions accordingly. This is known as mutual interdependence.
(b) Mutual interdependence creates an incentive to collude rather than to compete, because competition simply erodes potential profits for all firms in the industry.
(c) Once a collusive agreement is reached, each firm has an incentive to cheat on the agreement.

5. Because rival firms are mutually interdependent, any firm's demand curve, although downward sloping to reflect some monopoly power, is dependent upon the marketing strategy pursued by the other firms. The uncertainty that accompanies mutual interdependence makes it difficult for an oligopolist to estimate its demand curve. Different assumptions about the specific manner in which rivals will respond lead to different versions of the demand curve, and differing decisions for the profit-maximizing pricing and output. Economists have devised a number of oligopoly models based on different reaction assumptions. The chapter presents four such models to illustrate the range of pricing practices of oligopolists.

6. In the kinked demand curve model, which is a noncollusive model, each firm believes that when it lowers its price its rivals will lower their prices, and when it increases its price, its rivals will not increase their prices. The firm is, therefore, reluctant to change its price, and even if their variable cost curve shifts, they may change price unless the cost shift is large. This model, while providing a theory for inflexible prices, does not explain how prices are set in the first place.

7. The game theory approach to oligopolistic behaviour suggests that mutual interdependence can lead rival firms to collude to reach and maintain acceptable profit levels.
(a) Firms that collude tend to set their price and joint output at the same level at which a pure monopolist would set them.
(b) Among the several methods of collusion that firms may use are the cartel and gentlemen's agreement.
(c) Collusive arrangements tend to self-destruct over time. The obstacles to collusion are: demand and cost differences, too many firms, potential for entry by new firms, cheating on industry agreements, and legal prohibitions.
(d) In the OPEC oil cartel, collusion worked to increase price and profits during the 1970s, but obstacles to collusion reduced the market power of the cartel during the 1980s.

8. Price leadership is a form of covert collusion or gentlemen's agreement in which one firm initiates price changes and the other firms in the industry follow their lead.
(a) Price adjustments are made infrequently and occur only in response to significant changes in cost or demand conditions.
(b) The price leader communicates the price change to other firms through speeches, public announcements, etc.
(c) The announced price may not maximize short-run profits but may be designed to deter entry, and therefore maximize long-run profits.

9. In the cost-plus pricing model, a firm determines its per unit costs, and then adds some percentage markup in order to set the price. Such a markup is designed to yield a target rate of return on invested capital.
(a) Cost-plus pricing can produce similar results to collusion if rival firms have similar costs.
(b) Cost-plus pricing is more attractive to multiproduct oligopolists who find it difficult to estimate demand on many of their products.

10. Oligopolistic firms tend to avoid price competition, but where possible they engage in nonprice competition. Nonprice competition is preferred because: 1) price cuts are easily duplicated by rivals and could lead to price wars that devastate revenues; 2) nonprice competition is more unique and can be designed to influence a particular segment of the total market; and 3) oligopolists usually have the resources to devote to advertising and product development.

11. To compare the efficiency of an oligopolist with that of a pure competitor is difficult.
(a) Economists who hold the so called competitive view

believe that oligopoly is like monopoly in failing to generate either allocative or productive efficiency.
(b) Schumpeter and Galbraith have argued that oligopoly promotes rapid technological progress (dynamic efficiency).
(c) While the evidence is not conclusive, it appears that large firms have not been responsible for most of the world's important inventions, and the structure of an industry may not affect its technological progress.

12. The automobile industry in North America is an example of an oligopoly dominated by a few large firms; substantial barriers to entry; price leadership; styling competition among the sellers; and significant import competition from foreign producers. Over the long term the barriers to entry have proven less insurmountable than they once appeared.

Terms and Concepts

cartel
collusion
collusive oligopoly
competitive view
concentration ratio
cost-plus pricing
duopoly
game theory model
gentlemen's agreement
Herfindahl Index
homogeneous and differentiated oligopoly
import competition
interindustry competition
kinked demand curve
mutual interdependence
oligopoly
price leadership
price war
traditional and Schumpeter-Galbraith views

Hints and Tips

1. Table 10-1 should be reviewed to see exactly how the structural conditions of oligopoly compare with the conditions of the other market structures studied in Chapters 10, 11, and 12.

2. There is no standard model of oligopoly. You should be sure to know the different assumptions that give rise to each of the four models presented in this chapter.

Fill-In Questions

1. Oligopoly exists when a __________ large firms, producing a __________ or __________ product, dominate a market which is difficult for new firms to __________.

2. A four-firm concentration ratio is calculated by dividing the sales of the __________ firms in the industry by the sales of the __________. An industry is usually considered an oligopoly when this concentration ratio is at least _____%.

3. The concentration ratio measure does not reflect the __________ of market power among the __________ firms in the industry. The __________ Index overcomes this problem by calculating the __________ of the __________ market shares of __________ firms in the industry.

4. The three major underlying causes of oligopoly are economies of __________, ownership of __________, and __________.

5. The basics of strategic behaviour by oligopolists can be understood from a __________ theory perspective.

6. A __________ is a two-firm oligopoly.

7. Oligopolists are mutually __________ because one firm's actions have (significant, insignificant) __________ impacts on the profits of rival firms. This means that when setting price each producer must consider the __________ of rivals. The monopolist does not face this problem because it has __________ rivals;

the pure competitor and monopolistic competitor do not face it because they have __________ rivals.

8. A price-profit payoff matrix for two oligopolists indicates the __________ generated when the two firms charge various __________. The pay-off matrix calls attention to: (1) the __________, (2) the tendency to __________ that characterizes the oligopolistic market structure, and (3) the financial rewards from __________.

9. Unlike pure competition or monopoly there is no one economic model that can be applied to all oligopolistic industries. Oligopoly is in fact (one, a small number of, many) __________ specific market situation(s) determined by how rivals react to the marketing strategy pursued by the firm.

10. The four models of oligopolistic behaviour discussed in this chapter are:

(a) ____________________

(b) ____________________

(c) ____________________

(d) ____________________

11. Oligopoly prices tend to be (flexible, inflexible) __________ and oligopolists tend to change their prices (independently, simultaneously) __________.

12. The kinked demand curve that the individual noncolluding oligopolist sees for its product is highly (elastic, inelastic) __________ at prices above the current price, and tends to be only slightly __________ or __________ below that price. This kinked demand reflects the assumption that if the oligopolist raises its price, its rivals (will, will not) __________ raise their prices, and if it lowers its price its rivals __________ lower their prices.

13. Since there is a kink in the demand curve there will be a gap in the __________ curve so that small changes in the marginal cost curve (will, will not) __________ cause price to change.

14. When oligopolists collude, the price they set and their combined output tend to be the same as would be set in a __________ industry.

15. A cartel is a formal agreement among sellers in which the __________ and the total __________ of the product and each seller's __________ of the market are specified. A cartel is an example of a (collusive, noncollusive) __________ oligopoly. A gentlemen's agreement is (a formal, an informal) __________ agreement on prices or market shares.

16. A cartel is an example of (overt, tacit) __________ collusion, while a gentlemen's agreement is an example of (overt, tacit) __________ collusion.

17. Six obstacles to collusion among oligopolists are:

(a) ____________________

(b) ____________________

(c) ____________________

(d) ____________________

(e) ____________________

(f) ____________________

18. __________ is an international oil cartel whose market power has declined in recent years because of at least three obstacles to __________.

(a) One reason for the decline was the (increase, decrease) __________ in oil prices during the 1970s that (attracted, discouraged) __________ new entrants into oil production.

(b) A second reason was the (increase, decrease) __________ in the demand for oil during the early 1980s because of recession and (increased, decreased)

__________ use of alternative energy sources.

(c) A third reason was (fair-play, cheating) __________ among cartel members and the (similarity, diversity) __________ of economic circumstances among the members.

19. When one firm in an oligopoly is usually the first to change its price and the other firms follow with similar price changes, there is probably a type of (overt, tacit) __________ collusion called __________.

20. A strategy of setting price at a level that will discourage new entry is called __________ pricing.

21. A firm employing cost-plus pricing applies some __________ markup over their __________ cost of production to determine their price.

22. A market that firms can enter or leave with virtually no costs is called a __________ market. In such markets, the number of firms in the industry (is, is not) __________ predictive of pricing behaviour by existing firms.

23. There tends to be very little (price, nonprice) __________ competition among oligopolists and a great deal of __________ competition, which they use to determine each firm's __________.

24. The oligopolistic firm produces where price (is greater than, equals) __________ marginal cost and short of the output where average __________ is minimized. The firm (does, does not) __________ meet the conditions for __________ and __________ efficiency. The output and price of the oligopolist is more likely to be similar to that of a __________ rather than a pure __________.

25. In the Schumpeter-Galbraith view of oligopoly:

(a) only oligopolists have both the __________ and the __________ to be technologically progressive;

(b) over time the oligopolies will bring about a more rapid rate of __________, and lower __________ and prices than the same industry competitively organized.

26. The market structure of the North American auto industry can be characterized as (monopolistic, oligopolistic) __________, with price __________ and nonprice competition that has focused on __________.

(a) In recent decades, competition from __________ reduced the market power of the domestic industry. The industry responded by lobbying government for __________ on Japanese cars.

(b) The industry also arranged joint ventures with (domestic, foreign) __________ producers, thereby serving to (increase, decrease) __________ mutual interdependence worldwide among automobile producers.

(c) Foreign competition has also altered the role of __________ that was formerly played by General Motors.

Problems and Projects

1. The following are hypothetical sales data for VCR producers that manufacture in Canada:

Firm	1992 Sales million $	1992 Market Share	1995 Sales million $	1995 Market Share
Alpha	15	_____	15	_____
Beta	20	_____	20	_____
Delta	10	_____	10	_____
Poseidon	40	_____	30	_____
Gamma	60	_____	45	_____
Omicron	75	_____	100	_____
Omega	25	_____	25	_____
Epsilon	5	_____	5	_____

(a) Calculate the four firm concentration ratio for 1992 and use the result to determine what type of market structure these firms operate in.

(b) Calculate the Herfindahl index for 1992.
(c) Give at least two reasons why the concentration ratio or Herfindahl index might overstate the amount of monopoly power held by these Canadian manufacturers of VCRs.
(d) Recalculate the concentration ratio and Herfindahl ratio using 1995 data. What shortcoming of the concentration ratio calculation is revealed by comparing the 1992 and 1995 results on these two indicators of market power?

2. Suppose that the market for a particular computer chip is controlled by two manufacturers: Apogee and Bristol. There is no brand loyalty so each firm's profit depends only on their pricing strategy, and that of their rival. Each firm can set a high or low price, and neither firm knows what strategy its rival will follow. If both charge a high price, the profits will be $25 million for Apogee and $18 million for Bristol. If both charge a low price, profits will be $6 million for Apogee and $5 million for Bristol. If Apogee charges a high price and Bristol a low price, Apogee's profits will be $2 million and Bristol's profits will be $30 million. If Apogee charges a low price and Bristol charges a high price, Apogee's profits will be $35 million and Bristol's will be $3 million.
(a) Set up a profit-payoff matrix showing each firm's profits under the different possible pricing outcomes.
(b) If Bristol sets a high price, Apogee gets a higher profit by setting a (high, low) ________ price. If Bristol sets a low price, Apogee gets a higher profit by setting a ________ price. Therefore, if acting noncollusively, Apogee will set a ________ price.
(c) If Apogee sets a high price, Bristol gets a higher profit by setting a (high, low) ________ price. If Apogee sets a low price, Bristol gets a higher profit by setting a ________ price. Therefore, if acting noncollusively, Bristol will set a ________ price.
(d) If the two firms behave noncollusively, Apogee will get a profit of $________ and Bristol will get a profit of $________. Their combined profits will be $________. These profits (are, are not) ________ the maximum possible.
(e) Given the result in (d), Apogee and Bristol (will, will not) ________ have an incentive to collude. If they collude they would agree to set a ________ price, resulting in a combined profit of $________.
(f) If Apogee and Bristol form a collusive agreement, Apogee (will, will not) ________ have an incentive to cheat on the agreement. If Apogee cheats--and Bristol does not--Apogee's profits would (increase, decrease) ________ by $________. Similarly, if Bristol cheats--and Apogee does not--Bristol's profits would (increase, decrease) ________ by $________. Therefore, there is a strong possibility that the collusive agreement, if formed, (would, would not) ________ last long.

3. Mammoth Enterprises competes in homogeneous oligopoly in which all firms set price at $15. At this price Mammoth sells 10 units. Mammoth believes that if they raise their price their rivals will maintain a price of $15. Mammoth also believes that if they cut their price their rivals will match the price cut. Accordingly, Mammoth expects to sell 2 units less for every $1 price increase above $15, 1 unit more for every $1 cut in price.
(a) Fill in the table showing the firm's demand schedule, total revenue, marginal revenue, and marginal cost.

Price	Qd	TR	MR	MC
$18	____	$____		
			$____	$6
17	____	____		
			____	7
16	____	____		
			____	8
15	____	____		
			____	9
14	____	____		
			____	10
13	____	____		
			____	11
12	____	____		
			____	12
11	____	____		

(b) In the graph on the next page, plot Mammoth's demand, marginal revenue and marginal cost curves. (Be sure to plot the marginal revenue and marginal cost curves at the midpoint of the two quantities involved in the calculation for each.)
(c) Use the graph to confirm that Mammoth's profit-

maximizing price is $15 and output is 10 under these assumptions about costs and demand.
(d) How much can Mammoth's marginal cost shift up or down before Mammoth will choose to change their price?
(e) Suppose Mammoth's marginal cost shifts up by $3 at each and every level of output. Show the new marginal cost curve on the graph.
(f) Determine from the graph what Mammoth's new price and quantity would be after this increase in marginal costs.

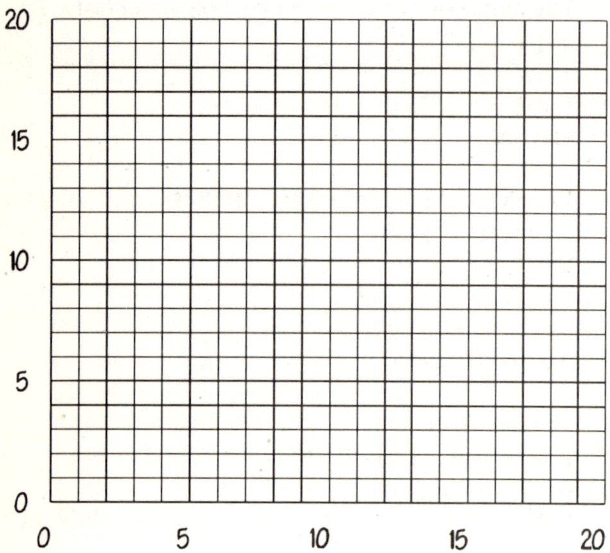

4. There are two firms, A and B, in an industry in which entry is blocked. The equation for the industry demand curve is: $P = 30 - 2Q$ where Q is the sum of the quantities sold by A and B. Neither firm has any costs. Firm A is the industry leader and Firm B always sells one-half of the number of units that Firm A sells; i.e., if A places 10 units on the market then B places 5 units.
(a) Fill in the table below.

A's Output	B's Output	Industry Output	Industry Price	A's Profit
1	_____	_____	_____	_____
2	_____	_____	_____	_____
3	_____	_____	_____	_____
4	_____	_____	_____	_____
5	_____	_____	_____	_____
6	_____	_____	_____	_____
7	_____	_____	_____	_____

(b) How many units should A place on the market to maximize its profits? What will be the industry price?

True-False

Circle T if the statement is true, F if it is false.

1. The products produced by oligopolistic firms may be either standardized or differentiated. **T F**

2. An oligopoly contains a few large firms that act independently of one another. **T F**

3. An oligopolistic firm ignores the possible reactions of its rivals to its decisions on price, advertising, or product development. **T F**

4. A four-firm concentration ratio of 64 percent in oil refining would mean that the largest four firms accounted for 64 percent of the industry's shipments. **T F**

5. Concentration ratios are used by economists as indicators of monopoly power. **T F**

6. Concentration ratios are low in those industries that are oligopolies. **T F**

7. Concentration ratios based on domestic firms understate monopoly power since they do not take into account competition from imports. **T F**

8. An alternative measure of industry concentration is the Herfindahl Index, which is calculated as the square of the number of firms in the industry. **T F**

9. The larger the Herfindahl Index the greater the degree of market power in the industry. **T F**

10. Two industries can have the same concentration ratio yet have different Herfindahl index values. **T F**

11. A key uncertainty that exists in oligopolies is the uncertainty faced by each firm on how its rivals will react if it changes its price. **T F**

12. Mergers can increase market concentration. **T F**

13. Entries in a profit-payoff matrix give the market shares of two firms resulting from pursuing various pricing strategies. **T F**

14. Entries in a profit-payoff matrix reflect the mutual interdependence that characterizes the oligopoly market model. **T F**

15. Oligopolistic prices tend to be inflexible or "sticky." **T F**

16. The kinked demand curve analysis provides an explanation of why prices tend to be "sticky" in oligopolistic industries. **T F**

17. Collusion occurs when firms in an industry reach an explicit or tacit agreement to fix prices, divide or share the market, and in some way restrict competition among firms. **T F**

18. Other things being equal, the larger the number of firms the easier it is to achieve a cartel. **T F**

19. The practice of price leadership is almost always based on a formal written or oral agreement. **T F**

20. The price leader determines and signals the profit-maximizing price for the industry and other firms then charge a near identical price. **T F**

21. The markup the firm uses in cost-plus pricing is determined by the rate of return the firm is seeking on its investment. **T F**

22. Price competition between firms is the most distinctive characteristic of oligopoly. **T F**

23. Nonprice competition is the typical method of determining each oligopolist's share of the total market. **T F**

24. Both productive and allocative efficiency are likely to be achieved in oligopolistic markets. **T F**

25. The Schumpeter-Galbraith view is that the oligopolistic market structure fosters product improvement and technological change. **T F**

26. Almost all the important technological advances between 1880 and 1965 can be attributed to research and development activities within firms operating in oligopolies or monopolies. **T F**

Multiple-Choice

Circle the letter that corresponds to the best answer.

1. The number of firms in an oligopolistic industry is:
(a) one
(b) a few
(c) many
(d) very many

2. Which of the following is the best example of a homogeneous oligopoly?
(a) the steel industry
(b) the beer industry
(c) the grain industry
(d) the breakfast cereal industry

3. Concentration ratios take into account:
(a) interindustry competition
(b) import competition
(c) the existence of separate local markets for products
(d) none of the above

4. Industry A is populated by four firms that hold market shares of 70, 15, 10, and 5. The Herfindahl Index value for this industry is:
(a) 100
(b) 10
(c) 5250
(d) 17.636

5. Which of the following does not contribute to the existence of oligopoly?
(a) the economies of large-scale production
(b) the gains in profits that result from mergers
(c) high barriers to entry
(d) the profits that result from cheating on a cartel agreement

Questions 6 through 10 are based on the following payoff matrix for a duopoly. The numbers in the matrix represent the profit in thousands of dollars for a high-price or low-price strategy.

		Firm A	
		High-price	Low-price
Firm B	High-price	A = 600 B = 600	A = 875 B = 200
	Low-price	A = 200 B = 875	A = 350 B = 350

6. If both firms collude to maximize joint profits, the total profits for the two firms will be:
(a) $700
(b) $1075
(c) $1200
(d) $1475

7. If Firm A pursues a high-price strategy and Firm B a low-price strategy, then Firm A's profit will be:
(a) $200
(b) $350
(c) $600
(d) $875

8. If Firm A always pursues a high-price strategy, the best strategy for Firm B is:
(a) a low-price strategy for earnings of $875
(b) a low-price strategy for earnings of $350
(c) a high-price strategy for earnings of $600
(d) a high-price strategy for earnings of $275

9. Suppose both firms collude and agree to follow a high-price strategy. If Firm B now cheats and follows a low-price strategy, it will:
(a) gain an extra $400
(b) gain an extra $275
(c) decrease its profit by $675
(d) decrease its profit by $150

10. If both firms act independently and do not collude, the most likely result is:
(a) $600 for Firm A and $600 for Firm B
(b) $875 for Firm A and $200 for Firm B
(c) $200 for Firm A and $875 for Firm B
(d) $350 for Firm A and $350 for Firm B

11. Mutual interdependence is only characteristic of:
(a) pure and monopolistic competition
(b) monopolistic competition and oligopoly
(c) pure competition and oligopoly
(d) oligopoly

12. Mutual interdependence means that:
(a) each firm produces a product similar but not identical to the products produced by its rivals
(b) each firm produces a product identical to the products produced by its rivals
(c) each firm must consider the reactions of its rivals when it determines its price policy
(d) each firm faces a perfectly elastic demand for its product

Use the following diagram to answer question 13.

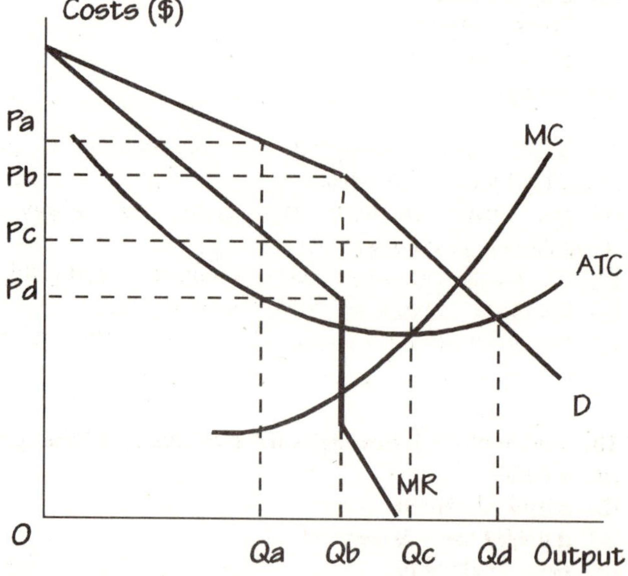

13. The profit-maximizing price and output for this oligopolistic firm is:
(a) P_a and Q_a
(b) P_b and Q_b
(c) P_c and Q_c
(d) P_d and Q_d

14. In the kinked demand curve model, an individual oligopolist's demand curve is:
(a) more inelastic above the going price than below the going price
(b) more elastic above the going price than below the going price
(c) elastic above the going price and inelastic below the

going price
(d) of unitary elasticity at the going price

15. There is a kink in the oligopolist's demand curve at the going price if the oligopolist believes that:
(a) competitor firms will match both price cuts and price increases
(b) competitor firms will match neither price cuts nor price increases
(c) competitor firms will not notice either price cuts or price increases
(d) competitor firms will match price cuts but not price increases

16. In the oligopolistic market structure the kinked demand analysis provides an explanation of:
(a) barriers to entry
(b) "sticky" prices
(c) price leadership
(d) mergers

17. Which of the following is a shortcoming of the kinked demand curve model?
(a) the model suggests that prices are relatively inflexible under oligopoly
(b) the model suggests that costs fluctuate unpredictably
(c) the model is based on product differentiation
(d) the model does not explain how price is determined in the first place

18. Which of the following is not a means of colluding?
(a) a cartel
(b) a kinked demand curve
(c) a gentlemen's agreement
(d) price leadership

19. Oligopolists tend to collude because collusive control over the price they charge permits them to:
(a) increase their profits
(b) decrease their uncertainties
(c) deter the entry of new firms into their industry
(d) do all of the above

20. For collusion to be successful, oligopolists must be able to:
(a) keep prices and profits as low as possible
(b) block or restrict the entry of new producers
(c) engage in technological improvements of their products
(d) reduce legal obstacles that protect market power

21. When oligopolists collude, the results are generally:
(a) greater output and higher price
(b) greater output and lower price
(c) smaller output and lower price
(d) smaller output and higher price

22. Which of the following constitutes an obstacle to collusion among oligopolists?
(a) a general business recession
(b) a small number of firms in the industry
(c) a homogeneous product
(d) the patent laws

23. The prices of products produced in an industry characterized by price leadership tend to be:
(a) relatively flexible and when firms change prices they are apt to change them at the same time
(b) relatively inflexible and when firms change prices they are not apt to change them at the same time
(c) relatively inflexible and when firms change prices they are apt to change them at the same time
(d) relatively flexible and when firms change prices they are not apt to change them at the same time

24. The price leader in an oligopolistic industry:
(a) necessarily sets the price that maximizes industry profit
(b) determines production quotas for each firm
(c) is usually the largest or most efficient firm in the industry
(d) is assured that other firms will initiate similar price changes

25. Oligopolistic firms that produce a variety of products and are unable to estimate demand for their products would tend to use which price strategy?
(a) cost-plus pricing
(b) price leadership
(c) price wars
(d) price inflexibility

26. Market shares in oligopolistic industries are usually determined on the basis of:
(a) tacit collusion
(b) nonprice competition
(c) gentlemen's agreements
(d) joint profit maximization

27. It is the belief of Schumpeter and Galbraith that an industry organized oligopolistically, when compared with

the same industry organized competitively, would, over time:
(a) foster more rapid improvement in the quality of the good or service produced
(b) bring about a greater reduction in the average cost of producing the product
(c) lower the price of the product by a larger percentage
(d) all of the above

Discussion Questions

1. What are the essential characteristics of an oligopoly? How does oligopoly differ from monopolistic competition? How is oligopoly like a chess game whereas monopolistic competition is not?

2. Explain how the concentration ratio and the Herfindahl Index in a particular industry are computed. What is the relationship between these measures and monopoly power?

3. What are the shortcomings of the concentration ratio and the Herfindahl index as measures of the extent of competition in an industry?

4. What are the underlying causes of oligopoly?

5. What do "mutual interdependence" and "uncertainty" mean with respect to oligopoly?

6. Why is it difficult to determine the demand curve for the output of a single oligopolist, and why does this result in the proliferation of oligopoly models rather than just one general model as in pure competition or monopoly?

7. What assumptions give rise to the kinked demand curve? How can the kinked demand curve be used to explain why oligopoly prices are relatively inflexible? Under what conditions will an oligopolist who believes it faces a kinked demand choose to change price?

8. Why do producers find it advantageous to collude? What are the obstacles to collusion?

9. Explain:
(a) a cartel
(b) gentlemen's agreement
(c) price leadership
(d) cost-plus pricing

10. Why do oligopolists engage in little price competition and in extensive nonprice competition?

11. Contrast the Schumpeter-Galbraith view on the dynamic economic efficiency of oligopoly with the traditional view. What does the empirical evidence have to say about sources of technological progress in industrialized countries?

12. Describe the North American automobile industry using the following criteria: (a) the number of firms and their market shares; (b) the barriers to entry; (c) the means used to establish the prices of automobiles; (d) the role of nonprice competition; (e) profits; (f) technological progress.

13. Explain the causes of and the effects of foreign competition on the North American automobile industry during the past two decades.

Answers

Fill-in questions

1. few, standardized, differentiated, enter

2. largest four, whole industry; 40

3. distribution; Herfindahl, sum, squares, all

4. scale, key resources, mergers

5. game

6. duopoly

7. interdependent, significant; reactions; no; many

8. profits; prices; (1) mutual interdependence, (2) collusion, (3) cheating

9. many

10. (a) kinked demand; (b) collusive pricing; (c) price

leadership; (d) cost-plus pricing

11. inflexible, simultaneously

12. elastic, elastic, inelastic; will not, will

13. marginal revenue, will not

14. pure monopoly

15. price, output, share; collusive; informal

16. overt, tacit

17. (a) demand and cost differences; (b) cheating (secret price concessions); (c) a large number of firms; (d) a recession; (e) potential entrants; (f) legal obstacles (anti-combines legislation)

18. OPEC, collusion; (a) increase, attracted; (b) decrease, increased; (c) cheating, diversity

19. tacit, price leadership

20. limit

21. percentage, average

22. contestable; is not

23. price, nonprice, market share

24. greater than, cost; does not, productive, allocative; monopolist, competitor

25. (a) means, incentive; (b) product improvement, costs

26. oligopolistic, leadership, styling and technology; (a) imports, import quotas; (b) foreign, increase; (c) price leadership

Problems and projects

1. (a) 80%; (b) 1952; (c) import competition is not reflected, competition from other industries that might produce substitutable products is not reflected; (d) 80%, 2288; The concentration ratio does not reflect distribution of market shares among firms. The total market share held by the largest firms did not change from 1992 to 1995, but Omicron grew larger relative to other large firms.

2. (a)

		APOGEE High-price	APOGEE Low-price
BRISTOL	High-price	A = 25 B = 18	A = 35 B = 3
	Low-price	A = 2 B = 30	A = 6 B = 5

(b) low, low, low; (c) low, low, low; (d) 6 million, 5 million; 11 million; are not; (e) will; high; 43 million; (f) will; increase, 10 million; increase, 12 million; would not.

3. (a) Quantity demanded: 4, 6, 8, 10, 11, 12, 13, 14; Total Revenue: $72, 102, 128, 150, 154, 156, 156, 154; Marginal Revenue: $15, 13, 11, 4, 2, 0, -2; (d) $1.50 per unit up or down; (f) new P = $15.50, new Q = 9.

4. Firm A Output: 1, 2, 3, 4, 5, 6, 7; Firm B Output: .5, 1, 1.5, 2, 2.5, 3, 3.5; Industry Output: 1.5, 3, 4.5, 6, 7.5, 9, 10.5; Industry Price: $27, $24, $21, $18, $15, $12, $9; A's Profit: $27, $48, $63, $72, $75, $72, $63; Profit-maximizing output Firm A: 5 units, Price: $15.

True-False

1. T **2.** F **3.** F **4.** T **5.** T **6.** F
7. T **8.** F **9.** T **10.** T **11.** T **12.** T
13. F **14.** T **15.** T **16.** T **17.** T **18.** F
19. F **20.** T **21.** T **22.** F **23.** T **24.** F
25. T **26.** F

Multiple-Choice

1. (b) **2.** (a) **3.** (d) **4.** (c) **5.** (d) **6.** (c)
7. (a) **8.** (a) **9.** (b) **10.** (d) **11.** (d) **12.** (c)
13. (b) **14.** (b) **15.** (d) **16.** (b) **17.** (d) **18.** (b)
19. (d) **20.** (b) **21.** (d) **22.** (a) **23.** (c) **24.** (c)
25. (a) **26.** (b) **27.** (d)

CHAPTER 14

Government Competition Policy and Regulation of Monopolies

Chapter 14 examines a number of ways in which the federal government has attempted to modify how industries operate. The first focus is on anti-combines laws and monopoly regulation--two approaches designed to prevent collusion or abuse of monopoly power. The second focus is on social regulations which are designed to lessen undesirable side effects that result from the production or consumption of certain goods. Finally, the chapter touches on industrial policies implemented by governments seeking to promote or deter the growth of production, technology, employment, etc., in particular industries or sectors of the economy.

Industrial concentration leads to monopoly power--whether the industry is a monopoly or an oligopoly. Monopoly power leads to inefficiency in resource allocation, may slow technological progress, and may promote income inequality. Defenders of concentration argue that concentration is often the result of superior product development or technological innovation, and that economies of scale can only be exploited if there are few firms. Perhaps because the effects of concentration are complicated and conflicting, the Canadian government's policies in this area have not been consistent.

Canada's earliest legislation to control monopoly was passed in 1889. By 1892 it became a criminal offence to restrict trade or competition. This was followed in 1910 by the Combines Investigation Act which established a specific mechanism for investigating and prosecuting alleged combines (conspiracies between firms to restrict competition). Despite numerous changes to the legislation over several decades, very few prosecutions occurred under this Act, largely because of the heavy burden of proof for prosecution under the Criminal Code. In 1986, the Competition Act was enacted to replace the Combines Investigation Act, and jurisdiction was shifted from the criminal law to civil law, making it easier to prosecute monopolies and mergers detrimental to the public interest. Another theme of the recent changes has been to recognize certain trade-offs between the goal of competition in the Canadian economy and other goals. Two key examples are efficiency justifications for mergers and monopolization, and international competitiveness considerations.

The basis for anti-combines law is that society will benefit from competition between firms. But in the case of natural monopoly, economies of scale are so extensive that one firm can serve the entire market at a lower cost per unit than could a number of competing firms. Having only one firm supply the product leads to the desired outcome of productive efficiency, but is likely to also lead to allocative inefficiency and unacceptably high prices unless the firm's exercise of monopoly power is held in check. In many public utilities the solution is government regulation of the monopolist's prices, with the price set just high enough to allow a fair rate of return on invested capital, but no more. Direct public ownership of certain enterprises has also been a common solution.

Mounting evidence that regulation was itself creating significant inefficiencies, and turning some potentially competitive industries into legal cartels led to a wave of deregulation in the 1970s and 1980s in industries such as airlines, trucking, and telecommunications. The overall results of the deregulation movement are somewhat mixed, but lower prices and greater efficiency are evident in some industries (including the airline industry which is discussed in this chapter).

Since the 1960s government has introduced a great many regulations aimed at improving health, safety and environmental conditions. Because such interventions usually apply across industries, they are called social regulations--as opposed to industrial regulations which are directed at particular industries. Social regulations have improved the quality of life in many respects, but not without opportunity costs. While there is no serious contention that we should not have social regulation, the appropriate level is controversial. Some critics claim that at current levels there are enough administrative costs, unintended side effects, and inappropriate applications of social regulation to cause higher prices for consumers and to slow the rate of technological innovation in new products and production processes.

Industrial policy refers to government actions to promote the economic vitality of specific firms or industries. Only recently has it become an important form of government influence on businesses in Canada. To date industrial policy has been used in Canada in reaction to crises in particular industries or firms. Bailouts in the auto industry, subsidies to stimulate development of alternative fuels, and subsidies and other incentives for export industries are a few examples. Many analysts are skeptical of industrial policy because international evidence shows that governments do not consistently pick the future industrial "winners." Thus, it is possible to devote large amounts of public resources to supporting industries that ultimately will not provide social benefits for Canada.

Checklist

When you have studied this chapter, you should be able to:

- ☐ Explain the meaning of the terms industrial concentration and monopoly power, and explain why they are used interchangeably in this chapter.
- ☐ Give four arguments against industrial concentration.
- ☐ Give four arguments in defense of industrial concentration.
- ☐ Differentiate between horizontal, vertical and conglomerate mergers.
- ☐ Outline the major provisions of the Combines Investigation Act as it existed before 1986.
- ☐ Outline the major changes brought about by the Competition Act in 1986.
- ☐ Give examples of groups that are exempt from the provisions of the Competition Act.
- ☐ Explain the significance of establishing anti-combines laws under a civil law framework versus a criminal law framework.
- ☐ Give examples of other social goals that may conflict with the goals of anti-combines law.
- ☐ Define a natural monopoly.
- ☐ State three problems that are encountered in the economic regulation of industries.
- ☐ Distinguish between the public interest theory and the legal cartel theory of regulation.
- ☐ Explain the forces that led to a trend of deregulation.
- ☐ Describe the outcomes of the deregulation of the airline industry.
- ☐ Contrast industrial (or economic) regulation with social regulation, and state the three principal distinguishing features of social regulation.
- ☐ Discuss the pros and cons of social regulation.
- ☐ Give examples of industrial policy in Canada.
- ☐ Discuss the pros and cons of industrial policy.

Chapter Outline

1. "Industrial concentration" occurs when one firm or a few firms control at least a substantial percentage of the output of an industry. The chapter is concerned mainly with firms that are large both in an absolute sense and in relation to the industry that they operate in.

2. Industrial concentration presents both disadvantages and advantages to our society. Those who oppose concentration and those who defend concentration sometimes make claims that directly contradict each other.

(a) The possible disadvantages are that:

(1) concentration leads to allocative inefficiency as firms restrict output to raise prices

(2) concentration is neither essential for achieving economies of scale nor conducive to technological progress

(3) concentration contributes to inequality of incomes

(4) concentration contributes to inequality of political power

(b) The possible advantages (or defenses) are that:

(1) concentration results from successful competition by firms that have developed superior products

(2) concentration calculations usually underestimate competition (from firms in other industries producing

substitutable products, from imported goods, and from potential new entrants to the market)
(3) concentration is a necessary condition if firms are to be large enough to exploit economies of scale
(4) in the Schumpeter-Galbraith view, concentration promotes technological research and development

3. In many industries the Canadian market is small enough that there is a fundamental trade-off between having enough firms for strong competition and having few enough plants to achieve economies of scale, or productive efficiency. For decades this trade-off has plagued Canadian governments who have tried various approaches to achieve both goals. In industries that are natural monopolies, regulatory agencies have been established. To combat tendencies toward collusion and mergers that would enable monopoly pricing in highly concentrated industries, anti-combines legislation has been enacted.
(a) In the 1880s, the slow expansion of the Canadian economy brought with it the creation of combines (or business monopolies) in some industries.
(b) Canadian anti-combines legislation began in 1889. This law and its successor, the Combines Investigation Act, have attempted to restrain both the growth and the exploitation of monopoly power.
(c) The combines legislation was periodically amended and updated in the light of court decisions, the emergence of new marketing strategies, and changing perceptions of the benefits and costs of particular business practices. By 1986 the anti-combines legislation applied to collusive agreements on prices and output of goods and services, formation of monopolies and mergers, and various marketing practices.

4. The effectiveness of the anti-combines law in preventing monopoly and maintaining competition was questionable, especially in the monopoly and merger areas. It was difficult to obtain convictions under the legislation because of 1) the presence of the undefined words "unduly" and "unreasonably" when defining prohibited practices, and 2) the heavy burden of proof required to obtain a conviction under criminal law.

5. The Competition Act, designed to tighten the rules for corporate behaviour, replaced the Combines Investigation Act in 1986. The new Act views competition not as an end in itself but as one means to promote efficiency. A quasi-judicial body called the Competition Tribunal has replaced the criminal courts and adjudicates under a civil law framework in treating the rewritten monopoly and merger sections. The conspiracy provisions now provide for larger fines, and allow for prosecutions based on circumstantial evidence.

6. Under the Competition Act the federal government has promoted monopoly and restricted competition in several ways.
(a) Canadian export combines, labour unions, agricultural marketing boards, credit unions, and (at the local and provincial levels) certain occupational groups are exempted from the provisions of the law.
(b) Mergers that result in greater gains from efficiency than costs from lessening of competition are permitted.
(c) The patent laws give temporary monopoly power to the producers of newly invented goods.

7. In addition to enacting anti-combines laws, the government regulates natural monopolies.
(a) If a single producer can provide a good or service at a lower average cost (because of economies of scale) than several producers, competition is then not economical, so a natural monopoly exists. Government may either itself produce the good or service or (following the public interest theory) regulate the private producer for the benefit of the public.
(b) The effectiveness of monopoly regulation has been questioned for three principal reasons. Critics argue that:
(1) Regulation increases costs and leads to an inefficient allocation of resources and higher prices.
(2) The regulatory agencies have been "captured" by the regulated industries and protect them rather than the public.
(3) Some regulated industries are not natural monopolies and would be competitive if they were not regulated.
(c) The legal cartel theory of regulation is that firms in potentially competitive industries want and support the regulation of their industries. They regard regulation as a way to increase their profits by limiting price and nonprice competition, and creating barriers that prevent the entry of new competitors.

8. The above criticisms of industrial regulation, and the advancement of the legal cartel theory of regulation, led during the 1970s and 1980s to the deregulation of a number of industries in Canada and the United States. The deregulation of the airlines is a case study of the effects of deregulation on prices, on customer service, on competition in the industry, and on the firms and workers in the industry. In Canada we have seen increased market concentration as a result. How the increased monopoly power will be exploited has yet to be fully revealed. It is too soon to declare deregulation a success or a failure in specific industries, but the overall effect of deregulation is regarded as positive so far. There are many signs in deregulated industries of lower prices, lower costs, and increased output. Yet, some industries are probably experiencing the replacement of the inefficiencies of regulation with the inefficiency of monopoly.

9. A "new" social regulation emerged in the early 1960s, rapidly leading to the creation of additional regulatory agencies. The realization that there could be a divergence between private and social benefits and also between private and social costs led to pressures for government to actively intervene in private market processes on behalf of society in general. Social regulation is not usually aimed at a specific industry or market, but applies across the economy. It is sometimes referred to as "health, safety, and environmental regulation," and typically sets mandatory standards for production processes, working conditions for employees, and physical characteristics of goods themselves.
(a) The central aim of social regulation is to improve the quality of life for Canadians.
(b) While the aim of social regulation is uncontroversial, the costs to the economy are high. Some critics argue that regulation is now so extensive that its marginal costs exceed its marginal benefits, meaning that regulation is now at an inefficient level. Furthermore, argue the critics, social regulation tends to have many unintended and undesirable side effects.
(c) This regulation raises prices (because compliance costs are passed on to consumers), slows the rate of innovation (because producers are less willing to take risks), and lessens competition (because the burden of compliance is greater for small firms).
(d) The defenders of the new regulation contend that it is needed to fight serious and neglected problems and that the social benefits will, over time, exceed the costs.

10. "Industrial policy" refers to government initiatives to promote the growth or health of particular businesses or industries. These initiatives may be tax concessions, subsidies, loan guarantees, or exemptions from certain rules or restrictions. Canada's federal government has no overall plan for industrial policy, but has employed industrial policy in numerous instances. Important examples include: 1) support of our auto industry when it faltered in the wake of Japanese competition, 2) a program to stimulate the development of alternate energy sources following the "oil crisis" of the mid-1970s, and 3) interest rate subsidies for loans to foreign buyers of goods exported by Canadian producers.

Terms and Concepts

anti-combines legislation
Combines Investigation Act
Competition Act
Competition Tribunal
conglomerate merger
foreign competition
horizontal merger
industrial concentration
industrial policy
industrial regulation
interindustry competition
legal cartel theory of regulation
natural monopoly
patent laws
potential competition
public interest theory of regulation
regulatory agencies
social regulation
vertical merger

Hints and Tips

1. This chapter shows that to really understand many aspects of the modern Canadian economy one must understand something of our economic history and of how we are influenced by developments elsewhere, especially in the United States. For example, the present Competition Act and regulatory framework reflect not only current economic and legal thinking, but also many decades of experience with previous laws and regulatory mechanisms in Canada and abroad.

Fill-In Questions

1. As used in Chapter 14, monopoly means that (many firms, no more than a few firms) __________ control at least a substantial portion of the output of a major industry; and this chapter is concerned with firms that are large (absolutely, relatively, both absolutely and relatively) __________.

2. On the whole it is not clear whether industrial concentration is __________ or __________ to the working of the economy.

3. Opponents of high levels of industrial concentration argue that concentration results in a(n) __________ of resources, (slows, speeds) __________ the rate of technological progress, makes the distribution of incomes more __________, and gives business undue influence over __________.

4. In defence of concentration, it can be claimed that: oligopolists dominate markets because they offer __________ products; oligopolies have lower costs by taking advantage of __________; oligopolies are conducive to a high rate of __________; and economists view competition too __________.

5. Mergers are of three basic types: __________, __________, and __________.

6. Canadian anti-combines legislation began in __________, and was administered under a (civil, criminal) __________ law framework. Under this legislative framework there were (few, many) __________ successful prosecutions.

7. The Combines Investigation Acts was replaced in 1986 by the __________ Act. Under the new law, mergers and monopolies (now called abuse of dominant position) are offenses only where they result in an unacceptable __________ of competition. Mergers that result in gains in __________ may be allowed even though they result in a __________ of competition.

8. Mergers and monopoly (abuse of dominant position) are no longer __________ offenses but are adjudicated under a __________ law by the Competition __________, which can issue __________ orders to restore and maintain market competition.

9. The Competition Act allows export consortia or cartels, provided the agreements apply only to their __________, even though such a cartel would have the unintended effect of __________ competition in the domestic market.

10. The Competition Tribunal may approve a specialization agreement between two competitors if the anticipated gains in __________ due to economies of __________ more than offset the costs due to the lessening of competition.

11. When a single firm can supply the entire market at a lower average cost than a number of competing firms, there is a __________ monopoly. In Canada, many of these monopolies are controlled by regulatory __________ or __________.

12. As an alternative to regulation, Canadian society has used __________ ownership as a means of industrial control.

13. The three main criticisms of regulation of industries by an agency or commission are:

(a) the regulated firms are allowed to charge a price that will cover costs plus provide a predetermined rate of return on __________. The regulated firms then have no incentive to reduce their __________ because the commission will then require them to lower their prices; and, because the prices they are allowed to charge are based on the value of their capital equipment, firms tend to use too much (labour, capital) __________ and too little __________.

(b) the regulatory commission has been "captured" or is controlled by the __________;

(c) regulation has been applied to industries that are not __________ monopolies and which, in the absence of regulation, would be __________.

14. The __________ theory of regulation assumes that the objective of industrial regulation is to protect society from abuses of monopoly power; but the __________ theory of regulation asserts that the firms wish to be regulated because it enables them to create a profitable and legal cartel.

15. The basic reason for the "new" social regulation and the creation of the new regulatory agencies has been the desire to improve the __________ of life in Canada. This type of regulation (is, is not) __________ usually directed at specific firms or industries.

16. Critics of "new" social regulation claim that it (increases, decreases) __________ product prices, that it reduces worker __________ by reallocating investment funds, that it causes a (slower, more rapid) __________ rate of innovation, and (more, less) __________ competition in the economy.

17. A government policy designed to promote investment and employment growth in a particular industry is called an __________ policy. A major objection to this type of government intervention is that governments cannot consistently identify the __________.

Problems and Projects

1. Below is a series of years. Following this is a series of facts about Canadian competition laws. Match each year with the appropriate fact by placing the appropriate letter after each fact.

A. 1889	B. 1910	C. 1952
D. 1969	E. 1976	F. 1971
G. 1981	H. 1986	

(a) First enactment of the Combines Investigation Act. _____

(b) Setting up of two separate agencies: Director of Investigation and Research and Restrictive Trade Practices Commission. _____

(c) Enactment of Competition Act. _____

(d) Initial introduction of the Bill that led to the Competition Act. _____

(e) Canada's first anti-combines legislation. _____

(f) Economic Council of Canada reported that the provisions of the Combines Investigation Act making mergers and monopolies criminal offenses were "all but inoperative." _____

(g) Combines Investigation Act became applicable to pure services. _____

2. Go to your library and find a copy of the Competition Act. Identify the specific section of the Act that applies to each of the following:

(a) a price-fixing agreement among five companies controlling 97 percent of the business of the compressed gas market

(b) the purchase of a controlling interest in a group of 38 community and real estate newspapers in the lower mainland region of British Columbia by a firm that controlled the dominant dailies in that area

(c) the purchase of waste disposal firms so that 87 per cent of the waste disposal market in three Vancouver Island areas was brought under the control of one firm

(d) a merger of two major firms in the oil refining industry

(e) misleading representation as to the price at which a product is ordinarily sold

3. Magna Carta and Maps for All are two retail chains that specialize in selling maps. Cartographica is a company that prints maps. Dogwood & Blandie is a restaurant chain.

(a) If Magna Carta merged with Maps for All it would be a __________ merger.

(b) If Magna Carta merged with Cartographica it would be a __________ merger.

(c) If Magna Carta merged with Dogwood & Blandie it would be a __________ merger.

(d) Of these mergers, the one most likely to be prohibited under the Competition Act is the __________ merger.

True-False

Circle T if the statement is true, F if it is false.

1. Since most wheat in Canada is produced on the Prairies, there is a high degree of industrial concentration in the wheat growing industry. **T F**

2. Although competition is beneficial to an economy, monopoly power benefits an individual firm. **T F**

3. Most economists agree that industrial concentration is seriously detrimental to the Canadian economy. **T F**

4. Empirical studies consistently show that economies of scale are only achieved in industries in which there are a few firms. **T F**

5. According to critics of concentration, oligopolists lack a competitive spur to productive efficiency. **T F**

6. Defenders of industrial concentration point out that large dominant firms have gained their position by offering the consumer superior products. **T F**

7. A horizontal merger is a merger between firms selling similar products in the same market. **T F**

8. A merger of Air Canada and Canadian International Airlines would be an example of a vertical merger. **T F**

9. A merger of Imperial Oil and Eaton's would be an example of a conglomerate merger. **T F**

10. Canadian anti-combines legislation began in 1889 with the passage of the Competition Act. **T F**

11. The latest major revision to Canada's anti-combines laws was passed in 1986. **T F**

12. The Competition Act makes some allowances for trade-offs between the goal of competition and other goals. **T F**

13. Under the Competition Act mergers and monopolies are no longer violations of Canada's criminal code. **T F**

14. Mergers that result in the merged firms controlling more than 50 percent of an industry's output are prohibited by the Competition Act. **T F**

15. Any collusive activity in Canada that results in reduced output or increased prices is prohibited by the Competition Act. **T F**

16. Labour unions are exempt from the Competition Act. **T F**

17. A natural monopoly exists when a single firm can supply the entire market at a lower unit cost than could a number of competing firms. **T F**

18. Natural monopolies tend to have relatively large fixed costs and relatively small variable costs. **T F**

19. Because the prices they are allowed to charge enable them to earn a "fair" return over their costs, regulated firms have a strong incentive to reduce their costs. **T F**

20. Potential competition can serve to restrain the price setting decisions of firms having monopoly power. **T F**

21. The CRTC is one of Canada's main federal regulatory agencies. **T F**

22. The legal cartel theory asserts that by legalizing cartels the government will save the cost of enforcing present anti-combines laws. **T F**

23. According to some critics, regulation protects the regulated firms from competitive forces and technological change. **T F**

24. Examples of the new social regulation are health, safety, and environmental laws. **T F**

25. Those who favour the "new" social regulation believe that it is needed in order to improve the quality of life in Canada. **T F**

26. Those who believe that X-inefficiency prevails under monopoly tend to support the government regulation of monopolies. **T F**

Multiple-Choice

Circle the letter that corresponds to the best answer.

1. "Industrial concentration" in this chapter refers to which one of the following?
(a) firms that are absolutely large
(b) firms that are relatively large
(c) firms that are either absolutely or relatively large
(d) firms that are both absolutely and relatively large

2. Which of the following is not a part of the case against industrial concentration?
(a) highly concentrated industries are larger than they need to be to take advantage of economies of scale
(b) highly concentrated industries earn economic profits that they use for research and technological development
(c) monopoly power leads to the misallocation of resources
(d) monopoly power leads to greater income inequality

3. A part of the defence of industrial concentration is that the market power of firms is limited by:
(a) interindustry competition
(b) foreign competition
(c) potential competition from new firms
(d) all of the above

4. The merger of a firm in one industry with a firm in an unrelated industry is called a:
(a) horizontal merger
(b) vertical merger
(c) conglomerate merger
(d) cartel

5. The Competition Tribunal is a quasi-judicial body that:
(a) has jurisdiction to determine cases on mergers and monopoly
(b) has recommended removal of interprovincial barriers to trade
(c) regulates agricultural marketing boards
(d) was replaced by the Restrictive Trade Practices commission in 1986

6. Suppose that two Canadian firms each produce a large furnace and a small furnace. How would the Competition Tribunal treat an agreement to split the market, with each firm specializing in one type of furnace?
(a) the Tribunal would have no jurisdiction over such an agreement
(b) the Tribunal must deny such an agreement
(c) the Tribunal would not care about such an agreement
(d) the Tribunal might allow such specialization if it allowed the firms to lower average costs

7. The conspiracy section in the Competition Act applies to:
(a) mergers
(b) monopolies
(c) misleading advertising
(d) price fixing

8. Which of the following have not been exempted from the anti-combines law?
(a) chartered banks
(b) labour unions
(c) credit unions
(d) agricultural marketing boards

9. All but one of the following have tended to reduce competition. Which one has not?
(a) occupational licensing
(b) the patent laws
(c) protective tariffs
(d) the Competition Act

10. A patent can be defined as:
(a) a remedial order set out by the Competition Tribunal to combat the abuse of dominant position
(b) the order set out by the Competition Tribunal approving a specialization agreement
(c) a grant of temporary monopoly rights by the government
(d) a discriminatory tax against the goods of a foreign firm

11. Legislation designed to regulate "natural monopolies" would be based on which theory of regulation?

(a) cartel
(b) public interest
(c) X-inefficiency
(d) public ownership

12. Supporters of the public interest theory of regulation argue that:
(a) if falling average costs render competition inappropriate, production and pricing should be controlled through a Crown Corporation
(b) in the competitive struggle for profits, firms ignore some social costs, so government regulation is required to protect the common good
(c) because of the lack of competition, monopolistic firms suffer from X-inefficiency, so government regulation is required to meet productive efficiency standards
(d) in industries where competition is inappropriate, regulated monopolies should be established to avoid the economic inefficiencies that accompany monopoly power

13. The legal cartel theory of regulating natural monopolies:
(a) would allow the forces of demand and supply to determine the prices of the good or service
(b) would attempt to protect the public from abuses of monopoly power
(c) assumes that the regulated industry wishes to be regulated and government officials provide the regulation in return for public support
(d) assumes that society is better off if certain cartels are legalized and operated in the open rather than underground

14. Critics of the deregulation of industry argue that (among other things) deregulation can lead to:
(a) higher prices for the products produced by the industry
(b) the monopolization of the industry by a few large firms
(c) a decline in the quantity or the quality of the product produced by the industry
(d) all of the above

15. Which of the following is not a concern of the "new" social regulation?
(a) the prices charged for goods
(b) the physical characteristics of goods produced
(c) the conditions under which goods are manufactured
(d) the environmental impact of production processes

16. Which of the following is not one of the criticisms levelled against the "new" social regulation?
(a) it results in higher prices
(b) it is too slow in achieving its objectives
(c) it will slow the rate of innovation in the economy
(d) it is anti-competitive

17. Airline deregulation in Canada has resulted in:
(a) increased airline fares
(b) improved airline safety
(c) increased airline service to smaller communities
(d) increasing industrial concentration in the industry

Discussion Questions

1. What is the difference between the way the term "monopoly" is used in this chapter and the way it is used in Chapter 11. What is "industrial concentration"?

2. List the arguments in favour of and against a high level of industrial concentration.

3. What is the historical background to the Competition Act?

4. Why was it difficult under the Combines Investigation Act to convict firms for forming a monopoly or a merger?

5. Section 1.1 of the Competition Act begins with: "The purpose of this act is to maintain and encourage competition in Canada in order to promote the efficiency and adaptability of the Canadian economy...." Why might there be a conflict between encouraging competition and efficiency? Which goal is emphasized more in the Act?

6. Find the Competition Act in your library and read Section 45. Now explain why the Ottawa Senators in the NHL had to pay millions of dollars to other NHL teams to be allowed to serve fans willing to pay for hockey entertainment.

7. Explain the role of the Bureau of Competition Policy in a hypothetical merger of Labatt's and Molson's brewing companies.

8. Why is the definition of the market an important issue in the application of anti-combines laws?

9. Give examples of how strict enforcement of anti-combines laws could conflict with other key social goals.

10. In what ways has the federal government restricted competition and fostered the growth of monopoly? How have the various protective tariffs fostered monopoly?

11. What is a natural monopoly? What are the two alternative methods for ensuring that it behaves in a socially acceptable fashion?

12. Explain the three major criticisms levelled against public interest regulation as it is practiced by commissions and agencies in Canada.

13. What is the legal cartel theory of regulation? Contrast it with the public interest theory of regulation.

14. How does the new social regulation differ from industrial (or economic) regulation? The critics of the new social regulation argue that it has resulted in over-regulation of the economy. How so? If there is over-regulation, what are its more important implications?

15. How has deregulation affected the airline industry in Canada?

16. Why does government use industrial policy? What arguments are made against using industrial policy?

Answers

Fill-in questions

1. no more than a few, both absolutely and relatively

2. advantageous, disadvantageous

3. misallocation, slows, unequal, government

4. superior; economies of scale; technological progress; narrowly

5. horizontal, vertical, conglomerate

6. 1889, criminal; few

7. Competition; lessening; efficiency, lessening

8. criminal, civil, Tribunal, remedial

9. exports, lessening

10. efficiency, scale

11. natural; agencies, commissions

12. public

13. (a) capital; costs; capital, labour (b) industries; (c) natural, competitive

14. public interest, legal cartel

15. quality; is not

16. increases, productivity, slower, less

17. industrial; winners

Problems and projects

1. (a) B; (b) C; (c) H; (d) F; (e) A; (f) D; (g) E

2. (a) section 45(1)(b); (b) section 79(1); (c) section 79(1); (d) section 79(1); (e) section 36(1)

3. (a) horizontal; (b) vertical; (c) conglomerate; (d) horizontal.

True-False

1. F	**2.** T	**3.** F	**4.** F	**5.** T	**6.** T
7. T	**8.** F	**9.** T	**10.** F	**11.** T	**12.** T
13. T	**14.** F	**15.** F	**16.** T	**17.** T	**18.** T
19. F	**20.** T	**21.** T	**22.** F	**23.** T	**24.** T
25. T	**26.** T				

Multiple-choice

1.(d)	**2.** (b)	**3.** (d)	**4.** (c)	**5.** (a)	**6.** (d)
7. (d)	**8.** (a)	**9.** (d)	**10.** (c)	**11.** (b)	**12.** (d)
13. (c)	**14.** (d)	**15.** (a)	**16.** (b)	**17.** (d)	

PART 4

Factor Markets and the Distribution of Income

CHAPTER 15

Production and the Demand for Resources

Chapters 10, 11, 12, and 13 considered how firms operating under different market conditions determine their profit-maximizing output levels. Of course, when a firm chooses to produce a given amount of output, they are also implicitly choosing to employ the amount of resources necessary to produce this amount of output. The output supply decision and the input demand decision go hand in hand, because they are linked by the firm's production function. (You should remember that the production function shows the resource inputs necessary to produce a given amount of output.) Profit maximization can be treated either from the output perspective, as in Chapters 10 through 13, or from the input perspective, as in this chapter.

Chapter 15 is the first of three chapters that examine markets for resources. In these markets, the interaction between employers of resources (demanders), and owners of these resources (suppliers), determines the prices at which resources will be employed and the quantities of resources that will be hired. These resources--you should recall--are labour, land, capital, and entrepreneurial ability. The price paid for labour is called a wage, the price paid for the use of land is rent, the price paid for the use of capital is interest, and the price paid for entrepreneurial ability is profit.

We begin with the demand for inputs. Inputs are employed because the firm can profit from selling the goods and services that inputs produce. The chapter stresses the most straightforward case: that of a firm that sells its product in a purely competitive market, and hires its inputs in a purely competitive market. This chapter does not explain the demand for a particular resource; it explains the demand for any resource. In Chapters 16 and 17 particular resources are examined in detail.

The list of important terms for Chapter 15 is quite short, but includes two crucial concepts--marginal revenue product and marginal resource cost. Marginal revenue product is the change in the firm's total revenue that results from employing an additional unit of input. Marginal resource cost is the change in the firm's total cost that results from hiring an additional unit of input. In order to maximize its profits, a firm will hire an extra unit of input as long as the added revenue it gets is greater than the added costs incurred to hire the input. Therefore, the firm hires additional units of each resource up to the point where the marginal revenue product and the marginal resource cost of that resource are equal. By hiring up to this point, the firm is also producing the output level where marginal revenue is equal to marginal cost. So the input demand decision and output supply decision are one and the same.

The marginal-revenue-product curve is the firm's resource demand curve. In the short run, the law of diminishing returns guarantees that this curve must eventually slope downward. Parallel to the analysis of product demand curves in Chapter 4, we find that input demand curves can shift, and that input demand curves vary with regard to their elasticity.

In the long run the firm is able to vary its employment of all resources. Thus, long-run resource demand decisions depend on the substitutability or complementarity of resources. Two key concepts are the "least-cost rule" and the "profit-maximizing rule" which address the interrelated issues of finding the optimal mix of inputs and producing the optimal amount of output.

Checklist

When you have studied this chapter, you should be able to:

- ☐ Present four reasons for studying resource pricing.

- ☐ Explain why a demand for a resource is a derived demand.
- ☐ Define marginal revenue product (MRP).
- ☐ Given a production schedule, calculate the marginal-revenue-product schedule for a competitive firm.
- ☐ Define marginal resource cost (MRC).
- ☐ State the rule used by a profit-maximizing firm to determine how much of a resource it will employ.
- ☐ Given the necessary data, use the MRP = MRC rule to find the quantity of a resource a firm will hire.
- ☐ Explain why the marginal-revenue-product schedule of a resource is the firm's demand for the resource.
- ☐ Explain the relationship between the law of diminishing returns and the shape of the short-run input demand curve for the competitive firm.
- ☐ Given the necessary data, find the MRP schedule of a resource employed by a firm that sells its product in an imperfectly competitive market.
- ☐ Explain how to derive a market demand curve for an input.
- ☐ List the three factors which would shift a firm's demand for a resource, and predict the effect on resource demand of an increase or decrease in each of the three factors.
- ☐ Explain how a change in the price of a substitute resource leads to a substitution effect and an output effect on the demand for a resource.
- ☐ Explain how a change in the price of a complementary resource changes the demand for a resource.
- ☐ List the four determinants of the price elasticity of demand for a resource.
- ☐ State how a change in each of these four determinants would affect the price elasticity of demand for a resource.
- ☐ State the rule employed by a firm to determine the least-cost combination of resources.
- ☐ Use the least-cost rule to find the least-cost combination when you are given the needed data.
- ☐ State the rule employed by a firm to determine how much of each of several resources to employ in order to maximize profits.
- ☐ Explain the relationship between the least-cost rule and the profit-maximizing rule.
- ☐ Apply the profit-maximizing rule to determine the quantity of each resource a firm will hire when the necessary data is given.
- ☐ Explain what is meant by the "marginal productivity theory of income distribution" and list the two major criticisms of this theory.

Chapter Outline

1. The firm can consider profit maximization from the viewpoint of the number of units of output to be produced or alternatively the number of inputs to be hired. Since the firm's production function relates the inputs to the output, the same profit-maximizing optimum is found under either approach. This chapter discusses how the demand for resources is determined, and how profit-maximizing firms choose what amounts of resources to employ.

2. The study of what determines the prices of resources is important because resource prices: 1) influence households' incomes and the distribution of income, 2) allocate scarce resources, 3) affect how firms combine resources to maximize profits, and 4) raise ethical questions about the distribution of income.

3. Economists generally agree upon the basic principles of resource pricing, but complexities of different market structures make these principles difficult to apply. The discussion in this chapter is mainly in terms of labour, but the principles outlined also apply to land, capital, and entrepreneurial ability.

4. The demand for a single resource is a derived demand because it flows from the demand for the good or service that the input makes.

(a) Because resource demand is a derived demand, the demand for a single resource depends upon its marginal productivity and the market price of the good or service it is used to produce.

(b) Marginal revenue product (MRP) combines these two factors--the marginal physical product of a resource and the market price of the product it produces--into a single tool, which indicates the amount that an extra unit of input adds to the firm's revenue.

(c) Marginal resource cost (MRC) is the addition to the firm's costs from hiring one more unit of the input.

(d) A profit-maximizing firm will hire a resource up to the quantity at which MRP = MRC.

(e) The firm's MRP curve is that firm's demand curve for the resource. In the short run this curve is downward sloping because of the law of diminishing returns which implies that the marginal physical product of a variable resource decreases as more units of it are employed, *ceteris paribus*.

(f) If a firm sells its output in an imperfectly competitive market, the more the firm sells, the lower becomes the price of the product. MRP then depends upon the marginal product of the resource and the marginal revenue of the output when it is sold. This causes the firm's resource-demand schedule to be less elastic than it would be if the firm sold its output in a purely competitive market.
(g) The market (or total) demand for a resource is derived from the demand schedules of all firms employing the resource.

5. Shifts in the demand for a resource can be caused by changes in the demand for the product being produced (which changes the output price); changes in the productivity of the resource (which changes its marginal physical product); or changes in prices of other resources.
(a) A change in the demand for a product produced by a resource will change the firm's demand for labour in the same direction.
(b) A change in the productivity of a resource such as labour (caused by an increase in the quantity of other resources such as capital, technological improvements, or improvement in resource quality) will change the firm's demand for the resource in the same direction.
(c) A change in the price of a substitute resource will change the demand for a resource in the same direction if the substitution effect outweighs the output effect, and in the opposite direction if the output effect outweighs the substitution effect. (The substitution effect occurs when a firm uses more of a resource that has become relatively less expensive, and less of resources that have become relatively more expensive. The output effect occurs when a change in the price of a resource leads to a change in output, and therefore, in input usage.)
(d) A change in the price of a complementary resource will change the demand for a resource in the opposite direction because of the output effect.

6. The price elasticity of resource demand measures the sensitivity of resource demand to changes in the price of the resource. It depends upon four factors:
(a) the rate at which the marginal physical product of that resource declines--the less rapid the rate, the more elastic the resource demand
(b) the ease with which firms can substitute other resources in the production process--the more good substitutes that are available, the more elastic the resource demand
(c) the elasticity of demand for the product the resource produces--the more elastic the product demand, the more elastic the resource demand
(d) the proportion of the firm's total costs represented by costs for the resource in question--the greater the proportion, the more elastic the resource demand.

7. Firms usually employ more than one resource in their production process and there is usually more than one combination of inputs that can produce a given level of output. In the case of purely competitive resource markets:
(a) The firm is hiring resources in the least-cost combination when the ratio of the marginal physical product of a resource to its price is the same for all the resources the firm hires.
(b) The firm is hiring resources in the most profitable combination if it hires resources to the point where the MRP of each resource is equal to the price of that resource.
(c) A firm that is hiring resources in the most profitable combination is also using a least-cost combination of inputs.
(d) A numerical example illustrates the least-cost and profit-maximizing rules for a hypothetical firm.

8. A controversial viewpoint in economics is that the marginal productivity theory results in an equitable distribution of income because each unit of a resource receives a payment equal to its marginal contribution to the firm's revenue; but the theory has at least two serious faults.
(a) The distribution of income will be unequal because resources are unequally distributed among individuals in the economy.
(b) The incomes of resource suppliers will not be based on their marginal productivities if there is monopsony or monopoly in resource markets.

Terms and Concepts

derived demand
least-cost combination of resources
marginal product
marginal productivity theory of income distribution
marginal resource cost
marginal revenue product

MRP = MRC rule
profit-maximizing combination of resources
substitution and output effects

Hints and Tips

1. When we view the firm's profit-maximizing decisions from the output perspective, marginal revenue and marginal cost are calculated with respect to changes in output, so we plot output on the horizontal axis of graphs. When the same decisions are viewed from the input perspective, marginal revenue product and marginal resource cost are calculated with respect to changes in input, so we plot input on the horizontal axis.

2. The marginal revenue product (MRP) of a resource is simply the marginal product of the resource (MP) times the marginal revenue from the sale of the product of that resource (MR), or MRP = MP x MR. Under pure competition in the firm's output market, MP changes, but MR is constant and equal to output price. Under imperfect competition in the firm's output market, price falls as the firm hires more resources and produce more output, so MR also falls.

3. The profit-maximizing rule for combining resources is easy enough to remember. Since the price of any resource must equal its marginal revenue product, the ratio must equal one.

Fill-In Questions

1. Resource prices allocate __________ and are a main determinant of household (costs, incomes) __________ and business __________. The price of labour is termed a __________; the price of capital is a __________; the price of land is a __________; and the price of entrepreneurial ability is a __________.

2. The demand for a resource is a __________ demand. This means that the demand for an input flows from the __________ for the good or service that the input helps to __________.

3. The impact of an additional unit of input on the firm's production is called the marginal __________, while the impact on the firm's total revenues is called the marginal __________.

4. The marginal revenue product schedule is obtained by multiplying the __________ of each unit of input by the __________ of the output.

5. The marginal resource cost is the change in the firm's __________ due to the hiring of __________ more unit of a(n) __________.

6. A firm will find it profitable to hire units of a resource up to the quantity at which the __________ equals __________.

7. A firm's demand schedule for a resource is the firm's __________ schedule for that resource because both indicate the quantities of the resource the firm will employ at various resource __________.

8. The marginal revenue product of the imperfectly competitive seller falls for two reasons: a) marginal product __________; and b) product price __________ as output increases. As a consequence, the MRP (or demand) schedule for the resource is (more, less) __________ elastic than it would be if the output were sold in a purely competitive market.

9. Other things being equal, an imperfectly competitive seller will produce (more, less) __________ of a product than a perfectly competitive seller and will demand (fewer, more) __________ resources.

10. The demand for a resource will shift if the demand for the __________ changes, if the __________ of the resource changes, or if the __________ of other resources change.

11. In the space to the right of each of the following, indicate whether the change would tend to increase (+), decrease (-), or have an uncertain effect (?) upon a manufacturer's demand for conveyor machines.

(a) an increase in the price of the manufacturer's product _____

(b) a decrease in the amounts of all other resources the manufacturer employs _____

(c) an increase in the productivity of the conveyor machines _____

(d) an increase in the price of a substitute resource when the output effect is greater than the substitution effect _____

(e) a decrease in the price of a complementary resource _____

12. The output of the firm being constant, a decrease in the price of resource A will induce the firm to hire (more, less) __________ of resource A and __________ of other resources; this is called the __________ effect. But if the decrease in the price of A results in lower total costs and an increase in output, the firm may hire __________ of both resources; this is called the __________ effect.

13. A firm's demand for labour will be *less* elastic: 1) the more (rapidly, slowly) __________ the marginal product of labour falls, 2) the (less, more) __________ elastic is the demand for the product the labour produces, 3) the (more, less) __________ difficult it is to substitute other resources in place of labour, 4) the (larger, smaller) __________ the percentage of the firm's total costs are represented by labour costs.

14. Suppose a firm employs resources in purely competitive markets. If the firm wishes to produce any given amount of its product in the least costly way, the ratio of the __________ of each resource to its __________ must be the same for all resources. In order to maximize __________, the firm must not only minimize costs, but also produce the optimal level of output. At this level, the firm employs the combination of resources where the ratio of the __________ of each resource to its __________ is equal to __________ for all resources.

15. In the marginal productivity theory, the distribution of income is claimed to be an equitable one because each unit of each resource is paid an amount equal to its __________.

16. The marginal productivity theory rests on the assumption of (competitive, imperfect) __________ markets. In the real world, this assumption fails because of monopsony or monopoly power, so wage rates and all other resource prices (do, do not) __________ measure contributions to a nation's output.

Problems and Projects

1. The following table shows production and input cost data for a firm buying and selling competitively. The firm uses one variable input and has fixed costs of $20. Complete the table and then use the information to answer the fill-in questions.

Input Units	Q	MP	Unit Input Price $	Price of Q $	MRP $	Profit $
1	17	____	20	2	____	____
2	32	____	20	2	____	____
3	45	____	20	2	____	____
4	56	____	20	2	____	____
5	65	____	20	2	____	____
6	72	____	20	2	____	____
7	77	____	20	2	____	____

(a) For the firm marginal resource cost is $_____.

(b) For the first unit of input marginal revenue product is $_____ and is found by multiplying __________ and __________.

(c) The firm should hire the first unit of input since the __________ is greater than the __________.

(d) For the second unit of input the marginal resource cost is $_____ and the marginal revenue product is $_____. The firm should hire the second unit of resource since the __________ is greater than the __________.

(e) To maximize profits the firm should hire _____ units of input and obtain profits of $_____.

(f) Suppose the firm was using 4 units of input and was considering using one more unit. For the 5th unit of input the increase in the firm's revenue is $_____ and the increase in the firm's costs is $_____. The firm (should, should not) __________ hire the 5th unit of input.

(g) Another way to show the firm should not hire the 5th unit of input is to compare the marginal revenue and marginal cost of an additional unit of output. Suppose the firm was using 4 units of input and decided to use 5 units. Total output would increase by _____ units and total cost would increase by $_____. Marginal cost of the extra output is defined as: (change in total cost/change in output) and equals $_____. Since this is a competitive firm, marginal revenue is the same as the __________ and equals $_____. Since marginal revenue of the output is (greater, less) __________ than its marginal cost, the firm (should, should not) __________ undertake the extra production.

2. The table below refers to the same firm as in problem 1 (above).

Unit Input Price	Qd of Input (Output P = $2)	Qd of Input (Output P = $3)
15	______	______
20	______	______
25	______	______
30	______	______
35	______	______
40	______	______

(a) In the first blank column of the table, fill in this firm's short-run input demand schedule if their product sells in a purely competitive market for $2.00 (the same price as assumed in Problem 1).

(b) In the second blank column, fill in the input demand schedule if the price of their product rises to $3.00.

3. Use the graph below to plot two input demand curves for the firm represented in Problems 1 and 2 above.

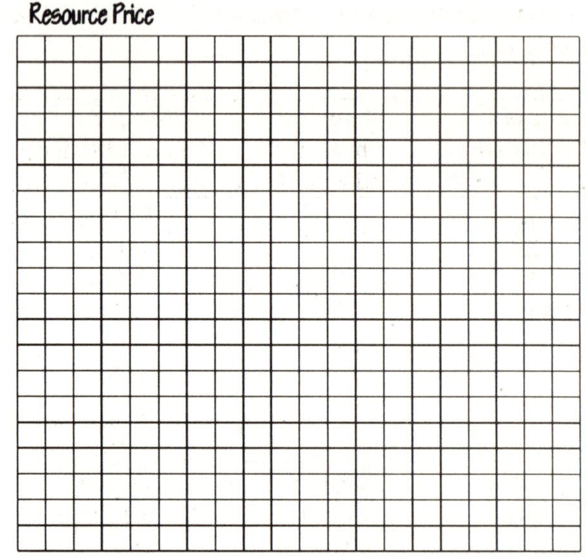

4. A manufacturer of toy wagons uses, among other resources, four wheels and one steel box to make a wagon. If there is an increase in the price of steel, what will happen to the firm's demand for wheels? Is this a result of a substitution effect, an output effect, or both?

5. A food processing firm combines carrots, corn, and other ingredients to produce tins of soup. The same vegetables are included in every tin, but the proportions can be varied according to cost and availability of specific vegetables. In 1994 the firm paid a lower price for carrots than they did in 1993. The price paid for corn was the same in both years. The firm participates in competitive markets for inputs and output.

(a) For this firm, are corn and carrots complementary resources or substitute resources?

(b) How would the typical contents of a can of this firm's soup have changed from 1993 to 1994?

(c) How would the firm's output level have changed?

(d) Would the firm be buying more or less carrots in total in 1994 than in 1993? Explain with reference to the substitution effect and the output effect.

(e) Would the firm be buying more or less carrots in total in 1994 than in 1993? Explain with reference to the substitution effect and the output effect.

6. The next two tables show the marginal physical product and marginal revenue product schedules for a particular firm's employment of resource C and resource D. Both resources are variable and are employed in purely competitive markets. The price of C is $2 and the price of D is $3.

Units of C Employed	Marginal Physical Product of C	Marginal Revenue Product of C
1	10	$5.00
2	8	4.00
3	6	3.00
4	5	2.50
5	4	2.00
6	3	1.50
7	2	1.00

Units of D Employed	Marginal Physical Product of D	Marginal Revenue Product of D
1	21	$10.50
2	18	9.00
3	15	7.50
4	12	6.00
5	9	4.50
6	6	3.00
7	3	1.50

(a) The least-cost combination of C and D that would enable the firm to produce:

(1) 64 units of output is _____ C and _____ D;

(2) 99 units of output is _____ C and _____ D.

(b) The profit-maximizing combination of C and D is _____ C and _____ D.

(c) When the firm employs the profit-maximizing combination of C and D, it is also employing C and D in the least-cost combination because __________ equals __________.

(d) Examination of the figures in the table reveals that the firm sells its product in a __________ competitive market at a price of $_____.

(e) Employing the profit-maximizing combination of C and D, calculate the firm's

(1) total output: __________

(2) total revenue: $__________

(3) total cost: $__________

(4) total profit: $__________

7. The table below shows three separate cases of a firm using two inputs and operating in competitive output and input markets. For each case, determine whether or not: (a) the firm is minimizing costs at current input levels; (b) the firm is maximizing profits at current input levels. (Note: MPP stands for the marginal physical product of a resource.)

	Case 1	Case 2	Case 3
Output Price	$1	$2	$3
MPP of Labour	12	3	6
MPP of Capital	8	2	6
Price of Labour	$6	$6	$6
Price of Capital	$4	$4	$4
Cost Minimization ?	Yes No	Yes No	Yes No
Profit Maximization ?	Yes No	Yes No	Yes No

True-False

Circle T if the statement is true, F if it is false.

1. In resource markets, resources are demanded by business firms and supplied by households. T F

2. The demand for resources is derived from the demand for the goods and services the resources produce. T F

3. The derived demand for a resource depends only on the price of the commodity it produces. T F

4. Marginal resource cost is the extra resource cost of producing an extra unit of output. T F

5. Marginal revenue product is the extra revenue the firm obtains when it hires an extra unit of input and sells the extra output produced. **T F**

6. For a firm in a competitive market the marginal revenue product is obtained by multiplying the marginal product of the extra input by the price of the output. **T F**

7. If the price of the product increases, the firm's demand curve for a resource will shift to the left. **T F**

8. An improvement in a resource's productivity will shift the firm's resource demand curve to the right. **T F**

9. An increase in the price of a resource will cause the demand for the resource to decrease. **T F**

10. The firm's resource demand curve slopes downward in the short run due to the law of diminishing returns. **T F**

11. A firm's demand schedule for a resource will be more elastic if it sells its product in a purely competitive market than it would be if it sold the product in an imperfectly competitive market. **T F**

12. When two resources are substitutable for each other, both the substitution effect and the output effect of a decrease in the price of one of these resources operate to increase the quantity the firm employs of the other resource. **T F**

13. Consider two inputs termed i and j. If an increase in the price of j results in a decrease in the use of i, then i and j are called complements. **T F**

14. If a firm wishes to produce any level of output at least-cost, resources should be combined so that their marginal products are equal. **T F**

15. If a factory's marginal product of labour falls sharply as more workers are hired, the factory's demand for labour will be quite elastic. **T F**

16. *Ceteris paribus*, a construction company that hires hundreds of manual workers and only a few supervisors will have a higher elasticity of demand for supervisors than for manual workers. **T F**

17. If there are no close substitutes for haircuts, but many close substitutes for massages, then the elasticity of demand for hair stylists will be less than the elasticity of demand for masseurs, *ceteris paribus*. **T F**

18. If labour is less expensive in India than in Canada, and capital is about equally expensive in India and Canada, the theories of this chapter predict a tendency towards the use of more labour-intensive production methods in India. **T F**

19. If individuals are paid according to the marginal products of their resources, society's income distribution will be fair and equal. **T F**

20. The existence of monopsony power helps resource suppliers gain a larger share of the income from their production. **T F**

Multiple-Choice

Circle the letter that corresponds to the best answer.

1. The price paid for resources affects:
(a) the money incomes of households in the economy
(b) the allocation of resources among different firms and industries in the economy
(c) the quantities of different resources employed to produce a particular product
(d) all of the above

2. The demand for a resource depends on:
(a) the marginal productivity of the resource and price of the good or service produced from it
(b) the marginal productivity of the resource and the price of the resource
(c) the price of the resource and the price of the good or service produced from it
(d) the price of the resource and the quantity of the resource demanded

3. The resource demand curve for a competitive firm slopes downward because of:
(a) the law of downward sloping demand
(b) the law of diminishing returns
(c) decreasing returns to scale

(d) the reduction in output price required to increase sales

4. All but one of the following would shift the demand curve for a resource. Which one?
(a) a change in technology
(b) a change in the price of the other inputs used in production
(c) a change in the price of the resource
(d) a change in the price of the output

5. Which of the following would increase a firm's demand for a particular resource?
(a) an increase in the prices of complementary resources used by the firm
(b) a decrease in the demand for the firm's product
(c) an increase in the productivity of the resource
(d) an increase in the productivity of a resource that is substitutable for this particular resource

6. Marginal resource cost is:
(a) the price paid for an input
(b) the slope of the input supply curve
(c) the increase in total cost when one more unit of the input is hired
(d) the increase in total cost when one more unit of output is produced

7. A profit-maximizing firm will hire an input up to the point where:
(a) the law of diminishing returns no longer holds
(b) average cost of production is minimized
(c) marginal product begins to fall
(d) marginal revenue product equals marginal resource cost

8. If a firm hires resources up to the point where marginal resource cost equals marginal revenue product, then the firm must also be operating where:
(a) marginal revenue equals marginal cost
(b) the marginal products of all inputs are equal
(c) the elasticity of resource demand equals 1
(d) marginal revenue is greater than the output price

9. As a firm that sells its product in an imperfectly competitive market increases the quantity of a resource it employs, the marginal revenue product of that resource falls because:
(a) the price paid by the firm for the resource falls
(b) the marginal physical product of the resource falls
(c) the price at which the firm sells its product falls
(d) both the marginal product and the price at which the firm sells its product fall

10. To maximize profits a competitive firm should hire additional units of a resource so long as:
(a) marginal resource cost is greater than output price
(b) input price is greater than marginal revenue product
(c) each successive resource unit adds more to the firm's revenues than to its costs
(d) the firm is earning economic profits

Use the total-product and marginal-physical-product schedules for a resource, below, to answer questions 11, 12, and 13. Assume that the quantities of other resources the firm employs remain constant.

Units of Resource	Total Product	Marginal Product
1	8	8
2	14	6
3	18	4
4	21	3
5	23	2

11. If the product the firm produces sells for a constant \$3 per unit, the marginal revenue product of the 4th unit of the resource is:
(a) \$3
(b) \$6
(c) \$9
(d) \$12

12. If the firm's product sells for a constant \$3 per unit and the price of the resource is a constant \$15, the firm will employ how many units of the resource?
(a) 2
(b) 3
(c) 4
(d) 5

13. If the firm can sell 14 units of output at a price of \$1 per unit and 18 units of output at a price of \$0.90 per unit, the marginal revenue product of the third unit of the resource is
(a) \$4
(b) \$3.60
(c) \$2.20
(d) \$0.40

14. A firm operating in competitive input and output markets is paying an input $6 per unit time period. If the last unit of this input hired produces $16 worth of output, the firm
(a) is maximizing profits
(b) should hire more units of the input
(c) should reduce employment of the input
(d) should raise the price paid to the input

15. Assume that a computer disk manufacturer is employing resources so that the MRP of the last unit hired for resource X is $240 and the MRP of the last unit hired for resource Y is $150. The price of resource X is $80 and the price of resource Y is $50 and both of these prices are constant. The firm should:
(a) hire more of resource X and less of resource Y
(b) hire less of resource X and more of resource Y
(c) hire less of both resource X and resource Y
(d) hire more of both resource X and resource Y

16. A firm that hires resources in competitive markets is not necessarily maximizing its profits when:
(a) the marginal revenue product of every resource is equal to 1
(b) the marginal revenue product of every resource is equal to its price
(c) the ratio of the marginal revenue product of every resource to its price is equal to 1
(d) the ratio of the price of every resource to its marginal revenue product is equal to 1

17. The effect on the employment of a resource when its price or the price of other inputs changes can be broken down into a substitution effect and an output effect. In finding the substitution effect which of the following is assumed to be constant?
(a) the total output of the firm
(b) the total expenditures of the firm
(c) the employment of all other resources
(d) the marginal physical products of all resources

18. Suppose resource A and resource B are substitutable and the price of A increases. If the output effect is greater than the substitution effect:
(a) the quantity of A employed by the firm will increase and the quantity of B employed will decrease
(b) the quantity of both A and B employed by the firm will decrease
(c) the quantity of neither A nor B employed will decrease
(d) the quantity of A employed will decrease and the quantity of B employed will increase

19. If decreases in the price of computers have decreased the employment of secretaries in medical clinics, then:
(a) computers and medical secretaries are complements
(b) there is no substitution effect on the demand for medical secretaries
(c) there is no output effect on the demand for medical secretaries
(d) the substitution effect on the demand for medical secretaries outweighs the output effect

20. Two inputs, capital and labour, are complementary. An increase in the price of capital will result in:
(a) a decrease in the demand for capital
(b) a decrease in the quantity demanded of labour
(c) a decrease in the demand for labour
(d) an increase in the demand for labour

21. Which of the following has no effect on the elasticity of demand of an input?
(a) the rate at which the marginal physical product of that resource declines
(b) the elasticity of demand for the product that the resource helps to produce
(c) the percentage of the firm's total costs accounted for by the resource
(d) the number of other resources that are good substitutes for the particular resource
(e) the marginal resource cost of the input

22. Which of the following is the best example of a pair of complementary inputs?
(a) land and fertilizer in agriculture
(b) bricks and lumber in house-building
(c) cars and drivers in the taxi business
(d) computers and typewriters in offices

23. A firm is allocating its expenditure on resources in a way that will result in the least total cost of producing any given output when:
(a) the amount the firm spends on each resource is the same
(b) the marginal revenue product of each resource is the same
(c) the marginal physical product of each resource is the same
(d) the marginal physical product per dollar spent on the last unit of each resource is the same

24. A competitive firm is currently using two inputs, A and B, and is producing its output at least cost. The input prices are $4 and $6 respectively. If the marginal product of A is 12 units, then the marginal product of B must be:
(a) 6 units
(b) 12 units
(c) 18 units
(d) 24 units

25. A business is employing inputs such that the marginal product of labour is 20 and the marginal product of capital is 45. The price of labour is $10 and the price of capital is $15. If the business wants to minimize costs, then it should:
(a) use more labour and less capital
(b) use less labour and more capital
(c) use less labour and less capital
(d) make no change in resource use

26. If a firm employs resources in imperfectly competitive markets, to maximize its profits the marginal revenue product of each resource must equal:
(a) its marginal physical product
(b) its marginal resource cost
(c) its price
(d) one

27. A major criticism of the marginal productivity theory of income distribution is that:
(a) markets are subject to imperfect competition
(b) the theory predicts that there will be equality in incomes
(c) the theory does not allow for losses in the short run
(d) in order to maximize profits, firms will pay their inputs as little as possible and not their marginal revenue product

Discussion Questions

1. Why is it important to study resource pricing?

2. Why is resource demand a derived demand, and upon what two factors does the strength of this derived demand depend?

3. What constitutes a firm's demand schedule for a resource? Why? What determines the total, or market, demand for a resource?

4. Explain why firms that wish to maximize their profits follow the MRP = MRC rule.

5. Explain the difference in the derivation of the resource demand curve for a competitive and imperfectly competitive firm.

6. Explain what will cause the demand for a resource to increase and what will cause it to decrease.

7. What are the "substitution effect" and the "output effect" which result from a change in the price of a resource?

8. What determines the elasticity of the demand for a resource? Explain the relationship between each of these four determinants and elasticity.

9. Considering the four determinants of elasticity of resource demand, which do you think would be more elastic, a hospital's demand for heart surgeons, or its demand for registered nurses? Explain your reasoning.

10. Assuming a firm employs resources in purely competitive markets, explain the rule for combining inputs so that it can produce a given output for the least total cost.

11. If highway engineers in Mexico have the same knowledge and expertise as Canadian engineers, why might they build highways using more labour-intensive methods than are used in Canada?

12. What is the marginal productivity theory of income distribution? What ethical proposition must be accepted if this distribution is to be fair and equitable? What are the two major shortcomings of the theory?

Answers

Fill-in questions

1. resources, incomes, costs; wages, interest, rent, profit

2. derived, demand, produce

3. physical product, revenue

4. marginal physical product, marginal revenue

5. costs, one, input

6. marginal revenue product, marginal resource cost

7. marginal revenue product, prices

8. declines, declines; less

9. less, fewer

10. product prices, productivity, prices

11. (a) +; (b) -; (c) +; (d) -; (e) +

12. more, less, substitution; more, output

13. 1) rapidly, 2) less, 3) more, 4) smaller

14. marginal physical product, price; profits; marginal physical product, price, one

15. marginal revenue product

16. competitive; do not

Problems and projects

1. Marginal Product: 17, 15, 13, 11, 9, 7, 5; Marginal Revenue Product: $34, $30, $26, $22, $18, $14, $10; Profit: -$6, $4, $10, $12, $10, $4, -$6
(a) $20; (b) $34, multiplying marginal product, output price; (c) marginal revenue product, marginal resource cost; (d) $20, $30; marginal revenue product, marginal resource cost; (e) 4, $12; (f) $18, $20; should not; (g) 9, $20; $2.22; price, $2.00; less, should not

2. (a) Qd at P = $2: 5, 4, 3, 2, 1, 0; (b) Qd at P = $3: 7, 6, 5, 4, 3, 2.

4. output effect leads to decreased demand for wheels.

5. (a) substitutes; (b) more carrots and less corn in 1994; (c) lower costs lead to increased output; (d) more because of both effects; (e) less because of substitution effect, more because of output effect; net effect is unknown

6. (a) (1) 1, 3; (2) 3, 5 (b) 5, 6 (c) the marginal physical product of C divided by its price, the marginal physical product of D divided by its price (d) purely, $0.50 (e) (1) 114, (2) $57 (3) $28 (4) $29

7. Case 1: Yes, No; Case 2: Yes, Yes; Case 3: No, No

True-False

1. T	**2.** T	**3.** F	**4.** F	**5.** T	**6.** T
7. F	**8.** T	**9.** F	**10.** T	**11.** T	**12.** F
13. T	**14.** F	**15.** F	**16.** F	**17.** T	**18.** T
19. F	**20.** F				

Multiple-choice

1. (d)	**2.** (a)	**3.** (b)	**4.** (c)	**5.** (c)	**6.** (c)
7. (d)	**8.** (a)	**9.** (d)	**10.** (c)	**11.** (c)	**12.** (a)
13. (c)	**14.** (b)	**15.** (d)	**16.** (a)	**17.** (a)	**18.** (b)
19. (d)	**20.** (c)	**21.** (e)	**22.** (c)	**23.** (d)	**24.** (c)
25. (b)	**26.** (b)	**27.** (a)			

CHAPTER 16

The Pricing and Employment of Resources: Wage Determination

Chapter 15 presented a theory of what determines the demand for any resource. Chapter 16 applies this theory specifically to the demand for labour, and also introduces some labour supply concepts. The first application of the labour market model is an explanation of the historical trend of rising real wages in Canadian labour markets. Then the chapter turns to a variety of issues concerning wage and employment determination under a number of different labour market models.

You learned in Chapters 10 to 13 that to understand how prices and quantities are determined in product markets one must pay attention to the competitive conditions of these markets. This led to the study of models of pure competition, monopoly, monopolistic competition and oligopoly. Because the same is true of labour markets, Chapter 16 examines wage and employment determination in six models that represent different conditions of competition: (1) the competitive market, in which there are many employers and many workers, all acting independently; (2) the monopsony market, in which a single employer hires labour under competitive (nonunion) conditions; (3) a market in which labour is supplied through a union to many employers, and the union seeks to increase labour demand; (4) a similar market in which the union attempts to reduce the supply of labour; (5) another similar market in which the union attempts--through threat of strike--to obtain a wage above the competitive equilibrium; and (6) the bilateral monopoly, in which a single employer hires workers whose supply is controlled by a union.

The wage and employment outcome in a particular labour market depends to a great extent on the characteristics of that market. In the first two types of market, the equilibrium wage rate and employment level are quite definite. When unions control the supply of labour, wage and employment levels are less certain. If the demand for labour is competitive, the wage rate and the amount of employment will depend upon how successful the union is in increasing the demand for labour, in restricting the supply of labour, or in setting a wage rate that employers will accept. If there is but a single employer, wages and employment will fall within certain limits; exactly where they occur within these limits will depend upon the relative bargaining strength and skills of the union and the firm.

The predictions that flow from the various models are the key theoretical content of the chapter. Following this material, the chapter discusses some empirical research and policy issues relating to labour markets in Canada. These include: (1) the case against, and the case for, minimum wage legislation; (2) the reasons for wage differentials between different workers; (3) the relationship between pay and performance under different compensation schemes; (4) the various effects of unions; (5) labour market discrimination.

Checklist

When you have studied this chapter, you should be able to:

- ☐ Define wages (or the wage rate); and distinguish between money and real wages.
- ☐ List at least five factors that led to the high and rising general level of real wages in Canada.
- ☐ List some possible explanations for why real wages in Canada have been stagnant in recent years.
- ☐ Using graphs or numerical data, explain the determination of wage rates and employment levels

in competitive labour markets.
- ☐ Give examples of labour markets that are competitive, or nearly so.
- ☐ Explain the difference between marginal resource cost in a competitive labour market and a monopsonistic labour market.
- ☐ Using graphs or numerical data, explain the determination of wage rates and employment levels in a monopsony labour market.
- ☐ Give examples of labour markets that are monopsonistic, or nearly so.
- ☐ List three techniques labour unions use to increase the demand for labour.
- ☐ Enumerate the ways in which exclusive or craft unions try to restrict the supply of labour, and show graphically the effects on wages and employment.
- ☐ Explain, using a graph, how the organization of an inclusive or industrial union in a previously competitive labour market would affect the wage rate and employment level.
- ☐ Explain, using a graph, why the wage and employment equilibrium is indeterminate when a labour market is a bilateral monopoly; and predict the range within which the wage rate will be found.
- ☐ Present the case for, and the the against, minimum wage legislation.
- ☐ List the three broad factors that explain why wage differentials exist between individual workers.
- ☐ Explain the sense in which the labour force can be seen to consist of a number of noncompeting groups.
- ☐ Give examples of nonmonetary aspects of job differences.
- ☐ Given three examples of imperfections in labour markets.
- ☐ Desribe the principal-agent problem and give five examples of pay or compensation schemes designed to solve the problem.
- ☐ Explain how the "solutions" to principal-agent problems can yield undesirable results.
- ☐ State the two generalizations that emerge from research on whether unions raise wages for their members, and whether unions effect wages of all workers taken as a whole.
- ☐ Discuss three main ways in which unions may reduce labour productivity, and three main ways in which unions may increase productivity.
- ☐ Define economic discrimination, list four types that can occur in labour markets, and explain the effects of discrimination for the victims and for the whole society.
- ☐ Give the crowding model explanation for occupational segregation of women in Canadian labour markets.
- ☐ List nondiscriminatory factors that also contribute to wage differentials between men and women.
- ☐ Define the comparable worth doctrine, and identify its pros and cons.

Chapter Outline

1. A wage (or the wage rate) is the price paid per unit of time for any type of labour and can be measured either in money or in real terms. Earnings are equal to the wage multiplied by the amount of time worked. It is real and not money wages that determine living standards.

2. The general level of wages in Canada is among the highest in the world because the demand for labour in Canada has been strong relative to the supply of labour.
(a) The strong demand for labour in Canada has been the result of high labour productivity in Canada, which can in turn be traced back to:
(1) the use of large amounts of capital per worker
(2) abundant natural resources
(3) improved work methods and the use of technologically superior equipment
(4) investment in training, education, and health
(5) a market oriented economy
(b) The real hourly wage rate and output per hour of labour input are closely related. Real income per worker can increase only at about the same rate as output per worker.
(c) The supply of labour depends ultimately on the size and age structure of a society's population.
(d) The increases in the demand for labour that have resulted from the increased productivity of labour over time have been greater than the increases in the supply of labour in Canada. As a result, the real wage rate has increased in the long run.
(e) However, since about 1980, real wage rates have been stagnant. Among the possible factors are falling rates of capital accumulation, shifts in employment to the low-productivity service sector, declining skill levels in the population, and globalization of production.

3. The wage rate received by a specific type of labour depends upon the demand for and the supply of that labour and upon the competitiveness of the markets in which that type of labour is hired and the output is sold.

4. In a purely competitive and nonunionized labour market, the total demand for and the total supply of labour determine the wage rate. From the point of view of the individual firm, the supply of labour is perfectly elastic at this wage rate (so the marginal labour cost is equal to the wage rate) and the firm will hire the amount of labour at which the marginal revenue product of labour is equal to the marginal labour cost.

5. In a monopsonistic and nonunionized labour market, the firm's marginal labour costs are greater than the wage rates it must pay to obtain various amounts of labour. It hires the amount of labour at which marginal labour cost and the marginal revenue product of labour are equal. The wage rate paid is less than either the marginal labour cost or the marginal revenue product of labour. The wage rate is set on the labour supply curve at the equilibrium employment level. Both the wage rate and the level of employment are less than they would be under purely competitive conditions.

6. In labour markets in which unions represent workers, the unions attempt to raise wage rates by:
(a) increasing the demand for labour by increasing the demands for the products produced by the union workers, by increasing the productivity of these workers, and by increasing the prices of resources that are substitutes for the labour provided by the members of the union;
(b) exclusive, or craft unionism, which is based on reducing the supply of labour by controlling entry to some occupations; or
(c) inclusive, or industrial unionism, which is based on organizing as many workers as possible, and then imposing upon employers wage rates that are higher than the equilibrium wage rate that would prevail in a purely competitive market.

7. Labour unions are aware that there is a trade-off between wage increases and employment for their members and may, therefore, limit their demands for higher wages. But the unemployment effect of higher wages could be lessened by increases in labour productivity or a relatively inelastic demand for labour.

8. In a labour market which is a bilateral monopoly, the wage rate depends, within certain limits, on the relative bargaining power of the union and of the employer.

9. A minimum wage imposed on a competitive labour market will result in higher wages and an increase in unemployment. In a monopsonistic labour market, an imposed minimum wage can result in both increased wages and increased employment. Empirical evidence suggests that, while minimum wages increase the incomes of employed workers, they also reduce the number of workers employed, especially among teenaged workers.

10. The unionization of workers has increased the wages received by union members significantly above what they would have received in the absence of unionization. However, these wage increases may have been at the expense of unorganized workers, and unionization probably has not increased the average real wages of workers as a whole.

11. Wage differentials between workers exist for three major reasons.
(a) Workers are not homogeneuous: they fall into noncompeting groups. The wages for each group may differ because of:
(1) differences in the abilities or skills possessed by workers, the number of workers in each group, and the labour market demand for these abilities or skills; and
(2) differences in human capital investment through education, training, or work experience.
(b) Wages differ as compensation for differences in the difficulty or attractiveness of different jobs. Some of the non-monetary differences include location, health risks, working conditions, and fringe benefits.
(c) Workers are not perfectly mobile because:
(1) relocation costs and attachments to families and friends may deter geographic movement;
(2) institutional barriers such as those imposed by regulatory bodies and unions may impede worker movement between occupations, or employers; and
(3) gender discrimination and racial discrimination may impede women and racial minorities from moving into higher paying jobs and occupations.

12. Many workers are not paid a fixed hourly wage, or monthly salary, but have a more complex pay system that is designed to relate pay to performance.
(a) A principal-agent problem arises when the interests of principals (firms) do not match the interests of their agents (workers). The workers may increase their own utility by shirking on the job.
(b) Firms may combat shirking by monitoring

(supervision), but this is sometimes ineffective, and always costly. An alternative solution is an incentive pay system. Some examples are: piece rates, commissions and royalties, bonuses and profit-sharing, seniority pay, and efficiency wages.
(c) Poorly designed incentive pay systems may solve the shirking problem but introduce other problems by creating incentives for the agents (workers) that are inconsistent with the goals of the principals (firms)

13. Considerable research and debate surrounds the effects of unions on wage rates.
(a) Empirical research overwhelmingly indicates that unions do raise the wages of their member relative to comparable nonunion workers.
(b) Unions appear to have little or no effect on the wages of all workers taken as a whole.
(c) The wage benefits that unions achieve for their members are to some extent at the expense of nonunion workers. If labour supply is restricted in the unionized sector (in order to raise wages), then in the nonunionized sector labour supply will be expanded, and wages will be reduced.
(d) However, unions also promote wage equality by advocating uniformity of wages within firms, and across firms in the same industry.
(e) There is some evidence that the net effect of unions is to reduce inequality of incomes.

14. There is also controversy over the effects of unions on the productivity of labour.
(a) In the negative view, unions decrease productivity by:
(1) feather-bedding and work rules that preclude firms from adopting new technologies, more effective organization of production techniques, etc.;
(2) strikes, whereby a withdrawal of labour services leads a shutdown of production; and
(3) labour misallocation because too few workers are employed by unionized firms and industries, and too many workers are employed by nonunionized firms and industries.
(b) In the positive view, unions increase productivity because:
(1) the shock effect of union wage increases may spur management to find ways to increase productivity;
(2) costly worker turnover is reduced as the union provides a "voice mechanism" as an alternative to the "exit mechanism" when workers are dissatisfied;
(3) the seniority system gives job security which makes experienced workers willing to train new workers who they might otherwise be in competition with.
(c) Empirical research has not yielded any firm conclusion regarding the effect of unions on labour productivity.

15. Labour market discrimination may be based on gender, race, ethnicity, or other minority status. It takes four main forms.
(a) Wage discrimination occurs when members of one group receive lower wages than another group for the same work and the same productivity.
(b) Employment discrimination occurs when one group experiences a higher unemployment rate than do other groups.
(c) Human capital discrimination occurs when members of one group enjoy less access to investments in education and training.
(d) Occupational discrimination occurs when members of one group are arbitrarily restricted from entering certain occupations.

16. In Canada, the most significant problem of labour market discrimination is probably the occupational segregation suffered by women.
(a) Discrimination has crowded women into a small number of occupations, causing the supply of labour in these occupations to be large relative to the demand for labour. Therefore, wages and incomes are depressed in "women's occupations."
(b) A simple supply-and-demand model also illustrates that crowding women into a limited number of occupations reduces output for society. Elimination of discrimination would lead to greater efficiency and greater income equality.
(c) Advocates of the doctrine of comparable worth propose that wage rates in different jobs be determined by the level of skill and effort required by the job, applying the principle of "equal pay for equal work." The practicality of this doctrine is questioned by many.
(d) Besides discrimination, there are a number of other factors that contribute to the earnings differentials between Canadian men and women.

Terms and Concepts

bilateral monopoly
collective voice

comparable worth doctrine--equal pay for work of equal value
compensating differentials
competitive labour markets
crowding model of occupational segregation
exclusive and inclusive unionism
exit and voice mechanisms
female participation rate
human capital investment
incentive pay plan
minimum wage
monopsonist
nominal and real wages
noncompeting groups
occupational discrimination
occupational licensing
principal-agent problem
shirking
wage differentials

Hints and Tips

1. To clarify the differences between the different models considered in this chapter, do two things:
(a) make up a table listing each model's assumptions regarding employer and worker behaviour;
(b) draw a supply and demand diagram to illustrate each model.

Fill-In Questions

1. A wage rate is the price paid for the use of labour per unit of __________, and the earnings of labour are equal to the __________ multiplied by __________; money or nominal wages are measured as an amount of money, while real wages are measured as an amount of __________ that can be purchased with the nominal wage.

2. The percentage change in real wages is found by subtracting the percentage change in the price level from the __________. Thus, a 3.5% increase in nominal wages in a year in which the price level rose by 2% yields a __________ increase in real wages for that year.

3. In general the average wage rate is determined by the __________ for and the __________ of labour in an economy. In the previous chapter it was stated that the demand for labour depends upon its marginal revenue product which, in turn, depends upon the __________ of the output and the __________ of the input.

4. The general level of wages is (higher, lower) __________ in Canada than in most foreign countries. The demand for labour in Canada is (great, small) __________ relative to the supply of labour.The demand for Canadian labour has been strong because of its high productivity, which results from:
(a) relatively large amounts of __________ with which to work;
(b) abundant __________ relative to population;
(c) technologically superior __________;
(d) the __________, __________, and __________ of the Canadian worker has resulted in a more __________ labour force;
(e) less tangible factors such as management __________ and __________; a favourable social and political __________; and an adequately sized __________.

5. In a competitive labour market:
(a) the supply curve slopes upward from left to right because it is necessary for employers to pay higher __________ to attract workers from alternative __________ and to attract nonworkers into the __________;
(b) the demand for labour services is the sum of the __________ of all firms hiring this type of labour;
(c) the wage rate will equal the rate at which the total __________ and the total __________ are equal.

6. Given the market wage rate, the individual firm can

hire all required workers at this rate. To the firm the marginal resource cost is __________ and equal to the market __________. The supply of labour service is perfectly __________ for the firm.

7. The individual employer who hires labour in a competitive market hires that quantity of labour at which the __________ of labour is equal to the __________.

8. A monopsonist faces an __________ sloping supply curve of labour and has to pay a __________ wage rate to hire more labour.

(a) Because the supply is upward sloping the extra cost of hiring an extra input is (greater than, less than) __________ the wage rate paid to that input. To the monopsonist the __________ is greater than the wage rate.

(b) The monopsonist hires labour up to the point where __________ equals __________.

(c) Other things being equal, the monopsonist hires __________ workers and pays a lower __________ than would a competitive employer.

9. Research in the baseball players' labour market (does, does not) __________ support the theory of monopsony. The researchers found that prior to free agency players were bound to individual teams, and were paid salaries significantly __________ their marginal revenue products. Once granted free agency, players were able to offer their services to a number of teams. This competition for their services caused players' salaries to become approximately __________ their marginal revenue products.

10. The basic economic objective of labour unions is to __________; they attempt to accomplish this goal either by increasing the __________ for labour, restricting the __________ of labour, or imposing demands for wages __________ their competitive equilibrium value.

11. Craft unions, which are examples of __________ unionism, typically try to increase wages by __________ the supply of labour. Industrial unions, which are examples of __________ unionism, try to increase wages by __________ the demand for labour.

12. Labour unions can increase the demand for the services of their members by increasing the __________ demand, by increasing the __________ of their members, and by increasing the __________ of resources that are substitutes for the services supplied by their members.

13. If craft unions are successful in restricting the supply of labour,

(a) the wage rate __________ and employment in the craft or industry (rises, falls, remains the same) __________.

(b) This effect on the employment of their members may lead unions to (increase, restrain) __________ their wage demands.

(c) But unions will not worry too much about the effect on employment of higher wage rates if the economy is (growing, declining, stationary) __________ or if the demand for labour is relatively (elastic, inelastic) __________.

14. In a bilateral monopoly labour market model, a union, which is a __________ seller of labour services, bargains with a __________ over wage rates. The outcome is __________ as economic theory makes no specific predictions as to the wage or employment result. The monopsonist will not pay a wage greater than __________; the union will ask for some wage greater than the __________; within these limits, the wage rate will depend on the relative __________ of the union and the employer.

15. The effect of the imposition of an effective minimum

wage rate (barring any shock effect):
(a) in a competitive labour market, is to (increase, decrease) __________ the wage rate and to __________ employment;
(b) in a monopsony market, is to __________ the wage rate and __________ employment.

16. There are differences in wage rates among occupations because workers differ as to __________ and __________, jobs differ as to __________, and because labour markets are __________. The labour force is composed of __________ groups and competition for jobs occurs within a particular grouping but not __________ groups.

17. An (agent, principal) __________ is someone hired by the (agent, principal) __________ to perform some job on the (agent's, principal's) __________ behalf.
(a) When the objectives of the principal and agent diverge, a __________-__________ problem arises.
(b) Once a contract has been agreed upon, agents may increase their own utility by __________ on the job. __________ pay plans that make pay a function of productivity can be instituted to dissuade agents from shirking. Examples of such schemes are:
1) ______________
2) ______________
3) ______________
4) ______________
5) ______________
(c) A prediction of the efficiency wage model is that the firm will maximize profits by paying the agents an amount (greater, less) __________ than can be earned in alternative employment.

18. The effect of the unionization of workers in the Canadian economy has been to (increase, decrease, have no effect on) __________ wage rates in the organized industries, to __________ them in the unorganized industries, and to __________ the average level of wages of organized and unorganized workers as a whole.

19. Unionism provides a collective __________ mechanism whereby worker grievances can be communicated to __________. Otherwise the only alternative would be to seek work elsewhere, a reaction termed the __________ mechanism.

20. Unions tend to (increase, reduce) __________ wage inequality within firms and __________ firms in the same industry.

21. In Canada, the average earnings of women working full-time are about __________% of the average earnings of men working full-time. Many analysts believe that some of this difference is explained by occupational discrimination which pushes women into a small number of __________ where the supply of labour ends up being large relative to the __________ for labour. This theory is known as the __________ hypothesis. Such discrimination (increases, lowers) __________ the relative wages of women and results in (increased, reduced) __________ domestic output.

22. The comparable worth doctrine can be summarized in the phrase "__________ pay for __________ work."

Problems and Projects

1. One construction firm has, for a particular type of labour, the marginal-revenue-product schedule given in the first table below.
(a) Assume there are 100 firms with the same marginal revenue product schedules. Compute the total or market demand for this labour by completing the first column of the table on the next page.
(b) Combining the total demand schedule for labour with the total supply schedule given in the same table,

the equilibrium wage rate is $______, and ______ units of labour will be hired in this market.

Units of Labour	MRP of Labour
1	$15
2	14
3	13
4	12
5	11
6	10
7	9

Quantity of Labour Demanded	Wage Rate	Quantity of Labour Supplied
______	$15	850
______	14	800
______	13	750
______	12	700
______	11	650
______	10	600
______	9	550

(c) At the equilibirum found in (b), the individual firm will have a marginal labour cost of $______, will employ ______ units of labour, and will pay a wage of $______.

(d) On the graph below, plot the market demand and supply curves for labour and indicate the equilibrium wage rate and the total quantity of labour employed.

(e) On the graph below, plot the individual firm's demand curve for labour, the supply curve for labour, and the marginal-labour-cost curve that confronts the individual firm. Indicate the quantity of labour the firm will hire and the wage it will pay.

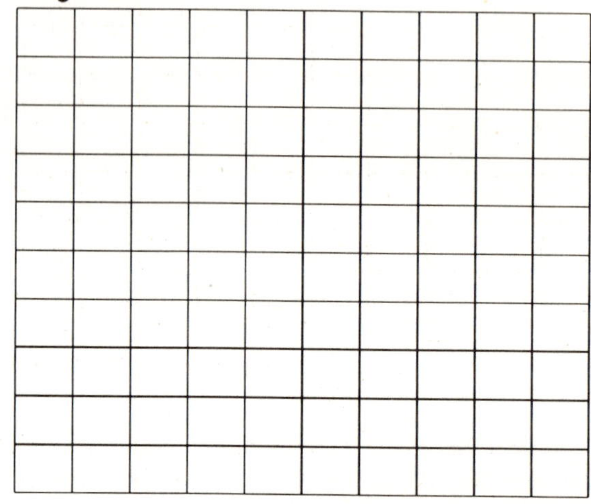

(f) The imposition of a $12 minimum wage rate would change the total amount of labour hired in this market to ______.

2. Assume a monopsonist has the marginal-revenue-product schedule for a particular type of labour given in columns 1 and 2 of the next table, and that the supply schedule for this labour is given in columns 1 and 3.

(1) Units of Labour	(2) MRP of Labour	(3) Wage Rate	(4) Total Labour Cost	(5) Marginal Labour Cost
0		$2	$______	
1	$36	4	______	______
2	32	6	______	______
3	28	8	______	______
4	24	10	______	______
5	20	12	______	______
6	16	14	______	______
7	12	16	______	______
8	8	18	______	______

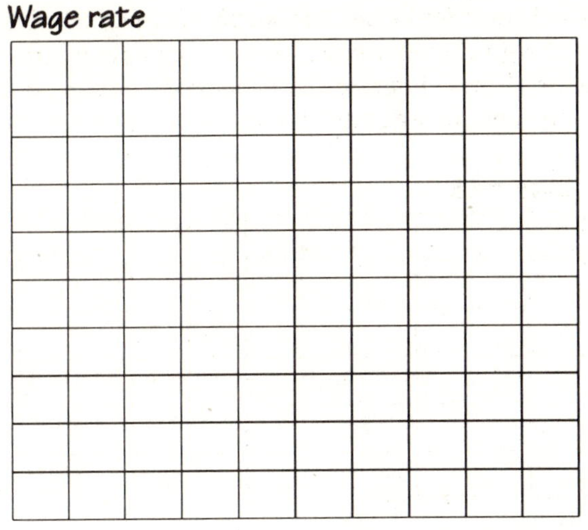

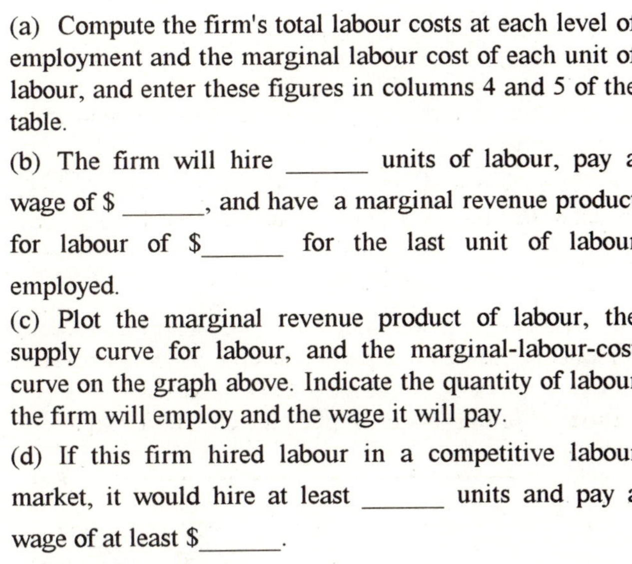

(a) Compute the firm's total labour costs at each level of employment and the marginal labour cost of each unit of labour, and enter these figures in columns 4 and 5 of the table.

(b) The firm will hire ______ units of labour, pay a wage of $ ______, and have a marginal revenue product for labour of $______ for the last unit of labour employed.

(c) Plot the marginal revenue product of labour, the supply curve for labour, and the marginal-labour-cost curve on the graph above. Indicate the quantity of labour the firm will employ and the wage it will pay.

(d) If this firm hired labour in a competitive labour market, it would hire at least ______ units and pay a wage of at least $______.

3. The graph in the next column illustrates the market for iron miners in an isolated Labrador community. The local iron mine is the only employer, and the miners are not unionized.

(a) From the graph, determine how many miners will be employed, and at what wage rate, if the employer behaves as a monopsonist.

(b) Suppose that the miners now unionize and demand a wage rate of $8 per hour. On the graph identify the new supply curve of labour.

(c) Why is the wage rate outcome uncertain when the union deals with the monopsony employer?

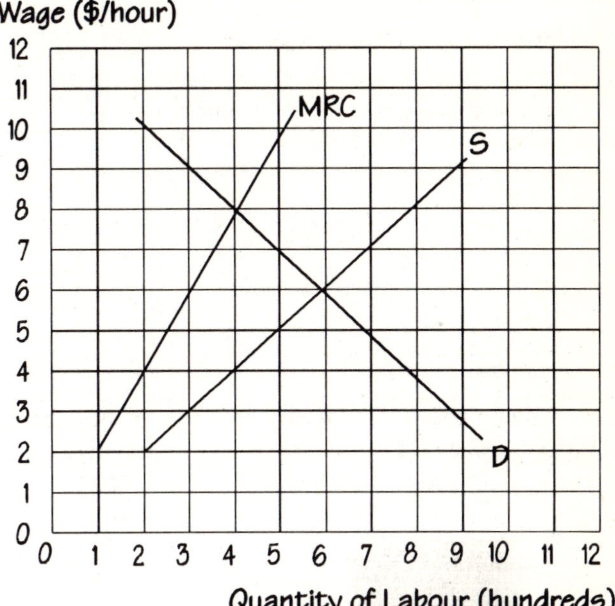

4. Suppose that there are two sectors of the economy that employ low skill workers: the retail sector and the domestic sector. Both are perfectly competitive labour markets. In the retail sector the marginal revenue product (in $ per month) is given by: $MRP_R = 3600\text{-}3L_R$ where L_R is the number of workers in this sector. For the domestic sector the marginal revenue product is given by $MRP_D = 2450\text{-}2L_D$ where L_D is the number of workers in this sector. Workers all have the same qualifications, are perfectly mobile between retail and domestic work, consider both kinds of jobs equally attractive, and seek the highest wage rate. There are 2000 of these workers in total. ($L_R + L_D = 2000$.) All workers must be employed.

(a) Under these assumptions, why must the wage rate in equilibrium be the same in both sectors?

(b) Given the total work force, find:

(1) how many are employed in the retail sector _____

(2) how many are employed in the domestic sector _____

(3) the wage rate (in $ per month) _____

(c) Suppose a minimum wage of $600 per month is set in the retail sector. No minimum applies for domestic workers. Find:

(1) how many are employed in the retail sector _____

(2) how many are employed in the domestic sector _____

(3) the wage rate in the retail sector _____

(4) the wage rate in the domestic sector _____

5. Suppose the economy consists of 100 workers; 50 men and 50 women. Men and women are equally productive workers, but at present the two groups are completely segregated in the labour market. All 50 men are employed in sector A where the marginal revenue product is given by MRP = 100-L. All 50 women are employed in sector B with a marginal revenue product given by MRP = 80-L.

(a) The wage rate for men will be $______, and the wage rate for women will be $______ in this complete segregation situation.

(b) If the causes of segregation are eliminated, and men and women are both free to work in either sector, employment in sector A will now be ______ workers, meaning that at least ______ women will be employed in this sector. Employment in sector B will now be ______ workers. The wage rates will be $______ in both sector A and sector B.

(c) This question is an example of the __________ model which shows that immobility of workers can lead to job __________ and lower wages for the group concentrated in a sector with lower productivity.

(d) Removing the impediments to mobility would definitely (decrease, increase) __________ the output of this society, because at the equilibrium found in part (a), the marginal revenue product of the 50th woman working in sector B is only $_____, whereas if she were working in sector A, her marginal revenue product would be $_____. Therefore, reallocating even just this one worker from B to A would (decrease, increase) __________ society's output by $_____.

True-False

Circle T if the statement is true, F if it is false.

1. The general level of real wages is lower in Canada than in foreign countries because the supply of labour in Canada is great relative to the demand for it. **T F**

2. The real income per worker can only increase at about the same rate as output per worker in the long term. **T F**

3. Nominal wages measure the purchasing power of wages. **T F**

4. If the price level should decline, a person's real wage could increase even if the nominal wage decreases. **T F**

5. The real income of males in Canada has increased substantially during the last decade. **T F**

6. If an individual firm employs labour in a competitive market, its marginal labour cost is equal to the wage rate in that market. **T F**

7. Given a competitive employer's wage rate, the more productive the labour input, the more will be hired. **T F**

8. For the monopsonist the extra cost of hiring one more unit of labour is greater than the wage paid to that additional worker. **T F**

9. Both a monopsonist and a firm hiring labour in a competitive market hire labour up to the point where the marginal revenue product of labour and wage rate are equal. **T F**

10. As compared to a competitive input market, the monopsonist hires fewer workers and pays a lower wage rate. **T F**

11. The basic economic objective of unions is job security for its members. **T F**

12. Restricting the supply of labour is a means of increasing wage rates more commonly used by craft unions than by industrial unions. **T F**

13. Unions attempt to increase the demand for the products they help to produce by lobbying for reduced import quotas and lower tariffs. **T F**

14. Craft unions are composed of members who possess specialized skills. **T F**

15. Occupational groups sometimes use licensing requirements as a method to artificially restrict entrants to specific occupations. **T F**

16. Exclusive unionism is a characteristic of industrial unions who attempt to exclude all nonunion workers from the place of employment **T F**

17. The imposition of an above-equilibrium wage rate will cause employment to drop more when demand for labour is inelastic than when demand is elastic. **T F**

18. On the whole, unions probably have caused the average wage in the unorganized sector to rise, as employers in this sector have raised wages as a defence against becoming unionized. **T F**

19. In the bilateral monopoly model the wage rate is set where the elasticity of labour demand equals one. **T F**

20. If a labour market is competitive, the imposition of an effective minimum wage will increase the wage rate paid and decrease employment in that market. **T F**

21. When an effective minimum wage is imposed upon a monopsonist, the wage rate paid by the firm will increase and the number of workers employed by it may also increase. **T F**

22. An increase in the minimum wage rate in the Canadian economy tends to increase the unemployment of teenagers and of others in low-wage occupations. **T F**

23. Noncompeting wage groups are composed of individuals who work for firms that produce goods and services that do not directly compete against each other in the marketplace. **T F**

24. The text argues that the main reason for the existence of wage differentials is the monopoly power of unions and monopsonistic employers. **T F**

25. The objective of the principal and agent are identical - the maximization of firm profit. **T F**

26. The efficiency wage theory suggests that the wage rate paid has an effect on worker productivity. **T F**

27. The principal-agent problem arises because it is not always possible to accurately assess the performance of the agent. **T F**

28. According to the crowding model of wage discrimination, differences in wages between men and women result from society placing impediments to female labour mobility. **T F**

29. Comparable worth reflects the notion that wages should reflect the level of skills, effort, responsibility, and working conditions in a consistent manner across different occupations. **T F**

30. Women suffer human-capital discrimination if they must have higher grades than men in order to be admitted to the same university programs. **T F**

Multiple-Choice

Circle the letter that corresponds to the best answer.

1. Real wages would decline if the:
(a) prices of goods and services rose more rapidly than money wage rates
(b) prices of goods and services rose less rapidly than money wage rates
(c) prices of goods and services fell while money wage rates rose
(d) prices of goods and services and money wage rates both increase by the same percent

2. Which of the following has not helped cause the generally high productivity of Canadian workers?
(a) the high level of real wage rates in Canada
(b) the superior quality of the Canadian labour force
(c) the advanced technology used in Canadian industries
(d) the large quantity of capital available to assist the average worker in Canada

3. The individual firm that hires labour under competitive conditions faces a supply curve for labour that:
(a) is perfectly inelastic
(b) is of unitary elasticity
(c) is perfectly elastic
(d) slopes upward from left to right

4. The key characteristic of the monopsony model is:
(a) many buyers and sellers of resources
(b) a single seller of resources
(c) a single seller of the product of the resources
(d) a single buyer of the resource

5. For the monopsonist:
(a) the marginal labour cost exceeds the wage rate
(b) the marginal labour cost is less than the wage rate
(c) each worker is paid a different wage rate
(d) there is a perfectly elastic supply of the input

6. A monopsonist pays a wage rate that is:
(a) greater than the marginal revenue product of labour
(b) equal to the marginal revenue product of labour
(c) equal to the firm's marginal labour cost
(d) less than the marginal revenue product of labour

7. Compared with a competitive labour market, a monopsonistic market will result in:
(a) higher wage rates and a higher level of employment
(b) higher wage rates and a lower level of employment
(c) lower wage rates and a higher level of employment
(d) lower wage rates and a lower level of employment

8. Higher wage rates and a higher level of employment are the usual consequences of:
(a) inclusive unionism
(b) exclusive unionism
(c) an above-equilibrium wage rate
(d) an increase in the productivity of labour

9. A craft union is composed of workers who:
(a) work for the same employer
(b) work in the same industry
(c) possess the same skill
(d) are members of noncompeting wage groups

10. Industrial unions typically attempt to increase wage rates by:
(a) imposing an above-equilibrium wage rate upon employers
(b) increasing the demand for labour
(c) decreasing the supply of labour
(d) forming a bilateral monopoly

11. The demand for labour can be increased by all but which one of the following?
(a) increasing labour productivity
(b) increasing the demand for products labour produces
(c) increasing the price of substitute resources
(d) occupational licensing

12. A negative impact on worker productivity results from the union effect on:
(a) worker turnover
(b) seniority and informal training
(c) managerial performance
(d) featherbedding and work rules

13. Which of the following may not be considered to be a union attempt to restrict the supply of labour?
(a) support for compulsory retirement
(b) long apprenticeships
(c) support for higher minimum wages
(d) seeking to have the employer hire only union members

14. Which of the following has been a consequence of unionization?
(a) higher wage rates for unionized workers
(b) greater employment of unionized workers
(c) greater employment of the workers in the entire labour force
(d) a higher level of real wages in the economy

Use the data in the following table to answer questions 15, 16, and 17.

Wage Rate	Quantity of Labour Supplied	Marginal Labour Cost	Marginal Revenue Product of Labour
$10	0	---	$18
11	100	$11	17
12	200	13	16
13	300	15	15
14	400	17	14
15	500	19	13
16	600	21	12

15. If the firm employing labour were a monopsonist, the wage rate and the quantity of labour employed would be, respectively:
(a) $14 and 300
(b) $13 and 400
(c) $14 and 400
(d) $13 and 300

16. But if the market for this labour were competitive, the wage rate and the quantity of labour employed would be, respectively:
(a) $14 and 300
(b) $13 and 400
(c) $14 and 400
(d) $13 and 300

17. If the firm employing labour were a monopsonist and the workers were represented by an industrial union, the wage rate would be:
(a) between $13 and $14
(b) between $13 and $15
(c) between $14 and $15
(d) below $13 or above $15

18. The fact that a star hockey player receives a wage of $1,500,000 a year can best be explained in terms of:
(a) noncompeting labour groups
(b) equalizing differences
(c) labour immobility
(d) imperfections in the labour market

19. About what percentage of the total labour force in Canada is women?
(a) 44%
(b) 41%
(c) 33%
(d) 28%

Questions 20, 21, and 22 use the next graph..

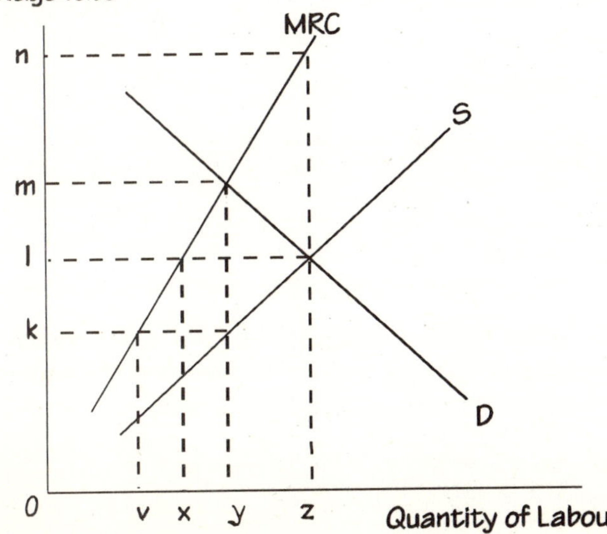

20. If this were a purely competitive labour market, the number of workers hired and the wage rate in equilibrium would be:
(a) 0*z* and 0*l*
(b) 0*z* and 0*n*
(c) 0*y* and 0*m*
(d) 0*y* and 0*n*

21. If this were a monopsonistic labour market, the number of workers hired and the wage rate in equilibrium would be:
(a) 0x and 0*l*
(b) 0*v* and 0*k*
(c) 0*y* and 0*m*
(d) 0*y* and 0*k*

22. If the market were characterized as a bilateral monopoly, the number of workers hired and the wage rate in equilibrium would be:
(a) 0x and 0*l*
(b) 0*v* and 0*k*
(c) 0*y* and 0*m*
(d) indeterminate

23. Incentive pay plans utilized to overcome shirking on the job do not include:
(a) piece rates
(b) commissions and royalties
(c) a wage premium for overtime work
(d) bonuses and profit-sharing

24. Efficiency wage theory suggests:
(a) the most efficient workers prefer to be paid piece rates
(b) gains in efficiency from using large size plants allow the payment of higher wages
(c) in any group of workers the more efficient should receive higher wages
(d) firms may find it profitable to pay wages higher than that available in alternative employment

25. Those who have suggested the crowding hypothesis assert that the crowding of women into certain occupations:
(a) is the result of occupational discrimination
(b) results in the misallocation of resources
(c) causes lower wage rates for women relative to men
(d) all of the above

Discussion Questions

1. Why is the general level of real wages higher in Canada than in most foreign nations? Why has the level of real wages continued to increase even though the supply of labour has continually increased?

2. Explain why the productivity of the Canadian labour force increased in the past to its present high level.

3. In the competitive model, what determines the market demand for labour and the wage rate? What kind of supply situation do all firms as a group confront? Why? What kind of supply situation does the individual firm confront? Why?

4. In the monopsony model, what determines employment and the wage rate? What kind of supply situation does the monopsonist face? Why? How does the wage rate paid and the level of employment compare with what would result if the market were competitive?

5. In what sense is a worker who is hired by a monopsonist "exploited," while one who is employed in a competitive labour market "justly" rewarded? Why does a monopsonist wish to restrict employment?

6. When the supply curve of labour is upward sloping, marginal labour cost is greater than the wage rate. Why?

7. What three methods might labour unions employ to increase the demand for labour? If these methods are successful, what effects do they have upon wage rates and employment?

8. When labour unions attempt to restrict the supply of labour to increase wage rates, what devices do they employ to do this for the economy as a whole, and what means do they use to restrict supply of workers?

9. Both exclusive and inclusive unions are able to raise the wage rates received by their members. Why might unions limit or temper their demands for higher wages? What two factors determine the extent to which they will or will not reduce their demands for higher wages?

10. What are the possible positive and negative effects that unions may have on productivity?

11. What is bilateral monopoly? What determines wage rates in a labour market of this type?

12. What is the effect of minimum wage laws upon wage rates and employment in (a) competitive labour markets, and (b) monopsony labour markets?

13. How do the wage rates paid to union members differ from those paid to nonunion employees? In the economy as a whole, is the effect of unions to promote wage equality or wage inequality?

14. Why are the wage rates received by workers in different occupations, by workers in the same occupations, and by workers in different localities different?

15. What reasons, other than discrimination, might explain why in Canada average incomes for workers are substantially lower for women than for men?

16. What is the principal-agent problem? In what way is the problem of the separation of ownership and control in corporations just another manifestation of this problem? How can the problem be overcome?

17. Discuss the reasons for, and the drawbacks of, using incentive pay schemes in some jobs that you have held, or that students typically hold (restaurant worker, retail clerk, and so on).

Answers

Fill-in questions

1. time, wage rate, time worked, goods and services

2. percentage change in nominal wages; 1.5%

3. demand, supply; price, marginal product

4. higher; great; (a) capital; (b) natural resources; (c) equipment; (d) health, education, training, efficient; (e) efficiency, flexibility; environment, market

5. (a) wages, employment, labour force; (b) marginal-revenue-products; (c) quantity of labour demanded, quantity of labour supplied (either order)

6. constant, wage; elastic

7. marginal revenue product, wage rate

8. upward, higher; (a) greater than; marginal resource cost; (b) marginal revenue product, marginal resource cost; (c) fewer, wage

9. does; below; equal to

10. increase wages; demand, supply, above

11. exclusive, restricting; inclusive, increasing

12. product, productivity, price

13. (a) rises, falls; (b) restrain; (c) growing, inelastic

14. single, monopsonist, indeterminate; the marginal revenue product of labour, competitive and monopsonistic equilibrium wage; the relative bargaining strength of the union and monopsonist

15. (a) increase, decrease; (b) increase, increase

16. ability, training, attractiveness, imperfect; noncompeting, between

17. agent, principal, principal's (a) principal-agent; (b) shirking; incentive; (1) piece rates; (2) commissions or royalties; (3) bonuses or profit-sharing; (4) seniority pay; (5) efficiency wages (c) greater

18. increase, decrease, have no effect on

19. voice, management; exit

20. reduce, between

21. 60; occupation; demand; crowding; decreases, reduced

22. equal, equal

Problems and projects

1. (a) Qd of Labour Demanded: 100, 200, 300, 400, 500, 600, 700; (b) $10, 600; (c) $10, 6, $10; (f) 400

2. (a) Total Labour Cost: 0, 4, 12, 24, 40, 60, 84, 112, 144; Marginal Labour Cost: 4, 8, 12, 16, 20, 24, 28, 32; (b) 5, $12, $ 20; (d) 6, $14

3. (a) 400 miners, $4 per hour; (b) horizontal at $8 to 800 miners, and then following the supply curve

4. (a) otherwise workers will move from low wage sector to high wage sector; (b) (1) 1030; (2) 970; (3) $510; (c) (1) 1000; (2) 1000; (3) $600; (4) $450

5. (a) 50; 30; (b) 60; 10; 40; 40; (c) crowding, segregation; (d) increase, 30, 50; increase, 20.

True-False

1. F	**2.** T	**3.** F	**4.** T	**5.** F	**6.** T
7. T	**8.** T	**9.** F	**10.** T	**11.** F	**12.** T
13. F	**14.** T	**15.** T	**16.** F	**17.** F	**18.** F
19. F	**20.** T	**21.** T	**22.** T	**23.** F	**24.** F
25. F	**26.** T	**27.** T	**28.** T	**29.** T	**30.** T

Multiple-choice

1. (a)	**2.** (a)	**3.** (c)	**4.** (d)	**5.** (a)	**6.** (d)
7. (d)	**8.** (d)	**9.** (c)	**10.** (a)	**11.** (d)	**12.** (d)
13. (c)	**14.** (a)	**15.** (d)	**16.** (c)	**17.** (b)	**18.** (a)
19. (a)	**20.** (a)	**21.** (d)	**22.** (d)	**23.** (c)	**24.** (d)
25. (d)					

CHAPTER 17

The Pricing and Employment of Resources: Rent, Interest and Profits

Chapter 17 concludes the study of the prices of resources by examining rent, interest, and profits. The discussion of each of these resource prices is considerably briefer and simpler than the discussion of wage of rates in Chapter 16. Various concepts that you are already familiar with from Chapters 15 and 16 are now applied to the study of rents, interest, and profits. You should recall that the marginal revenue product of a resource determines the demand for that resource. This principle is as true for land and capital as it is for labour.

It will be on the supply side of the land market that you will encounter whatever difficulties there are with Chapter 18. The supply of land is unique because it is perfectly *inelastic*: changes in rent do not change the quantity of land supplied. Demand, given the quantity of land available, is then the active determinant of rent. Land rents determine which land is allocated to which uses, but the rent is a surplus in the sense that its payment does not increase the total amount of land available.

Capital, as the economist defines it, means capital goods. Is the rate of interest, then, the price paid for the use of capital goods? No, not quite. Capital is not one kind of good; it is many different kinds. In order to be able to talk about the price paid for the use of capital goods, there must be a simple way of adding up different kinds of capital goods. The simple way is to measure the quantity of capital goods in terms of money. The rate of interest is, then, the price paid for the use of money (or of financial capital). It is the demand for and the supply of loanable funds that determine the market rate of interest. In the simple circular flow model we assumed that households supply and businesses demand loanable funds. In more sophisticated versions of the model, consumers, businesses, and governments all demand loanable funds; while other consumers and businesses supply loanable funds. Financial intermediaries such as banks, and trust companies act as middlemen who channel loanable funds from lenders to borrowers. The interest rate is a price and, as such, a rationing device that allocates financial capital to those firms that have the most product uses for capital

Profits cannot be understood with supply and demand analysis. Profits are not merely a wage for a particular type of labour; rather, they are rewards for taking risks and the gains of the monopolist. Such things as "the quantity of risk taken" or "the quantity of effort required to establish a monopoly" simply can't be measured; consequently, it is impossible to talk about the demand for or the supply of them. Nevertheless, profits are important in the economy. Part of the profit earned is called a "normal" profit and is the opportunity cost of the entrepreneurial input. Another part of profit is termed *economic* or *pure* profit, and it is a return for bearing uninsurable risk. It is the search for this profit that makes entrepreneurship such a dynamic element in the market economy. Economic profits are the lure or the bait that makes people willing to take the risks that result in efficiency and progress.

The final section of Chapter 17 examines the shares of national income going to labour and capital. What share goes to workers and what part goes to the capitalists--those who provide the economy with land, capital goods, and entrepreneurial ability? Have the shares going to workers and to capitalists changed much over the years? Perhaps surprisingly, ever since the 1920s labour's share has been about 80% of national income. There is no evidence that either labour's share or capital's share is showing any trend of increase or decrease.

Checklist

When you have studied this chapter, you should be able to:

- ☐ Define economic rent and explain what determines the amount of economic rent paid.

- ☐ Explain why economic rent is a surplus (or unearned income).
- ☐ State the proposal of Henry George and the socialists for how society should recover this surplus.
- ☐ State the criticisms of Henry George's proposal.
- ☐ Explain the functions of land rents in the market economy.
- ☐ Explain why owners of land do not all receive the same economic rent.
- ☐ Explain why a rent payment can be viewed as a surplus from society's viewpoint, but is a cost to the individual firm.
- ☐ Define the interest rate, outline how the equilibrium interest rate is determined in the loanable funds model.
- ☐ Give four reasons why different interest rates can exist simultaneously.
- ☐ State how the amount of financial capital a firm will borrow at any interest rate is determined.
- ☐ Explain the functions of interest rates in the market economy.
- ☐ Explain the effects of usury laws.
- ☐ Define economic profit and distinguish between economic profit, normal profit, and business profit.
- ☐ Explain the functions of economic profits in the market economy.
- ☐ Discuss the roles of uncertainty, risk, and monopoly in generating economic profits.
- ☐ State the current relative size of labour's and of capital's share of the national income; describe what has happened to these shares in the Canadian economy since 1926.

Chapter Outline

1. Economic rent is the price paid for the use of land or other natural resources whose supply is absolutely fixed (perfectly inelastic).
(a) Demand is the active determinant of economic rent because changes in the level of economic rent do not change the quantity of land supplied. Economic rent is, therefore, a payment that, in the aggregate, need not be paid to ensure that the land will be available.
(b) Although rent is a surplus payment from society's viewpoint, to the firm rent is a cost that must be paid to attract the land away from other entrepreneurs. Rent does not perform an incentive function, since the supply of land is fixed; but rent does allocate land to its most productive use in a market economy.

2. Some people have argued that land rents are unearned incomes and that either land should be nationalized or rents should be taxed away.
(a) In the late 1800s Henry George advocated a single tax on land, arguing that such a tax would have no adverse effects on resource allocation.
(b) Critics have pointed out three disadvantages of such a tax.
(c) Now there is a renewed interest in taxing land values to improve the equity and efficiency of local tax systems.

3. Economic rents on different types of land vary because land differs in its productivity. Land of very low productivity may be a free good, attracting no rent at all.

4. The interest rate is the price paid for the use of money.
(a) The interest rate is stated as a percentage annually of the amount borrowed.
(b) Money itself is not a resource, but it can be used to acquire physical capital resources.

5. The determination of interest rates can be explained in terms of the demand for and supply of loanable funds. Graphically, the interest rate is measured on the vertical axis, and the quantity of loanable funds is measured on the horizontal axis.
(a) The supply curve of loanable funds is upward sloping. Higher interest rates are needed to induce the household sector to defer more present consumption and to save more money, which can then be supplied (through the financial system) as loans to the business and government sector.
(b) The demand curve for loans is downward sloping. At higher interest rates, fewer of the investment projects that firms are considering will have rates of return that exceed the interest rate, hence firms will wish to borrow smaller amounts of funds to finance investment projects.
(c) The equilibrium interest rate is found where the quantity supplied and the quantity demanded are equal in the market for loanable funds.
(d) Shifts in the supply or demand curve in the loanable funds market will change the interest rate.

6. For convenience we speak as if there is but a single interest rate. In reality, there are a number of different rates of interest. The rates vary because of four loan factors--risk, maturity, size, and taxability-and because of market imperfections.

7. The interest rate plays two roles.
(a) Because of the inverse relationship between the interest rate and the total investment, the level of the interest rate affects the total output of capital goods and the equilibrium output of an economy.
(b) The interest rate rations (allocates) financial and real capital among competing firms and determines the composition of the total output of capital goods.

8. Usury laws specify maximum interest rates. They have been used in the United States, and are sometimes lobbied for in Canada, particularly with respect to credit card interest rates. Usury laws typically have the following effects:
(a) nonmarket rationing occurs;
(b) credit-worthy borrowers gain at the expense of lenders; and
(c) inefficiency arises in the allocation of capital.

9. Economic or pure profit is what remains of the firm's revenues after all its explicit and implicit opportunity costs have been deducted.
(a) Profit is a payment for entrepreneurial ability, which involves combining and directing the use of resources in an uncertain and innovating world.
(b) Profits are:
(1) rewards for assuming the risks in an economy in which the future is uncertain and subject to change;
(2) rewards for assuming the risks and uncertainties inherent in innovation; and
(3) surpluses that business firms obtain from the exploitation of monopoly power.
(c) The expectation of economic profits motivates business firms to innovate; and profits (and losses) guide business firms to produce products and to use resources in the way desired by society.

10. National income data for the Canadian economy indicate that:
(a) in the period 1971-94, wages and salaries were about 70% of the domestic income. But using a broader definition of labour income that adds net income of farmers and unincorporated businesses (which is mostly a payment for labour), labour's share was 80% and capital's share (rent, interest, and corporation profits) was about 20% of national income.
(b) since 1926, wages and salaries have increased from 55 to 73%.
(1) Because of changes in the industrial mix of the Canadian economy, the increased share going to wages does not indicate a larger share for labour. Employing the broader definition of labour income, labour's share has remained at about 80%.
(2) The growth of labour unions in Canada does not explain the increases in the wages and salaries received by workers.

Terms and Concepts

economic or pure profit
economic rent
explicit and implicit costs
incentive function
loanable funds theory of interest
normal profit
pure rate of interest
rate of return
single-tax movement
static economy
uninsurable risks

Hints and Tips

1. You may be confused by different uses of the term "rent." Usually it applies to income from land, but sometimes it refers to other incomes. In every case, rent retains the sense of a surplus earned when a resource earns more than it would take to retain that resource in its current use.

2. Remember that it is the expectation, not the certainty, of profit that drives the entrepreneur. Economics is never certain. In order to generate profit, the entrepreneur must take risks. You should distinguish between risks that are insurable and risks that are uninsurable. Assuming uninsurable risk is a major source of profit in a dynamic and unpredictable market economy.

Fill-In Questions

1. Rent is the price paid for the use of __________ and other __________ resources that have a completely (horizontal, vertical) __________ supply curve. Their supply can also be described as perfectly __________.

2. The active factor in determining rent is (demand, supply) __________.

3. When the demand for a fixed resource changes there is a large __________ effect and no __________ effect.

4. Because rent does not perform a(n) (rationing, incentive) __________ function, economists consider it to be a __________.

5. From the viewpoint of society rent is a surplus, but for a single firm a rent payment is a __________ if the fixed input has __________ uses.

6. If an individual receives a wage that exceeds the amount necessary to keep her/him in the present employment, the excess is a __________ or __________.

7. Socialists argue that land rents are (earned, unearned) __________ incomes and that land should be __________ so that these incomes can be used for the good of society as a whole. Proponents of the __________ tax argue that economic rent could be completely taxed away without affecting the amount of land available for productive purposes.

8. Rent payments for different pieces of land are not all the same but differ according to the land's __________ and __________. Such payments are called __________ rents and __________ land among alternative uses.

9. Interest is the price paid for the use of __________. Money itself is __________ an economic resource and when firms borrow money for investment they are ultimately purchasing the use of real __________ goods.

10. The equilibrium interest rate is the rate at which the quantity __________ is equal to the quantity __________ supplied in the market for loanable funds.

11. In the simple circular flow model, the supply of loanable funds is provided by __________ and the demand for loanable funds come from __________.

12. As far as the individual firm is concerned, the profit-maximizing amount of financial and real capital to invest in is the amount at which the rate of __________ and the expected rate of __________ are equal.

13. The firm's demand for loanable funds is __________ sloping because lower interest rates mean (higher, lower) __________ investment costs so (more, fewer) __________ investment projects will be profitable.

14. The firm's demand for loanable funds will shift to the right as a result of __________ improvements or an increase in __________ for the firm's product.

15. The supply curve of loanable funds is __________ sloping because (higher, lower) interest rates are required to induce households to __________ more.

16. In the simple model the supply of loanable funds would shift to the right if households became more __________.

17. There are differences in the rate of interest charged on loans due to differences in __________, __________, __________, and market __________.

18. The interest rate helps determine how much __________ will occur in the economy and also __________ financial and real capital among firms.

19. Normal profits are a payment for the resource called __________ ability, and this resource performs four functions: it combines the other __________ to produce goods and services; it makes (routine, non-routine) __________ decisions for the firm; it (invents, innovates) __________ products and production processes; and it bears the economic (costs, risks, criticisms) __________ associated with the other three functions.

20. Part of the return of an entrepreneur is called a __________ profit and part is a residual, which is the excess over the firm's opportunity __________. This residual arises because of the __________ risks the entrepreneur bears and/or the presence of __________ power, and it is called an __________ profit.

21. In an unchanging economy, which is called a __________ economy, uncertainty is __________ and if pure competition prevailed only __________ profits will exist.

22. When the future is __________, entrepreneurs necessarily assume risks, some of which are __________ and some of which are __________. The risks entrepreneurs cannot avoid arise either because of __________ and __________ changes in the economy or because the firm itself deliberately engages in __________.

23. Profits and losses promote the efficient __________ of resources in the economy unless the profits are the result of (competition, monopoly) __________.

24. Defining labour income broadly to include both wages and salaries and net income of farmers and unincorporated business (proprietors), since 1926, labour's share of national income has (increased, decreased, remained constant) __________, and is currently around _____%; capital's share is _____%.

Problems and Projects

1. Assume that there are 300,000 hectares available of a certain type of farmland, and that the demand for this land is that given in the following table:

Land Rent ($/hectare)	Land Demanded (hectares)
$125	100,000
100	200,000
75	300,000
50	400,000
25	500,000

(a) _____ hectares of this land that will be rented.

(b) The rent on this land will be $_____ per hectare.

(c) If the government placed a $50 per hectare tax on this farmland, there would be _____ hectares available.

(d) A tax of $50 per hectare would reduce the landowners' net income to $_____ per hectare.

2. There are three grades of land--A, B, and C--on which wheat is grown with the use of no other inputs but labour. The following table gives the output for various amounts of labour applied to the different land grades.

	Output by Land Grade (bushels)		
Labour	Grade A	Grade B	Grade C
1	50	45	20
2	90	75	30
3	120	95	37
4	140	105	41
5	150	110	43
6	155	112	44

If the price is a constant $1 per bushel, complete the following table showing the marginal revenue product for the various levels of labour input.

	Marginal Revenue Product ($)		
Labour	Grade A	Grade B	Grade C
1	_____	_____	_____
2	_____	_____	_____
3	_____	_____	_____
4	_____	_____	_____
5	_____	_____	_____
6	_____	_____	_____

Labour costs $20 per unit and is purchased in a perfectly competitive input market.

(a) A profit-maximizing firm would employ _____ units of labour on Grade A land; _____ units of labour on Grade B land; and _____ units of labour on Grade C land.

(b) The net income earned: on Grade A land _____; on Grade B land _____; and on Grade C land _____.

(c) If the firm sold the Grade A land, it would get $_____ in a competitive market for land.

(d) The amount the firm would get for the Grade A land is called ___________.

(e) The rent on Grade B land is $_____ and on Grade C land $_____.

(f) Suppose that the price of wheat increased to $2 a bushel. The rent on Grade A land becomes $_____; on Grade B land $_____; on Grade C land $_____.

3. The graph below shows the market for loanable funds.

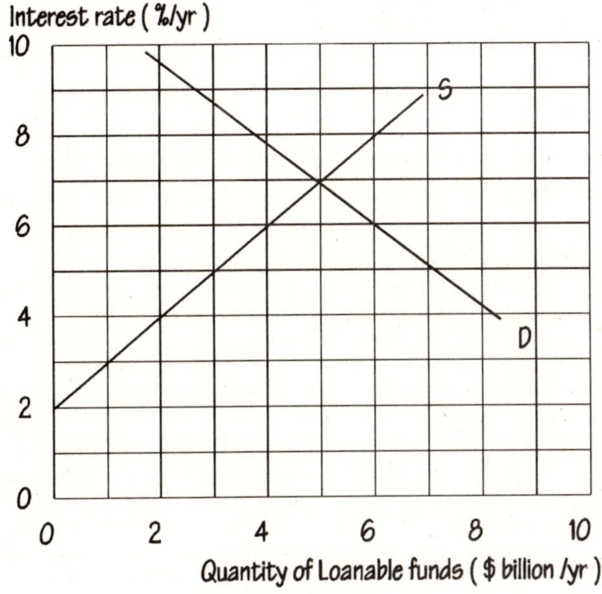

(a) The equilibrium interest rate is _____% per year.

(b) At this interest rate households save $_____ billion per year, and firms borrow $_____ billion per year.

(c) If a usury law was passed that set a maximum interest rate of 5% per year, households would save $_____ billion per year, and firms would wish to borrow $_____ billion per year, leaving a (shortage, surplus) __________ of $_____ billion per year.

True-False

Circle T if the statement is true, F if it is false.

1. Rent is the price paid for the use of land and buildings. **T F**

2. Rent is a surplus because it does not perform an incentive function. **T F**

3. Demand is the sole active determinant of rent. **T F**

4. Because the supply of land is fixed, rent does not change when demand increases. **T F**

5. The demand for land, and therefore the rent on land, would increase if there was an increase in the demand for the product obtained from the land. **T F**

6. Rent, which is a surplus from the viewpoint of society, is a cost from the viewpoint of the firm that pays the rent. **T F**

7. A person who receives in wages an amount greater than could be earned in an alternative occupation receives a rent or surplus. **T F**

8. A rent or surplus can arise because a tract of land is advantageously situated. **T F**

9. Rent payments on agricultural land on the Prairies are uniform. **T F**

10. Henry George claimed that land rents are unearned income so society should abolish all rent payments. **T F**

11. Money is an economic resource, and the interest rate is the price paid for this resource. **T F**

12. A decrease in the supply of loanable funds would tend to increase the interest rate and to decrease both investment spending and domestic output and employment. **T F**

13. An individual who borrows at a financial institution is a demander of loanable funds. **T F**

14. Charging different interest rates to individuals for loans of equal size is a form of discrimination and is illegal in Canada. **T F**

15. The pure rate of interest is the nominal rate of interest minus the rate of inflation. **T F**

16. Long-term loans or long-term government bonds always carry higher interest rates than short-term loans or short-term government bonds. **T F**

17. A normal profit is the minimum payment the entrepreneur must expect to receive to induce him or her to provide a firm with entrepreneurial ability. **T F**

18. If the economists' definition of profits were used, total profits in the economy would be greater than they would be if the business executive's definition were used. **T F**

19. One of the reasons why entrepreneurs earn economic profits is they are smart enough to buy insurance to cover insurable risks. **T F**

20. Uninsurable risks are the business risks that can be predicted and for which no insurance is required. **T F**

21. The expectation of profits is the basic motive for innovation, while actual profits and losses aid in the efficient allocation of resources. **T F**

22. The increasing importance of the corporation in the Canadian economy is a part of the explanation of why wages and salaries have increased and proprietors' incomes have decreased as shares of the national income. **T F**

23. The gain in the share of wages and salaries in national income has come at the expense of the capitalist share. **T F**

24. The growth of labour unions is the main cause of the expansion of wages and salaries as a share of the national income. **T F**

Multiple-Choice

Circle the letter that corresponds to the best answer.

1. The supply of land to society is:
(a) perfectly inelastic
(b) of unitary elasticity
(c) perfectly elastic
(d) elastic but not perfectly elastic

2. From the viewpoint of society, an increase in the demand for land results in:
(a) an increase in the supply of land
(b) an increase in the quantity supplied of land
(c) an increase in rent and an increase in the quantity supplied of land
(d) an increase in rent only

3. If an input, such as land, is fixed in supply:
(a) rent is supply determined
(b) rent is determined by the owner of that fixed supply
(c) rent is demand determined
(d) in some provinces rent payments are determined by a Rental Review Board

4. The factor payment to an input performs an incentive function if:
(a) the supply curve of the input is perfectly inelastic
(b) the price of the input is fixed
(c) the demand curve for the input is downward sloping
(d) the supply curve of the input is upward sloping

5. Economists consider rent to be a surplus because:
(a) no matter what the level of rent payment the same quantity of land is available to the economy
(b) agricultural products are grown from seeds using land and so a surplus results

(c) land owners are monopolists and charge a price greater than the competitive price
(d) there is a large quantity effect and little price effect when the demand for land changes

6. Which of the following is not true?
(a) the greater the demand for land, the greater will be the economic rent paid for the use of land
(b) a "windfall profits" tax on the increases in the profits of petroleum producers that would result from the rise in oil prices would be a good example of tax on economic rent
(c) individual users of land have to pay rent to its owners because that land has alternative uses
(d) the less productive a particular piece of land is, the greater will be the rent its owner is able to earn from it

7. Which of the following is *not* characteristic of the tax proposed by Henry George?
(a) it would be equal to 100% of all land rent
(b) it would be the only tax levied by government
(c) it would not affect the supply of land
(d) it would distort the allocation of resources

8. The economic rent from land will increase, *ceteris paribus*, whenever the:
(a) price of land decreases
(b) demand for land increases
(c) demand for land decreases
(d) supply curve for land increases

9. When the supply curve for land lies entirely to the right of the demand curve:
(a) landowners will receive an economic rent
(b) landowners will not receive an economic rent
(c) the interest rate on land will increase
(d) the interest rate on land will decrease

10. Differential rent payments can be due to:
(a) differences in land fertility
(b) differences in land location
(c) differences in the purity of natural resource deposits
(d) all of the above

11. The equilibrium interest rate is determined by:
(a) the demand and supply of land
(b) the demand and supply of entrepreneurship
(c) the demand and supply of loanable funds
(d) profits earned in the corporate sector

12. The supply of loanable funds is provided by all of the following except:
(a) borrowers at a commercial bank
(b) business savings
(c) buyers of Canada Savings Bonds
(d) credit creation by financial institutions

13. Demanders of loanable funds do not include:
(a) households
(b) buyers of Canada Savings Bonds
(c) businesses
(d) governments who borrow to finance budgetary deficits

14. Usually the smaller the rate of interest on a loan:
(a) the greater the risk involved
(b) the shorter the length of the loan
(c) the smaller the amount of the loan
(d) the greater the imperfections in the money market

15. The rate of interest does all of the following except:
(a) affect the total amount of investment in the economy
(b) affect the aggregate level of domestic output and employment
(c) allocate money and physical capital to those industries in which it will be most productive
(d) guarantee that there will be full employment in the economy

16. The profit-maximizing amount of financial and real capital an individual firm would employ is the amount at which the interest rate is equal to the:
(a) expected rate of net profit
(b) marginal physical product of capital
(c) marginal cost of capital
(d) marginal resource cost of capital

17. If the rate of interest were 12% and the rate of net profit a firm expects to earn by building a new plant were 14%, the firm would:
(a) not build the new plant
(b) build the new plant
(c) have to toss a coin to decide whether to build the new plant
(d) not be able to determine, from these figures, whether to build the plant

18. Which of the following is an economic cost?
(a) business profit

(b) normal profit
(c) economic profit
(d) windfall profit

19. Which of the following would *not* be a function of the entrepreneur?
(a) the introduction of a new product on the market
(b) the making of decisions in a static economy
(c) the incurring of unavoidable risks
(d) the combination and direction of resources in an uncertain environment

20. Business firms obtain profits because:
(a) not all risks are insurable
(b) not all markets are competitive
(c) the economy is dynamic
(d) all of these

21. Economic or pure profits result from all of the following except:
(a) innovation
(b) monopoly power
(c) the bearing of uninsurable risk
(d) decision making in a static economy

22. Using the broad definition of labour income, since 1926:
(a) capital's share of national income has increased
(b) labour's share has increased
(c) labour's share has decreased
(d) capital's share has been almost constant

23. Which of the following changes has contributed to an increase in wages as a share of national income?
(a) the growth of unions
(b) reduction in opportunities for new businesses
(c) a decrease in the number of owner-operated farms
(d) none of these

Discussion Questions

1. Explain what determines the economic rent paid for the use of land. What is unique about the supply of land?

2. Why is land rent a "surplus"? What economic difficulties would be encountered if the government adopted Henry George's single-tax proposal as a means of confiscating this surplus? What arguments are used to support the renewed interest in the heavy taxation of land values?

3. Even though land rent is an economic surplus, it is also an economic cost for the individual user of land. Why and how can it be both an economic surplus and an economic cost?

4. What is the interest rate? How is the equilibrium rate of interest determined?

5. How would a change in the supply of loanable funds affect: (a) the interest rate; (b) investment spending; (c) domestic output and employment?

6. Why are there actually many different interest rates in the economy at any given time?

7. What is the pure rate of interest and how does it differ from the real rate of interest?

8. Why does the amount of business investment increase when the interest rate falls?

9. What two important functions does the rate of interest perform in the economy?

10. What are profits? For what resource are they a payment? What tasks does this resource perform?

11. Why would there be no economic profits in a purely competitive static economy?

12. "The risks an entrepreneur assumes arise because of uncertainties that are external to the firm and because of uncertainties that are developed by the initiative of the firm itself." Explain.

13. What two important functions do profits or the expectations of profits perform in the economy? Why could monopoly power, such as a patent grant, both impede and enhance the effective performance of these functions?

14. What part of the Canadian national income is wages and salaries and what part is labour income? Why do your answers to these two questions differ? What part of the national income is the income of capitalists? What kinds of income are capitalist income? What are the long term trends in the labour and capital shares of national income?

Answers

Fill-in questions

1. land, natural resources, vertical; inelastic
2. demand
3. price, quantity
4. incentive, surplus
5. cost, alternative
6. surplus, rent
7. unearned, nationalized (or taxed); single
8. location, fertility; differential, allocate
9. money, not, capital
10. demanded, supplied
11. households, firms
12. interest, return
13. downward, lower, more
14. technological, demand
15. upward, higher, saving
16. thrifty
17. risk, maturity, loan size, imperfections
18. investment, allocate
19. entrepreneurial, resources, nonroutine, innovates, risks
20. normal, costs; uninsurable risks, monopoly, economic
21. static, nonexistent; normal
22. uncertain, insurable, uninsurable; cyclical, structural, risk-taking
23. allocation, monopoly
24. remained constant, 80%, 20%

Problems and projects

1. (a) 250; (b) 300,000; (d) 0, 300,000
2. (a) 71.3; (b) 79.1, 20.9
3. Grade A: $50, $40, $30, $20, $10, $5; Grade B: $45, $30, $20, $10, $5, $2; Grade C: $20, $10, $7, $4, $1, $1 (a) 4, 3, 1; (b) $60, $35, $0; (c) $60; (d) rent; (e) $35, $0; (f) $200, $130, $20

True-False

1. F	2. T	3. T	4. F	5. T	6. T
7. T	8. T	9. F	10. F	11. F	12. T
13. T	14. F	15. F	16. F	17. T	18. F
19. F	20. F	21. T	22. T	23. F	24. F

Multiple-choice

1. (a)	2. (d)	3. (c)	4. (d)	5. (a)	6. (d)
7. (d)	8. (b)	9. (b)	10. (d)	11. (c)	12. (a)
13. (b)	14. (b)	15. (d)	16. (a)	17. (b)	18. (b)
19. (b)	20. (d)	21. (d)	22. (d)	23. (c)	

CHAPTER 18

Income Inequality and Poverty

Chapter 18 examines the problems of unequal income distribution and poverty of many individuals and families in Canada. These problems are exacerbated, if not caused, by the market system and the institutions of capitalism. Therefore in a society whose goals include a reasonably equal income distribution and adequate incomes for all, there is an important role for government. In Canada there is a consensus for a mixed economy in which the government is actively engaged in modifying the economic results of market processes, and redistributing incomes.

The extent to which Canada's governments should redistribute incomes, and what the effects are of present income redistribution mechanisms, are under vigorous debate. Many critics of the market system argue that deteriorating incomes and opportunities for households in the lower income levels, along with a shrinking social safety net, are evidence that capitalism is fundamentally not working in Canada. Yet others believe that high taxes, government spending and the social safety net have sapped the vitality of the market system, hampering the investment, innovation, and risk-taking which could raise incomes for all Canadians.

The material in this chapter should help you understand some of the claims and arguments made by people who take different positions in this debate. The chapter deals first with the measurement of income distribution, and some data on the current Canadian situation. Then we turn to a summary of factors contributing to the unequal distribution of income in our nation.

The basic argument for an equal distribution of income--and therefore government intervention via income taxes, transfer payments, etc.--is that income equality is necessary if consumer utility is to be maximized for society as a whole. This is clearly a normative position, because one need not accept the goal of maximizing utility. But regardless of whether one accepts this goal, critics of income equality argue that income redistribution policies reduce the amount of income available for society to distribute amongst its members. Thus, there is a trade-off between equality and efficiency. This is a positive (as opposed to normative) proposition. The current debate in Canada over income maintenance programs is being contested both on the exact nature of the trade-off that we face, and on the issue of the relative importance of income growth vs. income distribution.

The final section of the chapter outlines the key elements of the Canadian income maintenance system, including government pensions, unemployment insurance, and welfare. in Canada. There is also an explanation of the negative income tax, an idea proposed by many economists and others as a way to overcome defects of other income maintenance programs.

Checklist

When you have studied this chapter, you should be able to:

- ☐ Present data from the textbook to support the conclusion that there is considerable income inequality in Canada.
- ☐ Report what has happened to the distribution of income in Canada since 1951.
- ☐ Given appropriate data, construct a Lorenz curve and interpret what the graph indicates about income inequality.
- ☐ Explain why looking at household incomes only from employment, and for only one year, can cause a distorted view of income inequality.
- ☐ Explain how much mobility between income classes there is in the short run (from one year to the next)

and in the long run (from one generation to the next).

- ☐ Enumerate seven causes of an unequal distribution of income.
- ☐ Show how utility theory can support the case for income equality.
- ☐ Explain the trade-off between equality and efficiency that is at the heart of the debate over how much income inequality is desirable.
- ☐ Explain the difference between absolute and relative poverty and why it can be claimed that "measures of poverty in Canada are primarily measures of income inequality."
- ☐ Use current Statistics Canada standards to define poverty and to describe the extent of poverty in Canada.
- ☐ Identify the groups in Canada where most poverty is concentrated.
- ☐ Give three reasons why poverty tends to be invisible.
- ☐ List components of the Canadian social security system; list three criticisms levelled against this system.
- ☐ Explain how a negative income tax (NIT) might be employed to reduce poverty, and state the two crucial elements in any NIT plan.
- ☐ List the three goals of any NIT plan and explain why it is impossible to devise a program in which these three objectives do not conflict.

Chapter Outline

1. There is considerable income inequality in the Canadian economy.
(a) The extent of the inequality can be seen by examining a personal-distribution-of-income table.
(b) Since 1951, the real incomes received by all income classes have increased but the relative distribution of personal income has been relatively stable.
(c) In the last decade there has been a slight increase in inequality, as shown by a drop in the percentage of total income received by the lowest quintile and a rise in the percentage received by the highest quintile.

2. Several possible reasons for the growing inequality of incomes are under investigation.
(a) Demographic changes have increased the proportion of less skilled and less experienced workers, and there are many more households headed by unmarried or divorced mothers (whose incomes are very likely to be low).
(b) Competition from imports produced in low-wage countries has put downward pressure on wages for Canadian workers whose goods compete with these imports.
(c) Technological change has sharply increased the demand for workers with high levels of education and skills. The wage gap between university graduates and workers with less education has grown.

3. The Lorenz curve is a geometric device for portraying the extent of inequality in any group at any time, for comparing the extent of inequality among different groups, and for contrasting the extent of inequality at different times.
(a) The relative distribution of income after taxes is about the same as it was before taxes were collected.
(b) Because earnings for most workers start at a low level, reach a peak during middle age, and then decline, there is significant income mobility over time, and the degree of income inequality is less if viewed over a lifetime.

4. The impersonal market system does not necessarily result in a distribution of income that society deems just. At least seven specific factors explain why income inequality exists:
(1) differences in ability and skills
(2) differences in education and training
(3) job tastes and risk
(4) unequal ownership of property and other wealth
(5) labour market discrimination
(6) market power in labour markets
(7) factors such as personal connections or influence, and plain luck--good or bad

5. An important question society must answer is what degree of income inequality it should strive for, given the trade-off between equality and efficiency.
(a) Those who argue for equality contend that it leads to the maximum satisfaction of consumer wants (utility) in the economy.
(b) But those who argue for inequality contend that equality would reduce the incentives to work, save, invest, and take risks. They maintain that these incentives are needed if the economy is to be efficient: to produce as large an output (and income) as possible given our available resources.

(c) In principle, economic research can shed light on how much efficiency is sacrificed by choosing a particular degree of equality.

6. Aside from inequality in the distribution of income, there is great concern today with the problem of poverty in Canada.
(a) Using Statistics Canada's definition of poverty, over 14% of families and more than 40% of unattached individuals in Canada live in poverty. These poor tend to be concentrated among certain groups, such as families headed by women.
(b) Poverty in Canada tends to be invisible because the poor are politically invisible, because the permanently poor increasingly live in isolation, and because there is considerable movement in and out of poverty.

7. The following are among the more important of the programs that make up Canada's income-maintenance system.
(a) The Old Age Security (OAS) Pension, for every one on reaching the age of 65, and the Guaranteed Income Supplement (GIS), for those with no other income than the OAS.
(b) The Canada and Quebec Pension Plans (CPP and QPP) at age 65; the amount of the pension depends on the size and number of the obligatory contributions previously made by the pensioner out of earnings.
(c) Unemployment Insurance benefits, paid to the unemployed on the basis of previous contributions.

8. The social insurance (or security) system has been criticized in recent years. Its critics argue that it impairs incentive to work, is abused by those who are not really in need, provides inadequate benefits to many of the most needy, and is costly to administer.

9. One comprehensive approach to income maintenance would employ a negative income tax (NIT) to subsidize families whose incomes are below a predetermined level.
(a) In any NIT plan, a family would be guaranteed a minimum income and the subsidy to a family would decrease as its earned income increases. But a comparison of three alternative plans reveals that the following may differ: the guaranteed income, the (benefit-loss) rate at which the subsidy declines as earned income increases, and the (break-even) income at which the subsidy is no longer paid.
(b) The comparison of the plans also indicates there is a conflict among the goals of taking families out of poverty, maintaining incentives to work, and keeping the costs of the plan at an acceptable level. A trade-off among the three goals is necessary because none of the three plans can achieve all three goals.

Terms and Concepts

absolute poverty
benefit-reduction rate (marginal transfer rate)
break-even income
Canada Pension Plan
equality-efficiency trade-off
guaranteed annual income
Guaranteed Income Supplement
income inequality
Lorenz curve
negative income tax
noncash transfers
Old Age Security
relative poverty
unemployment insurance benefits

Hints and Tips

1. Given how strongly people feel about income distribution issues, and given the current political turmoil over the overhaul of Canada's income maintenance programs, it is easy to lose track of the distinction between positive and normative statements. It is important that you keep the positive vs. normative distinction in mind in order to get the most out of this chapter.

Fill-In Questions

1. Data indicates that there is considerable income (equality, inequality) __________ in Canada. The percentage of total income received by the highest quintile is (much higher than, equal to, much lower than)

__________ the total income received by the lowest quintile.

2. Over time income has risen in __________ terms, but the relative distribution has been roughly __________ since 1951. In the last decade, __________ has increased somewhat.

3. Income inequality can be portrayed graphically by drawing a __________ curve.

(a) When such a curve is plotted, the cumulative percentage of (income, families) __________ is plotted on the horizontal axis and the cumulative percentage of __________ is plotted on the vertical axis.

(b) The curve that would show a completely (perfectly) equal distribution of income is a diagonal line, which would run from the (lower, upper) __________ left to the __________ right corner of the graph.

(c) The extent or degree of income inequality is measured by the area that lies between the __________ and the __________.

4. The important factors that explain (or cause) income inequality are differences in __________; in __________ and __________; in job __________; in the ownership of __________; in market __________; and in luck, connections, misfortune, and discrimination.

5. Those who argue for the:

(a) equal distribution of income contend that it results in the maximization of total (income, utility) __________ in the economy;

(b) unequal distribution of income believe income distribution is an important determinant of __________.

6. The so-called "big trade-off" is between economic __________ and economic __________. This means that:

(a) less income inequality leads to a (greater, smaller) __________ total output; and

(b) a larger total output requires (more, less) __________ income inequality.

7. Since, under the Canadian income maintenance system, basic material needs can be met, the poverty problem is one of __________ poverty rather than __________ poverty.

8. Using the Statistics Canada definition of poverty, in 1993:

(a) "the poor" included any big-city family of four with less than $__________ a year to spend;

(b) approximately ______% of the population would be classified as "poor."

9. Poverty tends to be concentrated:

(a) among the (young, old) __________;

(b) among (families, unattached individuals) __________;

(c) in families headed by __________;

(d) among those who are poorly __________;

(e) in (large, small) __________ families.

10. What three reasons explain why, in the affluent Canadian economy, those living in poverty remain hidden or invisible?

(a) ________________________

(b) ________________________

(c) ________________________

11. What do the following abbreviations stand for?

(a) OAS: __________

(b) GIS: __________

(c) CPP: __________

(d) UI: __________

12. Critics of the income-maintenance system often refer to "the welfare mess" and point to its three *ins*: they contend that it is administratively in-__________, is in-__________, and impairs work in-__________.

13. The two critical elements of any negative income tax plan are a __________ income below which family incomes would not be allowed to fall, and a __________ rate that specifies the rate at which the subsidy would be reduced if earned income increases.

14. The three goals of any negative income tax plan include:

(a) getting families out of __________,

(b) providing __________ to work,

(c) assuring the __________ of the program are reasonable.

These goals are (complementary, conflicting) __________.

Problems and Projects

1. The distribution of personal income among families in a hypothetical economy is shown in the table below.

(a) Complete the table by computing, beginning with the lowest income families:

(1) the percentage of all families in each income class and all lower classes. Enter these figures in column 4.

(2) the percentage of total income received by each income class and all lower classes. Enter these figures in column 5.

(b) From the distribution of income data in columns 4 and 5 it can be seen that:

(1) consumer units with less than $15,000 a year income constitute the lowest __________% of all families and receive __________% of the total income.

(2) families with incomes of $50,000 a year or more constitute the highest __________% of all families and receive __________% of the total income.

(c) Use the figures you entered in columns 4 and 5 to draw a Lorenz curve on the graph below. (Plot the seven points and the zero-zero point and connect them with a smooth curve.)

(1) On the same graph draw a diagonal line that would indicate complete equality in the distribution of income.

(2) Shade the area of the graph that shows the degree of income inequality.

(1) Personal Income Class	(2) % of All Families in This Class	(3) % of Total Income Received by This Class	(4) % of All Families in This and All Lower Classes	(5) % of Total Income Received by This and All Lower Classes
Under $10,000	18	4	______	______
$10,000-14,999	12	6	______	______
$15,000-24,999	14	12	______	______
$25,000-34,999	17	14	______	______
$35,000-49,999	19	15	______	______
$50,000-74,999	11	20	______	______
$75,000 and over	9	29	______	______

2. Following is a table containing different possible earned incomes for a family of a certain size.

Earned Income	NIT Subsidy	Total Income
$0	$5,000	$5,000
5,000	______	______
10,000	______	______
15,000	______	______
20,000	______	______
25,000	______	______

(a) Assume that $5,000 is the guaranteed annual income for a family of this size and that the benefit-loss rate is 20%. Enter the NIT subsidy and the total income at each of the five remaining earned-income levels. (*Hint*: 20% of $5,000 is $1,000.)

(1) This NIT program retains strong incentives to work because whenever the family earns an additional $5,000, its total income increases by $__________.

(2) But this program is costly because the family receives a subsidy until its earned income, the break-even income, is $__________.

(b) To reduce the break-even income, the benefit-loss rate is raised to 50%. Complete the next table.

Earned Income	NIT Subsidy	Total Income
$0	$5,000	$5,000
2,500	______	______
5,000	______	______
7,500	______	______
10,000	______	______

(1) This program is less costly than the previous one because the family only receives a subsidy until it earns the break-even income of $__________.

(2) But the incentives to work are less because, when ever the family earns an additional $5,000, its total income increases by only $__________.

(c) Both of the previous two NIT programs guaranteed an income of only $5,000. Assume the guaranteed income is raised to $7,500 and that the benefit-loss rate is kept at 50%. Complete the table below.

Earned Income	NIT Subsidy	Total Income
$0	$7,500	$7,500
3,000	______	______
6,000	______	______
9,000	______	______
12,000	______	______
15,000	______	______

(1) This program is more costly than the previous one because the break-even income has risen to $__________.

(2) The incentives to earn additional income are no better in this program than in the previous one. But to improve these incentives by reducing the benefit-loss rate to 40% would raise the break-even income to $__________. (Hint: Divide guaranteed income by the benefit-loss rate.)

(d) To summarize:

(1) given the guaranteed income, the lower the benefit--loss rate, the (greater, less) __________ are the incentives to earn additional income and the (greater, less) __________ is the break-even income and the cost of the NIT program;

(2) and given the benefit-loss rate, the greater the guaranteed income, the (greater, less) __________ is the break-even income and the cost of the program;

(3) but to reduce the break-even income and the cost of the program requires either a(n) (increase, decrease) __________ in the benefit-loss rate or a(n) __________ in the guaranteed income.

True-False

Circle T if the statement is true, F if it is false.

1. According to the text, there is considerable income inequality in Canada. **T F**

2. Until the last decade, real family income had increased steadily in Canada since World War II. **T F**

3. The progressive tax system in Canada has resulted in the before-tax and after-tax distribution of income being very much different. **T F**

4. The Lorenz curve is a means of visualizing differences in real wage rates paid in various countries. **T F**

5. There appears to be considerable mobility between income classes from one year to the next. **T F**

6. Differences in personal characteristics explains some of the differences in earned income common in the market economy. **T F**

7. A case can be made for an equal distribution of income based upon the notion that the marginal utility of extra income is greater for an individual with a lower income than for an individual with a higher income. **T F**

8. Those who favour inequality in the distribution of income contend that inequality will lead to stronger incentives to work, save, invest, and take risks. **T F**

9. In the trade-off between equality and economic efficiency, an increase in efficiency requires a decrease in inequality. **T F**

10. Relative poverty refers to an individual's or family's low income as compared to the incomes of other groups in society. **T F**

11. In Canada the "low income cutoff" for defining poverty is set by Statistics Canada on a relative rather than an absolute basis. **T F**

12. The low income cutoffs prepared by Statistics Canada are the same for every Canadian. **T F**

13. Currently, the top quintile of all families in Canada receives over 40% of before-tax personal incomes. **T F**

14. The incidence of poverty is extremely high among female-headed families. **T F**

15. Evidence suggests that the vast majority of the poor who obtain public assistance (welfare) are unable to support themselves. **T F**

16. Approximately half of the people below the poverty line in a given year will be above the poverty line the next year. **T F**

17. The Canada Pension Plan is funded by the federal government and benefits are payable to all Canadians upon reaching their 65th birthday. **T F**

18. Critics of the Canadian system of income maintenance contend that the welfare system impairs incentives to work. **T F**

19. A negative income tax program guarantees a specified income below which family income would not be allowed to fall. **T F**

20. In the NIT program, the benefit-loss rate is the rate at which subsidy benefits decrease as the earned income of a family increases. **T F**

21. The lower the benefit-loss rate, the smaller are the incentives to earn additional income. **T F**

Multiple-Choice

Circle the letter that corresponds to the best answer.

1. Approximately what percentage of all Canadian households had personal incomes of $75,000 and over annually in 1993?
(a) 5%
(b) 10%
(c) 20%
(d) 33%

2. Approximately what percentage of all Canadian households had personal incomes of less than $15,000 a year in 1993?
(a) 4%
(b) 6%
(c) 14%
(d) 20%

3. Which of the following applies to the distribution of incomes in Canada over time?
(a) incomes have fallen in absolute terms
(b) in relative terms inequality has decreased

(c) the relative distribution of income has been fairly stable since 1951
(d) the progressive tax system has resulted in a much more equal after-tax income distribution than the before-tax income distribution.

4. Which of the following would be evidence of a decrease in relative income inequality in Canada?
(a) a decrease in the percentage of total personal income received by the lowest quintile
(b) an increase in the percentage of total personal income received by the highest quintile
(c) an increase in the percentage of total personal income received by the four lowest quintiles
(d) a decrease in the percentage of total personal income received by the four lowest quintiles

5. When a Lorenz curve has been drawn, the degree of income inequality in an economy is measured by:
(a) the slope of the diagonal that runs from the south west to the northeast corner of the diagram
(b) the slope of the Lorenz curve
(c) the area between the Lorenz curve and the axes of the graph
(d) the area between the Lorenz curve and the southwest-northeast diagonal

6. Which of the following is not one of the causes of the unequal distribution of income in Canada?
(a) the unequal distribution of property
(b) the Guaranteed Income Supplement
(c) the inability of the poor to invest in human capital
(d) luck and the unequal distribution of misfortune

7. The case for income inequality is primarily made on the basis that income inequality:
(a) is reduced by the transfer payment programs for the poor
(b) is necessary to maintain incentives to work and produce output
(c) depends on luck and chance, which cannot be corrected by government action
(d) is created by education and training programs that distort the distribution of income

8. The debate over income redistribution focuses on the trade-off between equality and:
(a) efficiency
(b) unemployment
(c) economic growth
(d) economic freedom

9. Suppose that Ms. Carla obtains 5 units of utility from the last dollar of income received by her and that Mr. Robert obtains 8 units of utility from the last dollar of his income. Those who favour an equal distribution of income would:
(a) advocate redistributing income from Robert to Carla
(b) advocate redistributing income from Carla to Robert
(c) be content with this distribution of income between Carla and Robert
(d) argue that any redistribution of income between them would decrease total utility

10. Which of the following measures would tend to reduce income inequality?
(a) eliminating the Unemployment Insurance program
(b) increasing tax deductions for making investments
(c) taxing all personal income at a flat rate
(d) levying large taxes on inheritances

11. Statistics Canada's definition of the "poverty line" for a family of four living in a big city in 1993 is an annual income of about:
(a) $13,000
(b) $24,000
(c) $34,000
(d) $40,000

12. Which of the following is one of the parts of the Canadian income-maintenance system?
(a) public housing
(b) agricultural subsidies
(c) Old Age Security
(d) minimum-wage laws

13. Which of the following is designed to provide a nationwide income for all those aged 65 and over?
(a) Canada Pension Plan
(b) Guaranteed Income Supplement
(c) Canada Assistance Plan
(d) Old Age Security Pension

14. Under a negative income tax (NIT) plan the break-even income is:
(a) the level of income at which income and consumption expenditure are equal
(b) the level of income at which income tax payments equal zero

(c) the level of income equal to the low income cutoff as calculated by Statistics Canada
(d) the level of income at which the NIT subsidy equals zero

15. A negative income tax would provide:
(a) no tax revenues for the government
(b) no work incentives for low income individuals
(c) more work incentives than traditional welfare programs
(d) all Canadians with enough income to be above the poverty line

16. Negative income tax plans have been criticized because it is difficult to construct a plan that:
(a) provides reasonable income levels and incentives to work for the poor, but is not too costly
(b) is not subject to substantial administrative costs and bureaucratic red tape
(c) does not discriminate against those individuals with similar circumstances, but who have dissimilar needs
(d) all of the above are difficulties

Discussion Questions

1. How does the degree of income inequality in Canada compare with other nations, such as the United States, for instance? What causes income inequality in capitalism?

2. Has the distribution of income changed in Canada during the past 30 years? What does this imply about the efficiency of Canada's schemes for income redistribution?

3. If a nation's Lorenz curve becomes more sharply bowed over time, what does that indicate?

4. What difference is there, in your view, between a 19 year-old college student being below the poverty line, and a 39 year-old employed labourer, and father of three, being below the poverty line? Do these cases present different implications for government policy-makers who are attempting to combat poverty?

5. State the case for an equal distribution of income and the case for an unequal distribution. What would be traded for what in the "big trade-off?"

6. What is the currently accepted and more or less official definition of poverty? How many people and what percentage of the Canadian population are poor if we use this definition of poverty?

7. What characteristics-other than the small amounts of money they have to spend-do the greatest concentrations of the poor families of the nation tend to have?

8. Why does poverty in Canada tend to be invisible or hidden?

9. What are the economic incentives inherent in current income maintenance or social suppports mechanisms that lead to so-called "welfare dependence"?

10. Explain how poverty and the unequal distribution of income would be reduced by a negative income tax. In your explanation, be sure to include definitions of guaranteed income, the benefit-loss rate, and break-even income.

11. What are the three goals or objectives of any NIT plan? Explain why there is a conflict among these objectives-why all three goals cannot be achieved simultaneously.

Answers

Fill-in questions

1. inequality; much higher than

2. absolute, basically stable; inequality

3. Lorenz; (a) families, income; (b) lower, upper; (c) Lorenz curve, the line of complete equality (either order)

4. ability, education, training, tastes, property, power

5. (a) utility; (b) economic growth

6. equality, efficiency (either order); (a) smaller; (b) more

7. relative, absolute

8. (a) $23,934; (b) 14.5

9. (a) old; (b) unattached individuals; (c) females; (d) educated; (e) large

10. (a) sizeable year-to-year changes in the composition of the "poor"; (b) isolation of the permanent poor; (c) poor are politically invisible

11. (a) Old Age Security; (b) Guaranteed Income Supplement; (c) Canada Pension Plan; (d) Unemployment Insurance

12. efficient, equitable, incentives

13. guaranteed annual, benefit-loss

14. (a) poverty, (b) incentives, (c) costs; conflicting

Problems and projects

1. (a) (1) Column 4: 18, 30, 44, 61, 80, 91, 100; (2) Column 5: 4, 10, 22, 36, 51, 71, 100; (b) (1) 30, 10; (2) 20, 49

2. (a) NIT Subsidy: 4,000, 3,000, 2,000, 1,000, 0; Total Income: 9,000, 13,000, 17,000, 21,000, 25,000; (1) 4,000, (2) 25,000; (b) NIT Subsidy: 3,750, 2,500, 1250, 0; Total Income: 6,250, 7,500, 8,750, 10,000; (1) 10,000, (2) 2,500; (c) NIT Subsidy: 6,000, 4,500, 3,000, 1,500, 0; Total Income: 9,000, 10,500, 12,000, 13,500, 15,000; (1) 15,000, (2) 18,750; (d) (1) greater, greater, (2) greater, (3) increase, decrease

True-False

1. T	**2.** T	**3.** F	**4.** T	**5.** T	**6.** T
7. T	**8.** T	**9.** T	**10.** T	**11.** T	**12.** F
13. T	**14.** T	**15.** T	**16.** T	**17.** F	**18.** T
19. T	**20.** T	**21.** F			

Multiple-choice

1. (c)	**2.** (b)	**3.** (c)	**4.** (c)	**5.** (d)	**6.** (b)
7. (b)	**8.** (a)	**9.** (b)	**10.** (d)	**11.** (b)	**12.** (c)
13. (d)	**14.** (d)	**15.** (c)	**16.** (d)		

PART

Government and Current Economic Problems

CHAPTER 19

Government and Market Failure: Public Goods, the Environment, and Information Problems

One of the reasons for government interference in the competitive economy is market failure. Some of the major types of these failures lead government to intervene to provide public goods and services, to address externality problems such as pollution, and to improve the quality and amount of information for buyers and sellers in private markets.

The chapter begins by reviewing the characteristics of public goods. You should recall from Chapter 5 that a private good is divisible and subject to the exclusion principle, whereas a public good is indivisible and not subject to exclusion. In Chapter 19 you see how the demand curve and schedule for a public good is derived, and how the optimal production of a public good is determined. Government can employ benefit-cost analysis to determine which public goods government should provide, and to what level they should provide them. The optimal scale of government provision of public goods is the point at which the marginal benefit equals the marginal cost of providing the good or service. While the basic principles of benefit-cost analysis are straightforward, difficulties in evaluating and measuring the costs and benefits limits the application of benefit-cost analysis.

The second topic of Chapter 19 is externalities, a situation where a benefit or cost is imposed upon a third party who is not involved in a transaction. In the presence of externalities, a misallocation of resources occurs since the third party cost or benefit is not taken into account by the decision makers. In Chapter 5 you saw that governments can act to offset this resource misallocation by imposing a tax in the case of an external cost and a subsidy when external benefits occur. In addition to these policy approaches, Chapter 19 outlines other kinds of solutions.

There are situations where government interference is not required to offset externalities. Private lawsuits are sometimes an alternative, and therefore act as a deterrent to externalities. The Coase Theorem suggests that individual bargaining can settle externality problems where property rights are clearly defined, the number of people involved is small, and bargaining costs are low. For some externalities, property rights are held by society. When the effects of externalities are widely dispersed over the population it may be possible for the government to create externality rights and sell such rights to the agents responsible for creating the externality. In the case of pollution, the government would sell "rights" to pollute. However, there would still be a governmental presence in the marketplace as some authority must still determine the volume and disposition of the created property rights. Many of our current resource problems, including the state of the Atlantic and Pacific fisheries, can be viewed as the consequences of the lack of property rights in common resources.

Pollution is a prime example of a negative externality. The ultimate physical cause of pollution is the *law of conservation of energy*. The production of goods and services uses resources that ultimately become waste, which our environment cannot readily absorb. Over the years the government has developed a number of anti-pollution policies, some of which use market incentives to determine an optimal volume of pollution. You will also discover how the market forces of demand and supply in the recycling market help to reduce some of the demands for dumping solid waste in landfills.

The third main class of market failure addressed by Chapter 19 is asymmetric information. You probably have never thought about the role of information in the functioning of markets, but here you will discover how important information is to buyer and seller. For example, buyers need some assurance about the measurement standards or quality of products that they purchase, be it gasoline or medical care. The government may intervene in some markets to ensure that this information is made available.

Inadequate information in markets creates problems for sellers too. In certain markets, such as insurance, sellers experience a *moral hazard problem* because buyers change their attitude toward risk upon being insured, and this behaviour makes it more costly for the insurers. There is also an *adverse selection* problem in the insurance market because those buyers most likely to collect insurance benefits purchase large amounts of insurance. This group imposes higher costs on sellers than if the purchasers were randomly spread among the population. Because sellers will tend to screen buyers, fewer people will be covered by insurance, creating a situation that may provoke government to provide social insurance. Governments may also distribute information about workplace safety or enforce safety standards to address information problems in resource markets.

Many market failures require government intervention, but there are also many that can be handled more efficiently through individual negotiations, or the use of market incentives.

Checklist

When you have studied this chapter, you should be able to:

- ☐ Compare the characteristics of a public good with a private good.
- ☐ Calculate the demand (or collective willingness to pay) for a public good from data on individuals' demands for the good.
- ☐ Find the optimal allocation of a public good, given data on marginal costs and marginal benefits.
- ☐ Use benefit-cost analysis to determine the extent to which government should apply resources to a project or activity when you are given the cost and benefit data.
- ☐ Define a spillover cost and a spillover benefit, and give examples of each.
- ☐ Use supply and demand graphs to show how spillovers create inefficient resource allocation.
- ☐ State the conditions that are necessary for the Coase theorem and give an example of its use.
- ☐ Evaluate the conditions under which liability rules and private lawsuits may provide solutions to externalities.
- ☐ Identify two means governments can use to counter spillover costs.
- ☐ Identify three options governments have for dealing with cases of spillover benefits.
- ☐ Draw and explain a graph that illustrates the concept of an optimal amount of pollution abatement.
- ☐ Describe the dimensions of the pollution problem and provide some reasons for the continuing deterioration of the environment.
- ☐ Explain how the creation of a market for pollution rights could provide an incentive to control air pollution.
- ☐ Compare the advantages of a market for pollution rights to direct controls.
- ☐ Describe the solid waste disposal problem and the reason for the interest in recycling.
- ☐ Explain how government can influence the market for recyclable input.
- ☐ Define the meaning of "information failure" and "asymmetric information."
- ☐ Explain how lack of information about sellers can lead to market failure, and give two examples of how government can solve this problem.
- ☐ Define the meaning of "moral hazard" and "adverse selection."
- ☐ Explain the two problems that can arise in the insurance market because of incomplete information about buyers.
- ☐ Cite an example of how information difficulties have been overcome by the market economy without government intervention.

Chapter Outline

1. The market system fails to provide an optimal allocation of resources to the production of public goods. A public good is indivisible and not subject to exclusion--once it is provided for one person it is available for all.
(a) It is in the interest of consumers to conceal their preferences for such goods, since the benefits of the good will be obtained if someone else pays for its production. The market demand curve will underestimate the collective benefit from provision of the good.
(b) If the true demand by each individual for the public good is known, a collective demand schedule is obtained

by summing the prices that people are willing to pay collectively for the last unit of the public good at each quantity demanded. The optimal production of a public good is given at the intersection of the collective demand (or marginal benefit) curve and the supply (or marginal cost) curve.
(c) If the marginal benefit exceeds the marginal cost there is an underallocation of resources to the public good. This is likely to be the case in the absence of government intervention.

2. Benefit-cost analysis may be employed by government to determine whether it should employ resources for a project and to decide upon the total quantity of resources it should devote to a project. Additional resources should be devoted to a project only so long as the marginal benefit to society from using the additional resources for the project exceeds the marginal cost to society of the additional resources. In using benefit-cost analysis, however, government encounters the problem of measuring benefits and costs accurately.

3. Market failure can arise from externalities or spillovers, where a third party bears a cost resulting from the consumption or production of a good or service. Negative externalities lead to an overallocation of resources to a commodity and positive externalities lead to an underallocation of resources.
(a) Individual bargaining can be used to correct negative externalities, or to encourage positive externalities. The Coase Theorem suggests that private bargaining can overcome the externality problem when property rights are specified, the number of people involved is small, and the bargaining costs low.
(b) The legal system, which specifies liability rules and defines property rights, can also be used to adjudicate claims arising from externalities. Expense, length of time required, and uncertainty of the outcomes are deterrents to using the courts to resolve externalities.

4. When there is potential for severe harm to common resources, such as air or water, and when a large number of people are involved, two types of government intervention may be necessary.
(a) Direct controls use legislation to ban or limit the activities that produce negative externalities. The goal is to reduce the supply of an externality creating product to its allocatively efficient level.
(b) Specific taxes are also applied to activities that produce negative externalities. By increasing the cost of production, these taxes also decrease supply to the allocatively efficient level.
(c) When there are spillover benefits, other government actions may be necessary to correct for the underallocation of resources.
(1) Government can offer subsidies to buyers to encourage consumption of a good.
(2) Government can offer subsidies to producers to reduce the cost of production and increase output.
(3) When spillover benefits are extremely large, government may provide the good or service.

5. Another solution has been to create a market for externality rights. For example in an area where pollution is a problem:
(a) The government might set a limit for the permitted amount of pollution, and then allocate rights or permits based on willingness to pay.
(b) The permitted amount of pollution would be rationed to those polluters who are willing to pay the most.
(c) It is not economically efficient to totally eliminate a negative externality such as pollution. For society the optimal reduction occurs where the marginal cost to society and the marginal benefit of reducing the externality are equal (MB = MC).

6. Pollution provides a prime example of a major negative externality for our industrial society.
(a) The dimensions of the problem are extensive and include air pollution, toxic waste, solid-waste disposal, oil spills, and potential changes to the climate.
(b) The causes of the pollution problem relate to the *law of conservation of matter and energy*. Matter used for production of goods and services ultimately gets transformed into waste (in the form of matter and energy) after it is consumed. The problem arises when the amount of waste exceeds the amount that the environment can safely reabsorb. The result would be a rapidly changing environment requiring a large and rapid reallocation of resources. The standard of living of much of mankind would be threatened.
(c) Population density, rising income, changing technology, and economic incentives are all factors contributing to the pollution problem.
(d) Direct controls to limit the amount of pollutants have dominated public policy in Canada. In the United States pollution rights, whose quantity reflects the carrying capacity of the environment, have been created and issued to firms. A market has developed for these

pollution rights and provides an incentive for the most efficient use of the environmental resources.

7. Solid waste is usually deposited in garbage dumps or is incinerated. Dumps and incinerators create negative externalities, and they are becoming increasingly expensive. The situation has created a market for recycled items to help reduce this pollution problem. Government can use direct legislation or demand and supply incentives to encourage recycling as an alternative to dumping or incineration for solid waste.

8. Market failure can occur because of incomplete or inaccurate information. These failures arise from asymmetric information--unequal knowledge this is held by parties to a market transaction. When information about sellers is incomplete, inaccurate, or very costly, then there will be market failure. For example, consumers need accurate information about product quality of automobiles and assurance about the credentials of physicians. The cost would be prohibitive if each buyer had to verify the claims made by auto manufacturers and alleged physicians, so the market economy would be much less effective. Government can remedy such information failures by establishing measurement standards, testing requirements, and licensing bureaus.

9. The market economy also fails to achieve allocative efficiency because of inadequate information about buyers.
(a) A market may produce less than the optimal amount of goods from society's perspective because of a moral hazard problem. This problem results when buyers alter their behaviour and increase the cost to the seller. For example, the provision of insurance may cause the insured to be less cautious.
(b) There is also an adverse selection problem that occurs in many markets. In the case of insurance, the buyers most likely to need or benefit from insurance are the ones most likely to purchase it. These higher-risk buyers impose higher costs on sellers. Sellers then screen out the higher-risk buyers, but this action reduces the population covered by insurance in the private market. In some cases, government may establish a social insurance system that is designed to cover a much broader portion of the population than would be covered by the private insurers, such as with basic health insurance, or unemployment insurance.

10. Market failure can occur in resource markets when there is inadequate information for workers about the health hazards or safety of a workplace. Governments can correct these problems by publishing health and safety information, or by forcing businesses to publish more information. The more typical approach is for government to define acceptable standards and use the legal system for their enforcement.

11. Government does not always need to interfere in the private market to address information problems. Businesses have devised strategies to overcome the lack of information. In fact, some businesses, such as credit bureaus, exist specifically to profit from providing information to other businesses.

Terms and Concepts

adverse selection problem
asymmetric information
benefit-cost analysis
Coase theorem
law of conservation of matter and energy
marginal benefit = marginal cost rule
market for externality rights
moral hazard problem
optimal reduction of an externality

Hints and Tips

1. A review of Chapter 5 would be very useful because you might not have seen the concepts of externalities and public good for quite some time.

2. Table 19-3 is a useful summary of methods of dealing with externality problems. On this general topic, note the variety of interventions available to government, including some imaginative ways to harness market incentives.

3. Note that when one considers the existence of public goods, the notion of efficiency in government clearly does not mean that government should minimize its spending, or its activities.

Fill-In Questions

1. A public good is one which is __________ and which is not subject to the __________ principle. Once a public good is produced, the benefits flowing from the good cannot be confined to the purchaser and result in a __________-__________ effect. Because benefits can be obtained if someone else purchases the good buyers (will, will not) __________ reveal their true preferences. The market demand curve for a public good will be significantly __________.

2. If individual demand curves for a public good were known, a market demand curve could be constructed by adding the __________ people are collectively willing to pay for the last unit of the public good at each quantity demanded. The collective demand curve indicates the combined __________ for the individuals from consuming an extra unit of the public good, and is constructed as a (horizontal, vertical) __________ sum of all the individual demand curves.

3. In applying benefit-cost analysis, government should employ more resources in the public sector if the marginal (costs, benefits) __________ from the additional public goods exceed the marginal (costs, benefits) __________ of providing the goods.

4. Spillovers occur when benefits or costs associated with the production or consumption of a good impact on a __________ party. Spillovers are also called __________.

5. In the event of spillover benefits accompanying the production of a good, then resources will be __________ to the production of that good by the market economy. In the event of spillover costs, resources will be __________ to the production of that good.

6. The Coase theorem suggests that when there are __________ or __________ externalities in situations where __________ rights are clearly defined, the number of people involved is __________ and bargaining costs are __________, then government intervention (is, is not) __________ required.

7. The legal system is important for settling externality disputes between parties because it specifies __________ rights and specifies __________ rules that can be used for lawsuits.

8. One method to remedy a negative externality such as pollution is to create a market for __________.

9. Eliminating all pollution (may, may not) __________ be economically desirable even if it were technologically possible as the optimal amount of externality reduction occurs where, for society, the __________ of reduction equals the __________.

10. The pollution problem stems from the law of __________ of matter and energy. Matter used for the production of goods and services ultimately gets transformed into __________, which is another form of matter or energy that the environment may not be able to __________.

11. The immediate reasons for the pollution problem are increases in population __________, rising __________, changes in __________, and lack of economic __________ to refrain from polluting.

12. If a single firm in an industry is socially responsible and installs pollution-abating equipment, the result will be (higher, lower) __________ costs, a __________ market for its product, diminished __________ and the prospect of __________.

13. A specific tax on a pollution-producing substance would shift its supply curve __________, raise equilibrium __________, and __________ the equilibrium output.

14. Garbage dumps and incineration are becoming increasingly expensive due to the high __________ cost of land-fill sites and the __________ externalities created by dumps. An alternative to dumps or burning is __________. Government policies can be enacted to provide incentives on the __________ side or the __________ side of the market.

15. A recyclable material is an __________ in the productive process and its demand depends partly on the demand for the __________ it is used to produce. The demand also depends upon the cost of using original __________ rather than recycling. The more costly it is to use recycled material relative to original raw materials, the (greater, less) __________ the demand for recycled inputs. Government can take advantage of these facts to stimulate the market for recycled inputs by (subsidizing, taxing) __________ the use of recycled inputs, and __________ the use of original inputs.

16. Markets can produce information failures when information about sellers is incomplete or obtaining the information is very __________. To overcome these deficiencies, government establishes __________ for measurement or quality. In the medical market, the government protects consumers by __________ physicians.

17. Inadequate information about buyers can lead to two problems. First, if a market situation arises where buyers alter their behaviour and increase the cost to the seller, then a __________ problem has been created. Second, if buyers withhold information from sellers that would impose a large cost on sellers, then an adverse __________ problem has been created. The first problem occurs (at the same time, after) __________ a person makes a purchase, but the second problem occurs __________ the buyer makes a purchase.

18. The __________ problem eliminates the pooling of risk, which is the basis for profitable __________. Governments overcome this problem by requiring __________ participation in social insurance schemes.

19. Another example of information failure occurs in the labour markets where there is incomplete or inadequate information about workplace __________. The government will intervene in these situations to publish __________ or to enforce __________.

Problems and Projects

1. Given below are three individuals' demand schedules for mosquito control (a public good). Columns (2), (3) and (4) show the prices individuals A, B, and C are willing to pay for additional units of this program. Assume these three people are the only ones in society.
(a) Fill in the collective demand schedule column (5) below.
(b) Given the marginal cost schedule (6), would any of the individuals buy any mosquito control on their own? _____
(c) The optimal quantity of mosquito control is _____.
(d) The total net gain to this society is $_____ if the optimal quantity of mosquito control is undertaken.

(1) Quantity	(2) Pa	(3) Pb	(4) Pc	(5) Price	(6) MC
1	$15	$8	$10	$____	$16
2	12	7	8	____	18
3	8	6	6	____	20
4	6	5	4	____	22
5	5	4	3	____	24
6	4	3	2	____	26

2. Imagine that the city of Moose Jaw is considering the construction of a new arena for its Junior A hockey team. The city's estimate of the total costs and the total benefits of areas with various different seating capacities are shown below. (All figures are in millions of dollars.)

Seats	Total Cost	MC	Total Benefit	MB	Total Net Benefit
no arena	$0	- -	$0	- -	$0
3000	12	$___	20	$___	___
4000	15	___	26	___	___
5000	17	___	29	___	___
6000	20	___	31	___	___

(a) Fill in the marginal cost, marginal benefit, and total net benefit of 3000, 4000, 5000 and 6000 seat arenas.

(b) Will it benefit the city to allocate resources to construct an arena? ________

(c) If Moose Jaw builds an arena:

(1) it should be the ________ seat version

(2) the total cost will be $________

(3) the total benefit will be $________

(4) the net benefit to the city will be $________.

3. Assume the atmosphere of Metropolitan Toronto is unable to reabsorb more than 1,500 tonnes of pollutants per year. The following schedule shows the price polluters would be willing to pay for the right to dispose of 1 tonne of pollutants per year, and the total quantity of pollutants they would wish to dispose of at each price.

Price (per tonne of pollution rights)	Total Quantity of Pollution Rights Demanded (tonnes)
$ 0	4,000
1,000	3,500
2,000	3,000
3,000	2,500
4,000	2,000
5,000	1,500
6,000	1,000
7,000	500

(a) If there were no emission fee, polluters would put __________ tonnes of pollutants in the air each year; this quantity of pollutants would exceed the ability of nature to reabsorb them by _____ tonnes.

(b) To reduce pollution to the capacity of the atmosphere to recycle pollutants, an emission fee of $_____ per tonne should be set.

(c) Were this emission fee set, the total emission fees collected would be $_____.

(d) Were the quantity of pollution rights demanded at each price to increase by 500 tonnes, the emission fee could be increased by $_____ and total emission fees collected would increase by $_____.

4. The marginal cost of pollution abatement differs between two industrial firms. The data for the Acrid Acid Co. and the Smoky Smelter Ltd. are shown below:

Acrid Acid Unit of Abatement	MC	Smelly Smelter Unit of Abatement	MC
1	$1	1	$1
2	3	2	2
3	7	3	3
4	12	4	4
5	18	5	5
6	25	6	6

(a) The second unit of pollution abatement by Acrid would cost it $_____.

(b) The third unit of pollution abatement by Smelly would cost it $ _____. Suppose the government decides to reduce pollution by 6 units and demands a 3-unit reduction by both firms:

(c) the total cost to Acrid will be $_____,

(d) the total cost to Smelly will be $_____,

(e) the total cost of the 6-unit reduction will be $_____.

Instead of the above division, suppose that Acrid was required to reduce pollution by 2 units and Smelly by 4 units:

(f) the total cost to Acrid will be $_____

(g) the total cost to Smelly will be $_____

(h) the total cost of the 6-unit reduction will be $______. By requiring equal reductions by both firms, the cost of pollution reduction (will, will not) __________ be minimized. Suppose the government, instead of demanding a 6-unit reduction in pollution, placed a tax of $3.50 on each unit of pollution:

(i) Acrid would reduce pollution by __________ units.

(j) Smelly would reduce pollution by __________ units.

(k) with the tax each firm (will, will not) __________ reduce pollution by the same amount. The firm with the highest marginal cost of pollution abatement will reduce pollution the (most, least) __________, and this (is, is not) __________ socially efficient.

5. In question 4 suppose each firm was causing 6 units of pollution and the government wanted to reduce pollution to a total of 6 units by issuing 3 tradeable pollution rights to each firm.

(a) Without trading, Acrid must abate pollution by _____ units. If it obtained one more pollution right, it would have to abate pollution by _____ units and would save $_____. If Acrid could get a pollution right for less than $_____, it would (increase, decrease) __________ net income.

(b) Without trading, Smelly must abate pollution by _____ units. By giving up one of its pollution rights, Smelly will have to abate pollution by _____ units at an extra cost of $____. If Smelly could get more than $_____ for a pollution right, it would (increase, decrease) __________ its net income.

(c) Both firms would benefit if the pollution unit sold for more than $_____ but less than $_____.

(d) Explain why only one pollution right would be exchanged between the two profit-maximizing firms.

6. In the next column are two graphs.

(a) Use the first to draw in another curve that reflects the inclusion of spillover costs.

(b) Compare the current allocation of resources with the efficient allocation.

(c) How might the government solve the problem using a tax or subsidy?

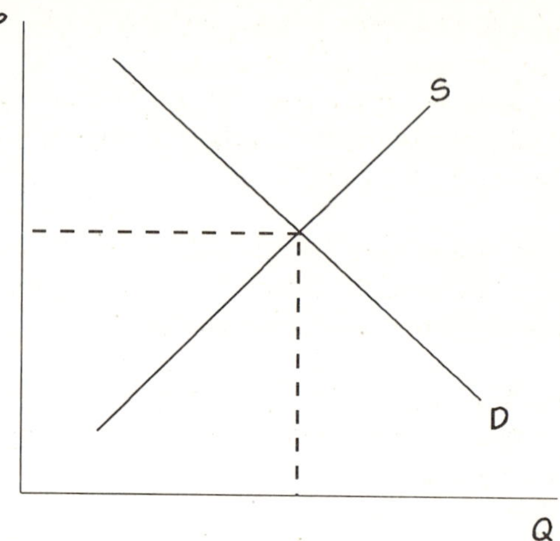

(d) Use the next graph to draw in another curve that reflects the inclusion of spillover benefits.

(e) Compare the current allocation of resources with the efficient allocation.

(f) How might the government solve the problem using a tax or subsidy?

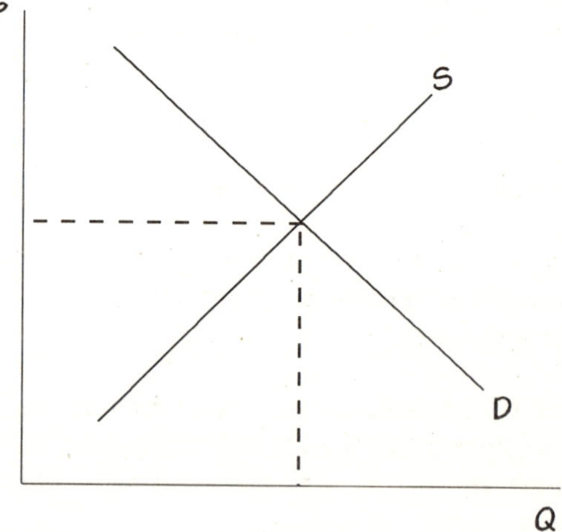

7. Singh has a tree that blocks Cohen's view of English Bay. The view can only be cleared by falling the tree.

(a) What would the Coase Theorem suggest as a way to determine whether the tree should be cut down or not? Does the Coase Theorem seem applicable in this case?

(b) Why would the Coase Theorem be less useful if Singh's tree obstructs the angle of view for ten or fifteen different houses in the neighbourhood?

True-False

Circle T if the statement is true, F if it is false.

1. For public goods the free-rider problem occurs when people can receive benefits without contributing to the cost of providing the good. **T F**

2. When determining the demand for a public good, we add the prices various individuals are willing to pay for the last unit at each quantity demanded. **T F**

3. Benefit-cost analysis is a method of evaluating public projects by comparing the marginal benefits and marginal costs attributed to the project. **T F**

4. In practice it is usually quite simple to estimate the costs and benefits of a project financed by the government. **T F**

5. A spillover or externality is a cost or benefit that is imposed upon an individual or group external to the market transaction. **T F**

6. When spillover costs exist, it means that private costs do not fully reflect all the costs flowing from the transaction. **T F**

7. Resources are overallocated to the production of goods that confer spillover benefits. **T F**

8. A government subsidy could be used to correct the misallocation of resources that results when spillover benefits are present. **T F**

9. The Coase theorem states that as long as private property rights exist, the market system will correct for the presence of externalities without government interference. **T F**

10. The optimal amount of pollution abatement occurs when the marginal benefit from further pollution reduction is zero. **T F**

11. The market system penalizes the socially conscious firm in comparison to its polluting competitors. **T F**

12. Taxes imposed on products that create pollution will lower the marginal cost of production and increase supply. **T F**

13. The issuing and the trading of pollution rights is the main policy initiative used by governments in Canada to control pollution. **T F**

14. When governments allow pollution rights to be bought and sold, the governments have created a form of property. **T F**

15. In the market for pollution rights, if a government sets a fixed level for pollution, the supply curve of pollution rights will be perfectly elastic. **T F**

16. The economically efficient level of pollution is zero, so the government is pursuing an inefficient solution when it issues pollution rights. **T F**

The next two questions assume that, at present, newsprint production uses no recycled inputs, although they are available.

17. If the government mandates that newsprint must be made up of 50% recycled products, the demand for used newsprint will shift to the left. **T F**

18. If the government mandates that newsprint must be made up of 50% recycled products, the price of a newspaper would rise, other things being equal. **T F**

19. The inspection of meat products by the federal government for quality is justified on the grounds that it reduces the costs of obtaining information in the marketplace. **T F**

20. If the provision of deposit insurance encourages financial firms to invest in more risky business ventures, then it has created a moral hazard. **T F**

21. The "lemon" principle states that goods available in second-hand markets are of below average quality. **T F**

22. The adverse selection problem results when information is known only by the first party to a contract and, as a result, the second party incurs major expenses. **T F**

Multiple-Choice

Circle the letter that corresponds to the best answer.

1. A spillover cost exists when:
(a) a part of the cost of a transaction is placed on an uninvolved third party
(b) a part of the cost of a transaction is paid for by the government
(c) the private and social costs of production are equal
(d) marginal cost is greater than average cost

2. If external benefits accompany the production of a good:
(a) resources will be overallocated to the production of the good
(b) resources will be underallocated to the production of the good
(c) a tax on the production of the good will result in the optimum production of the good
(d) the market demand curve for the good overstates the total benefit flowing from the consumption of the good

3. The government could promote the optimal output when the production of a good causes spillover costs by:
(a) applying the provisions of the Competition Act
(b) a tax on the production of the good
(c) a subsidy to consumers of the good
(d) a subsidy to producers of the good

4. According to the Coase theorem:
(a) government intervention is required to overcome the misallocation of resources when spillovers are present
(b) the best way to remedy negative externalities is to create pollution rights
(c) public goods should be financed by the government with tax revenue generated by a progressive tax
(d) negative externalities can be solved through bargaining--as long as one party to the dispute has clearly defined property rights, affected parties are few, and bargaining costs are small.

5. Which of the following would do little or nothing to reduce pollution?
(a) create a market for pollution rights
(b) charge polluters an emission fee
(c) enact legislation that prohibits pollution and fines polluters
(d) redesign the environmental regulation agencies

6. An emission fee levied against polluters will:
(a) encourage the use of pollution-abatement equipment
(b) eliminate pollution
(c) reduce the revenues of governments that levy the fee
(d) externalize the internal costs of pollution

7. An increase in the demand for pollution rights will:
(a) increase both the quantity of pollutants discharged and the market price of pollution rights
(b) increase the quantity discharged and have no effect on the market price
(c) have no effect on the quantity discharged and increase the market price
(d) have no effect on either the quantity discharged or the market price

8. User charges imposed on those who drive on urban expressways would tend to:
(a) relieve congestion on the expressways
(b) discourage the use of public transportation facilities
(c) reduce the funds available for the expansion of the expressway system
(d) do all of the above

9. Public goods differ from private goods in that public goods are:
(a) divisible
(b) subject to the exclusion principle
(c) not subject to the free-rider problem
(d) *not* divisible and *not* subject to exclusion

Answer the next four questions on the basis of the following information for a public good. Q_{d1} and Q_{d2} represent the quantities of the public good demanded at each price by individuals 1 and 2, the only two people in society. Q_S represents the supply curve for the public good in the society.

Price	Qd 1	Qd 2	Qs
$7	0	0	6
6	0	1	5
5	1	2	4
4	2	3	3
3	3	4	2
2	4	5	1
1	5	6	0

10. This society is willing to pay what amount for the third unit of the public good?

(a) $7
(b) $6
(c) $5
(d) $4

11. This society is willing to pay what amount for the fifth unit of the public good?
(a) $5
(b) $4
(c) $3
(d) $2

12. Given the supply Q_S, the optimal price and quantity of the public good in this society will be:
(a) $7 and 5 units
(b) $5 and 4 units
(c) $4 and 3 units
(d) $3 and 2 units

13. If this good were a private good instead of a public good, the total quantity demanded at the $2 price would be:
(a) 9 units
(b) 8 units
(c) 7 units
(d) 6 units

14. In the Canadian economy the reallocation of resources needed to provide for the production of public goods is accomplished by means of:
(a) government subsidies to the producers of public goods
(b) government purchases of public goods from producers
(c) direct control of producers of both private and public goods
(d) direct control of producers of public goods only

15. The ultimate cause of pollution is:
(a) profit-seeking in the market economy
(b) the law of conservation of matter and energy
(c) rising incomes
(d) the greenhouse effect

16. The optimal amount of pollution control occurs where:
(a) pollution is eliminated
(b) the marginal benefit from pollution control equals zero
(c) the marginal benefit from pollution control is maximized
(d) the marginal benefit from pollution control equals the marginal cost of the controls.

17. If the government places a $40 tax on each unit of pollution produced by a firm, all of the following hold with the exception of:
(a) the firm saves $40 for each unit of pollution it eliminates
(b) the tax creates an incentive to reduce the amount of pollution produced
(c) the firm will eliminate pollution completely if the cost of eliminating the last unit is less than $40
(d) the profits of the firm will decrease

18. Which of the following has not contributed to the pollution problem in Canada?
(a) increasing population density
(b) rising incomes
(c) more use of plastic and aluminum containers
(d) rising real price for gasoline

19. The result of government legislation, requiring a different and more costly production technique to reduce pollution in the newsprint-producing industry, will be:
(a) an increase in production and the price of newsprint
(b) a reduction in production and the price of newsprint
(c) increased employment in the industries supplying inputs for newsprint
(d) a reduction in production and an increase in the price of newsprint

20. Which of the following would tend to increase the demand for recycled paper?
(a) an increase in the price of regular paper
(b) an increase in taxes on paper production
(c) a decrease in interest in protecting the environment
(d) a decrease in the price of pulpwood used in the production of regular paper.

21. In order to encourage recycling instead of the use of dumps the government could carry out all of the following except:
(a) place specific taxes on the inputs substitutable for the recycled input
(b) legislate the use of recycled inputs in the production process
(c) subsidize garbage pickup

(d) shift its purchases toward goods produced with recycled inputs

22. In insurance, the moral hazard problem arises because:
(a) people tend to be untruthful when asked about their medical history
(b) large insurance payouts may prompt some people to act in an immoral manner
(c) people who have insurance coverage tend to alter their behaviour in a way that is costly to the seller of insurance
(d) of the random nature of accidents

23. The inclusion of a deductible clause (for example, the insured is responsible for the first $250 of an accident claim) will:
(a) decrease the problems arising out of adverse selection
(b) decrease the moral hazard problem
(c) increase insurance premiums
(d) none of the above

24. If the government mandates that deposit insurance on deposits at financial institutions be increased to $240,000 for each depositor, this action would create a moral hazard problem because it may:
(a) lead to careful screening of depositors and the source of their funds
(b) reduce the amount of deposits made by customers
(c) encourage the making of riskier loans
(d) reduce bank investments in real estate

25. The "lemon" principle can be phrased as:
(a) good money drives out bad money
(b) *caveat venditor*-let the seller beware
(c) poor-quality products will drive out high-quality products
(d) don't look a gift horse in the mouth

Discussion Questions

1. What is "market failure" and what are the three major kinds of such failures?

2. What basic method does government employ in Canada to reallocate resources away from the production of private goods and toward the production of public goods?

3. Describe benefit-cost analysis and state the rules used to make a decision from a marginal and total perspective. What are the two major problems encountered when benefit-cost analysis is utilized by government?

4. What rules can society use to determine the optimal level of pollution abatement? What are the problems with this approach?

5. If society creates pollution rights, how should the rights be distributed and who should receive the revenue from any subsequent sale of these rights?

6. According to widely accepted theories, the earth has been evolving for millions and millions of years and today's environment is the end result of that process. Why, then, all the recent fuss by economists over environmental changes?

7. Suppose the Canadian government decided to issue pollution rights and asked your advice on the following:
(a) What volume of pollution rights should be created?
(b) How should the pollution rights be distributed among firms and/or individuals?
(c) Should rights, once created, be purchased and sold on a "pollution rights market"? What are your answers?

8. Explain why economists claim that it might be optimal to allow some pollution.

9. The government can control pollution directly by setting pollution standards or indirectly by placing a tax on pollution. Enumerate some of the advantages and problems that are connected with both methods.

10. At most race tracks "claiming races" are quite popular as a device to classify horses. In the claiming race any horse entered to run can be claimed by any driver, trainer, or horse owner at the track for a predetermined price. Thus in a "$15,000 claimer" any horse entered in the race can be claimed for that price. Apply the "lemon principle" to predict the quality of horse to be found in cheap claimers. Explain how, as a horse owner, you could take advantage of your knowledge of the "lemon principle."

11. Explain what is meant by the "moral hazard problem'" and describe how it affects sellers. Should car insurance firms be allowed to refuse insurance to a client with a long list of accident claims on his/her record? Before you answer, remember there is an externality involved (insurance not only protects the insured but also other members of the travelling public).

12. In what way does workplace safety become an informational problem? How might this problem be resolved by government or business?

Answers

Fill-in questions

1. indivisible, exclusion; free, rider; will not, understated

2. prices; utilities; vertical

3. benefits, costs

4. third party, externality

5. underallocated; overallocated

6. positive,negative, property, small small, is not

7. property, liability

8. externality rights

9. may not, marginal benefit, marginal cost

10. conservation; waste, recycle (absorb)

11. density, incomes, technological, incentive

12. higher, smaller, profits, bankruptcy

13. leftward, price, decrease

14. opportunity, negative; recycling; demand, supply

15. input, product; raw materials; less; subsidizing, taxing

16. expensive; standards; licensing

17. moral hazard; selection; after, at the same time

18. adverse selection, insurance; universal

19. safety; information, standards

Problems and projects

1. (a) $33, 27, 20, 15, 12, 9; (b) no; (c) 3; (d) 26.

2. (a) MC: $12, 3, 2, 3; MB: $20, 6, 3, 2; (b) Yes; (c) (1) 5000, (2) $17 million, (3) $29 million, (4) $12 million.

3. (a) 4,000, 2,500; (b) 5,000; (c) 7,500,000; (d) 1,000, 1,500,000

4. (a) $3; (b) $3; (c) $11; (d) $6; (e) $17; (f) $4, (g) $10; (h) $14; will not; (i) 2; (j) 3; (k) will not; least, is.

5. (a) 3, 2, $7; $7, increase (b) 3, 4, $4; $4, increase (c) $4, $7

6. (b) overallocation; (c) impose per unit tax on the activity leading to spillover; (e) underallocation; (f) give a subsidy to producers or consumers of the activity

7. (a) bargaining between the individuals; if property rights are specified, then yes, since numbers are few and transactions costs seem to be low; (b) the increased numbers raise transactions costs

True-False

1. T	**2.** T	**3.** T	**4.** F	**5.** T	**6.** T
7. F	**8.** T	**9.** F	**10.** F	**11.** T	**12.** F
13. F	**14.** T	**15.** F	**16.** F	**17.** F	**18.** T
19. T	**20.** T	**21.** T	**22.** F		

Multiple-choice

1. (a)	**2.** (b)	**3.** (b)	**4.** (d)	**5.** (d)	**6.** (a)
7. (c)	**8.** (a)	**9.** (d)	**10.** (a)	**11.** (c)	**12.** (b)
13. (a)	**14.** (b)	**15.** (b)	**16.** (d)	**17.** (a)	**18.** (d)
19. (d)	**20.** (a)	**21.** (c)	**22.** (c)	**23.** (b)	**24.** (c)
25. (c)					

CHAPTER 20

Public Choice Theory and Taxation

Chapter 19 discussed instances of market failure in the competitive economy, making the case for government intervention to correct the misallocation of resources that accompanies market failure. Chapter 20 takes the opposite perspective, examining problems of government failure to make correct decisions that also lead to inefficient use of scarce resources. For this explanation, you will be introduced to public choice theory, which is the economic analysis of public decision making. Later in the chapter you will learn more about public finance, which deals with the principles of taxation and the effects of particular kinds of taxes. The chapter ends with a review of two recent tax reforms, and an outline of two divergent views on the relationship between the size of the public sector and the extent of individual freedoms.

Government decision making in Canada depends ultimately upon a democratic process that uses a majority voting rule. Yet it is possible for a majority voting rule to produce results that lead to an inefficient allocation of resources. In some cases the benefits from public goods are greater than the costs, but the majority vote against them; and then again, the costs can be greater than the benefits, and the majority vote in favour of providing the good. Sometimes the actions of interest groups and political logrolling overcome some of the inefficiencies of majority voting, but this is really a case of two wrongs maybe making a right.

Depending upon how the election is set up, majority voting can produce results that are inconsistent with the ranking of preferences by society. You should carefully work through the example presented in the chapter because it illustrates how opposing outcomes are possible under a system of majority voting. The median voter model predicts that in a system of majority voting the median voter, or the person holding the middle position, strongly determines the result of a vote.

The second part of the chapter discusses other reasons for inefficiency of government: (1) the special-interest effect and rent-seeking behaviour result in programs that transfer income among different groups through the exercise of market power; (2) politicians opt for programs that provide clear-cut benefits and hidden costs; (3) public choices are limited and inflexible because they tend to entail voting on "bundles" of programs; and (4) bureaucratic inefficiencies in the public sector arise from a lack of the economic incentives and competitive pressures found in most private sector industries.

Chapter 20 then turns from public choice theory to public finance. The basic philosophies on how taxes should be levied are introduced; along with a description of a progressive, a proportional, and a regressive tax system. The main types of Canadian taxes are discussed with respect to these attributes. Another key issue is the incidence of a tax (who ultimately ends up paying). The elasticity of demand and supply determine how much of a tax will be paid by buyers and how much of it will be paid by sellers. Taxes entail an efficiency loss for society, and the extent of this loss is also related to the elasticities of demand and supply.

The question arises as to whether an increase in the size of government's role in the economy reduces or expands the freedoms of individual Canadians. Two cases are presented: the case of those who argue that expanded governmental activity reduces personal freedom and the case of those who contend it may actually lead to greater individual freedom.

Checklist

When you have studied this chapter, you should be able to:

- ☐ Define public choice theory and describe how it can explain various inefficiencies in public decision making.
- ☐ Illustrate how majority voting can yield both an inefficient "yes" vote and an inefficient "no" vote.
- ☐ Describe how interest groups and political logrolling can affect the inefficiencies that may accompany majority voting.
- ☐ Give and analyse an example of the paradox of voting.
- ☐ Explain why the median voter is able to exert undue influence on the outcome in a majority voting process.
- ☐ Describe how rent-seeking behaviour and the special-interest effect influence public decision making.
- ☐ Compare the nature of choices available to citizens in the private realm with the choices available to them in the public realm.
- ☐ Compare the incentives for economic efficiency and the criteria used in determining success in the private sector with those that exist in public agencies and bureaucracies.
- ☐ Explain the two basic philosophies on the distribution of the tax burden among society's members.
- ☐ Define a progressive, a proportional, and a regressive tax system and provide examples of each from the array of taxes levied in Canada.
- ☐ Explain how the incidence of a tax is related to the elasticity of demand and supply.
- ☐ Explain what is meant by the "efficiency loss of a tax," and illustrate this loss using a demand-supply diagram. Show how the measure of this loss is related to the elasticities of the demand and supply curves.
- ☐ Outline key points of the 1987 tax reforms and of the GST.
- ☐ Outline the case for and the case against the proposition that an expanded public sector reduces individual freedom.

Chapter Outline

1. The competitive market does not always allocate resources efficiently and governments do interfere to alter the resource distribution. However, there is no assurance that government policies or programs will improve resource allocation; so government interference may hinder rather than promote efficiency. This chapter first analyses government decision making from a public choice perspective and then examines the effect of taxation on resource allocation.

2. Majority voting can result in decisions that impair efficiency.

(a) Voting outcomes can result in accepting projects in which total costs outweigh the benefits, or rejecting projects where benefits outweigh the costs. Special-interest groups and political logrolling can operate to offset some of the inefficiencies of majority voting, but there is no certainty of such an outcome.

(b) The paradox of voting suggests that under a majority voting rule the public may not always be able to make consistent choices that reflects the public's preferences.

(c) Under majority voting the median voter can determine the outcome of the election. Public decisions reflect the median view.

3. The theory of public choice suggests that the public sector has failed because the process it uses to make decisions is inherently weak and results in an economically inefficient allocation of resources.

(a) The weakness of the decision-making process in the public sector is often the result of pressures exerted on government and the bureaucracy by special interests. The power of the government to create and allocate property rights encourages rent-seeking behaviour, whereby wealth is transferred to specific groups. Since benefits are often concentrated and costs are widely diffused and not easily identified, politicians tend to support these special-interest programs even though they result in inefficiencies.

(b) Programs with clear and immediate benefits and vague costs that can be deferred are favoured by those seeking public office.

(c) From our choice of which candidates to support for office, to how we vote in important referenda, the public is forced to deal with "bundled" choices. We may not support our favoured candidate's position on all issues, and we may not support all elements of the option that we vote for in a referendum. Public programs are often not divisible. The public often accepts entire programs even if some parts are low on the list of priorities.

(d) Employees in the public sector generally lack the competitive pressures to perform that are prevalent in the market sector of the economy. The criteria used to measure success are not easily identified for the public sector.

4. The need for financing of public programs raises questions about how to distribute the tax burden among members of society.
(a) Two alternative principles on which a tax system can be based are:
(1) the benefits-received principle which holds that beneficiaries of a public program should bear the cost burden;
(2) the ability-to-pay principle which holds that public programs should be financed in direct relation to one's income and wealth.
(b) Taxes are classified as progressive, proportional, or regressive according to whether the average tax rate increases, stays the same, or decreases as income increases.
(c) In Canada the personal income tax is reasonably progressive, sales taxes and property taxes are regressive, and the corporate tax nominally proportional (with this tax becoming regressive if the tax is passed onto consumers).

5. The incidence of a tax refers to the final resting place of the tax. This must take into account that a tax might be shifted from those on which the tax is initially levied onto someone else. The price elasticities of demand and supply determine the incidence of a sales or an excise tax.
(a) A sales or excise tax shifts the supply curve upward by the amount of the tax and increases the price of the product. The price increase generally does not equal the tax and indicates the portion of the tax paid by the buyer; the seller pays the rest.
(1) Given supply, the more elastic the demand for the commodity, the greater the portion of the tax borne by the seller.
(2) Given supply, the more inelastic the demand, the greater the portion of the tax borne by the consumer.
(3) Given demand, the more inelastic the supply, the greater the portion of the tax borne by the seller.
(4) Given demand, the more elastic the supply, the greater the portion borne by the buyer.
(b) There is an efficiency loss connected with the imposition of a sales or excise tax. Because the tax causes an increase in price, output will decrease to some point where the marginal benefit, as measured by the price, is now greater than the marginal cost. In other words, an efficiency loss occurs because the imposition of the tax pushes output and consumption below the optimal level reached in a competitive market.
(1) The greater the elasticities of demand and supply, the greater the efficiency loss from the levying of a tax. Thus society's total tax burden may differ, even though two different taxes bring in the same amount of revenue.

6. In the last decade Canada has undergone some major tax reforms. In 1987 the income tax system was revamped. Major changes included reducing from 11 to 3 the number of income intervals at which different marginal tax rates apply, sharply reducing the highest marginal tax rate from 64% to around 45%, and changing the tax treatment of some transfer payments. The Goods and Services Tax (GST) has replaced the Manufacturers' Sales Tax. The GST is levied on the difference between the value of a firm's sales and the value of its purchases from other firms (making it a type of value-added tax).

7. Many people believe that the nature and amount of government activity and the extent of individual freedom are related.
(a) Conservatives (small "c") argue that the cost of government entails not only the economic cost from a growing public sector, but also a cost in terms of reduced economic freedom and choice for the individual, and a dangerous concentration of power in the hands of government, because government now makes more of the decisions over economic activity.
(b) Liberals (small "l") counter that the conservative position is subject to the fallacy of limited decisions. They argue also that appropriate government activity expands the range of free choice for society by providing public goods, correcting for externalities, and solving other market failure problems.

Terms and Concepts

ability-to-pay principle
benefits-received principle
efficiency loss of a tax
fallacy of limited decisions
Goods and Services Tax
logrolling
median-voter model
paradox of voting

progressive tax
proportional tax
public choice theory
public finance
public sector failure
regressive tax
rent-seeking behaviour
special-interest effect
tax incidence
value-added tax

Hints and Tips

1. See if you can apply the ideas from the first part of the chapter, dealing with political decision-making, to political behaviour in this country. The median-voter model, logrolling, the influence of special-interest groups, rent-seeking behaviour, and limited and bundled choices are important concepts. Real world examples abound.

2. The technical part of the chapter is that portion dealing with tax incidence. If elasticity is not fresh in your mind, review Chapter 7.

Fill-In Questions

1. The economic analysis of government decisions and the economic problems created by the public sector are studied under the theory of public (finance, choice) __________, while the study of public spending and taxation would be the subject of public __________.

2. Society's well-being can be improved whenever a public good is provided for which the __________ is greater than its __________.

3. Many public decisions are made on the basis of majority voting, but

(a) this procedure can produce outcomes that are __________, as projects can be accepted when public benefits are (greater than, less than) __________ total cost, or projects defeated where total benefits are __________ than total costs.

(1) The inefficiencies of majority voting may be offset by political pressure exerted by __________ groups or by political __________.

(2) Majority voting can lead to inefficient outcomes because it fails to incorporate the __________ of the individual voters.

(b) Another difficulty that can result from majority voting is an __________ ranking of preferences and is called the __________ of __________.

(c) Under a majority voting rule the __________ voter is likely to determine the outcome of a vote.

4. Sound economics call for the support of public projects when the marginal __________ exceed the __________; while political considerations may lead to the support of projects that maximize the probability of getting __________.

5. Four possible reasons for public sector failure are:

(a) that government, instead of promoting the general interests (or welfare) of its citizens, may promote the __________ interests of small groups in the economy;

(b) that the benefits from a program or project are often (clear, hidden) __________; and its costs are frequently __________;

(c) that individual voters are unable to __________ the particular quantities of each public good and service they wish the public sector to provide;

(d) that there are weak __________ to be efficient in the public sector and no way to __________ the efficiency of the public sector.

6. The two basic philosophies on apportioning the tax burden are: the __________ principle and the __________ principle.

7. With a progressive tax, the tax rate __________ as income increases; the tax rate decreases with increasing income for a __________ tax; and with a proportional tax the __________ stays the same as income increases.

8. In Canada the personal income tax is __________, while property and sales tax are __________. The exemption of food items from the Goods and Services tax makes this tax (more, less) __________ regressive.

9. Taxes (will always, may not) __________ be paid by the person or institution on which they are levied. The final resting place of the tax is called the __________ of the tax.

10. When a sales tax is levied on a commodity, the amount of the tax borne by the buyers of the commodity is equal to the amount the __________ of the commodity rises as a result of the tax. The incidence of the tax depends upon the price __________ of __________ and __________.

(a) The buyer's portion of the tax is larger the (more, less) __________ elastic the demand and the __________ elastic the supply.

(b) The seller's portion of the tax is larger, the __________ elastic the demand and the __________ elastic the supply.

11. When a tax reduces consumption and production below that achieved in a free market there exists an __________ loss. Other things being equal, the greater the __________ of supply and demand the greater this loss.

12. The Goods and Services Tax (GST) is a type of __________-added tax. The tax rate is applied to the __________ between the value of a firm's sales and the value of its __________ from other firms. When introduced the tax was set at __________% and is placed on both __________ and __________.

13. Many conservatives believe a larger public sector diminishes individuals' economic __________. Liberals counter that to believe that more governmental activity must decrease private decision making and economic activity is a case of the fallacy of limited __________.

Problems and Projects

1. Preferences are consistent if when Project A is preferred to Project B and Project B is preferred to Project C, then Project A is preferred to Project C. The tables below illustrate two cases where the preferences of the individual voters are consistent, but majority voting on pairs of alternatives yields consistent choices in one case and inconsistent choices in the other.

Case 1	Preference Rankings		
Public Project	Voter A	Voter B	Voter C
Park	1	3	3
School	2	2	1
Dam	3	1	2

In an election determined by majority vote, which project would win each of the following contests?
School vs. Dam __________
Dam vs. Park __________
School vs. Park __________

Case 2	Preference Rankings		
Public Project	Voter A	Voter B	Voter C
Park	1	2	3
School	2	3	1
Dam	3	1	2

In an election determined by majority vote, which project would win each of the following contests?
School vs. Dam __________
Dam vs. Park __________
School vs. Park __________

Majority voting has led to inconsistent public preferences in Case _____.

2. In the table below are five levels of income and the amount of tax that would be paid under two different tax systems: A and B.

(a) Compute for each tax system the average rate of taxation at each income level.

Income	Tax A		Tax B	
	Tax Paid	Average Tax Rate	Tax Paid	Average Tax Rate
$1500	$150	_____%	$300	_____%
3000	300	_____	390	_____
5000	500	_____	600	_____
7500	750	_____	825	_____
10,000	2,000	_____	1,000	_____

(b) Tax A is (regressive, progressive, proportional) __________ up to income level $__________ and then becomes __________. Tax B is consistently __________.

3. The graph below illustrates the market for some wine before and after the imposition of a new production tax.

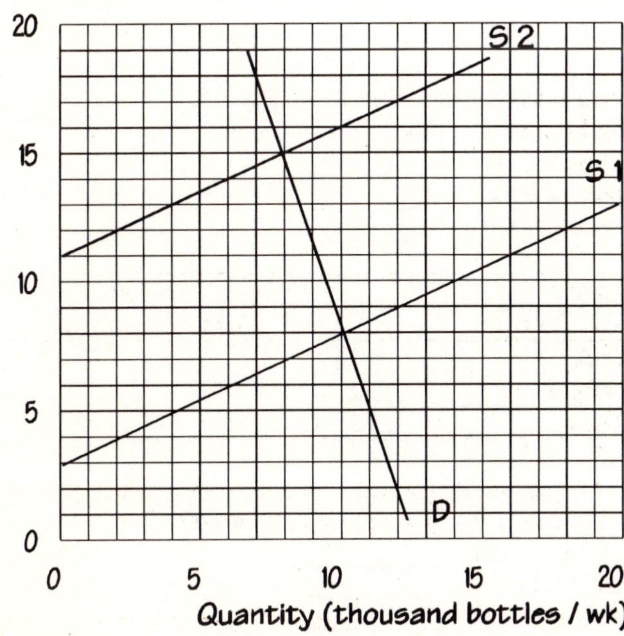

(a) Which of the two supply curves is the "before tax" supply curve? _____

(b) Before the tax, the price of this wine was $_____ per bottle and the quantity produced was _____ bottles per week.

(c) The amount of the tax is $_____ per bottle.

(d) After the tax, the price of this wine becomes $_____ per bottle and the quantity produced becomes _____ bottles per week.

(e) The government's tax revenue is $_____ per bottle times _____ bottles per week, for a total of $_____ per week.

(f) On the graph, shade in the area of tax revenue.

(g) Of the total tax per bottle, the consumers' burden is $_____, and the producers' burden is $_____. The consumers bear a (larger, smaller) __________ share relative to the producers because the demand curve is relatively __________ and the supply curve is relatively __________.

(h) On the graph shade in the area of efficiency loss due to the tax.

True-False

Circle T if the statement is true, F if it is false.

1. Certain characteristics of the public sector hinder the government's efforts to achieve an efficient allocation of resources. **T F**

2. Since majority voting reveals the demand of the electorate, programs based on an election's outcome will lead to an efficient use of society's resources. **T F**

3. By incorporating the preferences of individuals, majority voting produces efficient outcomes. **T F**

4. Logrolling and pressure by interest groups always diminish economic efficiency in government. **T F**

5. Majority voting sometimes fails to make consistent choices that reflect community preferences. **T F**

6. The suggestion that the person holding the middle position will, in a majority rule election, likely determine the outcome is called the paradox of voting. **T F**

7. Even though the market economy may not always result in an efficient allocation, it does not follow that the political process will yield superior results. **T F**

8. There is failure in the public sector whenever a government program or activity has been expanded to the level at which the marginal social cost exceeds the marginal social benefit. **T F**

9. The special-interest effect, it is argued by those concerned with the theory of public choice, tends to reduce public sector failures because the pressures exerted on government by one special-interest group are offset by the pressures brought to bear by other special-interest groups. **T F**

10. Rent-seeking behaviour occurs when one group seeks the transfer of wealth from others with the assistance of the government. **T F**

11. When the costs of programs are hidden and the benefits are clear, vote-seeking politicians tend to reject economically justifiable programs. **T F**

12. The limited choice of citizens refers to the inability of individual voters to select the precise bundle of public goods and services that best satisfies the citizen's wants **T F**

13. The benefits-received principle states that governments should spend tax receipts so that the benefits for society are maximized. **T F**

14. According to the ability-to-pay principle, people should be taxed according to their income. **T F**

15. A tax is progressive if the tax rate increases as income increases. **T F**

16. For a tax to be regressive the amount paid in taxes represents a smaller percentage of income as income increases. **T F**

17. A regressive tax takes more money from the poor than the rich. **T F**

18. A general sales tax is considered to be regressive. **T F**

19. The Canadian personal income tax is an example of a progressive tax. **T F**

20. The more inelastic the demand for a product, the more of an excise tax is borne by the consumers. **T F**

21. The efficiency loss of a tax results from the decreased production and consumption of the taxed article. **T F**

22. The degree of efficiency loss from an excise tax varies from market to market and depends on the price elasticities of supply and demand. **T F**

23. The GST is a value-added tax in that it is applied to the difference between the value of the firm's sales and purchases. **T F**

24. Canadians are not required to pay GST on exports and imports. **T F**

25. Both liberal and conservative economists agree that the expansion of government's role in the economy has reduced personal freedom in Canada. **T F**

Multiple-Choice

Circle the letter that corresponds to the best answer.

1. Deficiencies in the processes used to make collective decisions and economic inefficiencies caused by government are the primary focus of:
(a) public finance
(b) public choice theory
(c) the study of tax incidence
(d) the study of tax shifting

2. Majority voting may produce inefficient economic outcomes because:
(a) of poor voter turnout
(b) voters do not know all of the marginal social benefit and marginal social costs of proposals they are voting on
(c) majority voting fails to incorporate the preferences of individuals
(d) politicians do not keep election promises

3. The trading of votes to secure favourable outcomes on decisions that otherwise would be adverse is known as:
(a) rent-seeking behaviour
(b) special-interest effect
(c) due process
(d) logrolling

Questions 4 through 7 are based on the following table, which shows the ranking of three public goods by three voters A, B, and C.

Public Good	Voter A	Voter B	Voter C
Pool	2	3	1
Road	3	1	2
Day-care	1	2	3

4. In a choice between a pool and a road:
(a) a majority of voters favour the pool
(b) a majority of voters favour the road
(c) a majority of voters favour both the pool and the road
(d) there is not a majority of voters for either good

5. In a choice between a road and day-care:
(a) a majority of voters favour a road
(b) a majority of voters favour day-care
(c) a majority of voters favour both a road and day-care
(d) there is not a majority of voters for either good

6. In a choice between day-care and a pool:
(a) a majority of voters favour a pool
(b) a majority of voters favour day-care
(c) a majority of voters favour both day-care and a pool
(d) there is not a majority of voters for either good

7. What do the rankings in the table indicate about choices made under majority rule? Majority voting:
(a) reflects irrational preferences
(b) produces inconsistent choices
(c) produces consistent choices in spite of irrational preferences
(d) results in economically efficient outcomes since everyone had a vote to indicate their preferences

8. The suggestion that the middle position will be chosen under majority voting is called:
(a) the paradox of voting
(b) the special-interest effect
(c) logrolling
(d) the median voter model

9. All of the following can be considered rent seeking behaviour except:
(a) political pressure by farm groups to set an effective floor price for an agricultural good
(b) actions aimed at continuing the restrictions on the interprovincial movement of beer
(c) actions aimed at eliminating tariffs on foreign automobiles
(d) all are examples of rent-seeking

10. Which of the following is not among the reasons for the alleged greater efficiency of the private sector?
(a) the least efficient workers in the economy gravitate to the public sector
(b) strong incentives to be efficient are largely absent in the public sector
(c) there is no simple way to measure or test efficiency in the public sector
(d) in the public sector, agencies tend to be rewarded with larger budgets if they perform inefficiently

11. Which of the following would ***not*** be observed if society established taxes strictly on the benefits-received principle?
(a) the beneficiaries of public programs would pay for them
(b) families with more children would pay higher school taxes
(c) income would be redistributed from the wealthy to the poor
(d) there would be user charges for services provided by governments

12. Taxing people according to the ability-to-pay principle would be most characteristic of:
(a) a sales or excise tax
(b) a progressive income tax
(c) the GST
(d) property taxes

13. A tax that takes a greater amount of money the higher the income is called:
(a) progressive
(b) proportional
(c) regressive
(d) may be any of the above

14. In a competitive market the portion of a sales tax borne by the buyer is:
(a) equal to the amount of the tax
(b) equal to 50% of the amount of the tax
(c) equal to the rise in the price of the product
(d) any of the above is equally possible

15. Which of the following is incorrect with regard to the imposition of a sales or excise tax?
(a) given the supply, the more inelastic the demand, the larger the portion of the tax shifted onto the consumer
(b) given the demand, the more inelastic the supply, the larger the portion of the tax borne by the producer
(c) given the supply, the more elastic the demand, the greater the portion of the tax borne by the seller
(d) given the demand, the more inelastic the supply, the greater the portion of the tax borne by the buyer.

Answer questions 16 through 20 based on this graph showing the imposition of a per unit tax.

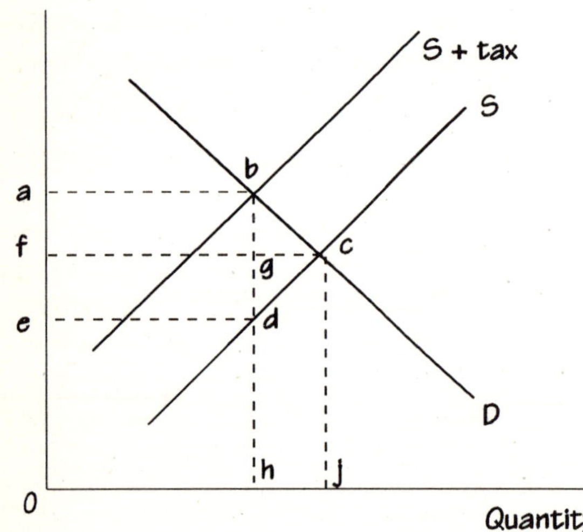

16. Before the tax is levied, the equilibrium price is:
(a) 0*e*
(b) 0*a*
(c) 0*f*
(d) 0*b*

17. The tax per unit of output is:
(a) 0*a*
(b) *af*
(c) *ef*
(d) *ae*

18. The consumer's burden of the tax, per unit, is:
(a) 0*a*
(b) *af*
(c) *ef*
(d) *ae*

19. The tax revenue for the government is:
(a) *abgf*
(b) *aebd*
(c) *fged*
(d) *bcd*

20. The efficiency loss of the tax is represented by the area:
(a) *bgc*
(b) *bdc*
(c) *bcjh*
(d) *abfc*

21. Which of the following statements concerning the efficiency loss of a tax is incorrect?
(a) the greater the elasticities of supply and demand, the greater the efficiency loss of the tax
(b) two taxes that yield the same tax revenue entail equal tax burdens for society
(c) the efficiency loss of a tax results from the loss of output for which marginal benefits exceed marginal cost
(d) the efficiency losses of taxes must be considered when designing an optimal tax system

22. A value-added tax would tax a firm's:
(a) revenues from the sale of a product
(b) revenue from sales less input costs
(c) purchases of inputs
(d) revenues from sales less purchases from other firms

23. The GST was introduced as a replacement for:
(a) the Manufacturer's Sales Tax
(b) import duties
(c) excise taxes on tobacco and alcohol
(d) royalties on oil and gas production

24. The GST most closely resembles:
(a) a personal income tax
(b) a corporate profits tax
(c) a consumption tax
(d) a property tax

Discussion Questions

1. Explain the difference between public choice theory and public finance. Why is a discussion of public choice theory included in a text on economics?

2. How do special-interest groups or the use of logrolling influence the efficiency of outcomes in the public sector? Construct an example to show that logrolling could result in an improvement in the efficiency of resource allocation.

3. What are consistent preferences? Why can there be a paradox with majority voting?

4. Describe how the median voter influences the results of majority rule elections on public issues.

5. The theory of public choice suggests that there are a number of possible causes of public sector failures. What are these causes? Explain how each would tend to result in the inefficient allocation of the economy's resources.

6. It is generally agreed that "the national defence must lie in the public sector, while wheat production can best be accomplished in the private sector." Why isn't there agreement on where many other goods or services should be produced?

7. Explain the two basic philosophies for apportioning the tax burden. What difficulties can be encountered when these two philosophies are put into practice?

8. Explain the difference between progressive, proportional, and regressive taxes. Which Canadian taxes fall into each category?

9. What is the GST? What tax did the GST replace and in what ways can it be said to be superior to the tax it replaced?

10. Define the *incidence* of a tax. Explain how the incidence of a sales or excise tax depends upon the elasticities of supply and demand.

11. Explain why a firm does not simply pass a sales tax on to the consumer by increasing the price of the taxed commodity by the full amount of the tax. Since the GST is added on the cash register, does this mean that 100% of the GST is passed on to the consumer?

12. How does an excise or sales tax produce an efficiency loss for society? How is this efficiency loss affected by the elasticity of supply or demand? All else equal, shouldn't the total tax burden be the same for two taxes that produce the same revenue?

13. Do you think that government limits or expands personal freedom? Do you think that the government's role in the economy should be increased or decreased?

Answers

Fill-in questions

1. choice, finance

2. marginal benefit, marginal cost

3. (a) inefficient, less than, greater than; (1) special interest groups, logrolling, (2) preferences, (b) inconsistent, paradox, voting; (c) median

4. benefits, marginal costs, elected

5. (a) special; (b) clear, hidden; (c) select; (d) incentives, test (measure)

6. benefits received, ability-to-pay

7. increases, regressive, tax rate

8. progressive, regressive, less

9. may not; incidence

10. price; elasticity, demand, supply; (a) less, more; (b) more, less

11. efficiency; elasticities

12. value; difference, purchases; 7, goods, services

13. freedom, decisions

Problems and projects

1. CASE 1; Winner: School; Dam; School
CASE 2; Winner: School; Dam; Park; 2

2. (a) Tax A: 10,10, 10, 10, 20; Tax B: 20, 13, 12, 11, 10; (b) proportional, 7500, progressive; regressive.

3. (a) S1; (b) 8, 10,000; (c) 8; (d) 15, 8,000; (e) 8, 8,000, 64,000; (g) 7, larger, inelastic, elastic.

True-False

1. T **2.** F **3.** F **4.** F **5.** T **6.** F
7. T **8.** T **9.** F **10.** T **11.** F **12.** T
13. F **14.**T **15.** T **16.** T **17.** F **18.** T
19. T **20.** T **21.** T **22.** T **23.** T **24.** F
25. F

Multiple-choice

1. (b) **2.** (c) **3.** (d) **4.** (a) **5.** (a) **6.** (b)
7. (b) **8.** (d) **9.** (d) **10.** (a) **11.** (c) **12.** (b)
13. (d) **14.** (c) **15.** (d) **16.** (c) **17.** (d) **18.** (b)
19. (b) **20.** (b) **21.** (b) **22.** (d) **23.** (a) **24.** (c)

CHAPTER 21

Agriculture: Economics and Policy

Chapter 22 is devoted to the economics of agriculture, and policy attempts to deal with problems in this sector of our economy. Probably no economic issue has aroused as much public interest, for as many years, as the farm problem has. It has concerned not only those directly or indirectly engaged in agriculture, but every Canadian consumer and taxpayer. The current focus of the problem relates to the globalization of markets, because national farm programs can distort agricultural trade flows and have been the centre of international trade disputes for the last number of years. As a trading nation, Canadian farm programs must be adjusted to fit in with the emphasis on the unimpeded flow of goods internationally.

Fundamentally, the farm problem can be analysed as two separate problems--a short-run problem and a long-run problem--each with its own particular causes. The chapter deals with each of the two problems in turn. The short-run problem is that farm prices and incomes have fluctuated sharply from year to year. The long-run problem is that farming is a declining industry, so farm incomes have tended to fall. A good understanding of these problems is easily within your grasp if you have mastered the concepts of elasticity, supply, demand, and competitive markets.

In Canada, both federal and provincial governments have been active in the area of farm policy since World War I. Most policies pursued over the years have been aimed at raising or stabilizing farm incomes by supporting prices of farm products. Various programs--including offers-to-purchase at guaranteed prices, deficiency payments, supply management, and the most recent farm revenue insurance--have all been tried at one time or another as income stabilizing devices. The programs resulted in higher consumer prices and smaller quantities consumed of the various farm products, but no lasting solution to the declining and unstable farm income. With the offers-to-purchase at prices supported by the federal government, there tended to be surpluses of some products. The federal government bought these surpluses to keep the price above the competitive market price. The purchases of the surpluses were financed by Canadian taxpayers. To eliminate these surpluses, government looked for ways to increase the demand for or to decrease the supply of these commodities. They switched from the offers-to-purchase to the deficiency payments method, often coupling this with crop restrictions. Since the 1970s, domestic supply of some agricultural products has been controlled in "supply management" industries by legalizing producer-controlled marketing boards, which determine price and limit production to the quantity demanded.

More recently, farm policy is being shaped by Canada's desire to reduce world trade barriers in agricultural markets, allowing Canadian producers to expand their exports. Our government is also under pressure in free trade talks, such as the GATT, to open Canadian markets to imports of agricultural commodities from other nations. These pressures suggest a bleak future for the supply management system. Under freer world trade in agricultural goods, it is expected that Canadian producers of some goods will thrive whereas others will be unable to compete, barring dramatic improvements in productivity. Emphasis is now being placed on farm risk management through revenue insurance schemes, as opposed to income support schemes.

Over the last half century the different farm policies have not worked well: farm population has kept falling; falling real prices of agricultural products have kept relative farm income low; incomes, especially in the grains sector, have been unstable; and trade restrictions in some products have been imposed. Farm policies have confused *symptoms* of the problem (low farm prices and incomes) with the *causes* of the problem (resource allocation). Structural change in an economy requires reallocation of resources: often a very difficult process for households who must drastically change their lifestyles. Most elements of Canadian farm policy have responded to short-run difficulties and have ignored the fundamental restructuring question.

At the global level, there exists an even more important agriculture-related issue: will the world be able to feed itself? The chapter closes with a look at both a pessimistic and an optimistic view on this question.

Checklist

When you have studied this chapter, you should be able to:

- ☐ Identify the short-run farm problem; and explain its three causes.
- ☐ Identify the long-run farm problem, and explain its two causes.
- ☐ Explain why the long-run farm problem is the result of a misallocation of resources in a dynamic economy.
- ☐ Enumerate three arguments that support government assistance to agriculture.
- ☐ With the help of supply and demand graphs, show the mechanics of the basic forms of price support policies: offers-to-purchase and deficiency payments.
- ☐ Explain the effects on consumers and taxpayers of price support and supply restriction mechanisms.
- ☐ Identify and comment on relevance of: The Canadian Wheat Board, provincial marketing boards, Canadian Dairy Commission, GATT, and the EU.
- ☐ Present four major criticisms of the farm policy.
- ☐ Explain why costly farm programs survive even when farm populations are declining.
- ☐ Give three reasons to support the prediction that farm subsidies will decline in the future.
- ☐ Explain how the movement towards free trade on a global basis is forcing Canada to reevaluate and change farm programs.
- ☐ Present the arguments for and against the contention that the world will not be able to feed itself a few decades from now.

Chapter Outline

1. There are five good reasons for devoting some of our time to the analysis of the Canadian farm sector. It is one of the nation's largest industries; it is a real-world example of the purely competitive model; it illustrates the effects of government intervention in markets; domestic agricultural policy is reflecting the increasing globalization of markets; and it provides illustrations of rent-seeking and the special-interest effect of public choice theory.

2. The farm problem is both a short-run and a long-run problem. The short-run problem is the frequent sharp changes in the incomes of farmers from one year to the next; the long-run problem is the tendency for farm prices and incomes to lag behind the upward trend of prices and incomes in the rest of the economy.

3. The causes of the short-run problem of unstable incomes are:
(a) the inelastic demand for farm products,
(b) fluctuations in the output of agricultural products,
(c) fluctuations in the domestic demand, and
(d) unstable foreign demand.
Particularly because of the way that demand and supply shifts interact with the highly inelastic demand curve, these factors produce relatively large and unpredictable changes in agricultural prices and farm incomes.

4. The causes of the long-run problem (low farm income and prices) flow from two basic factors:
(a) productivity in agriculture increased markedly over time resulting in significant increases in agricultural supply;
(b) the demand for agricultural products failed to meet the large increase in supply, even though there were large increases in income, because the demand for farm products is income inelastic.
(c) Another explanation of the long-run problem is that as productivity in Canadian agriculture has grown, our economy has been too slow to reallocate labour resources away from agriculture and into other industries. Hence, the average incomes of those remaining in agriculture are persistently low.

5. Farm interests present several arguments to justify special assistance: the poor incomes of farmers, the many uninsurable risks that are unavoidable in farming, the lack of market power for farmers when selling their products (whereas they purchase inputs in imperfectly competitive markets).

6. Farmers have been successful in obtaining various forms of public aid, and the policy of both the federal and provincial governments towards agriculture has included programs designed to raise and stabilize farm prices and incomes.

7. Historically the government has attempted to increase farm prices and income through subsidies, price floors, and marketing boards. Some important boards and agencies are: Canadian Wheat Board, Agricultural Stabilization Board, Canadian Dairy Commission, Agricultural Stabilization Board, and the National Farm Products Marketing Council. Due to international pressure against trade barriers and subsidies, more emphasis is now being placed on a market-oriented farm policy supplemented by farm revenue insurance.

8. Two types of price supports--offers-to-purchase and deficiency payments--were utilized. The price support scheme resulted in higher consumer prices, a surplus production purchased by government, and international trading difficulties when the surplus was disposed of in foreign markets. Deficiency payment plans are costly and impede the movement of resources out of agriculture. Supply management schemes have been used in some agricultural industries. They are a means to avoiding surplus production, but have the drawbacks of raising consumer prices, and of concentrating the economic benefits in the hands of those producers fortunate enough to be recipients of free quota rights.

9. Farm policies aimed at increasing producer incomes have not worked well and are subject to four criticisms.
(a) Policies have confused symptoms and causes of the problem and failed to move resources out of agriculture.
(b) The major benefits of the program were not directed toward the low-income farmers.
(c) The various farm programs of the federal govern ment have often operated to offset (or contradict) each other.
(d) Farm policy has also been less effective in achieving its goal of enhancing farm incomes because of the increased size of farm operations, and because the effects of these programs have sometimes been swamped by the harm done to farmers by rising interest rates or fluctuations in the international value of the dollar.

10. Given international pressures towards freer trade in agricultural products, Canada is under pressure to reduce subsidies to our farmers. The federal debt problem also makes massive subsidization of agriculture difficult to sustain. Some predict a shift in emphasis away from the goal of enhancing to the goal of stabilizing farm incomes by promoting farm revenue insurance.

11. Rent-seeking behaviour on the part of farmers, the special-interest effect that impairs public decision making, and the clear benefits to farmers and hidden costs to other Canadians--all explain the persistence of farm programs despite rising costs and falling farm population. Nevertheless, declining farm populations will spell declining political power of the farm sector. This in conjunction with the other factors mentioned in point 10 lead to the prediction that farm subsidies will decline over time.

12. Farm programs--such as those in Canada, the United States and the European Union--distort world agricultural trade. The recently concluded negotiations of the General Agreement on Tariffs and Trade (GATT) will lower trade barriers for farm products and will necessitate some change in Canada's farm programs.

13. It is unclear whether the world will be able to feed itself in the future. There are pessimists and optimists in the "feast or famine" debate. Key factors in the debate include population growth, environmental degradation, pressures on farmland supplies, and the room for growth in food production technologies.

Terms and Concepts

Agriculture Products Board
Agricultural Products Marketing Act
Agricultural Stabilization Board
Canadian Dairy Commission
Canadian Wheat Board
crop restrictions
deficiency payments
long-run farm problem
market-oriented income stabilization
offers-to-purchase
short-run farm problem

Hints and Tips

1. The chapters that you may wish to review are Chapter 4 (on supply and demand), Chapter 7 (on elasticities), and Chapter 20 (on public choice).

2. To comment intelligently on whether government policies in agriculture work or not, it is crucial that you understand the distinction between the short-run farm problem and the long-run farm problem. In principle, it would be perfectly possible to have either one of these problems exist without the other existing.

Fill-In Questions

1. It is important to study Canadian agriculture for at least five reasons: It is one of the __________ Canadian sectors; it is a real-world example of the __________ model; it reveals the effects of government __________; it reflects the increasing __________ of markets; and it provides illustrations of the __________ effect and __________ behaviour introduced in public choice theory.

2. The short-run farm problem is the (stability, instability) __________ of farm prices and incomes from one year to the next.

3. The basic cause of this short-run problem is the __________ demand for farm products. This demand occurs because farm products have few good __________, and because of rapidly diminishing __________.

4. Inelasticity of demand contributes to unstable farm prices and incomes in two ways. Relatively (large, small) __________ changes in the output of farm products result in relatively __________ changes in farm prices and incomes; and relatively __________ changes in demand result in relatively __________ changes in prices and incomes.

5. In addition to a highly inelastic demand, fluctuations in __________ sales have contributed to income instability.

6. The long-run farm problem is farm prices and incomes that (run ahead of, lag behind) __________ the trends of prices and incomes in the rest of the economy. The reason is that the (demand, supply) __________ has increased rapidly because of technological change, while the __________ for agricultural products has increased slowly over time because food demand is income __________. In addition, population growth has __________ in recent decades.

7. As the Canadian economy has grown and improved its agricultural technology, it has failed to reallocate enough __________ from __________ to __________ sectors of the economy.

8. Since the 1930s governments have used a combination of __________, __________ __________, and __________ __________ to enhance and stabilize farm __________ and __________.

9. Three of the reasons advanced to support the farmers' claim to assistance from the federal government are: (a) the low __________ of farmers; (b) uninsurable __________, such as drought, to which the industry is exposed; (c) farmers sell in __________ markets but purchase inputs from industries in which market __________ is exercised.

10. In the supply management industries, such as eggs and milk, farm policy is partly designed to restrict farm (prices and incomes, output) __________ in order to increase farm __________.

11. If government supports prices at a level above equilibrium, the result will be (shortages, surpluses) __________, which the government must __________ in order to maintain prices at their support level.
(a) Farmers benefit from this price-support program because it increases their __________.
(b) But the program hurts consumers who must pay higher __________ and consume __________ .
(c) Society (gains, loses) __________ because taxpayers will pay (higher, lower) __________ taxes to finance the purchase of the surplus by government, and because there is economic __________ from the (overallocation, underallocation) __________ of resources to agriculture.
(d) There are also __________ costs from distortion in worldwide supply and demand for agricultural products, the increased potential for __________ barriers, and a (positive, negative) __________ effect on less-developed countries.

12. As consumers, the public will prefer (an offers-to-purchase, a deficiency payments) __________ price support program. As taxpayers, the public (will, will not) __________ prefer one program to another because total payments by the public to farmers are (identical, more, less) __________ with offers-to-purchase compared to deficiency payments.

13. Supply restriction occurs whenever a marketing board has the power to allocate __________. Eventually, the benefits of this program are capitalized into high quota __________.

14. Agricultural policies to stabilize farm income and prices (have, have not) __________ worked well for at least four reasons:
(a) they have confused the __________ of the farm problem (low prices and incomes) with the __________ of the problem (misallocation of resources);
(b) most agricultural support goes to (high, low) _____ -income farmers rather than _____-income farmers.;
(c) the objectives of different farm programs have often offset or __________ each other;
(d) farm policy is (increasing, decreasing) __________ in its effectiveness because of the increasing __________ of farm enterprises, and because of the significant effects on farm incomes from changes in domestic __________ rates and the international value of the __________.

15. An appreciation of the Canadian dollar will (increase, decrease) __________ sales of Canadian farm products abroad.

16. Farm policies have received strong support from both the federal and provincial governments. This result can be explained by insights from __________ __________ theory. Farm representatives are displaying __________-__________ __________ when they lobby for programs that transfer income to themselves. There is also a __________-__________ effect because the cost to individual taxpayers is (large, small) __________ but the benefit to the farm group is __________.

17. Farm subsidies are likely to decline in the future due to
(a) __________ farm population
(b) pressures to control budget __________
(c) conflicts between domestic farm programs and __________ trade.

18. The farm programs of the United States and the European Economic Community have (increased, decreased) __________ Canadian farm sales in foreign markets. The farm programs of various nations, including Canada, have contributed to a __________ of the world's agricultural resources.

19. There is a global dimension to farm problems.

(a) The pessimistic view is one of possible famine as (supply, demand) __________ outpaces __________ because:

(1) the quantity of arable land is __________ and its quality is __________;

(2) urban sprawl reduces the availability of (agricultural, nonagricultural) __________ land;

(3) the underground water system is being depleted by increasing __________;

(4) world __________ continues to increase; and

(5) future agricultural production may be affected by long-run changes in the __________.

(b) Optimists contend global famine is not a serious prospect because:

(1) the arable land for production can be __________;

(2) agricultural __________ continues to rise, especially in __________ countries;

(3) the rate of world __________ growth is diminishing; and

(4) any food shortages would produce adjustments in the __________ system.

Problems and Projects

1. This table shows a demand schedule for some farm product.

Price ($/kg)	Quantity demanded (kg/yr)	Total Producer Income ($/yr)
3.00	9,000	________
2.50	10,000	________
2.00	11,000	________
1.50	12,000	________
1.00	13,000	________

(a) Fill in the column for producer income.

(b) Given that revenues (rise, fall) _____ when price rises, the demand for this product is (inelastic, elastic) __________, which (is, is not) __________ typical of agricultural products.

(c) Calculate elasticity to confirm your conclusion. (Reminder: E = % change in Qd / % change in P).

2. The graph shows the market for a hypothetical agricultural product, X.

(a) In the absence of any government intervention, the equilibrium price of X is $_____ per bushel, and producers will sell _______ bushels per year, for an annual income of $ ________.

Suppose that the government agrees to support the price of X at $4.80 per bushel.

(b) If this price support is implemented by an offers-to-purchase program, consumers will buy ________ bushels per year, farmers will produce ________ bushels per year, and the government will be required to purchase the (shortage, surplus) __________ of __________ bushels per year, at a total cost of $________ per year.

(c) If the government becomes committed to this price support, using an offers-to-purchase program, what pressure is there to also implement supply management?

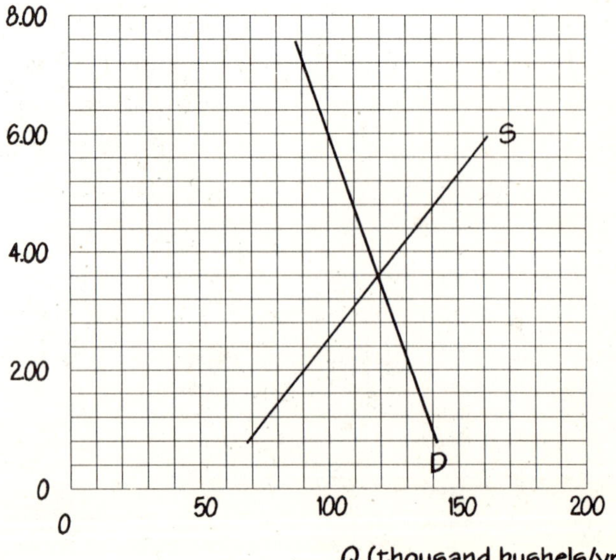

(d) If the same level of price support is done by a deficiency payments program, farmers will produce ________ bushels per year, consumers will buy ________ bushels per year, at a price of $_____ per bushel, and the government will be required to pay $______ per bushel for ________ bushels per year, at a total cost of $________ per year.

(e) Which of the two price support programs is the government (and taxpayers) likely to favour in this instance? ______________

(f) Which of the two price support programs are consumers likely to favour? ______________

(g) Farmers are indifferent between the two alternatives because their total annual income becomes $_______ under both schemes.

3. Consider the market for potatoes. Suppose the following:

i. potatoes are inferior, and incomes are increasing
ii. population is growing slowly
iii. potatoes are price inelastic
iv. technology for producing potatoes is improving

Draw and explain a supply and demand diagram for potatoes to predict what will happen to potato prices and incomes of potato farmers in the near future.

Price

Quantity

True-False

Circle T if the statement is true, F if it is false.

1. Agriculture employs about 30% of the Canadian labour force. **T F**

2. The short-run farm problem is the sharp year-to-year fluctuations in farm incomes and prices. **T F**

3. The short-run problem in agriculture arises because some countries are dumping subsidized farm products in the Canadian market. **T F**

4. The demand for most farm products is price inelastic. **T F**

5. Because of the inelasticity of demand for farm products a relatively large change in output will cause a relatively small change in price. **T F**

6. The supply of agricultural products tends to be subject to random variations due to weather and other unex pected factors. **T F**

7. Changes in crop production in other countries affects the demand and hence the income of Canadian farmers. **T F**

8. Changes in the farm programs of foreign countries have led to the loss of foreign markets for Canadian agricultural products. **T F**

9. Appreciation of the Canadian dollar against over seas currencies increases foreign demand for Canadian agricultural products. **T F**

10. The long-run farm problem is that the incomes of farmers have been low relative to incomes in the economy as a whole. **T F**

11. Since World War II productivity in agriculture has increased at about half the rate of the nonfarm economy. **T F**

12. Most of the recent technological advances in agriculture have been initiated by farmers. **T F**

13. The demand for farm products is income inelastic. **T F**

14. Increases in income of Canadian consumers lead to less-than-proportionate increases in expenditures on farm products. **T F**

15. The supply of agricultural products has tended to increase more rapidly than the demand for these products in Canada. **T F**

16. The Canadian Wheat Board is a Crown corporation that guarantees Prairie wheat farmers a "fair" price for their crop. **T F**

17. The Canadian Egg Marketing Agency is an example of a supply management marketing board. **T F**

18. The major aim of agricultural policy in Canada has been to enhance and stabilize farm prices and farm incomes. **T F**

19. When government supports farm prices at above-equilibrium levels, it can reduce the annual surpluses of agricultural commodities either by increasing the supply or by decreasing the demand. **T F**

20. The deficiency payments method of price supports is appropriate when demand is elastic. **T F**

21. As consumers, the public prefers the offers-to-purchase method of price support to deficiency payments. **T F**

22. Crop restriction programs cost the government more money than an offers-to-purchase program. **T F**

23. The offers-to-purchase method of price supports should be used when demand is elastic. **T F**

24. A market-oriented income stabilization policy would shift the goal of farm policy from enhancing to stabilizing farm incomes. **T F**

25. Placing an agricultural product under a supply management scheme is an example of rent-seeking behaviour. **T F**

26. One reason to predict that farm subsidies will decline in the future is a declining farm population. **T F**

27. If GATT negotiations are successful in lowering trade barriers, all sectors of Canadian agriculture will benefit. **T F**

Multiple-Choice

Circle the letter that corresponds to the best answer.

1. The percent of the labour force employed in Canadian agriculture is about:
(a) 12
(b) 9
(c) 6
(d) 3

2. Which of the following is *not* characteristic of Canadian agriculture?
(a) farmers sell their products in highly competitive markets
(b) farmers buy in markets that are largely noncompetitive
(c) the demand for agricultural products tends to be inelastic
(d) agricultural resources tend to be highly mobile

3. The short-run farm problem is the result of all the following except:
(a) an inelastic demand for agricultural products
(b) fluctuations in farm output
(c) rent-seeking behaviour by farm groups
(d) shifts in the demand curve for farm products

4. If both the demand for and the supply of a product increase:
(a) the quantity of the product bought and sold will increase
(b) the quantity of the product bought and sold will decrease
(c) the price of the product will increase
(d) the price of the product will decrease

5. Which one of the following is not a reason that increases in the demand for agricultural commodities have been relatively small?

(a) The population of Canada has not increased as rapidly as the productivity of agriculture.
(b) The increased per capita incomes of Canadian con sumers have resulted in less than proportionate increases in their expenditures for farm products.
(c) The demand for agricultural products is inelastic.
(d) The standard of living in Canada is well above the level of bare subsistence.

6. The market system has failed to solve the problem of low farm incomes because:
(a) the demand for agricultural products is relatively inelastic
(b) the supply of agricultural products is relatively elastic
(c) agricultural products have relatively few good substitutes
(d) agricultural resources are relatively immobile

7. If the demand for agricultural products is inelastic, a relatively small increase in supply will result in:
(a) a relatively small increase in farm prices and incomes
(b) a relatively small decrease in farm prices and a relatively large increase in farm incomes
(c) a relatively large decrease in farm prices and incomes
(d) a relatively large increase in farm prices and a relatively small decrease in farm incomes

8. All of the following have contributed to the long-run farm problem except:
(a) increased supply of agricultural products due to technological change
(b) declining farm population
(c) income inelastic demand
(d) declining population growth

9. Which of the following is *not* one of the arguments used in support of public aid for agriculture in Canada?
(a) Farmers have had to bear a disproportionate part of the cost of economic progress.
(b) Farmers are subject to hazards to which other indus tries are not subject.
(c) Farmers sell their products in highly competitive markets.
(d) Farmers are more affected by competition from foreign producers than are other parts of the economy.

10. A consequence of the government's offer-to-purchase program at a price above the equilibrium is:
(a) reduced farm incomes
(b) reduced consumer prices
(c) increased consumption of the farm product
(d) a surplus of the farm product

11. Deficiency payments mean that:
(a) the real income of the farmer remains constant
(b) through subsidies, the farmer enjoys a form of price support
(c) the purchasing power of the farmer's money income remains constant
(d) the money income of the farmer will buy a constant amount of goods and services

12. Which statement is correct?
(a) Deficiency payments can lead to surpluses, which the government must then buy.
(b) Crop restriction is not appropriate if supply is elastic.
(c) The offers-to-purchase method of price supports should not be used with an elastic demand.
(d) Consumers prefer the offers-to-purchase method of price supports.

Use the diagram below to answer questions 13 to 15.

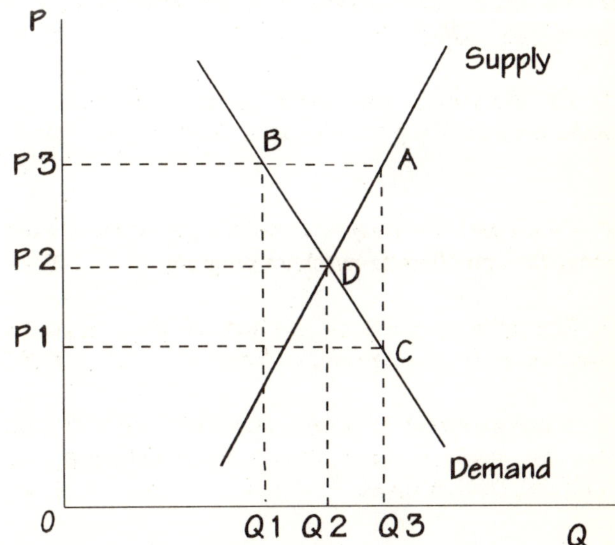

13. If the government supported the price of this product at P_3 through offers-to-purchase, the total amount it

would have to spend to purchase the surplus of the product would be:
(a) $0Q_3AP_3$
(b) Q_1Q3AB
(c) P_1CAP_3
(d) $0Q_1BP_3$

14. If the government supported the price of this product at P_3, the total deficiency payments made by the government to producers of the product would be:
(a) $0QAP_3$
(b) Q_1Q_3AB
(c) P_1CAP_3
(d) $0Q_1BP_3$

15. Regardless of whether the government supports the price of the product at P_3 through offers-to-purchase or deficiency payments, the total income of producers of the product will be:
(a) $0Q_3AP_3$
(b) $0Q_1BP_3$
(c) $0Q_3CP_1$
(d) $0Q_2DP_2$

16. Which of the following will reduce the foreign demand for Canadian farm products?
(a) a reduction in foreign tariffs on farm products
(b) a reduction in foreign quotas on farm products
(c) an appreciation of the Canadian dollar
(d) crop failures in foreign countries

Answer the next two questions (17 and 18) on the basis of the demand and supply schedules for agricultural product Z as shown below.

Kilograms of Z Demanded	Price of Z per Kilogram	Kilograms of Z Supplied
850	$1.30	1,150
900	1.20	1,100
950	1.10	1,050
1,000	1.00	1,000
1,050	0.90	950
1,100	0.80	850
1.150	0.70	800

17. If the federal government supports the price of Z at $1.30 a kilogram, then at this price, there is:
(a) a surplus of 200 kilograms of Z
(b) a surplus of 300 kilograms of Z
(c) a surplus of 400 kilograms of Z
(d) a shortage of 400 kilograms of Z

18. With a federal price support of $1.30 a kilogram, consumers spend:
(a) $1,040 - the federal government spends $410, and farmers receive income from product Z of $1,450
(b) $1,105 - the federal government spends $390, and farmers receive income from product Z of $1,495
(c) $1,296 - the federal government spends $240, and farmers receive income from product Z of $1,320
(d) $1,045 - the federal government spends $110, and farmers receive income from product Z of $1,155

19. High quota values in the supply management industries:
(a) are indicative of prices set below the equilibrium price
(b) are a help to new farmers entering the industry
(c) are the result of price and income benefits of the plan being capitalized into quota prices
(d) are a fixed cost and do not affect farm profitability

20. Criticisms of farm programs include all of the following except:
(a) farm programs entail huge and increasing budgetary costs
(b) farm program subsidies do not benefit the most needy farmers
(c) farm programs promote the reallocation of resources out of agriculture
(d) farm programs complicate international economic policies

21. The nonfarm policies of the federal government critical to the well-being of the agricultural sector of the economy are those that affect:
(a) interest rates in the economy
(b) the international value of the dollar
(c) the accessibility of foreign markets to farmers
(d) all of the above

22. The goal of a market-oriented income stabilization policy would be:
(a) to prevent farm prices and incomes from falling in the long run
(b) to prevent sharp fluctuations in farm prices and incomes from one year to the next
(c) to increase farm prices and incomes in the long run

(d) to prevent both sharp year-to-year fluctuations and falling long-run farm prices and incomes

23. The farm policy of the European Economic community has:
(a) opened markets in Europe for Canadian farm products
(b) reduced world prices in world markets for agricultural products, making these markets less attractive to Canadian farmers
(c) reduced the costs of farm programs in Canada
(d) resulted in a more efficient international allocation of farm resources

24. A good reason for an optimistic view of the capacity of the world to feed itself fifty years from now would be that:
(a) the population of the world is increasing
(b) the climate of the world is changing
(c) agricultural productivity is increasing
(d) land is being put to more productive uses in urban areas

Discussion Questions

1. Why is the economics of agriculture an important topic for study?

2. What is the short-run farm problem, and what are its causes?

3. Why does the demand for agricultural products tend to be inelastic? What effect does the elasticity of demand have on price and income instability in agriculture?

4. What have been the specific causes of the large increases in the supply of agricultural products since World War I?

5. Why has the demand for agricultural products failed to increase at the same rate as the supply of these products?

6. Explain why the farm population tends to be relatively immobile. If farmers were more mobile, how would the price system reallocate their labour away from agricul ture and into more prosperous occupations?

7. Why do agricultural interests claim that farmers have a special right to aid from government?

8. What devices does the government employ to support above-equilibrium agricultural prices? Why is the result of government-supported prices through offers-to-purchase invariably a surplus of farm commodities?

9. Why has the farm program not been successful in preventing falling farm prices and incomes, surpluses, and an unequal distribution of farm income?

10. Explain why in the supply management industries the quotas or rights to produce take on value.

11. Why and in what ways have the nonfarm policies of the federal government been critical to the well-being of the farm sector?

12. Explain how the farm policies of the United States and the European Community affect the export demand for Canadian farm products.

13. What insights does public choice theory provide about the persistence of government support for the agricultural sector?

14. What are the arguments of the pessimists and of the optimists on the issue of whether the world will be able to feed itself in the next century?

Answers

Fill-in questions

1. leading; purely competitive; interference; globalization; special-interest; rent-seeking

2. instability

3. inelastic; substitutes, marginal utility

4. small, large, small, large

5. export

6. lag behind; supply, demand, inelastic; slowed

7. resources, the agricultural, nonagricultural

8. subsidies, price floors, marketing boards, prices, incomes

9. (a) income; (b) risk; (c) competitive; (d) power

10. output, prices and incomes

11. surpluses, purchase; (a) incomes; (b) prices, less; (c) loses; higher, inefficiency, overallocation; (d) international, trade, negative

12. deficiency payments; will not, identical

13. production quotas, values

14. have not; (a) symptoms, cause; (b) high, low (c) contradicted; (d) decreasing, size; interest, dollar

15. decrease

16. public choice; rent-seeking behaviour; special-interest; small, large

17. declining, deficits, free

18. decreased, misallocation

19. (a) demand, supply; (1) fixed, poor, (2) agricultural, (3) irrigation, (4) population, (5) environment; (b) (1) increased, (2) productivity, less-developed, (3) population, (4) price (market)

Problems and projects

1. (a) 27,000, 25,000, 22,000, 18,000, 13,000; (b) rise, inelastic, is.

2. (a) 3.60, 120,000, 432,000; (b) 110,000, 140,000 surplus, 30,000 144,000: (c) there will be an ongoing surplus which government must buy; (d) 140,000, 140,000, 0.80, 4.00, 140,000, 560,000: (e) offers-to-purchase; (f) deficiency payments; (g) 672,000.

True-False

1. F	**2.** T	**3.** F	**4.** T	**5.** F	**6.** T
7. T	**8.** T	**9.** F	**10.** T	**11.** F	**12.** F
13. T	**14.**T	**15.** T	**16.** F	**17.** T	**18.** T
19. F	**20.** T	**21.** F	**22.** F	**23.** F	**24.** T
25. F	**26.** T	**27.** F			

Multiple-choice

1. (d)	**2.** (d)	**3.** (c)	**4.** (a)	**5.** (c)	**6.** (d)
7. (c)	**8.** (b)	**9.** (d)	**10.** (d)	**11.** (b)	**12.** (c)
13. (b)	**14.** (c)	**15.** (a)	**16.** (c)	**17.** (b)	**18.** (b)
19. (c)	**20.** (c)	**21.** (d)	**22.** (b)	**23.** (b)	**24.** (c)

Glossary

Ability-to-pay principle—The belief that those who have the greater income (or wealth) should be taxed absolutely and relatively more than those who have less.

Abstraction—Elimination of irrelevant and non-economic facts to obtain an economic principle.

Actual budget—The amount spent by the federal government to purchase goods and services and for transfer payments) less the amount of tax revenue collected by it in any (fiscal) year; and which can *not* reliably be used to determine whether it is pursuing an expansionary or contractionary fiscal policy. Compare with the Cyclically adjusted budget *(see).*

Actual deficit—The size of the federal government's Budget deficit *(see)* actually measured or recorded in any given year.

Actual investment—The amount that business Firms do invest; equal to Planned investment plus Unplanned investment.

Actual reserve—The amount a bank has as Vault cash and on deposit at the Bank of Canada.

Adaptive expectations theory—The idea that people determine their expectations about future events (for example, inflation) on the basis of past and present events (rates of inflation) and only change their expectations as events unfold.

Adjustable pegs—The device utilized in the Bretton Woods system *(see) to* change Exchange rates in an orderly way to eliminate persistent Payments deficits and surpluses; each nation defined its monetary unit in terms of (pegged it to) gold or the U.S. dollar, kept the Rate of exchange for its money stable in the short run, and changed (adjusted) it in the long run when faced with international disequilibrium.

Adverse selection problem—A problem arising when information known to one party to a contract is not known to the other party, causing the latter to incur major costs. Example: individuals who have the poorest health are more likely to buy health insurance.

Aggregate demand—A schedule or curve that shows the total quantity of goods and services demanded (purchased) at different price levels.

Aggregate demand-aggregate supply model—The macroeconomic model that uses Aggregate demand and Aggregate supply *(see both) to* determine and explain the Price level and the real Domestic output.

Aggregate expenditures—The total amount spent final for goods and services in the economy.

Aggregate expenditure-domestic output approach—Determination of the Equilibrium gross domestic product *(see)* by finding the real GDP at which Aggregate expenditures are equal to the real Domestic output.

Aggregate expenditures schedule—A schedule or curve showing the total amount spent for final goods and services at different levels of real GDP.

Aggregate supply—A schedule or curve showing the tool quantity of goods and services supplied (produced) at different Price levels.

Aggregation—Treating individual units or data as one unit or number. For example, all prices of individual goods and services are combined into a Price level, or all units of output are aggregated into Real GDP.

Agricultural Stabilization Board—The federal agency established in 1958 to support the following commodities at not less than 90% of their average price over the previous five years, with adjustments according to production costs: cattle, hogs, and sheep; industrial milk and cream; and oats and barley not produced on the Prairies [where the Canadian Wheat Board *(see)* has jurisdiction].

Allocative efficiency—The apportionment of resources among firms and industries to obtain the production of the products most wanted by society (consumers): the output of each product at which its Marginal cost and Price are equal.

Allocative factor—The ability of an economy to reallocate resources to achieve the Economic growth that the Supply factors *(see)* make possible.

American Federation of Labor (AFL)—The American organization of affiliated Craft unions formed in 1886.

Annually balanced budget—The equality of government expenditures and tax collections during a year.

Anticipated inflation - Inflation *(see)* at a rate that was equal to the rate expected in that period of time.

Anti-combines—*(See* Combines Investigation Act.)

Anti-Inflation Board—The federal agency established in 1975 (and disbanded in 1979) to administer the government's inflation control program.

Applied economics—*(See* Policy economics.)

Appreciation—An increase in the international price of a currency caused by market forces; not caused by the central bank; the opposite of Depreciation.

Arbitration—The designation of a neutral third to render a decision in a dispute by which both parties (the employer and the labour union) agree in advance to abide.

Asian tigers—The newly industrialised and rapidly growing nations of Hong Kong, Singapore, South Korea, and Taiwan.

Asset—Anything with a monetary value owned by a firm or an individual.

Asset demand for money—The amount of money people want to hold as a Store of value (the amount of their financial assets they wish to have in the form of Money); and which varies inversely with the Rate of interest.

Authoritarian capitalism—An economic system in which property resources are privately owned and government extensively directs and controls the economy.

Authoritarian socialism—*(See* Command economy.)

Average fixed cost—The total fixed cost *(see)* of a Firm divided by output (the quantity of product produced).

Average product—The total output produced per unit of a resource employed (total product divided by the quantity of a resource employed).

Average propensity to consume—Fraction of Disposable income that households spend for consumer goods and services; consumption divided by Disposable income.

Average propensity to save—Fraction of Disposable income that households save; Saving divided by Disposable income.

Average revenue—Total revenue from the sale of a product divided by the quantity of the product sold (demanded); equal to the price at which the product is sold so long as all units of the product are sold at the same price.

Average tax rate—Total tax paid divided by total (taxable) income; the tax rate on total (taxable) income.

Average total cost—The Total cost of a Firm divided by its output (the quantity of product produced); equal to Average fixed cost *(see)* plus Average variable cost *(see).*

Average variable cost—The total Variable cost *(see)* of a Firm divided by output (the quantity of product produced).

Balanced budget multiplier—The effect of equal increases (decreases) in government spending for goods and services and in taxes is to increase (decrease) the Equilibrium gross domestic product.

Balance of (international) payments—The annual statement of a nation's international economic dealings showing the Current account *(see)* balance and the Capital account *(see)* balance, the latter including the balance in Official international reserves *(see).*

Balance of payments deficit—When the balance in Official international reserves *(see) is* positive.

Balance of payments surplus—When the balance in Official international reserves *(see) is negative.*

Balance of trade—The addition of the balances on goods (merchandise) and services in the Current account *(see)* of the Balance of payments *(see).*

Balance on the capital account—The Capital inflows *(see)* of a nation less its Capital outflows *(see),* both of which include Official international reserves *(see).*

Balance on current account—The exports of goods (merchandise) and services of a nation less its imports of goods (merchandise) and services plus its Net investment income from nonresidents *(see)* and its Net transfers.

Balance on goods and services—The Balance of trade *(see).*

Balance sheet—A statement of the Assets *(see),* Liabilities *(see),* and Net worth *(see)* of a Firm or individual at some given time.

Bank rate—The interest rate that the Bank of Canada charges on advances *(normally* very short-term loans) made to the chartered banks.

Bankers' bank—The bank that accepts the deposits of and makes loans to chartered banks: the Bank of Canada.

Barrier to entry—Anything that artificially prevents the entry of Firms into an industry.

Barter—The exchange of one good or service for another good or service.

Base year—The year with which prices in other years are compared when a Price index *(see) is* constructed.

Benefit-cost analysis—Deciding whether to employ resources and the quantity of resources to employ for a project or program (for the production of a good or service) by comparing the marginal benefits with the marginal costs.

Benefit-reduction rate—The percentage of any increase in earned income by which subsidy benefits in a Negative income tax *(see)* plan are reduced.

Benefits-received principle—The belief that those who receive the benefits of goods and services provided by government should pay the taxes required to finance them.

Bid rigging—The illegal action of oligopolists who agree either that one or more will not bid on a request for bids or tenders or, alternatively, agree on what bids they will make, and forbidden under the Competition Act *(see).*

Big business—A business Firm that either produces a large percentage of the total output of an industry, is large (measured by number of employees or stockholders, sales, assets, or profits) compared with other Firms in the economy, or both.

Bilateral monopoly—A market in which there is a single seller (Monopoly) and a single buyer (Monopsony).

Brain drain—The emigration of highly educated, highly skilled workers from a country.

Break-even income—The level of Disposable income at which Households plan to consume (spend) all of their income (for consumer goods and services) and to save none of it; also denotes that level of earned income at which subsidy payments become zero in an income-maintenance program.

Break-even point—Any output that a (competitive) Firm might produce at which its Total cost and Total revenue would be equal; an output at which it has neither a profit nor a loss.

Bretton Woods system—The international monetary system developed after World War II in which Adjustable pegs *(see)* were employed, the International Monetary Fund *(see)* helped to stabilize exchange rates, and gold and the major currencies were used as Official international reserves *(see).*

Budget deficit—The amount by which the expenditures of the federal government exceed its revenues in any year.

Budget line—A curve that shows the different combinations of two products a consumer can purchase with a given money income.

Budget restraint—The limit imposed on the ability of an individual consumer to obtain goods and services by the size of the consumer's income (and by the prices that must be paid for the goods and services).

Budget surplus—The amount by which the revenues of the federal government exceed its expenditures in any year.

Built-in stability—The effect of Nondiscretionary fiscal policy *(see)* upon the economy; when Net taxes vary directly with the Gross domestic product, the fall (rise) in Net taxes during a recession (inflation) helps to eliminate unemployment (inflationary pressures).

Business cycle—Recurrent ups and downs over a period of years in the level of economic activity.

Canada Assistance Plan—The federal Act under which the federal government makes funds available to the provinces for their programs of assistance to disabled, handicapped, unemployed who are not entitled to unemployment insurance benefits, and other needy persons.

Canada Deposit Insurance Corporation—Federal Crown Corporation that, for a fee payable by the chartered banks and federally chartered trust companies, insures their customers' deposits up to a limit of $60,000 per customer per bank or trust company.

Canada Labour Code—The federal law of 1970 that consolidated previous legislation regulating employment practices, labour standards, and so on, in the federal jurisdiction.

Canada Pension Plan—The compulsory, contributory, earnings-related federal pension plan that covers most employed members of the labour force between the ages of 18 and 65, and payable at the latter age; it came into effect in 1965; there is transferability between the Plan and the Quebec Pension Plan, which applies to the people of that province.

Canada-United States Free Trade Agreement (FTA)—An accord that came into effect on January 1, 1989, to eliminate all Tariffs *(see)* between the two countries over the following ten years.

Canadian Congress of Labour (CCL)—The federation of Industrial unions *(see)* formed in 1940 and affiliated with the Congress of Industrial Organizations *(see)*; amalgamated into Canadian Labour Congress *(see)* in 1956.

Canadian International Development Agency (CIDA)—The federal agency responsible for the operation and administration of Canada's international development assistance programs of approximately $2.5 billion a year.

Canadian Labour Congress (CLC)—The largest federation of Labour unions *(see)* in Canada, with 3 million members in international and national unions; founded in 1956 on the amalgamation of the Canadian Congress of Labour *(see)* and the Trades and Labour Congress of Canada *(see)*.

Canadian Payments Association—The federal agency set up in 1982 to provide for Cheque clearing *(see)*.

Canadian Wheat Board—Federal Crown Corporation established in 1935, which does not own or operate grain-handling facilities but has complete control over the way western wheat is marketed and the price at which it is sold. The Board also acquired complete control of the supplies of all Prairie coarse grains in 1949.

Capacity-creating aspect of investment—The effect of investment spending on the productive capacity (the ability to produce goods and services) of an economy.

Capital—Human-made resources (machinery and equipment) used to produce goods and services; goods that do not directly satisfy human wants; capital goods.

Capital account—That part of the Balance of payments *(see)* that records the net inflows and outflows of liquid capital (money) for direct and portfolio investments at home and abroad, and includes the balance in Official international reserves *(see)*.

Capital account deficit—A negative Balance on the capital account *(see)*.

Capital account surplus—A positive Balance on the capital account *(see).*

Capital consumption allowances—Estimate of the amount of Capital worn out or used up (consumed) in producing the Gross domestic product; Depreciation.

Capital flight—The transfer of Savings from less developed to industrially advanced countries to avoid government expropriation, taxation, and high rates of inflation or to realise better investment opportunities.

Capital gain—The gain realised when securities or properties are sold for a price greater than the price paid for them.

Capital goods—*(See* Capital.)

Capital inflow—The expenditures made by the residents of foreign nations to purchase equity, shares, and bonds from the residents of a nation.

Capital intensive commodity—A product that requires a relatively large amount of Capital to produce.

Capital outflow—The expenditures made by the residents of a nation to purchase equity, shares, and bonds from the residents of foreign nations.

Capital-output ratio—The ratio of the stock of Capital to the productive (output) capacity of the economy; and the ratio of a change in the stock of Capital (net investment) to the resulting change in productive capacity.

Capital-saving technological advance—An improvement in technology that permits a greater quantity of a product to be produced with a specific amount of Capital (or the same amount of the product to be produced with a smaller amount of Capital).

Capital-using technological advance—An improvement in technology that requires the use of a greater amount of Capital to produce a specific quantity of a product.

Cartel—A formal written or oral agreement among Firms to set the price of the product and the outputs of the individual Firms or to divide the market for the product geographically.

Causation—A cause-and-effect relationship; one or several events bring about or result in another event.

Ceiling price—*(See* Price ceiling.)

Central bank—The bank whose chief function is the control of the nation's money supply: the Bank of Canada.

Central economic planning—Determination of the objectives of the economy and the direction of its resources to the attainment of these objectives by the national government.

***Ceteris Paribus* assumption**—*(See* "Other things being equal" assumption.)

Change in amount consumed—increase or decrease in consumption spending that results from an increase or decrease in Disposable income, the Consumption schedule (curve) remaining unchanged; movement from one line (point) to another on the same Consumption schedule (curve).

Change in amount saved—Increase or decrease in Saving that results from an increase or decrease in Disposable income, the Saving schedule (curve) remaining unchanged; movement from one line (point) to another on the same Saving schedule (curve).

Change in the consumption schedule—An increase or decrease in consumption at each level of Disposable income caused by changes in the Nonincome determinants of consumption and saving *(see);* an upward or downward movement of the Consumption schedule.

Change in the saving schedule—An increase or decrease in Saving at each level of Disposable income caused by changes in the Nonincome determinants of consumption and saving *(see);* an upward or downward movement of the Saving schedule.

Chartered bank—One of the 66 multibranched, privately owned, commercial, financial intermediaries that have received charters by Act of Parliament and that alone, with Quebec Savings Banks, may call themselves "banks"; and which accept Demand deposits *(see).*

Chartered banking system—All Chartered banks as a group.

Checkoff—The deduction by an employer of union dues from the pay of workers and the transfer of the amount deducted to a Labour union.

Chequable deposit—Any deposit in a Chartered bank or other financial intermediary (trust company, credit union, etc.) against which a cheque may be written and which deposit, if it is in a bank, is thus part of the M1 *(see)* money supply.

Cheque clearing—The process by which funds are transferred from the Chequing accounts of the writers of cheques to the Chequing accounts of the recipients of the cheques; also called the "collection" of cheques.

Chequing account—A Demand deposit *(see)* in a chartered bank.

Circular flow of income—The flow of resources from Households to Firms and of products from Firms to Households accompanied in an economy using money by flows of money from Households to Firms and from Firms to Households.

Civilian labour force—Persons 15 years of age and older who are not residents of the Yukon or the Northwest Territories, who are not in institutions or the armed forces, and who are employed for a wage or salary, seeking such employment, or self employed for gain.

Classical economics—The Macroeconomic generalizations accepted by most economists before the 1930s that led to the conclusion that a capitalistic economy would employ its resources fully.

Closed economy—An economy that neither exports nor imports goods and services.

Close-down case—The circumstance in which a Firm would experience a loss greater than its total fixed cost if it were to produce any output greater than zero; alternatively, a situation in which a firm would cease to operate when the price at which it can sell its product is less than its Average variable cost.

Coase theorem—The idea that Externality problems may be resolved through private negotiations of the affected parties.

Coincidence of wants—The item (good or service) that one trader wishes to obtain is the same as another trader desires to give up and the item the second trader wishes to acquire is the same as the first trader desires to surrender.

COLA—*(See* Cost-of-living adjustment.)

Collection of cheques—*(see* Cheque clearing.)

Collective bargaining—The negotiation of work agreements between Labour unions *(see)* and their employers.

Collective voice—The function a union performs for its members as a group when it communicates their problems and grievances to management and presses management for a satisfactory resolution.

Collusion—A situation in which Firms act together and in agreement (collude) to set the price of the product and the output each firm will produce or to determine the geographic area in which each firm will sell.

Collusive oligopoly—Occurs when the few firms composing an oligopolistic industry reach an explicit or unspoken agreement to fix prices, divide a market, or otherwise restrict competition; may be a Cartel *(see)*, Gentleman's agreement *(see)*, or Price leadership *(see)*.

Combined tax-transfer system—The percentage of income collected as taxes less the percentage of income received as transfer payments in different income classes.

Combines Investigation Act—The federal Act, first passed in 1910, whose avowed aim is to prevent agreements to lessen competition unduly; amended and renamed the Competition Act in June 1986.

Command economy—An economic system (method of organisation) in which property resources are publicly owned and Central economic planning *(see)* is used to direct and co-ordinate economic activities.

Commercial bank—*(See* Chartered bank.)

Communism—*(See* Command economy.)

Company union—An organization of employed that is dominated by the employer (the company) and does not engage in genuine collective bargaining with the employer.

Comparable worth doctrine—The belief that women should receive the same salaries (wages) as men when the levels of skill, effort, and responsibility in their different jobs are the same.

Comparative advantage—A lower relative or Comparative cost *(see)* than another producer.

Comparative cost—The amount the production of one product must be reduced to increase the production of another product; Opportunity cost *(see).*

Compensating differences—The differences in the Wages received by workers in different jobs which compensate for nonmonetary differences in the jobs.

Competing goods—*(See* Substitute goods.)

Competition—The presence in a market of a large number of independent buyers and sellers and the freedom of buyers and sellers to enter and to leave the market.

Competition Act—The Act that amended the Combines Investigation Act *(see)* in June 1986 and, in so doing, renamed it the Competition Act.

Competitive industry's short run supply curve—The horizontal summation of the short-run supply curves of the Firms in a purely competitive industry *(see* Pure competition); a curve that shows the total quantities offered for sale at various prices by the Firms in an industry in the Short run *(see).*

Competitive industry's short-run supply schedule—The summation of the short-run supply schedules of the Firms in a purely competitive industry *(see* Pure competition); a schedule that shows the total quantities that will be offered for sale at various prices by the Firms in an industry in the Short run *(see).*

Competitive labour market—A market in which a large number of (noncolluding) firm demand a particular type of labour from a large number of nonunionized workers.

Complementary goods—Goods or services for which there is an inverse relationship between the price of one and the demand for the other, when the price of one falls (rises) the demand for the other increases (decrease).

Complex multiplier—The Multiplier *(see)* when changes in the Gross domestic product change Net taxes and Imports, as well as Saving.

Concentration ratio—The percentage of the total sales of an industry made by the four (or some other number) largest sellers (Firms) in the industry

Conditional grant—A transfer to a province by the federal government for a Shared-cost program whereby the federal government undertakes to pay part of the costs (usually half) of programs run by the provinces in accordance with federally set standards; such grants are mostly for health, post-secondary education, and general welfare [mostly under the Canada Assistance Plan *(see)*].

Confederation of National Trade Unions (CNTU)—The Labour union *(see)* federation that represents approximately 20% of Quebec's union members; established in 1921 as the Federation of Catholic Workers of Canada, it was later renamed the Canadian and Catholic Confederation of Labour; it adopted its present name and became nonconfessional in 1956.

Conglomerate combination—A group of Plants *(see)* owned by a single Firm and engaged at one or more sages in the production of different products (of products that do not compete with each other).

Conglomerate merger—The merger of a Firm in one Industry with a Firm in another industry (with a Firm that is neither supplier, customer, nor competitor).

Congress of Industrial Organizations (CIO)—The organisation of affiliated Industrial unions formed in the United States in 1936.

Constant-cost industry—An Industry in which the expansion of the Industry by the entry of new Firms has no effect upon the prices the Firms in the Industry pay for resources and no effect, therefore, on their cost curve.

Consumer goods—Goods and services that satisfy human wants directly.

Consumer price index (CPI)—An index that measures the prices of a fixed Market basket" of some 300 consumer goods bought by a "typical" consumer

Consumer sovereignty—Determination by consumers of the types and quantities of goods and services produced from the scarce resources of the economy.

Consumption schedule—A schedule showing the amounts Households plan to spend for Consumer goods at different levels of Disposable income.

Contractionary fiscal policy—A decrease in Aggregate demand brought about by a decrease in government expenditures for goods and services, an increase in Net taxes, or some combination of the two.

Contractionary monetary policy—Contracting, or restricting the growth of, the nation's Money supply *(see).*

Corporate income tax—A tax levied on the net income (profit) of Corporations.

Corporation—A legal entity ("person") chartered by the federal or a provincial government, which is distinct and separate from the individuals who own it.

Correlation—Systematic and dependable association between two sets of data (two kinds of events); does not necessarily indicate causation.

Cost-of-living adjustment (COLA)—An increase in the incomes (wages) of workers that is automatically received by them when there is inflation and guaranteed by a clause in their labour contracts with their employer.

Cost-plus pricing—A procedure used by (oligopolistic) firms to determine the price they will charge for a product and in which a percentage markup is added to the estimated average total cost of producing the product.

Cost-push inflation—Inflation resulting from a decrease in Aggregate supply (from higher wage rates and raw material prices) and accompanied by decreases in real output and employment (by increases in the Unemployment rate).

Cost ratio—The ratio of the decrease in the production of one product to the increase in the production of another product when resources are shifted from the production of the first to the second product; the amount the production of one product decreases when the production of a second increases by one unit.

Craft union—A Labour union that limits its membership to workers with a particular skill (craft).

Credit—An accounting notation that the value of an asset (such as the foreign money owned by the residents of a nation) has increased.

Credit union—An association of persons who often have a common tie (such as being employees of the same Firm or members of the same Labour union) that sells shares to (accepts deposits from) its members and makes loans to them.

Creeping inflation—A slow rate of inflation; a 2 to 4% annual rise in the price level.

Crop restriction—A method of increasing farm revenue when demand for the product is inelastic. Usually done through a Farm products marketing board *(see)* allotting quotas.

Cross elasticity of demand—The ratio of the percentage change in Quantity demanded of one good to the percentage change in the price of some other good. A positive coefficient indicates the two products are Substitute goods; a negative coefficient indicates Complementary goods.

Crowding model of occupational discrimination—A model of labour markets that assumes Occupational discrimination *(see)* against women and minorities has kept them out of many occupations and forced them into a limited number of other occupations in which the large Supply of labour (relative to the Demand) results in lower wages and incomes.

Crowding-out effect—The rise in interest rates and the resulting decrease in planned investment spending in the economy caused by increased borrowing in the money market by the federal government.

Currency—Coins and Paper money.

Currency appreciation—*(See* Exchange rate appreciation.)

Currency depreciation—*(See* Exchange rate depreciation.)

Current account—That part of the Balance of payments *(see)* that records the total current receipts for merchandise exports, services, investment income from nonresidents, and transfers and the total current payments for merchandise imports, services, investment income to nonresidents, and transfers.

Current account deficit—A negative Balance on current account *(see).*

Current account surplus—A positive Balance on current account *(see).*

Customary economy—*(See* Traditional economy.)

Cyclical unemployment—Unemployment caused by insufficient Aggregate expenditures (or by insufficient Aggregate demand).

Cyclically adjusted budget—What the budget balance would be for the total government sector if the economy were operating at an average or cyclically adjusted level of activity.

Cyclically adjusted deficit—The budget deficit that would have occurred even though the economy was operating at an average or cyclically adjusted level of activity.

Cyclically balanced budget—The equality of Government expenditures for goods and services and Net taxes collections over the course of a Business cycle; deficits incurred during periods of recession are offset by surpluses obtained during periods of prosperity (inflation).

Debit—An accounting notation that the value of an asset (such as the foreign money owned by the residents of a nation) has decreased.

Debt-equity swaps—The transfer of stock in private or government owned enterprises of Less developed countries *(see)* to foreign creditors.

Declining economy—An economy in which Net investment *(see)* is less than zero (Gross private domestic investment is less than Depreciation).

Declining industry—An industry in which Economic profits are negative (losses are incurred) and which will, therefore, decrease its output as firms leave the industry.

Decrease in demand—A decrease in the Quantity demanded of a good or service at every price; a shift of the Demand curve to the left.

Decrease in supply—A decrease in the Quantity supplied of a good or service at every price; a shift of the Supply curve to the left.

Deduction—Reasoning from assumption to conclusions; a method of reasoning that tests a hypothesis (an assumption) by comparing the conclusions to which it leads with economic facts.

Deficiency payments—A method of Price support *(see)* whereby the government pays a subsidy to producers when the market price is below the minimum price demand suitable by the government.

Deflating—Finding the Real gross domestic product *(see)* by decreasing the dollar value of the Gross domestic product produced in a year in which prices were higher than in the Base year *(see).*

Deflation—A fall in the general (average) level of prices in the economy.

Demand—A Demand schedule or a Demand curve *(see* both).

Demand curve—A curve showing the amounts of a good or service buyers wish to purchase at various prices during some period of time.

Demand deposit—A deposit in a Chartered bank against which cheques may be written for immediate payment; bank-created money.

Demand factor—The increase in the level of Aggregate expenditures that brings about the Economic growth made possible by an increase in the productive potential of the economy.

Demand management—The use of Fiscal policy *(see)* and Monetary policy *(see)* to increase or decrease Aggregate expenditures.

Demand-pull inflation—Inflation resulting from an increase in Aggregate demand.

Demand schedule—A schedule showing the amounts of a good or service buyers will purchase at various prices during some period of time.

Dependent variable—A variable that changes as a consequence of a change in some other (independent) variable; the "effect" or outcome.

Deposit multiplier—*(See* Monetary multiplier.)

Depository institution—A Firm that accepts the deposits of Money of the public (businesses and persons); Chartered banks and other Financial intermediaries *(see).*

Depreciation (1)—*(See* Capital consumption allowances.)

Depreciation (2)—A decrease in the international price of a currency caused by market forces; not caused by the Central bank; the opposite of Appreciation.

Derived demand—The demand for a good or service that is dependent on or related to the demand for some other good or service; the demand for a resource that depends on the demand for the products it can be used to produce.

Descriptive economics—The gathering or collection of relevant economic facts (data).

Desired reserves—The amount of vault cash each chartered bank chooses to keep on hand for daily transaction. This amount includes reserves held at the Bank of Canada for cheque settlements among the chartered banks.

Determinants of aggregate demand—Factors such as consumption, investment, government, and net export spending that, if they change, will shift the Aggregate demand curve.

Determinants of aggregate supply—Factors such as input prices, productivity, and the legal-institutional environment that, if they change, will shift the Aggregate supply curve.

Determinants of demand—Factors other than its price that determine the quantities demanded of a good or service.

Determinants of supply—Factors other than its price that determine the quantities supplied of a good or service.

Devaluation—A decrease in the government-defined value of a currency brought about by the Central bank; the opposite of Revaluation.

DI—*(See* Disposable income.)

Differentiated oligopoly—An Oligopoly in which the firms produce a Differentiated product *(see).*

Differentiated product—A product that differs physically or in some other way from the similar products produced by other Firms; a product such that buyers are not indifferent to the seller from whom they purchase it when the price charged by all sellers is the same.

Dilemma of regulation—When a Regulatory agency *(see)* must establish the maximum price a monopolist may charge, it finds that if it sets the price at the Optimal social price *(see)*, this price is below Average total cost (and either bankrupts the Firm or requires that it be subsidized); and if it sets the price at the Fair return price *(see)*, it has failed to eliminate the underallocation of resources that is the consequence of unregulated monopoly.

Direct investment—Investment by nonresidents in a firm they thereby establish or control or come to control through the investment. *(see* also Portfolio investment.)

Directing function of prices—*(see* Guiding function of prices.)

Directly related—Two sets of economic data that change in the same direction; when one variable increases (decreases) the other increases (decreases).

Direct relationship—The relationship between two variables that change in the same direction, for example, product price and quantity supplied.

Discouraged workers—Workers who have left the Civilian labour force *(see)* because they have not been able to find employment.

Discretionary fiscal policy—Deliberate changes in taxes (tax rates) and government spending (spending for goods and services and transfer payment programs) by Parliament for the purpose of achieving a full-employment, noninflationary Gross domestic product and economic growth.

Diseconomies of scale—The forces that increase the Average total cost of producing a product as the Firm expands the size of its Plant (its output) in the Long run *(see)*.

Disinflation—A reduction in the rate of Inflation *(see)*.

Disposable income—Personal income *(see)* less Personal taxes *(see)*; income available for Personal consumption expenditures *(see)* and Personal saving *(see)*.

Dissaving—Spending for consumer goods and services in excess of Disposable income; the amount by which Personal consumption expenditures *(see)* exceed Disposable income.

Dividend tax credit—A federal government method of reducing the Double taxation *(see)* of corporation income.

Division of labour—Dividing the work required to produce a product into a number of different tasks that are performed by different workers; Specialization *(see)* of workers.

Dollar votes—The "votes" consumers and entrepreneurs in effect cast for the production of the different kinds of consumer and capital goods, respectively, when they purchase them in the markets of the economy.

Domestic economic goal—Assumed to be full employment with little or no Inflation.

Domestic income—*(See* Net domestic income.)

Domestic output—Gross domestic product *(see)*.

Domestic price—The price of a good or service within a country, determined by domestic demand and supply.

Doomsday models—Computer-based models that predict that continued growth of population and production will exhaust available resources and the environment, causing an economic collapse.

Double counting—Including the value of Intermediate goods *(see)* in the Gross domestic product; counting the same good or service more than once.

Double taxation—Taxation of both corporation net income (profits) and the dividends paid from this net income when they become the Personal income of households.

Dumping—The sale of products below cost in a foreign country.

Duopoly—A Market in which there are only two sellers; an industry in which there are two firms.

Durable good—A consumer good with an expected life (use) of three years or more.

Dynamic progress—The development over time of more efficient (less costly) techniques of producing existing products and of improved products; technological progress.

Earnings—The Money income received by a worker; equal to the Wage (rate) multiplied by the quantity of labour supplied (the amount of time worked) by the worker.

Easy money policy—Central bank expanding the Money supply in an effort to decrease interest rates.

EC—European Economic Community *(see* European Union) .

Economic analysis—Deriving Economic principles *(see)* from relevant economic facts.

Economic cost—A payment that must be made to obtain and retain the services of a resource; the income a Firm must provide to a resource supplier to attract the resource away from an alternative use; equal to the quantity of other products that cannot be produced when resources are employed to produce a particular product.

Economic efficiency—The relationship between the input of scarce resources and the resulting output of a good or service; production of an output with a specific dollar-and-cents value with the smallest total expenditure for resources; obtaining the largest total production of a good or service with resources of a specific dollar and-cents value.

Economic growth—(1) An increase in the Production possibilities schedule or curve that results from an increase in resource supplies or an improvement in Technology; (2) an increase either in real output (Gross domestic product) or in real output per capita.

Economic integration—Co-operation among and the complete or partial unification of the economies of different nations; the elimination of the barriers to trade among these nations; the bringing together of the markets in each of the separate economies to form one large (a common) market.

Economic law—*(See* Economic principle.)

Economic model—A simplified picture of reality; an abstract generalisation.

Economic perspective—A viewpoint that sees individuals and institutions making rational or purposeful decisions based on a consideration of the Marginal benefits and Marginal costs associated with one's actions.

Economic policy—Course of action that will correct or avoid a problem.

Economic principle—Generalization of the economic behaviour of individuals and institutions.

Economic profit—The total receipts (revenue) of a firm less all its Economic costs; also called "pure profit" and Above normal profit."

Economic regulation—*(See* Industrial regulation.)

Economic rent—The price paid for the use of land and other natural resources, the supply of which is fixed (perfectly inelastic).

Economic resources—Land, labour, capital, and entrepreneurial ability which are used in the production of goods and services.

Economics—Social science concerned with using scarce resources to obtain the maximum satisfaction of the unlimited human wants of society.

Economic theory—Deriving Economic principles *(see)* from relevant economic facts; an Economic principle *(see)*.

Economies of scale—The forces that reduce the Average total cost of producing a product as the Firm expands the size of its Plant (its output) in the Long run *(see)*; the economies of mass production.

Economizing problem—Society's material wants are unlimited but the resources available to produce the goods and services that satisfy wants are limited (scarce); the inability to produce unlimited quantities of goods and services.

Efficiency factors in growth—The capacity of an economy to combine resources effectively to achieve the growth of real output that the Supply factors *(see)* make possible.

Efficiency loss of a tax—The loss of net benefits to society because a tax reduces the production and consumption of a taxed good below the economically efficient level.

Efficiency wage—A wage that minimizes wage costs per unit of output.

Efficient allocation of resources—The allocation of the resources of an economy among the production of different products that leads to the maximum satisfaction of the wants of consumers; producing the optimal mix of output.

Elastic demand—The Elasticity coefficient *(see) is* greater than one; the percentage change in Quantity demanded is greater than the percentage change in price.

Elasticity coefficient—The number obtained when the percentage change in quantity demanded (or supplied) is divided by the percentage change in the price of the commodity

Elasticity formula—The price elasticity of demand (supply) is equal to:

$$\frac{\text{Percentage change in quantity demanded (supplied)}}{\text{Percentage change in price}}$$

Elastic supply—The Elasticity coefficient *(see) is* greater than one; the percentage change in Quantity supplied is greater than the percentage change in price.

Emission fees—Special fees that might be levied against those who discharge pollutants into the environment.

Employment and training policy—Policies and programs involving vocational training, job information, and anti-discrimination that are designed to improve labour market efficiency and lower unemployment at any level of aggregate demand.

Employment rate—The percentage of the Civilian labour force *(see)* employed at any time.

End products—Finished commodities that have attained their final degree of processing, such as commodities used directly for consumption, and machinery.

Entrepreneurial ability—The human resource that combines the other resources to produce a product, makes nonroutine decisions, innovates, and bears risks.

Equality vs. efficiency trade-off—The decrease in Economic efficiency *(see)* that may accompany a decrease in Income inequality *(see);* the presumption that an increase in Income inequality is required to increase Economic efficiency.

Equalization payment—An Unconditional grant *(see)* made by the federal government to the seven less wealthy provinces in an attempt to equalize incomes and opportunities across Canada.

Equalizing differences—The differences in the Wages received by workers in different jobs that compensate for nonmonetary differences in the jobs.

Equation of exchange—MV = PQ; in which M is the Money supply *(see),* V is the Velocity of money *(see), P* is the Price level, and Q is the physical volume of final goods and services produced.

Equilibrium GDP—The Gross domestic product at which the total quantity of final goods and services produced (the Domestic output) is equal to the total quantity of final goods and services purchased (Aggregate expenditures); the real Domestic output at which the Aggregate demand curve intersects the Aggregate supply curve.

Equilibrium position—The point at which the Budget line *(see) is* tangent to an Indifference curve *(see)* in the indifference curve approach to the theory of consumer behaviour.

Equilibrium price—The price in a competitive market where the Quantity demanded *(see)* and the Quantity supplied *(see)* are equal; where there is neither a shortage nor a surplus; and where there is no tendency for price to rise or fall.

Equilibrium price level—The Price level at which the Aggregate demand curve intersects the Aggregate supply curve.

Equilibrium quantity—The Quantity demanded *(see)* and Quantity supplied *(see)* at the Equilibrium price *(see)* in a competitive market.

European Common Market—*(See* European Union.)

European Union (EU)—The association of European nations initiated in 1958 to abolish gradually the Tariffs and Import quotas that exist among them, to establish common Tariffs for goods imported from outside the member nations, to allow the eventual free movement of labour and capital among them, and to create other common economic policies. (Earlier known as "European Economic Community" and the "Common Market.")

Excess capacity—A situation where an imperfectly competitive firm produces an output less than the minimum Average total cost output, thereby necessitating a higher product price than a purely competitive firm would charge.

Excess reserves—The amount by which a Chartered bank's Actual reserves *(see)* exceeds its Desired cash reserve *(see);* Actual reserves minus Desired reserves.

Exchange control—*(See* Foreign exchange control.)

Exchange Fund Account—The account operated by the Bank of Canada on the government's behalf wherein are held Canada's Official international reserves *(see).*

Exchange rate—The Rate of exchange *(see).*

Exchange rate appreciation—An increase in the value of a nation's money in foreign exchange markets caused by free market forces; a decrease in the Rates of exchange for foreign monies.

Exchange rate depreciation—A decrease in the value of a nation's money in foreign exchange markets caused by free market forces; an increase in the Rates of exchange for foreign monies.

Exchange rate determinant—Any factor other than the Rate of exchange *(see)* that determines the demand for and the supply of a currency in the Foreign exchange market *(see).*

Excise tax—A tax levied on the expenditure for a specific product or on the quantity of the product purchased.

Exclusion principle—The exclusion of those who do not pay for a product from the benefits of the product.

Exclusive dealing and tied selling—The illegal action whereby a supplier sells a product only on the condition that the buyer acquire other products from the same seller and not from competitors; and forbidden under the Competition Act *(see).*

Exclusive unionism—The policies employed by a Labour union to restrict the supply of labour by excluding potential members to increase the Wages received by its members; the policies typically employed by a Craft union *(see).*

Exhaustive expenditure—An expenditure by government resulting directly in the employment of economic resources and in the absorption by government of the goods and services these resources produce; Government purchase *(see).*

Exit mechanism—Leaving a job and searching for another one to improve the conditions under which a worker is employed.

Expanding economy—An economy in which Net investment *(see)* is greater than zero (Gross investment is greater than Depreciation).

Expanding industry—An industry in which Economic profits are obtained by the firms in the industry and which will, therefore, increase its output as new firms enter the industry.

Expansionary fiscal policy—An increase in Aggregate demand brought about by an increase in Government expenditures for goods and services, a decrease in Net taxes, or some combination of the two.

Expectations—What consumers, business Firms, and others believe will happen or what conditions will be in the future.

Expected rate of net profits—Annual profits a firm anticipates it will obtain by purchasing Capital (by investing) expressed as a percentage of the price (cost) of the Capital.

Expenditure approach—The method that adds all the expenditures made for Final goods and services to measure the Gross domestic product.

Expenditures-output approach—*(See* Aggregate expenditures-domestic output approach.)

Explicit cost—The monetary payment a Firm must make to an outsider to obtain a resource.

Export controls—The limitation or prohibition of the export of certain high-technology products on the basis of foreign policy or national security objectives.

Exports—Goods and services produced in a nation and sold to customers in other nations.

Export subsidies—Government payments that reduce the price of a product to foreign buyers.

Export supply curve—An upsloping curve showing the amount of a product domestic firms will export at each World price *(see)* above the Domestic price *(see)*.

Export transaction—A sale of a good or service that increases the amount of foreign money (or of their own money) held by the citizens, firms, and governments of a nation.

External benefit—*(See* Spillover benefit.)

External cost—*(See* Spillover cost.)

External debt—Debt *(see)* owed to foreign citizens, firms, and institutions.

Externality—*(See* Spillover.)

Externally held public debt—Public debt *(see)* owed to (Canadian government securities owned by) foreign citizens, firms, and institutions.

Face value—The dollar or cents value stamped on a coin.

Factors of production—Economic resources: Land, Capital, Labour, and Entrepreneurial ability.

Fair-return price—The price of a product that enables its producer to obtain a Normal profit *(see)*, and that is equal to the Average total cost of producing it.

Fallacy of composition—Incorrectly reasoning that what is true for the individual (or part) is therefore necessarily true for the group (or whole).

Fallacy of limited decisions—The false notion that there are a limited number of economic decisions to be made so that, if government makes more decisions, there will be fewer private decisions to render.

Farm problem—Technological advance, coupled with a price inelastic and relatively constant demand has made agriculture a Declining industry; also the tendency for the prices farmers receive and their incomes to fluctuate sharply from year to year.

Farm products and marketing boards—The federal and provincial boards, numbering more than 100, that set marketing regulations for commodities ranging from asparagus to turkeys. The boards have the power to allocate quotas, set prices, issue licences, collect fees, and require that the commodity be marketed through them.

Featherbedding—Payment by an employer to a worker for work not actually performed.

Feedback effects—The effects a change in the money supply will have (because it affects the Interest rate, Planned investment, and the Equilibrium GDP) on the demand for money, which is itself directly related to the GDP.

Female participation rate—The percentage of the female population of working age in the Civilian labour force *(see)*.

Fewness—A relatively small number of sellers (or buyers) of a good or service.

Fiat money—Anything that is Money because government has decreed it to be Money.

Final goods—Goods that have been purchased for final use and not for resale or further processing or manufacturing (during the year).

Financial capital—*(See* Money capital.)

Financial intermediary—A Chartered bank or other financial institution (trust or mortgage loan company, credit union, caisse populaire), which uses the funds (savings) deposited with it to make loans (for consumption or investment).

Financing exports and imports—The use of Foreign exchange markets by exporters and importers to receive and make payments for goods and services they sell and buy in foreign nations.

Firm—An organisation that employs Resources to produce a good or service for profit and owns and operates one or more Plants *(see)*.

Fiscal policy—Changes in government spending and tax collections designed to achieve a full-employment and noninflationary domestic output.

Five fundamental economic questions—The five questions every economy must answer: what to produce, how to produce, how to divide the total output, how to maintain Full employment, and how to assure economic flexibility.

Fixed cost—Any cost that in total does not change when the Firm changes its output; the cost of Fixed resources *(see).*

Fixed exchange rate—A Rate of exchange that is prevented from rising or falling by the intervention of government.

Fixed resource—Any resource employed by a Firm in a quantity that the firm cannot change.

Flat-rate income tax—A tax that taxes all incomes at the same rate.

Flexible exchange rate—A Rate of exchange determined by the demand for and supply of the foreign money and is free to rise or fall without government interference.

Floating exchange rate—*(See* Flexible exchange rate.)

Floor price—A price set by government that is above the Equilibrium price.

Food and Drugs Act—The federal law enacted in 1920 as outgrowth of legislation dating back to 1875; subsequently amended, the Act and its Regulations now provide for controls over all foods, drugs, cosmetics, and medical devices sold in Canada.

Foreign competition—*(See* Import competition.)

Foreign exchange—*(See* Official international reserves.)

Foreign exchange control—The control a government may exercise over the quantity of foreign money demanded by its citizens and business firms and over the Rates of exchange in order to limit its outpayments to its inpayments (to eliminate a Payments deficit) *(see).*

Foreign exchange market—A market in which the money (currency) used by one nation is used to purchase (is exchanged for) the money used by another nation.

Foreign exchange rate—*(See* Rate of exchange.)

Foreign-trade effect—The inverse relationship between the Net exports *(see)* of an economy and its Price level *(see)* relative to foreign Price levels.

Foreign investment—*(see* Direct investment and Portfolio investment.)

45° line—A curve along which the value of the GDP (measured horizontally) is equal to the value of Aggregate expenditures (measured vertically).

Fractional reserve—A Reserve ratio *(see)* that is less than 100% of the deposit liabilities of a Chartered bank.

Freedom of choice—Freedom of owners of property resources and money to employ or dispose of these resources as they see fit, of workers to enter any line of work for which they are qualified, and of consumers to spend their incomes in a manner they deem appropriate (best for them).

Freedom of enterprise—Freedom of business Firms to employ economic resources, to use these resources to produce products of the firm's own choosing, and to sell these products in markets of their choice.

Freely floating exchange rates—Rates of exchange *(see)* that are not controlled and that may, therefore, rise and fall; and that are determined by the demand for and the supply of foreign monies.

Free-rider problem—The inability of potential providers of an economically desirable and indivisible good or service to obtain payment from those who benefit because the Exclusion principle *(see) is* not applicable.

Free trade—The absence of artificial (government imposed) barriers to trade among individuals and Arms in different nations.

Frictional unemployment—Unemployment caused by workers voluntarily changing jobs and by temporary lay-offs; unemployed workers between jobs.

Fringe benefits—The rewards other than Wages that employees receive from their employers and that include pensions, medical and dental insurance, paid vacations, and sick leaves.

Full employment—(1) Using all available economic resources to produce goods and services; (2) when the Unemployment rate is equal to the Full-employment unemployment rate and there is Frictional and Structural but no Cyclical unemployment (and the real output of the economy is equal to its Potential real output).

Full-employment unemployment rate—The Unemployment rate *(see)* at which there is no Cyclical unemployment *(see)* of the Civilian labour force *(see)* and, because some Frictional and Structural unemployment is unavoidable, equal to about 7.5 to 8%.

Full production—The maximum amount of goods and services that can be produced from the employed resources of an economy; occurs when both Allocative efficiency and Productive efficiency are realized.

Functional distribution of income—The manner in which national income is divided among those who perform different functions (provide the economy with different kinds of resources); the division of Net domestic income *(see)* into wages and salaries, corporation profits, farmers' income, unincorporated business income, interest, and rent.

Functional finance—Use of Fiscal policy to achieve a full-employment, noninflationary Gross domestic product without regard to the effect on the Public debt *(see)*.

G 7 nations—A group of seven major industrial powers that meet regularly to discuss common economic problems and try to co-ordinate economic policies; Canada, the United States, Japan, Germany, United Kingdom, France, and Italy.

Game theory—A theory that compares the behaviour of participants in games of strategy, such as poker and chess, with that of a small group of mutually interdependent firm (an Oligopoly).

GATT—*(See* General Agreement on Tariffs and Trade.)

GDP—*(See* Gross domestic product.)

GDP deflator—The Price index *(see)* for all final goods and services used to adjust nominal GDP to derive real GDP.

GDP gap—Potential Real gross domestic product less actual Real gross domestic product.

General Agreement on Tariffs and Trade—The international agreement reached in 1947 in which 23 nations agreed to give equal and nondiscriminatory treatment to the other nations, to reduce tariff rates by multinational negotiations, and to eliminate import quotas. Now includes 123 nations.

Generalisation—Statistical or probability statement; statement of the nature of the relation between two or more sets of facts.

Gentlemen's agreement—An informal understanding on the price to be charged among the firms in an Oligopoly *(see)*.

GNP—*(See* Gross national product.)

Gold export point—The Rate of exchange for a foreign money above which—when nations participate in the International gold standard *(see)*—the foreign money will not be purchased and gold will be sent (exported) to the foreign country to make payments there.

Gold flow—The movement of gold into or out of a nation.

Gold import point—The Rate of exchange for a foreign money below which—when nations participate in the International gold standard *(see)*—a nation's own money will not be purchased and gold will be sent (imported) into that country by foreigners to make payments there.

Gorbachev's reforms—A mid-1980s series of reforms designed to revitalise the Soviet economy. The reforms stressed the modernization of productive facilities, less centralized control, improved worker discipline and productivity, more emphasis on market prices, and an expansion of private economic activity.

Government purchases—Disbursements of money by government for which government receives a currently produced good or service in return; the expenditures of all governments in the economy for Final goods *(see)* and services.

Government transfer payment—The disbursement of money (or goods and services) by government for which government receives no currently produced good or service in return.

Grievance procedure—The methods used by a Labour union and the Firm to settle disputes that arise during the life of the collective bargaining agreement between them.

Gross domestic product (GDP)—The total market value of all Final goods *(see)* and services produced annually within the boundaries of Canada, whether by Canadian or foreign-supplied resources.

Gross national product (GNP)—The total market value of all Final goods *(see)* and services produced annually by land, labour, and capital, and entrepreneurial talent supplied by Canadian residents, whether these resources are located in Canada or abroad.

Gross private domestic investment—Expenditures for newly produced Capital goods *(see)*—machinery, equipment, tools, and buildings—and for additions to inventories.

Guaranteed annual income—The minimum income a family (or individual) would receive if a Negative income tax *(see)* were to be adopted.

Guaranteed Income Supplement—A 1966 amendment to the Old Age Security Act *(see)* provides for the payment of a full supplement to pensioners with no other income and a partial supplement to those with other, but still low, income.

Guiding function of prices—The ability of price changes to bring about changes in the quantities of products and resources demanded and supplied. *(see* Incentive function of price.)

Herfindahl index—A measure of the concentration and competitiveness of an industry; calculated as the sum of the squared market shares of the individual firms.

Homogeneous oligopoly—An Oligopoly in which the firms produce a Standardized product *(see)*.

Horizontal axis—The Left—right" or "west—east" axis on a graph or grid.

Horizontal combination—A group of Plants *(see)* in the same stage of production owned by a single Firm *(see)*.

Horizontal merger—The merger of one or more Firms producing the same product into a single Firm.

Horizontal range—The horizontal segment of the short-run Aggregate supply curve, indicating much slack in the economy.

Household—An economic unit (of one or more persons) that provides the economy with resources and uses the money paid to it for these resources to purchase goods and services to satisfy material wants.

Human capital investment—Any action taken to increase the productivity (by improving the skills and abilities) of workers; expenditures made to improve the education, health, or mobility of workers.

Hyperinflation—A very rapid rise in the price level.

IMF—*(See* International Monetary Fund.)

Immobility—The inability or unwillingness of a worker or another resource to move from one geographic area or occupation to another or from a lower-paying to a higher paying job.

Imperfect competition—All markets except Pure competition *(see)*; Monopoly, Monopolistic competition, Oligopoly *(see all)*.

Implicit cost—The monetary income a Firm sacrifices when it employs a resource it owns to produce a product rather than supplying the resource in the market; equal to what the resource could have earned in the best-paying alternative employment.

Import competition—Competition that domestic firms encounter from the products and services of foreign suppliers.

Import demand curve—A downsloping curve showing the amount of a product that an economy will import at each World price *(see)* below the Domestic price *(see).*

Import quota—A limit imposed by a nation on the quantity of a good may be imported during some period of time.

Imports—Spending by individuals, Firms, and governments for goods and services produced in foreign nations.

Import transaction—The purchase of a good or service that decreases the amount of foreign money held by citizens, firms, and governments of a nation.

Incentive function of price—The inducement that an increase (a decrease) in the price of a commodity offers to sellers of the commodity to make more (less) of it available; and the inducement that an increase (decrease) in price offers to buyers to purchase smaller (larger) quantities; the Guiding function of prices *(see).*

Incentive pay plan—A compensation scheme that ties worker pay directly to performance. Such plans include piece rates, bonuses, commissions, and profit sharing.

Inclusive unionism—A union that attempts to include all workers employed in an industry as members.

Income approach—The method that adds all the incomes generated by the production of Final goods and services to measure the Gross domestic product.

Income effect—The effect of a change in price of a product on a consumer's Real income (purchasing power) and thus on the quantity of the product purchased, after the Substitution effect *(see)* has been determined and eliminated.

Income elasticity of demand—The ratio of the percentage change in the Quantity demanded of a good to the percentage change in income; it measures the responsiveness of consumer purchases to income changes.

Income inequality—The unequal distribution of an economy's total income among persons or families.

Income-maintenance system—The programs designed to eliminate poverty and to reduce inequality in the distribution of income.

Incomes policy—Government policy that affects the Nominal incomes of individuals (the wages workers receive) and the prices they pay for goods and services and alters their Real incomes; *(see* Wage-price policy).

Income velocity of money—*(see* Velocity of money.)

Increase in demand—An increase in the Quantity demanded of a good or service at every price; a shift in the Demand curve to the right.

Increase in supply—An increase in the Quantity supplied of a good or service at every price; a shift in the Supply curve to the right.

Increasing-cost industry—An industry in which expansion through the entry of new firms increases the prices the firms in the Industry must pay for resources and, therefore, increases their cost schedules (shifts their cost curves upward).

Increasing returns—An increase in the Marginal product *(see)* of a resource as successive units of the resource are employed.

Independent goods—Goods or services for which there is no relationship between the price of one and the demand for the other; when the price of one rises or falls the demand for the other remains constant.

Independent variable—The variable causing a change in some other (dependent) variable.

Indifference curve—A curve showing the different combinations of two products that give a consumer the same satisfaction or Utility *(see).*

Indifference map—A series of indifference curves *(see),* each representing a different level of Utility; and which together are the preferences of the consumer.

Indirect taxes—Such taxes as Sales, Excise, and business Property taxes *(see all),* licence fees, and Tariffs *(see),* which Firms treat as costs of producing a product and pass on (in whole or in part) to buyers of the product by charging them higher prices

Individual demand—The Demand schedule *(see)* or Demand curve *(see)* of a single buyer of a good or service.

Individual supply—The Supply schedule *(see)* or Supply curve *(see)* of a single seller of a good or service.

Induction—A method of reasoning that proceeds from facts to Generalization *(see).*

Industrial Disputes Investigation Act—The 1907 law that marked the beginning of federal labour legislation; it required disputes in the federal jurisdiction to be submitted to a Board of Conciliation and Investigation; replaced by Canada Labour Code *(see).*

Industrial policy—Any policy in which government takes a direct and active role in promoting firms or industries to expand output and achieve economic growth.

Industrial regulation—The older and more traditional type of regulation in which government is concerned with the prices charged and the services provided the public in specific industries; in contrast to Social regulation *(see).*

Industrial union—A Labour union that accepts as members all workers employed in a particular industry (or by a particular firm).

Industrially advanced countries (IACs)—Countries such as Canada, the United States, Japan, and the nations of western Europe that have developed Market economies based on large stocks of technologically advanced capital goods and skilled labour forces.

Industry—A group of (one or more) Firms that produce identical or similar products.

Inelastic demand—The Elasticity coefficient *(see)* is less than one; the percentage change in Quantity demanded is less than the percentage change in Price.

Inelastic supply—The Elasticity coefficient *(see)* is less than one; the percentage change in Quantity supplied is less than the percentage change in Price.

Inferior good—A good or service of which consumers purchase less (more) at every price when their incomes increase (decrease).

Inflating—Finding the Real gross domestic product *(see)* by increasing the dollar value of the Gross domestic product produced in a year in which prices are lower than in the Base year *(see).*

Inflation—A rise in the general (average) level of prices in the economy.

Inflation premium—The component of the nominal interest rate that reflects anticipated inflation.

Inflationary expectations—The belief of workers, business Firms, and consumers that there will be substantial inflation in the future.

Inflationary gap—The amount by which equilibrium GDP exceeds full employment GDP.

Inflationary recession—*(See* Stagflation.)

Infrastructure—The capital goods usually provided by the Public sector for the use of its citizens and Firms (e.g., highways, bridges, transit systems, waste-water treatment facilities, municipal water systems, and airports).

Injection—An addition of spending to the income-expenditure stream: Investment, Government purchases, and Exports.

Injunction—A court order directing a person or organization not to perform a certain act because the act would do irreparable damage to some other person or Persons; a restraining order.

In-kind investment—Nonfinancial investment *(see).*

In-kind transfer—The distribution by government of goods and services to individuals and for which the government receives no currently produced good or service in return; a Government transfer payment *(see)* made in goods or services rather than in money.

Innovation—The introduction of a new product, the use of a new method of production, or the employment of a new form of business organization.

Inpayments—The receipts of (its own or foreign) money that the individuals, Firms, and governments of one nation obtain from the sale of goods and services, investment income, Remittances, and Capital inflows from abroad.

Insurable risk—An event—the average occurrence of which can be estimated with considerable accuracy that would result in a loss that can be avoided by purchasing insurance.

Interest—The payment made for the use of money (of borrowed funds).

Interest income—Income of those who supply the economy with Capital *(see)*.

Interest rate—The Rate of interest *(see)*.

Interest-rate effect—The tendency for increases (decreases) in the Price level to increase (decrease) the demand for money; raise (lower) interest rates; and, as a result, to reduce (expand) total spending in the economy.

Intergovernmental grant—A transfer payment from the federal government to a provincial government or from a provincial to a local government *(see* Conditional grant and Unconditional grant.)

Interindustry competition—Competition or rivalry between the products of one industry *(see)* and the products of another Industry (or of other Industries)..

Interlocking directorate—A situation where one or more members of the board of directors of a Corporation are also on the board of directors of a competing Corporation; and which is illegal in the United States—but not in Canada—when it tends to reduce competition among the Corporations.

Intermediate goods—Goods that are purchased for resale or further processing or manufacturing during the year.

Intermediate range—The upsloping segment of the Aggregate supply curve lying between the Horizontal range and the Vertical range *(see both)*.

Internal economic goal—*(See* Domestic economic goal.)

Internal economies—The reduction in the unit cost of producing or marketing a product that results from an increase in output of the Firm *(see* Economies of (large) scale).

Internally held public debt—Public debt *(see)* owed to (Government of Canada securities owned by) Canadian residents, Firms, and institutions.

International Bank for Reconstruction and Development—*(See* World Bank.)

International economic goal—Assumed to be a current account balance of zero.

International gold standard—An international monetary system employed in the nineteenth and early twentieth centuries in which each nation defined its money in terms of a quantity of gold, maintained a fixed relationship between its gold stock and money supply, and allowed the free importation and exportation of gold.

International Monetary Fund (IMF)—The international association of nations that was formed after World War 11 to make loans of foreign monies to nations with temporary Payments deficits *(see)* and to administer the Adjustable pegs *(see)*; and which today creates Special Drawing Rights *(see)*.

International monetary reserves—The foreign monies —in Canada mostly U.S. dollars—and such other assets as gold and Special Drawing Rights *(see)* that a nation may use to settle a Payments deficit *(see)*.

International value of the dollar—The price that must be paid in foreign currency (money) to obtain one Canadian dollar.

Intrinsic value—The value in the market of the metal in a coin.

Inverse relationship—The relationship between two variables that change in opposite directions, for example, product price and quantity demanded.

Investment—Spending for (the production and accumulation of) Capital goods *(see)* and additions to inventories.

Investment curve (schedule)—A curve (schedule) that shows the amounts firms plan to invest (along the vertical axis) at different income (Gross domestic product) levels (along the horizontal axis).

Investment-demand curve (schedule)—A curve (schedule) that shows real Rates of interest (along the vertical axis) and the amount of Investment (along the horizontal axis) at each Rate of interest.

Investment in human capital—*(See* Human capital investment.))

Invisible hand—The tendency of Firms and resource suppliers seeking to further their self-interests in competitive markets that furthers the best interest of society as a whole (the maximum satisfaction of wants).

Jurisdictional strike—A Labour union's withholding of its labour from an employer because of the union's dispute with another Labour union over which is to perform a specific kind of work.

Keynesian economics—The macroeconomic generalizations that lead to the conclusion that a capitalist economy does not always employ its resources fully and that Fiscal policy *(see)* and Monetary policy *(see)* can be used to promote Full employment *(see)*.

Keynesianism—The philosophical, ideological, and analytical views pertaining to Keynesian economics *(see)*.

Kinked demand curve—The demand curve for a noncollusive oligopolist, based on the assumption that rivals will follow a price decrease and will ignore a price increase.

Labour—The physical and mental talents (efforts) of people that can be used to produce goods and services.

Labour force—*(See* Civilian labour force.)

Labour force participation rate—The percentage of the working-age population that is actually in the labour force.

Labour-intensive commodity—A product that requires much labour to produce.

Labour productivity—Total output divided by the quantity of labour employed to produce the output; the Average product *(see)* of labour or output per worker per hour or per year.

Labour theory of value—The Marxian notion that the economic value of any commodity is determined solely by the amount of labour required to produce it.

Labour union—A group of workers organized to advance the interests of the group (to increase wages, shorten the hours worked, improve working conditions, and so on).

Laffer curve—A curve showing the relationship between tax rates and the tax revenues of government and on which there is a tax rate (between 0 and 100%) where tax revenues are at a maximum.

Laissez-faire capitalism—*(See* Pure capitalism.)

Land—Natural resources ("free gifts of nature") used to produce goods and services.

Land-intensive commodity—A product requiring a relatively large amount of Land to produce.

Law of conservation of matter and energy—The notion that matter can be changed to other matter or into energy but cannot disappear; all production inputs are ultimately transformed into an equal amount of finished product, energy, and waste (potentially pollution).

Law of demand—The inverse relationship between the price and the Quantity demanded *(see)* of a good or service during some period of time.

Law of diminishing marginal utility—As a consumer increases the consumption of a good or service, the

Marginal utility *(see)* obtained from each additional unit of the good or service decreases.

Law of diminishing returns—When successive equal increments of a Variable resource *(see)* are added to the Fixed resources *(see)*, beyond some level of employment, the Marginal product *(see)* of the Variable resource will decrease.

Law of increasing opportunity cost—As the amount of a product produced is increased, the Opportunity cost *(see)*—the Marginal cost *(see)*—of producing an additional unit of the product increases.

Law of supply—The direct relationship between the price and the Quantity supplied *(see)* of a good or service during some period.

Leakage—(1) a withdrawal of potential spending from the income-expenditures stream: Saving *(see)*, tax payment, and Imports *(see)*; (2) a withdrawal that reduces the lending potential of the Chartered banking system.

Leakages-injections approach—Determination of the Equilibrium gross domestic product *(see)* by finding the GDP at which Leakages *(see)* are equal to Injections *(see)*.

Least-cost combination rule (of resources)—The quantity of each resource a Firm must employ if it is to produce an output at the lowest total cost; the combination in which the ratio of the Marginal product *(see)* of a resource to its Marginal resource cost *(see)* (to its price if the resource is employed in a competitive market) is the same for all resources employed.

Legal cartel theory of regulation—The hypothesis that industries want to be regulated so that they may form legal Cartels *(see)* and that government officials (the government) provide the regulation in return for their political and financial support.

Legal tender—Anything that government has decreed must be accepted in payment of a debt.

Lending potential of an individual chartered bank—The amount by which a single Chartered bank can safely increase the Money supply by making new loans to (or buying securities from) the public; equal to the Chartered bank's Excess cash reserve *(see)*.

Lending potential of the banking system—The amount the Chartered banking system *(see)* can increase the Money supply by making new loans to (or buying securities from) the public; equal to the Excess reserve *(see)* of the Chartered banking system multiplied by the Money multiplier *(see)*.

Less-developed countries (LDCs)—Many countries of Africa, Asia, and Latin America that are characterised by a lack of capital goods, primitive production technologies, low literacy rate, high unemployment, rapid population growth, and labour forces heavily committed to agriculture.

Liability—A debt with a monetary value; an amount owed by a Firm or an individual.

Limited liability—Restriction of the maximum loss to a predetermined amount; for the owners (stockholders) of a Corporation, the maximum loss is the amount they paid for their share of stock.

Limited-liability company—An unincorporated business whose owners are protected by Limited liability *(see)*.

Liquidity—Money or things that can be quickly and easily converted into Money with little or no loss of purchasing power.

Loaded terminology—Terms that arouse emotions and elicit approval or disapproval.

Loanable funds theory of interest—The concept that the supply of and demand for loanable funds determines the equilibrium rate of interest.

Log-rolling—The trading of votes by legislators to secure favourable outcomes on decisions to provide public goods and services.

Long run—A period of time long enough to enable producers of a product to change the quantities of all the resources they employ; in which all resources and costs are variable and no resources or costs are fixed.

Long-run aggregate supply curve—The aggregate supply curve associated with a time period in which input prices (specially nominal wages) are fully responsive to changes in the price level.

Long-run competitive equilibrium—The price at which the Firms in Pure competition *(see)* neither obtain Economic profit nor suffer losses in the Long run and the total quantity demanded and supplied at that price are equal; a price equal to the minimum long-run average total cost of producing the produce

Long-run farm problem—The tendency for agriculture to be a declining industry as technological progress increases supply relative to an inelastic and relatively constant demand.

Long-run supply—A schedule or curve showing the prices at which a Purely competitive industry will make various quantities of the product available in the Long run.

Lorenz curve—A curve showing the distribution of income in an economy; and when used for this purpose, the cumulated percentage of families (income receivers) is measured along the horizontal axis and the cumulated percentage of income is measured along the vertical axis.

Loss-minimizing case—The circumstances where a firm loses less than its Total fixed cost; when the price at which the firm can sell its product is less than Average total but greater than Average variable cost.

Lotteries—Games of chance where people buy numbered tickets and winners are drawn by lot; a source of provincial government revenue.

Lump-sum tax—A tax that is a constant amount (the tax revenue of government is the same) at all levels of GDP.

M1 —The narrowly defined Money supply; the Currency (coins and Paper money) and Demand deposits in chartered banks *(see)* not owned by the federal government or banks.

M2—Includes, in addition to M1, Canadian dollar personal savings deposits and nonpersonal notice deposits at chartered banks.

M2+—Includes, in addition to M2, deposits at trust and mortgage loan companies, and deposits and shares at *caisses populaires* and credit unions.

M3—Includes, in addition to M2, Canadian dollar nonpersonal fixed term deposits plus all foreign currency deposits of Canadian residents booked at chartered banks in Canada.

Macroeconomics—The part of economics concerned with the economy as a whole; with such major aggregates as the households, business, international trade, and governmental sectors and with totals for the economy.

Managed floating exchange rate—An Exchange rate allowed to change (float) to eliminate Payments deficits and surpluses and is controlled (managed) to eliminate day-to-day fluctuations.

Marginal analysis—Decision making that involves a comparison or marginal ("extra" or "additional") benefits.

Marginal cost—The extra (additional) cost of producing one more unit of output; equal to the change in Total cost divided by the change in output (and in the short run to the change in total Variable cost divided by the change in output).

Marginal labour cost—The amount the total cost of employing Labour increases when a Firm employs one additional unit of Labour (the quantity of other resources employed remaining constant); equal to the change in the total cost of Labour divided by the change in the quantity of Labour employed.

Marginal product—The additional output produced when one additional unit of a resource is employed (the quantity of all other resources employed remaining constant); equal to the change in total product divided by the change in the quantity of a resource employed.

Marginal productivity theory of income distribution—The contention that the distribution of income is equitable when each unit of each resource receives a money payment equal to its marginal contribution to the firm's revenue (its Marginal revenue product).

Marginal propensity to consume—Fraction of any change in Disposable income spent for Consumer goods; equal to the change in consumption divided by the change in Disposable income.

Marginal propensity to import—The fraction of any change in income (Gross domestic product) spent for imported goods and services; equal to the change in Imports *(see)* divided by the change in income.

Marginal propensity to save—Fraction of any change in Disposable income that households save; equal to change in Saving *(see)* divided by the change in Disposable income.

Marginal rate of substitution—The rate (at the margin) at which a consumer is prepared to substitute one good or service for another and remain equally satisfied (have the same total Utility); and equal to the slope of an Indifference curve *(see)*.

Marginal resource cost—The amount the total cost of employing a resource increases when a Firm employs one additional unit of the resource (the quantity of all other resources employed remaining constant); equal to the change in the total cost of the resource divided by the change in the quantity of the resource employed.

Marginal revenue—The change in the Total revenue of the Firm that results from the sale of one additional unit of its product; equal to the change in Total revenue divided by the change in the quantity of the product sold (demanded).

Marginal-revenue-marginal-cost approach — The method that finds the total output where Economic profit *(see)* is a maximum (or losses a minimum) by comparing the Marginal revenue *(see)* and the Marginal cost *(see)* of additional units of output.

Marginal revenue product—The change in the Total revenue of the Firm when it employs one additional unit of a resource (the quantity of all other resources employed remaining constant); equal to the change in Total revenue divided by the change in the quantity of the resource employed.

Marginal tax rate—The fraction of additional (taxable) income that must be paid in taxes.

Marginal utility—The extra Utility *(see)* a consumer obtains from the consumption of one additional unit of a good or service; equal to the change in total Utility divided by the change in the quantity consumed.

Market—Any institution or mechanism that brings together the buyers (demanders) and sellers (suppliers) of a particular good or service.

Market demand—*(See* Total demand.)

Market economy—An economy in which only the private decisions of consumers, resource suppliers, and business Firms determine how resources are allocated; the Market system *(see)*.

Market failure—The failure of a market to bring about the allocation of resources that best satisfies the wants of society (that maximizes the satisfaction of wants). In particular, the over- or underallocation of resources to the production of a particular good or service (because of Spillovers) and no allocation of resources to the production of Public (social) goods *(see)*.

Market for eternality rights—A market in which the Perfectly inelastic supply *(see)* of the right to pollute the environment and the demand for the right to pollute would determine the price a polluter would have to pay for the right.

Market period—A period in which producers of a product are unable to change the quantity produced in response to a change in its price; in which there is Perfect inelasticity of supply *(see)*; and where all resources are fixed resources *(see)*.

Market policies—Government policies designed to reduce the market power of Labour unions and large business firms and to reduce or eliminate imbalances and bottlenecks in labour markets.

Market socialism—An economic system (method of organisation) in which property resources are publicly owned and markets and prices are used to direct and coordinate economic activities.

Market system—All the product and resource markets of the economy and the relationships among them; a method that allows the prices determined in these markets to allocate the economy's Scarce resources and to communicate and co-ordinate the decisions made by consumers, business firms, and resource suppliers.

Median-voter model—The view that under majority rule the median (middle) voter will be in the dominant position to determine the outcome of an election.

Medium of exchange—Money *(see)*; a convenient means of exchanging goods and services without engaging in Barter *(see)*; what sellers generally accept and buyers generally use to pay for a good or service.

Microeconomics—The part of economics concerned with such individual units within the economy as Industries, Firms, and Households, and with individual markets, particular prices, and specific goods and services.

Minimum wage—The lowest Wage (rate) employers may legally pay for an hour of Labour.

Mixed capitalism—An economy in which both government and private decisions determine how resources are allocated.

Monetarism—An alternative to Keynesianism *(see);* the macroeconomic view that the main cause of changes in aggregate output and the price level are fluctuations in the money supply; advocates a Monetary rule *(see).*

Monetary control instruments—Techniques the Bank of Canada employs to change the size of the nation's Money supply *(see);* Open-market operations *(see),* and Switching Government of Canada deposits *(see).*

Monetary policy—Changing the Money supply *(see)* in order to assist the economy to achieve a full-employment, noninflationary level of total output.

Monetary rule—The rule suggested by the Monetarists *(see):* the Money supply should be expanded each year at the same annual rate as the potential rate of growth of the Real gross domestic product; the supply of money should be increased steadily at from 3 to 5% per year.

Money—Any item that is generally acceptable to sellers in exchange for goods and services.

Money capital—Money available to purchase Capital goods *(see).*

Money income—*(See* Nominal income.)

Money interest rate—The Nominal interest rate *(see).*

Money market—The Market in which the demand for and the supply of Money determine the Interest rate (or the level of interest rates) in the economy.

Money multiplier—The multiple of its Excess reserve *(see)* by which the Chartered banking system *(see)* can expand deposits and the Money supply by making new loans (or buying securities); equal to one divided by the Reserve ratio *(see).*

Money supply—Narrowly defined: M1 *(see);* more broadly defined: M2, M3, and M2+ *(see).*

Money wage—The amount of Money received by a worker per unit of time (hour, day, and so on).

Money wage rate—*(See* Money wage.)

Monopolistic competition—A Market in which many Firms sell a Differentiated product *(see),* into which entry is relatively easy, in which the Firm has some control over its product prices, and in which there is considerable Nonprice competition *(see).*

Monopoly—(1) A Market in which the number of sellers is so few that each seller is able to influence the total supply and the price of the good or service; (2) a major industry in which a small number of Firms control all or a large portion of its output. *(see also* Pure Monopoly.)

Monopsony—A Market in which there is only one buyer of a good or service.

Moral hazard problem—The possibility that individuals or institutions will change their behaviour as the result of a contract or agreement. Example: A bank whose deposits are insured against loss may make riskier loans and investments.

Moral suasion—The statements, pronouncements, and appeals made by the Bank of Canada that are intended to influence the lending policies of Chartered banks.

Most-favoured-nation (MFN) clause—A clause in a trade agreement between Canada and another nation that provides that the other nation's Imports into Canada will be subjected to the lowest tariff rates levied then or later on any other nation's Imports into Canada.

MR = MC rule—A Firm will maximise its Economic profit (or minimize its losses) by producing the output at which Marginal revenue *(see)* and Marginal cost *(see)* are equal—provided the price at which it can sell its product is equal to or greater than Average variable cost *(see).*

MRP = MRC rule—To maximize Economic profit (or minimize losses), a Firm should employ the quantity of a resource where its Marginal revenue product *(see) is* equal to its Marginal resource cost *(see).*

Multinational corporation—A Firm that owns production facilities in other countries and produces and sells its products abroad.

Multiplier—The ratio of the change in the Equilibrium GDP to the change in Investment *(see),* or to the change in any other component in the Aggregate expenditures schedule or to the change in Net taxes; the number by which a change in any component in the Aggregate expenditures schedule or in Net taxes must be multiplied to find the resulting change in the Equilibrium GDP.

Multiplier effect—The effect on the Equilibrium gross domestic product of a change in the Aggregate- expenditures schedule (caused by a change in the Consumption schedule, Investment, Net taxes, Government expenditures, or Net exports).

Mutual interdependence—Situation in which a change in price (or in some other policy) by one Firm will affect the sales and profits of another Firm (or other Firms) and any Firm that makes such a change can expect the other Firm(s) to react in an unpredictable (uncertain) way.

Mutually exclusive goals—Goals that conflict and cannot be achieved simultaneously.

National income—Total income earned by resource suppliers for their contributions to the production of the Gross national product *(see);* equal to the Gross national product minus the Nonincome charges *(see).*

National income accounting—The techniques employed to measure the overall production of the economy and other related totals for the nation as a whole.

National Policy—Sir John A. Macdonald's 1879 policy of high tariff protection for Canadian (Ontario and Quebec) secondary manufacturers.

Natural monopoly—An industry in which Economies of scale *(see)* are so great the product can be produced by one Firm at a lower average total cost than if the product were produced by more than one Firm.

Natural rate hypothesis—Contends that the economy is stable in the Long run at the natural rate of unemployment; views the long-run Phillips curve *(see)* as vertical at the natural rate of unemployment.

Natural rate of unemployment—*(See* Full-employment unemployment rate.)

Near-money—Financial assets, the most important of which are savings, term, and notice deposits in Chartered banks, trust companies, credit unions, and other savings institutions, that can be readily converted into Money.

Negative income tax—The proposal to subsidize families and individuals with money payments when their incomes fall below a Guaranteed (annual) income *(see);* the negative tax would decrease as earned income increases *(see* Benefit-reduction rate).

Negative relationship—*(See* Inverse relationship.)

Net capital movement—The difference between the real and financial investments and loans made by individuals and Firms of one nation in the other nations of the world and the investments and loans made by individuals and Firms from other nations in a nation.

Net domestic income—The sum of the incomes earned through the production of the Gross domestic product *(see).*

Net exports effect—The notion that the impact of a change in Monetary policy (fiscal policy) will be strengthened (weakened) by the consequent change in Net exports *(see).* For example, a contractionary (expansionary) monetary policy will increase (decrease) domestic interest rates, increasing (decreasing) the foreign demand for dollars. The dollar appreciates (depreciates) and causes Canadian Net exports to decrease (increase).

Net exports—Exports *(see)* minus Imports *(see).*

Net investment—Gross investment *(see)* less Capital consumption allowances *(see);* the addition to the nation's stock of Capital during a year.

Net investment income—The interest and dividend income received by the residents of a nation from residents of other nations less the interest and dividend payments made by the residents of that nation to the residents of other nations. In Canada, always a negative quantity.

Net national income—National income *(see).*

Net national product—Gross national product *(see)* less that part of the output needed to replace the Capital goods worn out in producing the output (Capital consumption allowances *[see]*).

Net taxes—The taxes collected by government less Government transfer payments *(see).*

Net transfers—The personal and government Transfer payments made to residents of foreign nations less the personal and government Transfer payments received from residents of foreign nations.

Net worth—The total Assets *(see)* less the total Liabilities *(see)* of a Firm or an individual; the claims of the owners of a firm against its total Assets.

New classical economics—The theory that, although unanticipated price level changes may create macroeconomic instability in the Short run, the economy is stable at the full-employment level of domestic output in the Long run because of price and wage flexibility.

New global compact—A reform agenda by which Less-developed countries *(see)* seek more foreign aid, debt relief, greater access to a world market, freer immigration, and an end to neocolonialism.

NIT—*(See* Negative income tax.)

New perspective view of advertising—Envisions advertising as a low-cost source of consumer information that increases competition by making consumers more aware of substitute products.

NNP—*(See* Net national product.)

Nominal gross domestic output (GDP)—The GDP *(see)* measured in terms of the price level at the time of measurement (unadjusted for changes in the price level).

Nominal income—The number of dollars received by an individual or group during some period of time; the money income.

Nominal interest rate—The rate of interest expressed in dollars of current value (not adjusted for inflation).

Nominal wage rate—The Money wage *(see).*

Noncollusive oligopoly—An Oligopoly *(see)* in which the Firms do not act together and in agreement to determine the price of the product and the output each Firm will produce or to determine the geographic area in which each Firm will sell.

Noncompeting groups—Groups of workers in the economy who do not compete with each other for employment because the skill and training of the workers in one group are substantially different from those in other groups.

Nondiscretionary fiscal policy—The increases (decreases) in Net taxes *(see)* that occur without Parliamentary action when the Gross domestic product rises (falls) and that tend to stabilize the economy; also called Built-in stability.

Nondurable good—A Consumer good *(see)* with an expected life (use) of less than three years.

Nonexhaustive expenditure—An expenditure by government that does not result directly in the employment of economic resources or the production of goods and services; *see* Government transfer payment.

Nonfinancial investment—An investment that does not require Households to save a part of their money incomes; but that uses Surplus (unproductive) labour to build Capital goods.

Nonincome charges—Capital consumption allowances *(see)* and Indirect-taxes *(see).*

Nonincome determinants of consumption and saving—All influences on consumption spending and saving other than the level of Disposable income.

Noninterest determinants of investment—All influences on the level of investment spending other than the Rate of interest.

Noninvestment transaction—An expenditure for stocks, bonds, or second-hand Capital goods.

Nonmarket transactions—The production of goods and services not included in the measurement of the Gross domestic product because the goods and services are not bought and sold.

Nonmerchandise balance—The addition of the balances on services, investment income, and transfers in the Current account *(see)* of the Balance of payments *(see).*

Nonprice competition—The means other than decreasing the prices of their products that Firms employ to increase the sale of their products and that includes Product differentiation *(see),* advertising, and sales promotion activities.

Nonproduction transaction—The purchase and sale of any item that is not a currently produced good or service.

Nontariff barriers (NTBs)—All barriers other than Tariffs *(see)* that nations erect to impede international trade: Import quotas *(see),* licensing requirements, unreasonable product-quality standards, unnecessary red tape in customs procedures, and so on.

Nonunion shop—A place of employment at which none of the employees are members of a Labour union (and at which the employer attempts to hire only workers who are not apt to join a union).

Normal good—A good or service whose consumption increases (decreases) when income increases (decreases).

Normal profit—Payment that must be made by a Firm to obtain and retain Entrepreneurial ability *(see)*; the minimum payment (income) Entrepreneurial ability must (expect to) receive to induce it to perform the entrepreneurial functions for a Firm; an Implicit cost *(see).*

Normative economics—That part of economics pertaining to value judgements about what the economy should be like; concerned with economic goals and policies.

North American Free Trade Agreement (NAFTA)—A 1993 agreement establishing a Trade block *(see)* comprising Canada, Mexico, and the United Sates. The goal is to establish free trade between the three nations.

Notice, term, and savings deposit—A deposit in a Chartered bank against which cheques may or may not be written but for which the bank has the right to demand notice of withdrawal.

NTBs—*(See* Nontariff barriers.)

Occupational discrimination—The form of discrimination that excludes women from certain occupations and the higher wages paid workers in these occupations.

Occupational licensing—The laws of provincial governments that require a worker to obtain a licence from a provincial board (by satisfying certain specified requirements) before engaging in a particular occupation.

Offers to purchase—A method of Price support *(see)* whereby the government buys the Surplus created when it sets the minimum price above the Equilibrium price *(see).*

Official international reserves—The international monetary assets *(see)* owned by the federal government and held in its behalf by the Bank of Canada in the Exchange Fund Account.

Official reserves—Official international reserves *(see).*

Okun's law—The generalization that any one percentage point rise in the Unemployment rate above the Full-employment unemployment rate will increase the GDP gap by 2.5% of the Potential output (GDP) of the economy.

Old Age Security Act—The 1951 federal Act, as subsequently amended, by which a pension is payable to every person aged 65 and older provided the person has resided in Canada for ten years immediately preceding the approval of an application for pension; in addition a Guaranteed Income Supplement *(see)* may be paid; the pension is payable in addition to the Canada Pension *(see)*.

Oligopoly—A Market in which a few Firms sell either a Standardized or Differentiated product, into which entry is difficult, in which the Firm has limited control over product price because of Mutual interdependence *(see)* (except when there is Collusion among firms), and in which there is typically Nonprice Competition *(see)*.

Oligopsony—A market in which there are a few buyers.

OPEC—An acronym for the Organization of Petroleum Exporting Countries *(see)*.

Open economy—An economy that both exports and imports goods and services.

Open-economy multiplier—The Multiplier *(see)* in an economy in which some part of any increase in the income (Gross domestic product) of the economy is used to purchase additional goods and services from abroad; and which is equal to the reciprocal of the sum of the Marginal propensity to save *(see)* and the Marginal propensity to import *(see)*.

Open-market operations—The buying and selling of Government of Canada securities by the Bank of Canada.

Open shop—A place of employment where the employer may hire either Labour union members or workers who are not (and need not become) members of the union.

Opportunity cost—The amount of other products that must be forgone or sacrificed to produce a unit of a product.

Optimal amount of externality reduction—That reduction of pollution or other negative externality where society's marginal benefit and marginal cost of reducing the externality are equal.

Optimal social price—The price of a product that results in the most efficient allocation of an economy's resources and that is equal to the Marginal cost *(see)* of the last unit of the product produced.

Organization of Petroleum Exporting Countries—The cartel formed in 1970 by 13 oil-producing countries to control the price and quantity of crude oil exported by its members, and which accounts for a large proportion of the world's export of oil.

"Other things being equal" assumption—Assuming that the factors other than those being considered are constant.

Outpayments—The expenditures of (its own or foreign) money that the individuals, Firms, and governments of one nation make to purchase goods, services, and investment income, for Remittances, for government loans and grants, and (liquid) capital outflows abroad.

Output effect—The change in labour input resulting from the effect of a change in the wage rate on a Firm's cost of production and the subsequent change in the desired level of output, after the Substitution effect *(see)* has been determined and eliminated.

Paper money—Pieces of paper used as a Medium of exchange *(see)*; in Canada, Bank of Canada notes.

Paradox of voting—A situation wherein voting by majority rule fails to provide a consistent ranking of society's preferences for public goods or services.

Partnership—An unincorporated business Firm owned and operated by two or more persons.

Patent laws—The federal laws granting to inventors and innovators the exclusive right to produce and sell a new product or machine for a period of 17 years.

Payments deficit—*(See* Balance of payments deficit.)

Payments surplus—*(See* Balance of payments surplus.)

Perestroika—The essential feature of Mikhail Gorbachev's reform program to "restructure" the Soviet economy; includes modernization, decentralisation, some privatisation, and improved worker incentives.

Perfect elastic demand—A change in the Quantity demanded requires no change in the price of the product or resource; buyers will purchase as much of a product or resource as is available at a constant price.

Perfect elastic supply—A change in the Quantity supplied requires no change in the price of the product or resource; sellers will make available as much of the product or resource as buyers will purchase at a constant price.

Perfect inelastic demand—A change in price results in no change in the Quantity demanded of a product or resource; the Quantity demanded is the same at all prices.

Perfect inelastic supply—A change in price results in no change in the Quantity supplied of a product or resource; the Quantity supplied is the same at all prices.

Personal consumption expenditures—The expenditures of Households for Durable, semidurable, and nondurable consumer goods and for services.

Personal distribution of income—The manner in which the economy's Personal or Disposable income is divided among different income classes or different Households.

Personal income—The income earned and unearned, available to resource suppliers and others before the payment of Personal taxes *(see)*.

Personal income tax—A tax levied on the taxable income of individuals (Households and unincorporated Firms).

Personal saving—The Personal income of Households less Personal taxes *(see)* and Personal consumption expenditures *(see)*; Disposable income less Personal consumption expenditures; that part of Disposable income not spent for Consumer goods *(see)*.

Phillips curve—A curve showing the relationship between the Unemployment rate *(see)* (on the horizontal axis) and the annual rate of increase in the Price level (on the vertical axis).

Planned economy—An economy in which government determines how resources are allocated.

Planned investment—The amount that business firms plan or intent to invest.

Plant—A physical establishment (Land and Capital) that performs one or more of the functions in the production (fabrication and distribution) of goods and services.

P = MC rule—A Firm in Pure competition *(see)* will maximize its Economic profit *(see)* or minimize its losses by producing the output at which the price of the product is equal to Marginal *cost (see),* provided that price is equal to or greater than Average variable cost *(see)* in the short run and equal to or greater than Average total cost *(see)* in the long run.

Policy economics—The formulation of courses of action to bring about desired results or to prevent undesired occurrences (to control economic events).

Political business cycle—The tendency of Parliament to destabilize the economy by reducing taxes and increasing government expenditures before elections and to raise taxes and lower expenditures after the elections.

Portfolio investment—The buying of bonds and shares by nonresidents, the number of shares bought being insufficient to attain control of the firm. *(see* also Direct Investment.)

Positive economics—The analysis of facts or data for the purpose of establishing scientific generalisations about economic behaviour; compare Normative economics.

Positive relationship—The relationship between two variables that change in the same direction, for example, product price and quantity supplied.

***Post hoc, ergo propter hoc* fallacy**—Incorrectly reasoning that when one event precedes another, the first event necessarily is the cause of the second.

Potential competition—The possibility that new competitors will be induced to enter an industry if Firms at present in that industry are realizing large economic profits.

Potential output—The real output (GDP) an economy is able to produce when it fully employs its available resources.

Poverty—An existence in which the basic needs of an individual or family exceed the means available to satisfy them.

Poverty rate—The percentage of the population with incomes below the official poverty income levels established by Statistics Canada.

Predatory pricing—A general, illegal policy of selling at prices unreasonably low with a view to eliminating competition; forbidden under the Competition Act *(see)*.

Premature inflation—Inflation *(see)* that occurs be-fore the economy has reached Full employment *(see)*.

Price—The quantity of Money (or of other goods and services) paid and received for a unit of a good or service.

Price ceiling—A government-fixed maximum price for a good or service.

Price-decreasing effect—The effect in a competitive market of a Decrease in Demand or an Increase in Supply upon the Equilibrium price *(see)*.

Price discrimination—The selling of a product to different buyers at different prices when the price differences are not justified by differences in production costs; an illegal trade practice under the Competition Act *(see)* when it consists of giving a trade purchaser an unfair advantage over its competitors by selling to it at a lower price.

Price elasticity of demand—The ratio of the percentage change in Quantity demanded of a product or resource to the percentage change in its price; the responsiveness or sensitivity of the quantity of a product or resource buyers demand to a change in the price of the product or resource.

Price elasticity of supply—The ratio of the percentage change in the Quantity supplied of a product or resource to the percentage change in its price; the responsiveness or sensitivity of the quantity sellers of a product or resource supply to a change in the price of the product or resource.

Price guidepost—The price charged by an Industry for its product should increase by no more than the increase in the Unit labour cost *(see)* of producing the product.

Price-increasing effect—The effect in a competitive market of an Increase in Demand or a Decrease in Supply upon the Equilibrium price *(see)*.

Price index—An index number that shows how the average price of a "market basket" of goods changes through time. A price index is used to change nominal output (income) into real output (income).

Price leadership—An informal method that Firms in an Oligopoly *(see)* may employ to set the price of their product: one firm (the leader) is the first to announce a change in price and the other firms (the followers) quickly announce identical (or similar) changes in price.

Price level—The weighted average of the Prices paid for the final goods and services produced in the economy.

Price level surprises—Unanticipated changes in the price level.

Price-maker—A seller (or buyer) of a product or resource that is able to affect the product or resource price by changing the amount it sells (buys).

Price support—The minimum price government allows sellers to receive for a good or service; a price that is the established or maintained minimum price.

Price-taker—A seller (or buyer) of a product or resource that is unable to affect the price at which a product or resource sells by changing the amount it sells (or buys).

Price-wage flexibility—Changes in the prices of products and in the Wages paid to workers the ability of prices and Wages to rise or to fall.

Price war—Successive and continued decreases in the prices charged by the firms in an oligopolistic industry by which each firm hopes to increase its sales and revenues and from which firms seldom benefit.

Primary reserve—*(See* Cash reserve.)

Prime rate—The interest rate the Chartered banks *(see)* charge on demand note loans to their best corporate customers.

Principal-agent problem—A conflict of interest that occurs when agents (workers) pursue their own objectives to the detriment of the principal's (employer's) goals.

Private good—A good or service subject to the Exclusion principle *(see)* and which is provided by privately owned firms to those who are willing to pay for it.

Private property—The right of private persons and Firms to obtain, own, control, employ, dispose of, and bequeath Land, Capital, and other Assets.

Private sector—The Households and business Firms of the economy.

Product differentiation—Physical or other differences between the products of different Firms that result in individual buyers preferring (so long as the price charged by all sellers is the same) the product of one firm to the products of the other Firms.

Production possibilities curve (table)—A curve (table) showing the different combinations of two goods or services that can be produced in a Full-employment *(see)*, Full-production *(see)* economy where the available supplies of resources and technology are constant.

Productive efficiency—The production of a good in the least-costly way: employing the minimum quantity of resources needed to produce a given output and producing the output at which Average total cost is a minimum.

Productivity—A measure of average output or real output per unit of input. For example, the productivity of labour may be determined by dividing hours of work into real output.

Productivity slowdown—The recent decline in the rate at which Labour productivity *(see)* in Canada has increased.

Product market—A market in which Households buy and Firms sell the products they have produced.

Profit—*(see)* Economic profit and Normal profit; without an adjective preceding it, the income of those who supply the economy with Entrepreneurial ability *(see)* or Normal profit.

Profit-maximizing case—The circumstances that result in an Economic profit *(see)* for a (competitive) Firm when it produces the output at which Economic profit is a maximum: when the price at which the Firm can sell its product is greater than the Average total cost of producing it.

Profit-maximizing rule (combination of resources)—The quantity of each resource a Firm must employ if its Economic profit *(see)* is to be a maximum or its losses a minimum; the combination in which the Marginal revenue product *(see)* of each resource is equal to its Marginal resource cost *(see)* (to its price if the resource is employed in a competitive market).

Progressive tax—A tax such that the tax rate increases as the taxpayer's income increases and decreases as income decreases.

Property tax—A tax on the value of property (Capital, Land, stocks and bonds, and other Assets) owned by Firms and Households.

Proportional tax—A tax such that the tax rate remains constant as the taxpayer's income increases and decreases.

Proprietors' income—The net income of the owners of unincorporated Firms (proprietorships and partnerships); the sum of the accrued net income of farm operators from farm production plus the net income of nonfarm unincorporated business, including rent.

Prosperous industry—*(See* Expanding industry.)

Protective tariff—A Tariff *(see)* designed to protect domestic producers of a good from the competition of foreign producers.

Public assistance programs—Programs that pay benefits to those who are unable to earn income (because of permanent handicaps or because they are dependent children), that are financed by general tax revenues, and that are viewed as public charity (rather than earned rights).

Public choice theory—Generalisations that describe how government (the Public sector) makes decisions for the use of economic resources.

Public debt—The amount owed by the Government of Canada to the owners of its securities and equal to the sum of its past Budget deficits (less its Budget surpluses).

Public finance—The branch of economics that analyses government revenues and expenditures.

Public good—A good or service to which the Exclusion principle *(see)* is not applicable and that is provided by government if it yields substantial benefits to society.

Public interest theory of regulation—The presumption that the purpose of the regulation of an Industry is to protect the public (consumers) from the abuse of the power possessed by Natural monopolies *(see)*.

Public sector—The part of the economy that contains all its governments; government.

Public-sector failure—The failure of the Public sector (government) to resolve socioeconomic problems because it performs its functions inefficiently.

Public utility—A Firm that produces an essential good or service, that has obtained from a government the right to be the sole supplier of the good or service in an area, and that is regulated by that government to prevent the abuse of its monopoly power.

Purchasing power parity—The idea that exchange rates between nations equate the purchasing power of various currencies; exchange rates between any two nations adjust to reflect the price level differences between the countries.

Pure capitalism—An economic system in which property resources are privately owned and Markets and Prices are used to direct and co-ordinate economic activities.

Pure competition—(1) A market in which a very large number of Firms sells a Standardised product *(see)*, into which entry is very easy, in which the individual seller has no control over the price at which the product sells, and in which there is no Nonprice competition *(see)*; (2) a Market in which there is a very large number of buyers.

Pure monopoly—A Market in which one Firm sells a unique product (one for which there are no close substitutes), into which entry is blocked, in which the Firm has considerable control over the price at which the product sells, and in which Nonprice competition *(see)* may or may not be found.

Pure profit—*(See* Economic profit.)

Pure rate of interest—*(See The* Rate of interest.)

Quantity decreasing effect—The effect in a competitive market of a decrease in Demand or a decrease in Supply on the Equilibrium quantity *(see)*.

Quantity demanded—The amount of a good or service buyers wish (or a buyer wishes) to purchase at a particular price during some period of time.

Quantity-increasing effect—The effect in a competitive market of an increase in Demand or an increase in Supply on the Equilibrium quantity *(see)*.

Quantity supplied—The amount of a good or service sellers offer (or a seller offers) to sell at a particular price during some period of time.

Quasi-public good—A good or service to which the Exclusion principle *(see)* could be applied, but which has such a large Spillover benefit *(see)* that government sponsors its production to prevent an underallocation of resources.

R&D—Research and development; activities undertaken to bring about progress in Technology.

Rate of exchange—The price paid in one's own Money to acquire one unit of a foreign Money; the rate at which the money of one nation is exchanged for the Money of another nation.

Rate of interest—Price paid for the use of Money or for the use of Capital; interest rate.

Rational—An adjective that describes the behaviour of an individual who consistently does those things enabling the achievement of the declared objective of the individual; describes the behaviour of a consumer who uses money income to buy the collection of goods and services that yields the maximum amount of Utility *(see)*.

Rational expectations theory—The hypothesis that business firms and Households expect monetary and fiscal policies to have certain effects on the economy and, in pursuit of their own self-interests, take actions that make these policies ineffective.

Rationing function of price—The ability of Price in a competitive market to equalise Quantity demanded and Quantity supplied and to eliminate shortages and surpluses by rising or falling.

Reaganomics—The policies of the United States Reagan Administration based on Supply-side economics *(see)* and intended to reduce Inflation and the Unemployment rate (Stagflation).

Real-balances effect—*(See* Wealth effect.)

Real capital—*(See* Capital.)

Real gross domestic product—Gross domestic product *(see)* adjusted for changes in the price level; Gross domestic product in a year divided by the GDP deflator *(see)* for that year.

Real income—The amount of goods and services an individual or group can purchase with his, her, or its Nominal income during some period of time; Nominal income adjusted for changes in the Price level.

Real interest rate—The Rate of interest expressed in dollars of constant value (adjusted for Inflation); and equal to the Nominal interest rate *(see)* less the expected rate of Inflation.

Real rate of interest—The Real interest rate *(see).*

Real wage—The amount of goods and services a worker can purchase with his or her Money wage *(see)*; the purchasing power of the Money wage; the Money wage adjusted for changes in the Price level.

Real wage rate—*(see* Real wage.)

Recessionary gap—The amount by which equilibrium GDP falls short of full employment GDP.

Reciprocal selling—The practice in which one Firm agrees to buy a product from a second Firm, and the second Firm agrees, in return, to buy another product from the first Firm.

Reciprocal Trade Agreements Act of 1934 (U.S.)—The federal Act that gave the U.S. president the authority to negotiate agreements with other nations and lower American tariff rates by up to 50% if the other nations would reduce tariff rates on American goods, and which incorporated Most-favoured nation clauses *(see)* in the agreements reached with these nations.

Refinancing the public debt—Paying owners of maturing Government of Canada securities with Money obtained by selling new securities or with new securities.

Regional Development Incentives Act—The federal Act of 1970 designed to create jobs in Canada's slow-growth or "designated" areas.

Regressive tax—A tax such that the tax rate decreases (increases) as the taxpayer's income increases (decreases).

Regulatory agency—An agency (commission or board) established by the federal or a provincial government to control the prices charged and the services offered (output produced) by a Natural monopoly *(see).*

Remittance—A gift or grant; a payment for which no good or service is received in return; the funds sent by workers who have legally or illegally entered a foreign nation to their families in the nations from which they have migrated.

Rental income—Income received by those who supply the economy with Land *(see).*

Rent-seeking behaviour—The pursuit through government of a transfer of income or wealth to a resource supplier, business, or consumer at someone else's or society's expense.

Required reserve—The weighted average of demand deposit and notice deposits Chartered banks were requited to keep as Vault cash *(see)* or on deposit with the Bank of Canada up to the end of 1994, when these were eliminated.

Reserve ratio—The ratio of a Chartered bank's desired reserves to its deposit liabilities.

Reserves—Cash in a Chartered bank's vault plus its deposit with the Bank of Canada.

Resource market—A market in which Households sell and Firms buy the services of resources.

Retiring the public debt—Reducing the size of the Public debt *(see)* by paying money to owners of maturing Government of Canada securities.

Revaluation—An increase in the government-defined currency brought about by the Central bank the opposite of Devaluation.

Revenue sharing—The distribution by the federal government of some of its tax revenues to provincial governments.

Revenue tariff—A Tariff *(see)* designed to produce income for the (federal) government

Ricardian equivalence theorem—The idea that an increase in the public debt will have little or no effect on real output and employment because taxpayers will save more in anticipation of future higher taxes to pay the higher interest expense on the debt.

Roundabout production—The construction and use of Capital *(see)* to aid in the production of Consumer goods *(see)*.

Ruble overhang—The large amount of forced saving formerly held by Russian Households due to the scarcity of Consumer goods; these savings fuelled Inflation when Russian prices were decontrolled.

Rule of 70—A method for determining the number of years it will take for the Price level to double; divide 70 by the annual rate of inflation (the raw of increase).

Sales tax—A tax levied on expenditures for a broad group of products.

Saving—Disposable income not spent for Consumer goods *(see)*; equal to Disposable income minus Personal consumption expenditures *(see)*.

Savings account—A deposit in a financial institution that is interest-earning and that can normally be withdrawn by the depositor at any time (though the institution may legally require notice for withdrawal).

Saving schedule—Schedule that shows the amounts Households plan to save (plan not to spend for Consumer goods, *see)* at different levels of Disposable income.

Say's Law—The (discredited) macroeconomic generalization that the production of goods and services (supply) creates an equal demand for these goods and services.

Scarce resources—The fixed (limited) quantities of Land, Capital, Labour, and Entrepreneurial ability *(see* all) that are never sufficient to satisfy the wants of human beings because their wants are unlimited.

Schumpeter-Galbraith view (of oligopoly)—The belief shared by these two economists that large oligopolistic firms are necessary for rapid technological progress (because only this kind of firm has both the means and the incentive to introduce technological changes).

SDRs—*(see* Special Drawing Rights.)

Seasonal variation—An increase or decrease during a single year in the level of economic activity caused by a change in the season.

Secular trend—The expansion or contraction in the level of economic activity over a long period of years.

Self-interest—What each Firm, property owner, worker, and consumer believes is best for itself and seeks to obtain.

Seniority—The length of time a worker has been employed by an employer relative to the lengths of time the employer's other workers have been employed; the principle that is used to determine which workers will be laid off when there is insufficient work for them all, and which will be rehired when more work becomes available.

Separation of ownership and control—Difference between the group that owns the Corporation (the stockholders) and the group that manages it (the directors and officers) and between the interests (goals) of the two groups.

Service—That which is intangible (invisible) and for which a consumer, Firm, or government is willing to exchange something of value.

Shared-cost programs—*(see* Conditional grant.)

Shirking—Attempts by workers to increase their utility or well-being by neglecting or evading work.

Shortage—The amount by which the Quantity demanded of a product exceeds the Quantity supplied at a particular (below-equilibrium) price.

Short run—A period of time in which producers of a product are able to change the quantity of some but not all of the resources they employ; in which some resources—the Plant *(see)*—are Fixed resources *(see)* and some are Variable resources *(see);* in which some costs are Fixed costs *(see)* and some are Variable costs *(see);* a period of time too brief to allow a Firm *(see) to* vary its plant capacity but long enough to permit it to change the level at which the plant capacity is utilized a period of time not long enough to enable Firms to enter or to leave an Industry *(see).*

Short-run aggregate supply curve—The aggregate supply curve relevant to a time period in which input prices (particularly nominal wages) remain constant when the price level changes.

Short-run competitive equilibrium—The price at which the total quantity of a product supplied in the Short run *(see)* by a purely competitive industry and the total quantity of the product demanded are equal and which is equal to or greater than the Average variable cost *(see)* of producing the products and the quantity of the product demanded and supplied at this price.

Short-run farm problem—The sharp year-to-year changes in the prices of agricultural products and in the incomes of farmers.

Short-run supply curve—A curve that shows the quantities of a product a Firm in a purely competitive industry *(see* Pure competition) will offer to sell at various prices in the Short run *(see)*; the portion of the Firm's short-run Marginal cost *(see)* curve that lies above the Average variable cost curve.

Simple multiplier—The Multiplier *(see)* in an economy in which government collects no Net taxes *(see),* there are no Imports *(see)*, and Investment *(see)* is independent of the level of income (Gross domestic product); equal to one divided by the Marginal propensity to save *(see).*

Single-tax movement—The attempt of a group that followed the teachings of Henry George to eliminate all taxes except one that would tax all Rental income *(see)* at a rate of 100%.

Slope of a line—The ratio of the vertical change (the rise or fall) to the horizontal change (the run) in moving between two points on a line. The slope of an upward sloping line is positive, reflecting a direct relationship between two variables; the slope of a downward sloping line is negative, reflecting an inverse relationship between two variables.

Smoot Hawley Tariff Act—Passed in 1930, this legislation established some of the highest Tariffs in U.S. history. Its objective was to reduce imports and stimulate the American economy.

Social accounting—*(See* National income accounting.)

Social good—*(See* Public good.)

Social insurance programs—The programs that replace the earnings lost when people retire or are temporarily unemployed, that are financed by pay deductions, and that are viewed as earned rights (rather than charity).

Social regulation—The newer and different type of regulation in which government is concerned with the conditions under which goods and services are produced, their physical characteristics, and the impact of their production on society; in contrast to Industrial regulation *(see).*

Sole proprietorship—An unincorporated business Firm owned and operated by a single person.

Special Drawing Rights—Credit created by the International Monetary Fund *(see)*, which a member of the IMF may borrow to finance a Payments deficit *(see)* or to increase its Official international reserves *(see)*; "paper gold."

Special-interest effect—Effect on public decision making and the allocation of resources in the economy when government promotes the interests (goals) of small groups to the detriment of society as a whole.

Specialisation—The use of the resources of an individual, a Firm, a region, or a nation to produce one or a few goods and services.

Speculation—The activity of buying or selling with the motive of then reselling or rebuking to make a profit.

Spillover—A benefit or cost from production or consumption, accruing without compensation to nonbuyers and nonsellers of the product *(see* Spillover benefit and Spillover cost).

Spillover benefit—A benefit obtained without compensation by third parties from the production or consumption of other parties. Example: A beekeeper benefits when the neighbouring farmer plants clover.

Spillover Cyst—A cost imposed without compensation on third parties by the production or consumption of other parties. Example: A manufacturer dumps toxic chemicals into a river, killing the fish sought by sport fishers.

Stabilization funds—International monetary reserves *(see)* and domestic monies used to augment the supply of, or demand for, any Currency required to avoid or restrict fluctuations in the Rate of exchange; in Canada held in the Exchange Fund Account by the Bank of Canada on behalf of the government.

Stabilization policy dilemma—The use of monetary and fiscal policy to decrease the Unemployment rate increases the rate of Inflation, and the use of monetary and fiscal policy to decrease the rate of Inflation increases the Unemployment rate; see the Phillips curve.

Stagflation—Inflation accompanied by stagnation in the rate of growth of output and a high unemployment rate in the economy; simultaneous increases in both the price level and the Unemployment rate *(see)*.

Standardised product—A product such that buyers are indifferent to the seller from whom they purchase it so long as the price charged by all sellers is the same; a product such that all units of the product are perfect substitutes for each other (are identical).

Staple—An exported raw material.

State ownership—The ownership of property (Land and Capital) by government (the state); in the former Soviet Union by the central government (the nation).

Static economy—(1) An economy in which Net investment *(see)* is zero—Gross investment *(see)* is equal to the Capital consumption allowances *(see)*; (2) an economy in which the supplies of resources, technology, and the tastes of consumers do not change and in which, therefore, the economic future is perfectly predictable and there is no uncertain

Store of value—Any Asset *(see)* or wealth set aside for future use; functions of Money.

Strategic trade policy—The use of trade barriers to reduce the risk of product development by domestic Arms, particularly products involving advanced technology.

Strike—The withholding of their labour services by an organized group of workers (a Labour union).

Structural deficit—The difference between federal tax revenues and expenditures when the economy is at Full employment.

Structural unemployment—Unemployment caused by changes in the stature of demand for Consumer goods and in technology; workers who are unemployed because their skills are not demanded by employers, they lack sufficient skills to obtain employment, or they cannot easily move to locations where jobs for which they have skills are available.

Subsidy—A payment of funds (or goods and services) by a government, business Firm, or Household for which it receives no good or service in return. When made by a government, it is a Government transfer payment *(see)* or the reverse of a tax.

Substitutability—The ability of consumers to use one good or service instead of another to satisfy their wants and of Firms to use one resource instead of another to produce products.

Substitute goods—Goods or services for which there is a direct relationship between the price of one and the Demand for the other; when the price of one falls (rises) the Demand for the other decreases (increases).

Substitution effect—(I) The effect a change in the price of a Consumer good would have on the relative expensiveness of that good and the resulting effect on the quantity of the good a consumer would purchase if the consumer's Real income *(see)* remained constant; (I) the effect a change in the price of a resource would have on the quantity of the resource employed by a Arm if the firm did not change its output.

Superior good—*(see* Normal good.)

Supplementary labour income—The payments by employers into unemployment insurance, worker's compensation, and a variety of private and public pension and welfare funds for workers: "fringe benefits."

Supply—A Supply schedule or a Supply curve *(see both).*

Supply curve—A curve showing the amounts of a good or service sellers (a seller) will offer to sell at various prices during some period.

Supply factor—An increase in the available quantity of a resource, an improvement in its quality, or an expansion of technological knowledge, which makes it possible for an economy to produce a greater output of goods and services.

Supply schedule—A schedule showing the amounts of a good or service sellers (a seller) will offer to sell at various prices during some period.

Supply shock—One of several events of the 1970s and early 1980s that increased production costs, decreased Aggregate supply, and helped generate Stagflation in Canada.

Supply-side economics—The part of modern Macroeconomics that emphasises the role of costs and Aggregate supply in explaining Inflation, unemployed labour, and Economic growth.

Supply-side view—The view of fiscal policy held by the advocates of Supply-side economics that emphasizes increasing Aggregate supply *(see)* as a means of reducing the Unemployment rate and Inflation and encouraging Economic growth.

Support price—*(see* Price support.)

Surplus—The amount by which the Quantity supplied of product exceeds the Quantity demanded at a specific (above-equilibrium) price.

Surplus value—A Marxian term; the amount by which the value of a worker's daily output exceeds his or her daily wage; the output of workers appropriated by capitalists as profit.

Switching Government of Canada deposits—Action of Bank of Canada to increase (decrease) backing for Money supply *(see)* by switching government deposits from (to) itself to (from) the Chartered banks *(see).*

Tacit collusion—Any method utilized in a Collusive oligopoly *(see) to* set prices and outputs that does not involve outright (or overt) collusion (formal agreements or secret meetings); and of which Price leadership *(see) is* a frequent example.

Tangent—The point where a line touches, but does not intersect, a curve.

Target dilemma—A problem arising because the central bank cannot simultaneously stabilize both the money supply and the level of interest rates.

Tariff—A tax imposed by a nation on an imported good.

Tax—A nonvoluntary payment of money (or goods and services) to a government by a Household or Firm for which the Household or Firm receives no good or service directly in return.

Tax-based incomes policies (TIP)—An Incomes policy *(see)* that would include special tax penalties for those who do not comply and tax rebates for those who do comply with the Wage-price guideposts *(see).*

Tax incidence—The income or purchasing power different persons and groups lose as a result of the imposition of a tax after Tax shifting *(see)* has occurred.

Tax shifting—The transfer to others of all or part of a tax by charging them a higher price or by paying them a lower price for a good or service.

Tax subsidy—The subsidisation of individuals or industries through favourable tax treatment.

Tax transfer disincentives—Decreases in the incentives to work, save, invest, innovate, and take risks that allegedly result Tom high Marginal tax rates and Transfer payment programs.

Tax "wedge"—Such taxes as Indirect taxes *(see)* and pay deductions for Social insurance programs *(see)*, which are treated as a cost by business Arms and reflected in the prices of their products; equal to the price of the product less the cost of the resources required to produce it.

Technology—The body of knowledge that can be used to produce goods and services Tom Economic resources.

Term deposit—A deposit in a Chartered bank or other Financial intermediary against which cheques may not be written; a form of savings account; part of M2, M3, and M2+ *(see* all).

Terms of trade—The rate at which units of one product can be exchanged for units of another product; the Price *(see)* of a good or service; the amount of one good or service given up to obtain one unit of another good or service.

Theory of human capital—Generalization that Wage differentials *(see)* are the result of differences in the amount of Human capital investment *(see)*; and that the incomes of lower-paid workers are increased by increasing the amount of such investment.

The rate of interest—The Rate of interest *(see)* that is paid solely for the use of Money over an extended period of time and that excludes the charges made for the riskiness of the loan and its administrative costs; and that is approximately equal to the rate of interest paid on the long-term and virtually riskless bonds of the Government of Canada.

Third World—The semideveloped and less-developed nations; nations other than the industrially advanced market economies and the centrally planned economies.

Tied Dealing—*(see* Exclusive dealing.)

Tight money policy—Contracting the nation's Money supply *(see)*. See also Contractionary monetary policy.

Till money—*(see* Vault cash.)

TIP—*(see* Tax-based incomes policies.)

Token money—Coins having a Face value *(see)* greater than their Intrinsic value *(see)*.

Total cost—The sum of Fixed cost *(see)* and Variable cost *(see)*.

Total demand—The Demand schedule *(see)* or the Demand curve *(see)* of all buyers of a good or service.

Total demand for money—The sum of the Transactions demand for money *(see)* and Asset demand for money *(see)*; the relationship between the total amount of money demanded and nominal GDP and the Rate of interest.

Total product—The total output of a particular good or service produced by a Firm, a group of Firms or the entire economy.

Total revenue—The total number of dollars received by a Firm (or Firms) from the sale of a product; equal to the total expenditures for the product produced by the Firm (or Firms); equal to the quantity sold (demanded) multiplied by the price at which it is sold—by the Average revenue *(see)* from its sale.

Total-revenue test—A test to determine whether Demand is Elastic *(see)*, Inelastic *(see)*, or of Unitary elasticity *(see)* between any two prices: demand is elastic (inelastic, unit elastic) if the Total revenue *(see)* of sellers of the commodity increases (decreases, remains constant) when the price of the commodity falls; or Total revenue decreases (increases, remains constant) when its price rises.

Total-revenue-total-cost approach—The method that Ends the output at which Economic profit *(see)* is a maximum or losses a minimum by comparing the total receipts (revenue) and the total costs of a Firm at different outputs.

Total spending—The total amount buyers of goods and services spend or plan to spend. Also called Aggregate expenditure.

Total supply—The Supply schedule *(see)* or the Supply curve *(see)* of all sellers of a good or service.

Total utility—The total amount of satisfaction derived from the consumption of some particular amount of a product.

Trade balance—The export of merchandise (goods) of a nation less its imports of merchandise (goods).

Trade bloc—A group of nations that lowers or abolishes trade barriers among members. Examples include the European Union *(see)* and the North American Free Trade Agreement *(see)*.

Trade controls—Tariffs *(see)*, export subsidies, Import quotas *(see)*, and other means a nation may employ to reduce Imports *(see)* and expand Exports *(see)*.

Trade deficit—The amount a nation's imports of merchandise (goods) exceed its exports of merchandise (goods).

Trade-offs—The notion that one economic goal or objective must be sacrificed to achieve some other goal.

Trade surplus—The amount a nation's exports of merchandise (goods) and services exceed its imports of merchandise (goods) and services.

Trades and Labour Congress of Canada (TLC)—The federation of Craft unions *(see)* formed in 1886 and affiliated with the American Federation of Labor *(see)*; amalgamated into the Canadian Labour Congress *(see)* in 1956.

Trading possibilities line—A line that shows the different combinations of two products an economy is able to obtain (consume) when it specialises in the production of one product and trades (exports) this product to obtain the other product.

Traditional economy—An economic system in which traditions and customs determine how the economy will use its scarce resources.

Traditional view of advertising—The position that advertising is persuasive rather than informative; promotes industrial concentration; and is essentially inefficient and wasteful.

Transactions demand for money—The amount of Money people want to hold to use as a Medium of exchange (to make payments); and which varies directly with the nominal GDP.

Transfer payment—A payment of Money (or goods and services) by a government or a Firm to a Household or Firm for which the payer receives no good or service directly in return.

Tying agreement—A promise made by a buyer when allowed to purchase a patented product from a seller that it will make all its purchases of certain other (unpatented) products from the same seller

Unanticipated inflation—Inflation *(see)* at a rate greater than the saw expected in that period of time.

Unconditional grant—A transfer to a province by the federal government that goes into the general revenues of the province to be used as it sees fit; such grants are made for two reasons: (1) as an Equalisation payment *(see)* and (I) to make up for the general inadequacy of provincial revenues in relation to provincial responsibilities.

Underemployment—Failure to produce the maximum amount of goods and services that can be produced from the resources employed; failure to achieve Full production *(see)*.

Undistributed corporation profits—After-tax corporate profits not distributed as dividends to stockholders; corporate or business saving.

Unemployment—Failure to use all available Economic resources to produce goods and services; failure of the economy to employ fully its Civilian labour force *(see)*.

Unemployment insurance—The insurance program that in Canada is financed by compulsory contributions from employers and employees and from the general tax revenues of the federal government with benefits (income) made available to insured workers who are unable to find jobs.

Unemployment rate—The percentage of the Civilian labour force *(see)* unemployed at any time.

Uninsurable risk—An event—the occurrence of which is uncontrollable and unpredictable—that would result in a 105S that cannot be avoided by purchasing insurance and must be assumed by an entrepreneur *(see* Entrepreneurial ability); sometimes called "uncertainty."

Union shop—A place of employment where the employer may hire either Labour union members or non members, but where nonmembers must become members within a specified period of time or lose their jobs.

Unitary elasticity—The Elasticity coefficient *(see)* is equal to one; the percentage change in the quantity (demanded or supplied) is equal to the percentage change in price.

Unit labour cost—Labour costs per unit of output; equal to the Money wage rate *(see)* divided by the Average product *(see)* of labour.

Unlimited Liability—Absence of any limit on the maximum amount that may be lost by an individual and that the individual may become legally required to pay; the maximum amount that may be lost and that a sole proprietor or partner may be required to pay.

Unlimited wants—The insatiable desire of consumers (people) for goods and services that will give them pleasure or satisfaction.

Unplanned investment—Actual investment less Planned investment; increases or decreases in the inventories of business firms resulting from production greater than or less than sales.

Unprosperous industry—*(see* Declining industry.)

Uruguay Round—The eight round of trade negotiations under GATT *(see)*.

Vertical combination—A group of Plants *(see)* engaged in different stages of the production of a final product and owned by a single Firm *(see)*.

Utility—The want-satisfying power of a good or service; the satisfaction or pleasure a consumer obtains from the consumption of a good or service (or from the consumption of a collection of goods and services).

Utility-maximizing rule—To obtain the greatest Utility *(see)* the consumer should allocate Money income so that the last dollar spent on each good or service yields the same Marginal utility *(see)*; so that the Marginal utility of each good or service divided by its price is the same for all goods and services.

Value added—The value of the product sold by a Firm less the value of the goods (materials) purchased and used by the Firm to produce the product; and equal to the revenue that can be used for Wages, rent, interest, and profits.

Value-added tax—A tax imposed upon the difference between the value of the goods sold by a Arm and the value of the goods purchased by the firm from other firms.

Value judgement—Opinion of what is desirable or undesirable; belief regarding what ought or ought not to be (regarding what is right or just and wrong or unjust).

Value of money—The quantity of goods and services for which a unit of money (a dollar) can be exchanged; the purchasing power of a unit of money; the reciprocal of the Price level.

Variable cost—A cost that, in total, increases (decreases) when the firm increases (decreases) its output; the cost of Variable resources *(see)*.

Variable resource—Any resource employed by a Arm the quantity of which can be increased or decreased (varied) in quantity

VAT—Value-added tax *(see)*.

Vault cash—The Currency *(see)* a bank has in its safe (vault) and cash drawers; till money.

Velocity of money—The number of times per year the average dollar in the Money supply *(see)* is spent for Final goods and services *(see)*.

VERs—*(see* Voluntary export restrictions.)

Vertical axis—The "up-down" or "north-south" axis on a graph or grid.

Vertical intercept—The point at which a line meets the vertical axis of a graph.

Vertical merger—The merger of one or more Firms engaged in different stages of the production of a final product.

Vertical range—Vertical segment of the short-run Aggregate supply curve along which the economy is operating at full capacity.

Voluntary export restrictions—The limitation by firms of their exports to particular foreign nations in order to avoid the erection of other trade barriers by the foreign nations.

Wage—The price paid for Labour [for the use or services of Labour *(see)*l per unit of time (per hour, per day, and so on).

Wage differential—The difference between the Wage *(see)* received by one worker or group of workers and that received by another worker or group of workers.

Wage discrimination—The payment to women (or minority groups) of a wage lower than that paid to men (or established groups) for doing the same work.

Wage guidepost—Wages *(see)* in all industries in the economy should increase at an annual rate equal to the rate of increase in the Average product *(see)* of Labour in the economy.

Wage-price controls—A Wage-price policy *(see)* that legally Axes the maximum amounts Wages *(see)* and prices may be increased in any period of time.

Wage-price guideposts—A Wage-price policy *(see)* that depends upon the voluntary co-operation of Labour unions and business firms.

Wage-price inflationary spiral—Increases in wage rates that bring about increases in prices and in turn result in further increases in wage rates and in prices.

Wage-price policy—Government policy that attempts to alter the behaviour of Labour unions and business firms to make their Wage and price decisions more nearly compatible with the goals of Full employment and stable prices.

Wage rate—*(see* Wages.)

Wages—The income of those who supply the economy with Labour *(see)*.

Wastes of monopolistic competition—The waste of economic resources that is the result of producing an output at which price is greater than marginal cost and average cost is greater than the minimum average cost.

Wealth effect—The tendency for increases (decreases) in the price level to lower (raise) the real value (or purchasing power) of financial assets with Axed money values; and, as a result, to reduce (expand) total spending in the economy.

Welfare programs—*(see* Public assistance programs.)

(The) "will to develop"—Wanting economic growth strongly enough to change from old to new ways of doing things.

World Bangs—A bank supported by 151 nations, which lends (and guarantees loans) to less-developed nations to assist them to grow; formally, the International Bank for Reconstruction and Development.

World Price—The international price of a good or service, determined by world demand and supply.

World Trade Organization (WTO)—An organizaticn established in 1994 by GATT *(see)* to oversee the provisions of the Uruguay Round *(see)* and resolve any disputes stemming therefrom.

X-inefficiency—Failure to produce any given output at the lowest average (and total) cost possible.

cut here

STUDENT REPLY CARD

In order to improve future editions, we are seeking your comments on the *STUDY GUIDE to accompany MICROECONOMICS*, Seventh Canadian Edition McConnell/Brue/Barbiero by Walstad, Bingham, and Andersen. After you have read this text, please answer the following questions and return this form via Business Reply Mail.
Your opinions matter! Thank you in advance for your feedback!

Name of your college or university: ______________________________

Major program of study: ______________________________

Course title: ______________________________

Were you required to buy this book? ______ yes ______ no

Did you buy this book new or used? ______ new ______ used ($ _____)

Do you plan to keep or sell this book? ______ keep ______ sell

Is the order of topic coverage consistent with what was taught in your course?

fold here

cut here

Are there chapters or sections of this text that were not assigned for your course? Please specify:

Were there topics covered in your course that are not included in this text? Please specify:

What did you like most about this text?

What did you like least?

If you would like to say more, we'd love to hear from you. Please write to us at the address shown on the reverse of this card.

cut here

cut here

fold here

Postage will be paid by

Canada Post Corporation / Société canadienne des postes

Postage paid if mailed in Canada | **Port payé** si posté au Canada

Business Reply | **Réponse d'affaires**

0183560299 01

0183560299-L1N9B6-BR01

Attn.: Sponsoring Editor
College Division

MCGRAW-HILL RYERSON LIMITED
300 WATER ST
WHITBY ON L1N 9Z9